MEDICAL MALPRACTICE SERIES

MEDICAL MALPRACTICE

Handling Urology Cases

William J. Morton, M.D., J.D.

SHEPARD'S/McGRAW-HILL, INC.
P.O. Box 1235
Colorado Springs, CO 80901

McGRAW-HILL, INC.

New York • St. Louis • San Francisco • Auckland • Bogotá
Caracas • Colorado Springs • Hamburg • Lisbon • London
Mardrid • Mexico • Milan • Montreal • New Delhi • Panama
Paris • San Juan • São Paulo • Singapore • Sydney • Tokyo
Toronto

Copyright © 1990 by McGraw-Hill, Inc. All rights reserved. Printed in the United States of America. Except as permitted under the United States Copyright Act of 1976, no part of this publication may be reproduced or distributed in any form or by any means, or stored in a data base or retrieval system, without the prior written permission of the publisher.

Information has been obtained by Shepard's/McGraw-Hill, Inc. from sources believed to be reliable. However, because of the possibility of human or mechanical error by our sources, Shepard's/McGraw-Hill, Inc., or others, Shepard's/McGraw-Hill, Inc. does not guarantee the accuracy, adequacy, or completeness of any information and is not responsible for any errors or omissions or for the results obtained from use of such information.

1234567890 SHHI 909876543210

Library of Congress Cataloging-in-Publication Data

Morton, William J.
    Medical malpractice—handling urology cases / William J. Morton.
       p.   cm. — (Medical malpractice series)
    Includes bibliographical references and index.
    ISBN 0-07-172192-4
    1. Urologists—Malpractice—United States. 2. Jurisprudence—United States. I. Title. II. Title: Handling urology cases.
III. Series.
KF2910.U753M67   1990
346.7303'32—dc20
[347.306332]   90-38363
                                                                                    CIP

ISBN 0-07-172192-4

The sponsoring editor for this book was Bradley S. Abramson and the editor was Stephen F. Lynch.

Shepard's Medical Malpractice Series

Medical Malpractice: Bases of Liability
Medical Malpractice: Handling Dental Cases
Medical Malpractice: Handling General Surgery Cases
Medical Malpractice: Handling Obstetric and Neonatal Cases
Medical Malpractice: Handling Plastic Surgery Cases
Medical Malpractice: Pharmacy Law
Medical Malpractice: Psychiatric Care

Dedication

This book is dedicated to my mother, Eve Alpert Morton. I hope I told her how much of an influence she was on my life, although I probably didn't. In my solitude, I think of her and hope that somehow and in some way, wherever her soul is, she now knows it!

She was a gentle Georgia girl who came real close to being married for 50 years, and put aside whatever her own personal goals were to bring up her children.

You did a great job, Mother. I'm only sorry you didn't get to see this book in print.

Acknowledgments

I really wanted to write every chapter myself, but after spending hours and hours in the library, I realized I could be more efficient by asking others to write a few chapters for me. The chapters on the plaintiff's and defendant's perspective about urological medical malpractice were absolutely essential to the book and, frankly, an area in which I have had not enough experience to claim expertise. Tommy Malone and Bob Tanner quickly agreed to help me out, and their chapters are really the finest I have seen on that topic.

My urology/lawyer friends volunteered to do the chapters on anatomy and urological instruments which greatly relieved my workload and gave them something to do in their spare time.

I have compiled a brief biography of each of my collaborators which will be included in this Acknowledgments. Much more could be written of each of them, but the interested reader may contact any of them, if necessary, for further information.

ROBERT M. FRANK, M.D. graduated from Western Reserve University School of Medicine, Cleveland, Ohio in 1954 and did his Urology Residency at the Veterans Administration Hospital in Hines, Illinois from 1956 to 1959. He has been in the private practice of urology as Chief of the Urological Service with the Southern California Permanente Medical Group from 1959 to 1986. Dr. Frank graduated in 1985 from the Southwestern University School of Law, Los Angeles, California with the Juris Doctor degree. Dr. Frank also is a Diplomate of the American Board of Urology and belongs to numerous professional organizations.

DAVID G. McLEOD, M.D. is a Colonel in the United States Army and is presently the Chief of Urology at Walter Reed Army Medical Center, Washington, D. C. Prior to this position, he has taken a Pediatric Urology Fellowship in London, England, and was Chief of Urology at DeWitt Army Hosptial, Fort Belvoir, Virginia. He is a Diplomate of the American Board of Urology, a Fellow of the American College of Surgeons, Professor of Surgery (Urology) at the Uniformed Services University of the Health Sciences, Bethesda,

Maryland, and Clinical Assistant Professor, Department of Surgery, Georgetown University, Washington, D. C. Colonel McLeod belongs to eighteen professional societies and two heraldry societies. Additionally, he has been an active Principal Investigator for many national cancer and bladder investigations. Colonel McLeod is also a member of the District of Columbia Bar.

THOMAS WILLIAM MALONE is a sole practitioner in Atlanta, Georgia. He attended the University of Georgia from 1960 to 1963 and then entered Walter F. George School of Law, Mercer University, graduating in 1966 with an L.L.B. degree. Mr. Malone specializes in plaintiff's personal injury with an emphasis on medical malpractice. He is a member of the State Bar of Georgia, American Bar Association, Georgia Trial Lawyers Association, Association of Trial Lawyers of America, Dougherty Circuit Bar Association, Atlanta Bar Associaton, and the Atlanta Lawyers Club. He is also a member of the Law Science Academy of America, The Belli Society, and American Judicature Society. Mr. Malone is a Fellow of the Georgia Bar Foundation, Inc. and The International Academy of Trial Lawyers and is recognized in *The Best Lawyers in America, 1989-1990* (Woodward/White Publications 1989). He has served as an officer in numerous professional organizations and was President of the Georgia Trial Lawyers Associaton in 1980. He has written extensively concerning trial practice, personal injury issues, and wrongful death, and is the author of *Maximizing Damages through Voir Dire and Summation.*

ROBERT G. TANNER is a partner in the Atlanta, Georgia law firm of Long, Weinberg, Ansley & Wheeler, one of the largest litigation firms in the Southeast and among the largest in the nation. Mr. Tanner specializes in the defense of medical malpractice claims, an area in which he has probably tried more lawsuits than any lawyer in Georgia. He is a 1973 graduate of the Wake Forest University School of Law. He also lists over a dozen professional societies of which he is a member.

Preface

I learned a lot from writing this book—more, I am sure, than those who read it. I think the teacher always learns more than the student when preparing and presenting lessons, but, hopefully, if the teacher has done a good job, the student will eventually surpass him or her, and I hope, you, too, will eventually surpass me.

My motivation, besides my own need for expression and self-gratification, was to teach attorneys about the urological discipline and help prepare them to understand the issues and better represent their clients. Of course, being a urologist, I have somewhat of a conflict—I'm sure most urologists would view it that way—in telling attorneys how to handle a urology medical malpractice case. Most urologists feel they would be a lot better off if no one would handle a urology medical malpractice case, but that's not reality, and since there are a lot of urological medical malpractice actions being filed every day, I felt I was better prepared than anyone else to try to approach and decipher the subject for my attorney brethren.

This is not a book about medical malpractice—this book is beyond that. This book is about urology and how to prepare and understand and do a urology medical malpractice case. This book is for lawyers, written by a lawyer (me) and intended to assist lawyers in their job. Doctors have a difficult time separating the attorney as a professional representing a client whose cases they may or may not personally embrace from the patient who is suing them, but that's the doctor's problem. This text is intended for attorneys to understand a rather arcane topic; it is not intended to inflame physicians.

I need to thank many people for help in this endeavor, especially Dave McLeod, Bob Frank, Bob Tanner, and Tommy Malone for their contributions. I'm not going to mention any other names because I'm sure I would insult someone who got left out.

Will I do this again? Right now, I doubt it, because the energy and effort required is tremendous, and my wandering mind is considering other areas to investigate, but at least I've done it once, and that's important to me. On the other hand, seeing my name in print is infectious, and I do have some other ideas. . . .

Contents

Summary

    Acknowledgments

    Preface

1   Medical Malpractice Considerations

2   Opening the File

3   Medical Records

4   Urology as a Specialty

5   Urologic Anatomy, Physiology, and Common Laboratory Tests

6 The Use of Instruments and Devices in Diagnosis, Evaluation, and Treatment of the Urogenital Tract

7 Radiology of the Urinary Tract

8 Common Urological Surgical Procedures

9 Common Urological Complications

10 Handling the Plaintiff's Case

11 The Defense Perspective

12 Evolution of Hospital Liability

Tables

Index

Detailed

Acknowledgments

Preface

1 Medical Malpractice Considerations

§1.01	Introduction
§1.02	Elements of a Malpractice Action
§1.03	—Duty
§1.04	—Breach of Duty
§1.05	—Causation
§1.06	—Damages
§1.07	—Why Do Patients Sue?
§1.08	—Incompetent Doctors
§1.09	—Abandonment
§1.10	—Failure to Refer
§1.11	—Egregious Conduct
§1.12	—Litigious Society
§1.13	—Patients' Expectations
§1.14	—Technological Failures
§1.15	—Patients' Rights
§1.16	—Organized Medicine
§1.17	—Lawyers
§1.18	Physician/Attorney Relationships
§1.19	—Statement on Interprofessional Relationships
§1.20	Code of Ethics
§1.21	Standard of Care
§1.22	—Reasons for Substandard Care
§1.23	Informed Consent
§1.24	Burden of Proof
§1.25	Res Ipsa Loquitur
§1.26	Damages
§1.27	—Categories
§1.28	—Pain and Suffering
§1.29	—Pre- and Post-Judgment Interest
§1.30	Negligent Infliction of Emotional Distress
§1.31	Collateral Source
§1.32	Comparative Negligence
§1.33	Assumption of the Risk
§1.34	Joint and Several Liability
§1.35	—Contribution
§1.36	—Indemnity
§1.37	Release

§1.38 Countersuits
§1.39 Peer Review
§1.40 Health Care Quality Improvement Act of 1986
§1.41 Tort Reform
§1.42 —Collateral Source
§1.43 —Attorney's Fees
§1.44 —Limitation of Awards
§1.45 —Statutes of Limitations
§1.46 —Joint and Several Liability
§1.47 —Pre-Screening Panels and Arbitration
§1.48 Reference

2 Opening the File

§2.01 Introduction
§2.02 Initial Interview
§2.03 Realistic Elements to Consider—Is There a Case?
§2.04 How Good Is the Plaintiff?
§2.05 How Good Is the Defendant?
§2.06 Getting an Expert
§2.07 Procedural Requirements
§2.08 —Jurisdiction
§2.09 —Venue
§2.10 —Forum Non Conveniens
§2.11 —Service of Process
§2.12 —Prior Dismissals
§2.13 Wrongful Death and Survival
§2.14 Derivative Actions
§2.15 Statute of Limitations—Generally
§2.16 —Torts
§2.17 —Tolling
§2.18 —Foreign Body
§2.19 Affirmative Defenses
§2.20 —Contributory Negligence
§2.21 —Last Clear Chance
§2.22 —Comparative Negligence

§2.23 —Assumption of the Risk
§2.24 Procedural Defenses
§2.25 Compromise and Settlement
§2.26 —Settlement Brochure
§2.27 —Types of Settlement
§2.28 References

3 Medical Records

§3.01 Function of the Records
§3.02 Hospital Records
§3.03 —Certified Copy
§3.04 —Patient Information Sheet
§3.05 —Admission Note, History, and Physical
§3.06 —Progress Notes
§3.07 —Doctor's Orders
§3.08 —Nurses' Notes
§3.09 —Laboratory Data
§3.10 —X-Ray Data
§3.11 —Operative Notes
§3.12 —Anesthesia Record
§3.13 —Recovery Room Record
§3.14 —Consultation Notes
§3.15 —Ancillary Records
§3.16 —Discharge Summary
§3.17 —Consent Form
§3.18 —Graphic Sheet
§3.19 —Circulating Nurse's Records (Operating Room Records)
§3.20 —Pathology Report
§3.21 —Medication Sheets
§3.22 —Emergency Room Records
§3.23 Abbreviations
§3.24 Office Records
§3.25 Lost or Altered Medical Records
Appendix 3-A Sample Forms

4 Urology as a Specialty

- §4.01 Historical Background
- §4.02 Glossary
- §4.03 The Making of a Urologist
- §4.04 Licensure
- §4.05 Board Certification
- §4.06 —Recertification
- §4.07 Demographics and Socioeconomics
- §4.08 Subspecialization
- §4.09 Standard Texts and Jouranls
- §4.10 Urological Societies

5 Urologic Anatomy, Physiology, and Common Laboratory Tests

Anatomy
- §5.01 Introduction
- §5.02 The Retroperitoneum
- §5.03 The Adrenal Glands
- §5.04 The Kidneys
- §5.05 —Internal Anatomy of the Kidneys
- §5.06 —External Anatomy of the Kidneys
- §5.07 The Urinary Transport System
- §5.08 —The Ureter
- §5.09 The Urinary Storage System
- §5.10 —The Urethra
- §5.11 The Prostate Gland
- §5.12 The Penis
- §5.13 The Testicular and Spermatic Cord Structures
- §5.14 The Seminal Vesicles

Physiology
- §5.15 Nephrology and Urology
- §5.16 The Formation of Urine
- §5.17 Urine Transport and Micturition
- §5.18 —Transporting the Urine

§5.19 —The Bladder
§5.20 —Voiding the Urine
§5.21 The Male Reproductive System
§5.22 Sexual Dysfunction Generally
§5.23 Impotency
§5.24 —Psychological Causes
§5.25 —Physical Causes
§5.26 —Drugs
§5.27 Other Sexual Dysfunction
Common Laboratory Tests
§5.28 Overview
§5.29 Urinalysis
§5.30 Hemogram
§5.31 —Chemical Analysis of the Blood
References
§5.32 References
Appendix 5-A Illustrations

6 The Use of Instruments and Devices in Diagnosis, Evaluation, and Treatment of the Urogenital Tract

§6.01 Introduction
§6.02 Urethral Catheters
§6.03 Ureteral Catheters
§6.04 Urethral Sounds
§6.05 Cystoscopic Instruments
§6.06 Resectoscope
§6.07 Lithotrite
§6.08 Urethrotome
§6.09 Stone Baskets and Ureteroscopes
§6.10 Biopsy Instruments
§6.11 Penile Prosthesis
Appendix 6-A Illustrations

7 Radiology of the Urinary Tract

§7.01 Introduction

§7.02 Excretory Urography
§7.03 Tomography
§7.04 Retrograde Pyelography
§7.05 Antegrade Pyelography
§7.06 Cystography
§7.07 Loopogram
§7.08 Urethrography
§7.09 Vasogram
§7.10 Angiography
§7.11 Radionuclides
§7.12 Renal Ultrasound
§7.13 Computerized Tomography
Appendix 7-A Sample Radiological Procedures

8 Common Urological Surgical Procedures

§8.01 Overview
§8.02 Pyelolithotomy
§8.03 Nephrolithotomy
§8.04 Lithotripsy
§8.05 Percutaneous Nephrostomy
§8.06 Nephrectomy
§8.07 Ureterolithotomy
§8.08 Deligation with Anastomosis
§8.09 Ureteral Reimplantation
§8.10 Vesicourethropexy
§8.11 Vesicovaginal Fistula Repair
§8.12 Cystectomy and Ileal Conduit
§8.13 Open Prostatectomy
§8.14 Radical Prostatectomy
§8.15 Circumcision
§8.16 Vasectomy
§8.17 Insertion of Penile Prosthesis
§8.18 Orchiectomy
§8.19 Detorsion and Orchiopexy
§8.20 Transurethral Resection of Prostate

9 Common Urological Complications

§9.01 Overview
§9.02 Injury to Ureter during Abdominal Hysterectomy
§9.03 Damage to Urinary Sphincter during TUR
§9.04 Hyponatremia or Low-Salt Syndrome
§9.05 Failure to Diagnose Torsion of the Testicle
§9.06 IVP Dye Reactions
§9.07 Allergic or Toxic Drug Reactions
§9.08 Damage to Internal Organs during the Percutaneous Approach to the Kidney
§9.09 Penile Prosthesis: Infections and Improper Placement
§9.10 Failure to Timely Remove Ureteral Stent
§9.11 Damage to Testicle during Hernia Repair
§9.12 Complications of Vasectomy
§9.13 Urethral Perforation
§9.14 Suture through Catheter after Marshall-Marchetti-Krantz Procedure
§9.15 Potpourri

10 Handling the Plaintiff's Case

§10.01 Introduction
§10.02 Screening
§10.03 Evaluation
§10.04 Settlement or Suit
§10.05 The Complaint
§10.06 Discovery
§10.07 Initial Discovery
§10.08 —Interrogatories and Request for Production of Documents to Defendant Doctor

§10.09 —Interrogatories and Request for Production of Documents to Defendant Hospital
§10.10 Depositions
§10.11 —Deponents
§10.12 —Deposition of the Defendant Doctor
§10.13 —Deposition of Defense Experts
§10.14 Voir Dire
§10.15 Direct Examination
§10.16 Cross-Examination
§10.17 Summation

11 The Defense Perspective

§11.01 Introduction
§11.02 Defense on Law
§11.03 —Substantive Technicalities

Discovery

§11.04 Marshaling the Facts
§11.05 Exploring the Case: Depositions
§11.06 —Deposition of the Plaintiff
§11.07 —Deposition of the Defendant
§11.08 —Deposition of the Plaintiff's Expert

The Pretrial Phase

§11.09 Evaluating the Case
§11.10 Exhibit Preparation
§11.11 Establishing the Theme of the Defense

The Trial

§11.12 Rejecting the Jury
§11.13 Opening Statement
§11.14 Cross-Examination
§11.15 Direct Examination
§11.16 Closing Argument

Conclusion

§11.17 Conclusion
Appendix 11-A Model Interrogatories
Appendix 11-B Case Summary Chart

12 Evolution of Hospital Liability

§12.01 Overview
§12.02 Immunity
§12.03 —Charitable Immunity
§12.04 Agency
§12.05 —Principal and Agent
§12.06 —Respondeat Superior
§12.07 —Apparent Agency
§12.08 —Borrowed Servant
§12.09 —Agency by Necessity
§12.10 Expert Witness
§12.11 Corporations
§12.12 Joint Commission on Accreditation of Healthcare Organizations
§12.13 Corporate Practice of Medicine
§12.14 —Physician Credentialing
§12.15 —Independent Contractors
§12.16 —Substantial Evidence Test
§12.17 —Fairness
§12.18 —Antitrust
§12.19 —Grounds, Buildings, and Vendors
§12.20 Consolidated Omnibus Budget Reconciliation Act (COBRA)

Tables

Cases
Statutes
Authorities

Index

1

Medical Malpractice Considerations

§1.01   Introduction
§1.02   Elements of a Malpractice Action
§1.03   —Duty
§1.04   —Breach of Duty
§1.05   —Causation
§1.06   —Damages
§1.07   Why Do Patients Sue?
§1.08   —Incompetent Doctors
§1.09   —Abandonment
§1.10   —Failure to Refer
§1.11   —Egregious Conduct
§1.12   —Litigious Society
§1.13   —Patients' Expectations
§1.14   —Technological Failures
§1.15   —Patients' Rights
§1.16   —Organized Medicine
§1.17   —Lawyers
§1.18   Physician/Attorney Relationships
§1.19   —Statement on Interprofessional Relationships
§1.20   Code of Ethics
§1.21   Standard of Care
§1.22   —Reasons for Substandard Care
§1.23   Informed Consent
§1.24   Burden of Proof
§1.25   Res Ipsa Loquitur
§1.26   Damages
§1.27   —Categories
§1.28   —Pain and Suffering

§1.29 —Pre- and Post-Judgment Interest
§1.30 Negligent Infliction of Emotional Distress
§1.31 Collateral Source
§1.32 Comparative Negligence
§1.33 Assumption of the Risk
§1.34 Joint and Several Liability
§1.35 —Contribution
§1.36 —Indemnity
§1.37 Release
§1.38 Countersuits
§1.39 Peer Review
§1.40 Health Care Quality Improvement Act of 1986
§1.41 Tort Reform
§1.42 —Collateral Source
§1.43 —Attorney's Fees
§1.44 —Limitation of Awards
§1.45 —Statutes of Limitations
§1.46 —Joint and Several Liability
§1.47 —Pre-Screening Panels and Arbitration
§1.48 References

§1.01 Introduction

While this book is devoted to the understanding of the discipline of urology and the handling of a urological medical malpractice case, this chapter deals with some of the generics (i.e., basics) of medical malpractice cases generally. These topics are not specific to urology, and probably can be found in any of the other textbooks dealing with specialized medical malpractice cases, but to leave them out of this discussion would be an injustice to the topic.

Attorneys dealing in the highly specialized area of medical malpractice litigation not only must understand the individual specifics of their particular case, but also must have a good understanding of the speciality involved. In addition, they must also understand the general concepts and historical background of medical malpractice. Certain legal components such as the elements of the tort of negligence, as well as issues of standards of care, burden of proof, and damages, should be completely understood. Current controversial topics of tort reform, peer review statutes, and informed consent all contribute to the totality of knowledge required for the attorney to better understand the "big picture." All of these topics are briefly considered in this chapter as a starting point and stepping stone for the attorney to better represent his or her client.

§1.02 Elements of a Malpractice Action

The elements of a medical malpractice action are, with certain exceptions, the same as any other tort. Professor Prosser, in the Fifth Edition of his *Handbook of the Law of Torts,* describes the necessary elements for any cause of action involving negligence. These include:

1. A duty recognized by law requiring the person to conform to a certain standard of conduct for the protection of others against unreasonable risks
2. A failure on the person's part to conform to the standard required—i.e., a breach of that duty
3. A reasonably close and causal connection between the conduct and the resultant injury
4. Actual loss or damage resulting to the interests of another[1]

Confining this discussion to a medical malpractice action will not change the elements of the cause of action, but this specific type of tort does have certain aspects indigenous to it as opposed to other negligence types of causes of action.

§1.03 —Duty

A physician/patient relationship must be established before any duty can exist between the two parties. Occasionally, the establishment of that relationship may be difficult to ascertain, but once that relationship is established, the physician has the responsibility imposed by law to use due care. The physician/patient relationship must be established with mutual consent and, as was enunciated in 1951 in *Rice v Rinaldo*.[2]

> In the absence of statute, a physician or surgeon is under no legal obligation to render professional services to everyone who applies to him or who seeks to engage him. Physicians are not public servants who are bound to serve all who seek them, as are innkeepers, common carriers, and the like.

Peace v Weisman[3] illustrates the physician/patient relationship and the duty the physician has toward the patient. In this case, a wife brought an action on behalf of her deceased husband against the doctor based on the physician's failure to diagnose and notify the husband of lung cancer during an examination performed by the physician for the husband's Social Security Disability benefits. The Georgia court held in that case:

---

[1] W. Prosser, Handbook of the Law of Torts (1982).
[2] 67 Abs 183, 119 NE2d 657 (Mass 1951).
[3] 186 Ga App 697, 368 SE2d 319 (1988).

The physician's only duty to the applicant when he examines on behalf of the State Department of Human Resources is to determine Social Security Disability benefits and to conduct the examination in such a manner as though as to not injure the applicant. Courts further hold that it is a well-settled principle of Georgia law that there can be no liability for malpractice in the absence of the physician/patient relationship and it is this relationship which is a result of a consensual transaction that establishes the legal duty to conform to a standard of conduct. A physician who has been retained by a third party to undertake a physical examination of an individual cannot be held liable to that individual for malpractice where he neither intended to treat nor care for or otherwise benefit the individual and did not injure him during the course of the exam.[4]

Generally, consideration and reliance determine when the physician/patient relationship is established. In most jurisdictions, gratuitous rendering of care will shield a physician from liability if a Good Samaritan situation exists. In addition, it is important to understand that the failure of a patient to pay his or her medical bill does not limit or terminate the duty of the physician to provide care to the patient.

In a 1927 case, *Dunn v Beck*,[5] the court described the nature of the duty which exists once the relationship has been established:

The law requires a physician or surgeon to possess the skill and learning which is possessed by the average member of the medical profession in good standing and to apply such skill and learning with ordinary and reasonable care. He is not an insurer, nor is a good result impliedly guaranteed. His obligation is merely to exercise such reasonable care and skill in the treatment of the patient as is usually exercised by physicians or surgeons of good standing of the same school of practice in the community in which he resides with due regard to the condition of the patient and the progress of medical or surgical science at the time.[6]

Thus, this case set the requirement for the locality rule which measured the physician's level of care against the standards of the community in which he or she practiced. However, because of our increasingly mobile society, the locality rule has been sociologically abrogated, and there is now a national standard of care which has been adopted by all courts.

Additionally, the term "reasonable" was introduced and remains such that the standard of care is measured against that care rendered to a patient which was reasonable and equated with the general care and skill as held by other physicians generally.

---

[4] *Id.* at 700, 368 SE2d at 320.
[5] 80 Mont 414, 260 P 1047 (1927).
[6] *Id* at 416, 260 P at 1049.

The standard of care was more completely articulated in *Boyce v Brown*,[7] a 1938 Arizona case. Here, the court established that one licensed to practice medicine is presumed to possess the degree of skill and learning which is possessed by the average member of the medical profession in good standing in the community in which he or she practices and to apply that skill and learning with ordinary and reasonable care to patients who come to him or her for treatment.

> Before a physician or surgeon can be held liable, he must have done something in his treatment of the patient which the recognized standard of good medical practice in the community in which he is practicing forbids, or he must have neglected to do something which such standard requires.
>
> In order to sustain a verdict for the plaintiffs in an action for malpractice, the standard of medical practice in the community must be shown by affirmative evidence and, unless there is evidence of such a standard, a jury may not be permitted to speculate as to what the required standard is or whether the defendant has departed therefrom.
>
> Negligence on the part of a physician or surgeon in the treatment of a case is never presumed, but must be affirmatively proven, and no presumption of negligence nor want of skill arises from the mere fact that a treatment was unsuccessful, failed to bring the best results, or that the patient died.[8]

Although a physician has the duty to use reasonable care and diligence in the treatment of his or her patients, additional duties arise. Most states have informed consent statutes which require the physician to inform the patient of the ramifications of treatment of a particular problem, the risks and complications attendant to that treatment, and alternative modalities of treatment. Additionally, the physician has the duty to provide the care consistent with his or her own education and training level and, if such care requires additional knowledge, the physician has the duty to refer the patient for conditions beyond his or her knowledge and skill.

Finally, the physician has the duty to attend the patient diligently and to continue that rendering of care until the care necessitated by the illness is no longer required.

The physician/patient relationship may be terminated by the physician if he or she gives the patient notice of this termination and a reasonable opportunity to find alternative care. Of course, it goes without saying that a patient may also terminate the relationship, and usually does so in a much freer manner than allowed the physician. Failure of the physician to properly terminate the relationship may constitute abandonment of the patient and will increase the physician's liability.

---

[7] 51 Ariz 416, 77 P2d 455 (1938).
[8] *Id* at 419, 77 P2d at 460.

§1.04 —Breach of Duty

It is the breach of the duty established by the physician/patient relationship that is the next element required in the cause of action.

Generally, this breach of duty is the most difficult element to prove. Evidence must be presented and articulated as to what the standard of care is, and the defendant's role must be shown to have violated that standard. It is unique in a medical malpractice action that another physician must testify as to the standard of care and how that standard was violated. If the breach of duty is so obvious that the ordinary layperson could recognize it—i.e., operating on the wrong leg of a patient or leaving an instrument behind in the patient after surgery—an expert witness is not required.

A poor result is not necessarily an example of a breach of duty unless that poor result can be shown to have occurred as a result of actions which were a deviation from the standard of care.

Likewise, failure to make the proper diagnosis may also not be a departure from the standard of care if the physician used that skill and care ordinarily employed by physicians under like or similar circumstances in determining the diagnosis. If the final diagnosis was made as a result of actions that were a departure from the standard of care, that can also be a breach of duty owed the patient.

§1.05 —Causation

The question whether the breach of duty was a substantial factor in causing injury to the patient is known as "proximate cause." Without proximate cause, there can be no cause of action. Great malpractice may occur, but if no nexus can be shown between the breach and the resultant injury, an action may not be forthcoming.

If the patient's conduct was the slightest reason for the damages resulting from a breach of duty owed, earlier courts held, under the doctrine of contributory negligence, that no recovery was available. A more modern and generally accepted theory is that of comparative negligence. Here, where the plaintiff is responsible for some or most of the damages, a setoff occurs with the amount of damages awarded to the patient dependent on the extent of comparative negligence which the plaintiff provided.

§1.06 —Damages

According to Professor Prosser's Seventh Edition *Cases and Materials on Torts* (1982), there are three basic kinds of damages in tort law.

Nominal damages consist of a small sum of money awarded to the plaintiff to vindicate his or her rights, make the judgment available as a matter of record to prevent the defendant from acquiring prescriptive rights, and carry a part of the costs of the action. The amount of the award, as long as it is paltry, is unimportant. Current practice among juries has been to award nominal damages of one dollar.

Compensatory damages are intended to represent the closest possible financial equivalent of the loss or harm suffered by the plaintiff and restore him or her to the position he or she occupied before the tort.

Punitive damages are an additional sum over and above the proper compensation of the plaintiff awarded to punish the defendant, to make an example of him or her, and to deter others from committing similar torts.

In reality, although all elements of the cause of action must be present as a matter of law for the lawsuit to proceed, most plaintiffs' attorneys will not become involved in a case with minimal injury to the patient. The old saw, "Great liability, no damage," rears its ugly head frequently in the medical malpractice arena.

While there is significant evidence of real medical malpractice happening to patients, most of the misconduct is relatively harmless. Unfortunately, what is harmless to you and me may not be viewed as such by the patient.

I recall one recent case where, as part of a serious cancer operation, a urologist inserted a ureteral stent in a 70-year-old, quite ill patient. This stent was meant to be left in place for a few months at most, but five years later, because of a recent bout of recurrent urinary tract infections, the stent was finally noticed by her physicians and removed. The family and the patient were horrified, of course, but a careful review of the records revealed that very little damage had actually occurred to the patient as a result of the stent being left behind. The patient survived the cancer and the cancer surgery and had several episodes of infection, but, given the total picture, the patient had overcome what appeared to be a fatal course of widespread cancer and was now functioning in a successful and productive manner.

Great liability, minimal damage! No plaintiff's attorney, recognizing the hours of work required to prevail as well as the significant financial commitment involved, would pursue that case.

From an altruistic viewpoint, this is probably where the system involving compensation of some sort to the patient for injuries suffered breaks down. While this is also the topic for another time, the reader should be aware that before proceeding with a client's case, he or she must weigh all of the issues carefully. Chapter 2, Opening the File, discusses this aspect more fully.

§1.07 Why Do Patients Sue?

The fifth element of a medical malpractice action involves the reasons patients sue. While the law has strict guidelines about all the elements necessary for a cause of action, patients do not know the law, and it is important to understand what makes the patient decide to go to a lawyer.

Forgetting the anger aspect of the case because of injury to the patient, what really initiates the visit to the lawyer is, as Strother Martin said in *Cool Hand Luke,* "What we have here is a failure to communicate!" Physicians can cause all sorts of horrible things in patients, but if the relationship between the two is such that the patient earnestly believes the doctor is doing the best he or she can, that patient will never consider a lawsuit.

Because of the exposure that litigation is getting from the media and the thought of large awards, the idea of going to a lawyer about one's physician is no longer foreign or repugnant to the average layperson. Yet, if the doctor has a genuine concern and maintains a very open dialogue with his or her patient and the family, most patients will have continued faith in their doctor in spite of serious complications in their healthcare management.

I have seen this happen much more often than not, and it is well known that a "good bedside manner" is one of the most important aspects of any patient care.

The failure to communicate is what is often neglected in our high-tech world, where diagnosis and treatment are sometimes more dependent on computers than humans. Some physicians also have a haughty attitude toward their patients because they are programmed to believe the information they have is too technical and complicated for the average patient to understand. While this general supercilious attitude is disappearing, that posture has created the current situation in the medical malpractice arena.

This is not to say that the failure of communications between the physician and the patient is always the fault of the doctor. Patients, too, can make unreasonable demands on their physician which alienates him or her and which may oftentimes escalate the tension between the two. Every patient handles his or her illness differently—some with resignation, some with fear, and some with anger—and the physician must recognize that the patient at this particular moment in life is probably not his or her usual self. If these emotional needs of the patient in addition to the physical needs are not recognized by the physician, the communication gap invariably widens.

A physician can go to great lengths explaining to a patient the problem and the route necessary to resolve the problem along with all risks and complications, but if the patient is so terrified at that particular moment of even being in the doctor's office, all of this dialogue will not even be heard by the patient.

This situation is the genesis of the belief by the patient that "my doctor never talks to me." The physician must recognize this mental orientation of the patient and, if he or she sees that the communication is not getting through to the patient, the physician must take alternate steps. He or she can further discuss this with the patient at a later time, he or she can bring in other family members for communication, and he or she can give the patient written communication. But, the physician must absolutely recognize whether he or she is communicating with the patient, and if the physician fails to appreciate this fact, this certainly can be the source of a lawsuit at a later date.

While I believe the failure to communicate to be the main reason why patients sue, there are other factors to consider.

§1.08 —Incompetent Doctors

While it is important for the reader to understand that this text is about the failure to provide quality and successful healthcare to patients, the overwhelming and vast majority of care rendered is superior and successful. We must not lose sight of the fact that, although we are discussing the failure of this system, failure is not the norm. The quality of medical education, training, selection of physicians, technological advances, treatment modalities, and results to the American public is by far the most advanced and successful in the world. It is only the vast minority of physicians who are involved in medical malpractice and about which this text is concerned. There certainly are incompetent physicians, as there are incompetent lawyers, pilots, police officers, or any other members of any organized business or professional group.

Additionally, a certain number of physicians have an alcohol- or drug-related problem and, of course, this can rapidly come to the surface and be the source of the medical malpractice action.

Physicians may be technically unskilled, and this poor surgical technique may result in catastrophes with severe damage to the patient. Turning a simple gallbladder operation into a complicated surgical problem by injuring the bowel and requiring a colostomy is an example. Performing a vasectomy improperly such that a pregnancy results may also be the basis for a lawsuit.

§1.09 —Abandonment

Patients have been abandoned by their physicians for various reasons. The most common example is the physician who operates successfully, but is then unavailable for follow-up over the next several hours or days. A successful result can have an unexpected complication and, if the physician is unavailable—for whatever reason—the patient is abandoned. The physician may have failed to provide for coverage while he or she is out of town, or he or she may be at a social function and choose not to respond to a call, or he or she may even talk to the patient and refer the patient to the emergency room where less sophisticated physicians attempt to resolve the problem. All of these actions can bring about the abandonment charge.

§1.10 —Failure to Refer

Physicians may have the inability to properly recognize when a referral to another specialist is demanded. Failure to use the current and appropriate treatment modalities may also be the basis for a lawsuit. An example is the urologist who fails to refer a patient for ultrasonic lithotripsy of a ureteral or renal stone and who instead subjects the patient to surgery, a now outmoded method of treatment for this problem. Another example of failure to refer can involve a urologist who encounters a medical problem beyond his or her area of expertise. The failure to refer the patient to an appropriate physician may be a departure from the standard of care.

§1.11 —Egregious Conduct

Blatantly egregious conduct may also involve a physician in a lawsuit. In a recent case, a surgeon failed to properly perform *any* preoperative testing of his patient for a medical problem and swiftly subjected her to surgery based on his "clinical impression" not supported by any preoperative laboratory or radiological investigation. The surgery was performed poorly, resulting in a permanent complication, and the patient was found to have an illness which could have been treated with medicine rather than surgery, resulting in a lawsuit against the urologist.

§1.12 —Litigious Society

The specter of a litigious society is also the source of medical malpractice lawsuits. The media exposure of large jury verdicts titillates an unhappy patient and encourages him or her to proceed with a lawsuit. Sensationalizing and focusing on patients who successfully sue their doctors because of negligence suggests that litigation is an easy and acceptable way to handle the injured patient. Products liability lawsuits with the larger awards, probably because of greater injury to claimants, also encourage laypersons to see their attorneys.

§1.13 —Patients' Expectations

The greater expectation of patients in their physicians and the healthcare system generally can also be an underlying basis for a lawsuit. Patients have the perception, perhaps fostered by the medical community, that all ills and healthcare problems can be resolved swiftly, easily, and successfully. Patients read about artificial hearts, artificial kidneys, artificial joints, and even artificial erections, and the perception is that nothing is too difficult for physicians to resolve. When the outcome of that healthcare rendered to the patient breaks down, it is easy to see how this expectation is destroyed.

§1.14 —Technological Failures

Failures of highly sophisticated technological equipment such as cautery machines, monitoring devices, or even inflatable penile prostheses are other examples wherein patients file lawsuits. This situation can give rise to two types of actions: medical malpractice and products liability.

§1.15 —Patients' Rights

The advancement and encouragement of patients' rights promote additional lawsuits. The entire civil rights movement of the early 1960s has given patients a heightened awareness of their rights and certainly the perception that their own involvement be a part of the decisionmaking healthcare process. With the generalized increased knowledge of medicine and its technological advances, patients now demand to have the utmost of modern devices available to them. Patients demand to know the basis for their physicians' approach to a particular problem and will seek redress if they are not included in this process. Indeed, the topic of informed consent, discussed in §1.23, is a perfect example of this.

§1.16 —Organized Medicine

The final reason, but certainly not the least, for why patients sue is the reaction of organized medicine. Patients perceive that physicians generally are poorly responsive not only to the problem of physician discipline, but also to the monitoring and requirement of physicians to maintain their education and training. While some states have mandatory continuing medical education for physicians to maintain their licenses, these states are in a minority. Certain medical specialty societies require a physician to be recertified in that specialty, but these societies are also in the vast minority.

Physician discipline in the form of license suspension, revocation, or curtailment is at a minimum. Most investigations of physicians for quality issues are self-serving. While drug- and alcohol-impaired physicians seem to be properly handled by the medical profession generally, this is only a recent approach to a distinct problem.

§1.17 —Lawyers

There is a widespread belief amongst physicians that unscrupulous attorneys promote frivolous lawsuits. Patients do not have this perception because, in their mind, their case is egregious and based on sound facts of negligence, and they perceive their lawyers as their champions of justice. Physicians, however, believe almost every case of medical malpractice filed is trivial and frivolous, and that it is the unscrupulous, money-hungry, greedy attorney who is encouraging the client to sue.

While there may exist a percentage (hopefully de minimis) of lawyers who promote the filing and pursuing of a medical malpractice case at any cost, my personal experience has not shown that to be the case. The contingency fee structure, in my opinion, abrogates that approach. While physicians perceive the lawyer as promoting any medical malpractice case, they fail to understand that attorneys ordinarily consider pursuing the medical malpractice litigation very carefully prior to getting involved because of the tremendous amount of time and costs involved.

§1.18 Physician/Attorney Relationships

The highly charged and emotionally heightened topic of medical malpractice litigation has fostered tension between the physician and attorney. There are at least three components of the relationship between the two disciplines that must be clarified and understood by both professionals. While the attorney acts as a sword or a shield for a client, the physician may have several roles in this medical malpractice arena. The attorney's role is clear and self-defined, and one which the attorney and client understand very easily. The physician, on the other hand, has several roles he or she can assume, ranging from that of the defendant to the subsequent treating physician to an expert witness. Physicians confuse the difference between a subsequent treating physician and an expert, but will never confuse the role played as the defendant. It is this role, of course, that engenders the most hostility and anger toward the attorney.

The Defendant Physician

Physicians absolutely cannot perceive and refuse to accept the idea that the attorney is a professional representing a client zealously and to the best of his or her ability. Doctors view issues as right or wrong, black or white, and they fail to perceive the attorney as one who must represent the client in the context of winning within the boundaries of proper professional conduct.

The doctor transfers anger about being sued from the patient to the lawyer because he or she perceives that the lawyer is encouraging the client to pursue the litigation. Physicians, perhaps subconsciously, recognize that without the skill and guidance of an attorney a patient would never be able to successfully promulgate the lawsuit and, therefore, the doctor's anger focuses on the lawyer.

This book is written for an attorney audience, but certain comments are more important for physicians to read. Lawyers must recognize the antipathy they arouse in physicians and must be prepared to handle this emotion appropriately. While physicians absolutely do not understand the power of the subpoena and the control an attorney has over them, attorneys rarely exercise that power until the communication between the two absolutely deteriorates.

From the plaintiff's attorney standpoint, the relationship rarely will be one of trust and confidence. Because of this, the plaintiff's attorney must detach himself or herself totally, ignore the emotional diatribes of the defendant physician, and act in an objective and professional manner. The requirement for this is absolute, because if the attorney allows himself or herself to become vindictive or personally antagonistic, he or she loses the ability to properly manage and coordinate tactics and strategy.

The Expert Witness

In every medical malpractice action, attorneys are at the mercy and whim of their expert witness. Since no cause of action can go forward without the opinion and support of the expert witness, attorneys generally tend to patronize their experts at almost any cost.

The relationship between the expert witness and the attorney is usually warm and comforting. The attorney is (sigh of relief) grateful that he or she has a physician who will explain the case and agree to testify as to the standard of care, and the physician believes he or she is doing a great service to an injured patient, and getting paid (usually handsomely) for it.

The Subsequent Treating Physician

Subsequent treating physicians come in many forms. Some physicians have an inexplicable hatred for all attorneys, and will resist (but never successfully) at all costs the attorney's request for testimony or medical records. Some subsequent treating physicians believe they can be of assistance to their patients yet noncommittal regarding the rendering of an opinion concerning one of their peers, and will cautiously agree to help. Finally, a certain proportion of subsequent treating physicians just do not want to get involved and verbalize this to the attorney or the client.

It is the first type of subsequent treating physician that will be the most problematical for plaintiffs' attorneys. The plaintiff's attorney must recognize that when this type of physician is involved in the relationship, even though the attorney can force testimony from that physician, the antagonism created by that physician may be such that it could be detrimental to the plaintiff's case. These types of individuals frequently will change their testimony or alter the facts in such a way as to be more harmful than of value to the plaintiff's case.

By the way, defendants' attorneys do not have this problem at all. Physicians jump at the chance to be of service for their fellow physician, sometimes perhaps even twisting the facts to be accommodating. However, the plaintiff's attorney has a terrible burden of selecting an expert witness and then attempting to get all subsequent treating physicians to cooperate.

§1.19 —Statement on Interprofessional Relationships

In 1981, the National Conference of Representatives of the American Bar Association and the American Medical Association adopted a statement by the respective associations which, although advisory and voluntary, was adopted with the request that the report be widely disseminated to physicians and medical societies. The following is the statement:

> *Preamble:* This statement recognizes that with the growing interrelationship of medicine and law it is inevitable that physicians and attorneys will be drawn into steadily increasing association. It will serve its purpose if it promotes the public welfare, improves the practical working relationships of the two professions, and facilitates the administration of justice.
>
> *Medical Reports:* The physicians, upon proper authorization, should promptly furnish the attorney with a complete medical report, and should realize that delays in providing medical information may prejudice the opportunity of the patient either to settle his claim or suit,

delay the trial of a case or cause additional expense or the loss of important testimony. The attorney should give the physician reasonable notice of the need for a report, and clearly specify the medical information which he seeks.

Conferences: It is the duty of each profession to present fairly and adequately the medical information involved in legal controversies. To that end, the practice of discussion in advance of the trial between the physician and the attorney is encouraged and recommended. Such discussion should be had in all instances unless it is mutually agreed that it is unnecessary. Conferences should be held at a time and place mutually convenient to the parties. The attorney and physician should fully disclose and discuss the medical information involved in the controversy.

Subpoena for Medical Witness: Because of conditions in a particular case or jurisdiction or because of the necessity for protecting himself or his client, the attorney is sometimes required to subpoena the physician as a witness. Although the physician should not take offense at being subpoenaed, the attorney should not cause the subpoena to be issued without prior notification to the physician. The duty of the physician is the same as that of any other person to respond to judicial process.

Arrangement for Court Appearances: While it is recognized that the conduct of the business of the courts cannot depend upon the convenience of litigants, lawyers or witnesses, arrangements can and should be made for the attendance of the physician as a witness which takes into consideration the professional demands upon his time. Such arrangements contemplate reasonable notice to the physician of the intention to call him as a witness and to advise him by telephone after the trial has commenced of the approximate time of his required attendance. The attorney should make every effort to conserve the time of the physician.

Physician Called as Witness: The attorney and the physician should treat one another with dignity and respect in the courtroom. The physician should testify solely as to the medical facts in the case and should frankly state his medical opinion. He should never be an advocate, and should realize that his testimony is intended to enlighten rather than to impress or prejudice the court or the jury. It is improper for the attorney to abuse a medical witness or to seek to influence his medical opinion. Established rules of evidence afford ample opportunity to test the qualifications, competence and credibility of a medical witness, and it is always improper and unnecessary for the attorney to embarrass or harass the physician.

Fees for Services of Physician Relative to Litigation: The physician is entitled to reasonable compensation for time spent in conferences, preparation of medical reports and for court or other appearances. These are proper and necessary items of expense in litigation involving medical questions. The attorney should do everything possible to assure payment for services rendered by the physician for himself or his client.

When the physician has not been fully paid, the attorney should request permission of the patient to pay the physician from any recovery which the attorney may receive in behalf of the patient.

I have noted that some attorneys in their requests for production of medical records to physicians have included the preceding statement in hopes that the physician, when reading the request for production, will be more inclined to cooperate fully, knowing that this is a joint statement between the physicians and attorneys.

§1.20 Code of Ethics

In 1980, the American Medical Association revised its "Principles of Medical Ethics." The following are the seven points outlined as the Principles of Medical Ethics by the American Medical Association:

Preamble:

The medical profession has long subscribed to a body of ethical statements developed primarily for the benefit of the patient. As a member of this profession, a physician must recognize responsibility not only to patients, but also to society, to other health professionals, and to self. The following Principles adopted by the American Medical Association are not laws, but standards of conduct which define the essentials of honorable behavior for the physician.

I. A physician shall be dedicated to providing competent medical service with compassion and respect to human dignity.

II. A physician shall deal honestly with patients and colleagues and strive to expose those physicians deficient in character or competence or who engage in fraud or deception.

III. A physician shall respect the law and also recognize a responsibility to seek changes in those requirements which are contrary to the best interest of the patient.

IV. A physician shall respect the rights of the patients of colleagues and of other health professionals and shall safeguard patient confidences within the constraints of the law.

V. A physician shall continue to study, apply and advance scientific knowledge, make relevant information available to patients, colleagues and the public, obtain consultation and use the talents of other health professionals when indicated.

VI. A physician shall, in the provision of appropriate patient care except in emergencies, be free to choose whom to serve, with whom to associate and the environment in which to provide medical services.

VII. A physician shall recognize a responsibility to participate in activities contributing to an improved community.

§1.21 Standard of Care

A standard of care is required when there is a need to identify acceptable levels of healthcare rendered to a patient. Physicians are not the only ones to have standards, since attorneys, accountants, businesspeople, and tradespeople of all kinds define a standard as a level of quality of service rendered. Standards are constantly being changed as awareness, experience, education, and technological advances improve. A primary care physician standard in the treatment of a patient with a kidney stone is at a different level than the standard to which a urologist would adhere. In this context of urological medical malpractice, courts are reluctant and indeed do not set a level or standard of care, but rather the standard is set by expert witnesses called at trial to inform the jury as to that standard. The expert witness is asked to opine as to the negligence of the defendant physician, but only in the context as to whether any departure from the standard of care occurred.

Perhaps one of the earliest articulations of this standard of care occurred in the 1937 case of *Vaughan v Menlove*.[9] Here, Chief Justice Tindall said,

> Instead, therefore, of saying that the liability for negligence should be coextensive with the judgment of each individual which would be as variable as the length of the foot of each individual, we ought rather to adhere to the rule which requires in all cases a regard to caution such as a man of ordinary prudence would observe.

This "ordinary prudence" term was later stated by Justice Holmes in *Texas & Pacific Railroad Co v Behymer*[10] as follows: "What usually is done may be evidence of what ought to be done, but what ought to be done is fixed by a standard of reasonable prudence, whether it usually is complied with or not."

Courts gradually moved to the standard of care which concerns the professional, and, in *Heath v Swift Wings, Inc,*[11] a 1979 case, it was said:

> It is a familiar rule of law that the standard of care required of an individual, unless altered by statute, is the conduct of the reasonably prudent man under the same or similar circumstances. While the standard of care of the reasonably prudent man remains constant, the quantity or degree of care required varies significantly with the attendant circumstances. Indeed, our courts have long recognized that one who engages in a business, occupation or profession must exercise the requisite degree of learning, skill and ability of that calling with reasonable and ordinary care. Furthermore, the specialist within a profession may be held to a standard of care greater than the required of the general practitioner.

---

[9] 3 Bing (NC) 467, 132 Eng Rep 490 (1887).
[10] 189 US 468 (1903).
[11] 40 NC App 158, 252 SE2d 256 (1979).

It is important to deal with terms such as "reasonable" and "prudent," and understand how courts use these words. M. Hill, H. Rossen, & W. Soggs' *Torts for Law School and Bar Examinations* (3d ed 1975) says: "This so-called reasonable, prudent man is a nonexistent imaginary person who is set up as a standard ideal person whose presumed conduct would represent the conduct of the average person in the community...." And, finally, as was stated in *Gillette v Tucker*,[12] "The traditional standard for doctors is that he exercise the average degree of skill, care and diligence exercised by members of the same profession practicing in the same or a similar locality in light of the present state of medical and surgical science."

It is important to understand that physicians are not held to the highest standard of care, but only to that standard of care practiced by the reasonable and prudent physician.

§1.22 —Reasons for Substandard Care

Hopefully, the concept of standard of care has been dissected enough so that the reader understands what the actual standard must concern. While terms such as "malpractice" or "negligence" may be used generically, it is the standard of care which must be defined, and the departure from that standard of care which must be shown for the plaintiff to prevail. The standard of care may be applicable regarding issues of consent, diagnosis, treatment, or patient referral. The duty which the physician owes to the patient is to comply with the standard of care regarding those and other issues. It is that departure from the standard of care which becomes the basis for a lawsuit if it causes injury to the patient.

It should now be possible to understand the complexity of the medical malpractice lawsuit. The elements of duty and failure to comply with the standard of care must be present in order to initiate the case, and *any* departure from the standard of care involving all of the multitudinous aspects of the physician/patient relationship can be a basis for the cause of action. Failure of the physician to provide coverage for a patient when the physician is out of town, failure of the physician to respond appropriately and timely to the emergency room call, failure of the physician to prescribe the appropriate drug dose, or failure of the physician to provide follow-up care and treatment for a patient all have been the bases for medical malpractice lawsuits.

§1.23 Informed Consent

The concept of consent with regard to the practice of medicine is unique to the twentieth century. The Hippocratic Oath certainly does not mention consent, and the development of "informed" consent is strongly based on traditional American moral and legal concepts of basic human rights. To do no harm is the first consideration of physicians, while the second is diag-

---

[12] 67 Ohio St 106, 65 NE 865 (1966).

nosing and hopefully curing the patient's illness. These two concepts bring us to the current dilemma of providing information to the patients in such a way that they can and indeed must play a part in the process. It is the basic right of every competent person to be involved in decisions about his or her medical care and, while physicians may not understand the need for this concept to be superior to the concept of providing healthcare per se, the vehicle of informed consent has forced physicians to be more aware of basic patient rights. The doctrine encompasses two elements: (1) the physician's duty of disclosure; and (2) acquisition of the permission or consent of the patient for the proposed treatment. The duty of disclosure has been generally described as the obligation to reveal to the patient: (a) the nature of the recommended therapy; (b) the expected benefits; (c) any serious risks or side effects of that therapy; (d) alternatives to that therapy or the risk of no therapy at all; and (e) any additional information that physicians would disclose in similar circumstances as a matter of good medical practice.

Two judicial schools of thought have emerged with reference to measuring the scope of the physician's duty to disclose, one being the professional or medical customs standard, and the other being the lay or reasonable patient standard.

According to the professional or medical customs standard, the information to be disclosed to the patient is that which a reasonable practitioner in the same or similar circumstances would have disclosed. As such, the professional or medical standard is essentially a matter of professional judgment to be measured against what reasonable practitioners would disclose after considering all the attendant circumstances. Those jurisdictions adhering to the professional or medical standard in measuring the physician's duty to disclose require the plaintiff to supply expert medical testimony as to what that professional standard is.

The lay or reasonable patient standard requires that the physician disclose all risks that would be material to a reasonable and prudent person in the patient's position. A material risk is one which a physician knows or ought to know would be significant to a reasonable person in the patient's position in deciding whether or not to submit to a particular medical treatment or procedure. Those jurisdictions which measure the duty of disclosure by the lay or reasonable patient standard do not require expert medical testimony since this standard is measured by the patient's right to know, and liability does not flow from any medical standard.

The second element of informed consent involves permission from the patient. If a physician fails to obtain the patient's consent before administering treatment, the treatment is an unauthorized touching of the patient's body which is technically a battery. The most commonly cited early pronouncement of this rule was given by Justice Cardozo, who stated, "Any human being of adult years and sound mind has the right to determine what should be done with his own body, and that surgeon who performs an operation without his patient's consent commits an assault for which he is liable for damage."[13]

A cause of action in battery may arise from the touching of a person in an unauthorized or unprivileged manner during the course of medical examination, treatment, or surgery. This cause of action is not dependent on the skill or care involved in the performance of the procedure, and is distinct from an action based on malpractice or negligence. The primary issue under the battery theory is whether the patient consented to the actual treatment administered, and not whether the physician violated the duty to use skill and care in the treatment.

The court in *Salgo v Leland Stanford, Jr, University Board of Trustees*[14] discussed the issue of the patient's consent in the context of negligence rather than battery. The court reasoned that "A physician violates his duty to his patient and subjects himself to liability if he withholds any facts which are necessary to form the basis of an intelligent consent by the patient to the proposed treatment."

In 1960, the Kansas Supreme Court, in *Natanson v Kline*,[15] became the first court to hold that a physician's liability for failure to inform the patient of the risks and alternatives to a proposed therapy should be grounded in negligence law rather than battery.

Thus, the right to informed consent means that every patient for whom any therapeutic or diagnostic procedure might be planned must be given all pertinent and material information about the medical situation, and that care and management cannot legally be started unless and until the patient has received such information and given consent to that procedure. The courts have declared that this is a constitutional right embodied in the First Amendment of the United States Constitution governing the right to privacy, including the right to control over one's own body.

§1.24 Burden of Proof

The burden of proof technically includes the burden of persuasion which is that requirement of one party to convince the judge or jury of the elements of his or her case. The other aspect of burden of proof is the level of proof required, which follows three standards: (1) a preponderance of the evidence, or (2) clear or convincing evidence, or (3) evidence beyond a reasonable doubt.

In a medical malpractice case, the plaintiff has the burden of proof to establish by a preponderance of the evidence that the defendant has departed from the standard of care, proximately causing damage to the plaintiff. In *Price v Neyland*,[16] the court said:

> In order to fasten liability in a malpractice case, it is necessary that the plaintiff prove, by a preponderance of the evidence, (1) the recog-

---

[13] Schloendorf v Society of NY Hosps, 211 NY 125, 102 NE 92 (1914).
[14] 154 Cal App 560, 317 P2d 170 (1957).
[15] 186 Kan 393, 350 P2d 1093, *clarified*, 187 Kan 186, 354 P2d 670 (1960).
[16] 115 US App DC 355, 320 F2d 674 (1963).

nized standards of medical care in the community which would be exercised by physicians in the same specialty under similar circumstances, and (2) the physician in suit departed from that standard in his treatment of the plaintiff.

The essential element is proving the departure from the standard of care. A bad result or an error in judgment is not necessarily a departure from the standard of care, and the classic example may be the situation of torsion of the testicle.

Torsion, or twisting, of the testicle is a urological emergency which, if not treated promptly, will result in compromise of the vascular supply to the testicle with subsequent death and shrinkage of that testicle. Torsion is most frequently seen in prepubertal males and most often involves a sudden onset of sharp testicular pain which brings the patient to the emergency room. Proper evaluation includes taking a proper history, doing an appropriate physical examination, obtaining certain laboratory data including urinalysis and testicular scan, and, if necessary, surgical exploration. It is not uncommon that a urologist will do all these tests and yet make a judgmental decision that torsion is not present, but that the diagnosis is epididymitis, an infection of the tissues surrounding the testicle which closely mimics torsion.

If the patient subsequently turns out to have torsion, which will become very apparent in a few weeks when the testicle dies and shrinks, he may then go to his lawyer, seeking advice. Based on the previous facts, there may be no basis for a lawsuit because the standard of care was met, yet the wrong diagnosis was made and a bad result occurred.

This case is merely descriptive of the point that each case is individual and different, but the bottom line is that a poor result is not necessarily an indication of a departure from the standard of care.

§1.25 Res Ipsa Loquitur

The doctrine of res ipsa loquitur may be somewhat overrated in medical malpractice cases, but a brief description is certainly warranted here. This doctrine is a rule of evidence that may have several effects, depending on the jurisdiction. The three elements of this doctrine which must be present are:

1. The injury must be one that would not have occurred in the absence of negligence
2. The injury must have been caused solely by the exclusive control of the defendant
3. The plaintiff must not have contributed in any way to the injury

Because of the complexity of medical malpractice cases, rarely can this doctrine alone support the plaintiff's case. Unless the trier of fact can ascertain as a matter of common knowledge as to the negligence suggested, expert medical testimony is invariably required to establish the departure from the standard of care.

If the jurisdiction allows the doctrine to be used, the jury may accept the fact that the defendant was negligent. The doctrine can also be used as a burden-shifting device, requiring the defendant to establish that his or her conduct was within the accepted standard of care. Finally, the doctrine may be seen as a presumption of negligence which the defendant must rebut. In any of these situations, it is only the very narrow case wherein the doctrine solely applies.

57A Am Jur 2d *Negligence* §305 (1989) sets out the following rules:

> There is a sharp conflict of authority as to whether pleading a specific act of negligence waives the pleader's right to rely upon the doctrine of res ipsa loquitur. Some jurisdictions adopt the view that if the case is a proper one for the application of the doctrine, the plaintiff, by pleading the particular cause of the accident in no way loses his right to rely upon the doctrine, and any specific allegations of negligence in the complaint are wholly immaterial, provided of course the complaint otherwise contains a general allegation of negligence. In other words, by the mere allegation of a specific act of negligence, he is not deprived of the benefit of the doctrine so far as the specific act of negligence itself is concerned. The application of the doctrine is limited to the establishment of the particular acts of negligence alleged, just as any proof which the plaintiff might seek to introduce would be limited to the establishment of the negligence alleged.[17]

If res ipsa loquitur is found to apply in a specific case, the majority view is that it creates a permissible inference of negligence, thereby shifting the burden of proof to the defendant.

The two most common examples of applying the doctrine occur when foreign objects are left in a patient after surgery and expert testimony is not required to explain this fact to the jury, or when a patient, after an anesthetic, sustains an otherwise inexplicable injury such as damage to an extremity because of the positioning of the patient on the surgical table. In either case, if an expert witness is used to describe the standard of care, the mere presumption of negligence will not be enough to prevail.

In Georgia, the doctrine of res ipsa loquitur does not apply in malpractice suits. "An unintended result does not raise an inference of negligence. It is presumed that medical or surgical services were performed in an ordinarily skillful manner."[18]

---

[17] Reprinted by permission of The Lawyers
[18] Hayes v Brown, 108 Ga App 360, 133 SE2d 102 (1963).

22 Malpractice Considerations

In the case of *Terrell v West Paces Ferry Hospital, Inc,*[19] wherein a leaking duodenal suture line required several more operations, the court said, "We cannot conclude that actionable negligence appears clearly from the record and that expert opinion evidence is unnecessary to prove the plaintiff's case. We must similarly reject the plaintiff's contention that a prima facie case is created by the doctrine of res ipsa loquitur."

§1.26 Damages

A definition of somewhat confusing terms is appropriate for this discussion. Confusion usually arises between terms of damage, damages, and injury. Rather than use a dictionary for a strict definition of these terms, quotes from specific cases more clearly define the similarities and contrast the differences of the terms. " 'Damages' is a word which expresses in dollars and cents the injury sustained by the plaintiff."[20] " 'Legal injury' must be a violation of some legal right, and is distinct in meaning from the damage that may flow from the injury."[21] " 'Damage' may be defined to be the loss, injury or deterioration caused by negligence, design or accident of one person to another. . . ."[22] " 'Damages' are simply a measure of injury."[23]

Purposes

The *Restatement (Second) of Torts* §901 (1977) says that the purposes of damages are: "(a) to give compensation, indemnity or restitution for harm, (b) to determine rights, (c) to punish wrongdoers and deter wrongful conduct, and (d) to vindicate parties and deter retaliation or violent and unlawful self-help."

Elements

For each injury—bodily, property, or death—there are certain elements of damages recoverable. Personal injury lawsuits allow compensatory (both general and special) damages, while property damage actions only allow market value recovery. Survival or wrongful death actions allow other types of recovery such as conscious pain and suffering, funeral expenses, loss of earning power, and actual employment losses. This discussion focuses only on the personal injury elements of damages.

The *Restatement (Second) of Torts* §904 (1977) provides: "One whose interests of personalty have been tortiously invaded is entitled to recover damages for past or prospective (a) bodily harm and emotional distress, (b) loss or

---

[19] 162 Ga App 783, 292 SE2d 433 (1982). Co-operative Publishing Company, Rochester, New York.

[20] Turcotte v DeWitt, 333 Mass 389, 131 NE2d 195 (1955).

[21] Combs v Hargis Bank & Trust Co, 234 Ky 202, 27 SW2d 955 (1930).

[22] Hanna v Martin, 49 So 2d 585 (Fla 1950).

[23] Kozar v Chesapeake & Ohio RR, 449 F2d 1238 (DC Cir 1971).

impairment of earning capacity, (c) reasonable medical and other expenses, and (d) harm to property or business caused by the invasion."

§1.27 —Categories

There are three general categories of damages: compensatory, nominal, and punitive.

Compensatory Damages

Compensatory damages are further subdivided into special and general. Special or pecuniary damages are the actual monies lost as a result of the injury and must be specially pleaded. The special damages include harm to property, loss of earning capacity, and any creation of liability such as medical bills. Loss of wages, impairment of earning capacity, and aggravation of a pre-existing condition must be specifically set out in the complaint. The purpose of specifically pleading special damages is to give proper notice of the damages sought and to give the defendant an opportunity to defend against them.

General damages, also known as nonpecuniary damages, need not be specially pleaded and involve such issues as past and future pain and suffering, loss of enjoyment of life, loss of consortium, etc. These general damages are "those which the law would impute as the natural, necessary and logical consequences of the defendant's wrongful act, and such damages do not have to be specifically pleaded, but upon the proper averment of the wrongful act, they are recoverable under a claim of general damages."[24]

Juries have a wide latitude in fixing an amount allocated to general damages, and this amount will not be altered unless it is clear that the jury acted from bias or mistake of law, or when the verdict is clearly against the weight of the evidence.

Nominal Damages

Nominal damages are usually thought of as vindicating the plaintiff in a moral victory, but, because significant damage was not sustained, the jury awards a trifling sum—usually one dollar. These damages are rarely seen in medical malpractice actions because of the usually significant injury and damage to the patient. Certain jurisdictions will allow cost of the lawsuit recoverable to the plaintiff if even nominal damages are awarded.

Punitive Damages

Terms such as "exemplary" or "vindictive" may occasionally be interchanged with punitive damages. These money damages are in the nature of punishment to the defendant and act as a deterrent for repeating the same or similar actions in the future. Punitive damages are usually awarded only in instances of egregious, malicious, reckless, or wanton conduct.

---

[24] Johnson v Flex-O-Lite Mfg Corp, 314 SW2d 75 (Mo 1958).

Georgia law provides, "In a tort action in which there are aggravating circumstances in either the act or the intention, the jury may give additional damages to deter the wrongdoer from repeating the trespass, or as compensation for the wounded feelings of the plaintiff."[25]

Interestingly, it is well known in Georgia and exemplified by a 1981 case, *Mayfield v Ideal Enterprises, Inc*,[26] that "[e]ven though aggravating circumstances may exist, it is improper to award punitive damages unless general damages have also been awarded, for exemplary damages are 'additional damages', and a claim for them will not lie unless general damages are not recovered."

Punitive damages are usually not an issue in medical malpractice cases because the circumstances are usually not of a reckless, wanton, or aggravating nature. On the other hand, there is at least one pending action in Georgia wherein a general surgeon operated on a patient claiming concern over the possibility of her enlarged thyroid gland being a "bleed into a cancer" without doing one single preoperative test on her. She subsequently turned out to have an overactive thyroid which responded to medication. Punitive damages are being sought in that action because of the defendant's grossly reckless and aggravating conduct.

It is also important to know that some states have a limit on the amount of monies allowed to be awarded as punitive damages. Georgia[27] has a $250,000 cap, unless the tort is a products liability one, while Colorado[28] and Oklahoma[29] limit punitive damages to the amount of actual compensatory damages.

Finally, numerous states have statutory provisions which apportion a certain percentage of the punitive damage recovery to the state. Kansas[30] provides that 50 per cent is paid to the state, while Colorado[31] provides for the state to receive one-third, and Georgia[32] provides for the state to receive 75 per cent, but only of any products liability punitive award.

§1.28 —Pain and Suffering

This type of recoverable damages is discussed separately and not under general compensatory damages because these damages, when awarded, are usually the largest amount in any medical malpractice lawsuit.

There are usually various elements involved in defining pain and suffering. Both physical pain and mental pain are involved, and the suffering can

---

[25] Ga Code Ann §51-12-5 (1987).

[26] 157 Ga App 266, 277 SE2d 62 (1981).

[27] Ga Code Ann §51-12-5.1(F), (G) (1987).

[28] Colo Rev Stat §13-21-102(1)(A) (1986).

[29] Okla Stat Ann tit 23, §9(A) (West 1987).

[30] Kan HB 2025, §1(H) (1987).

[31] Colo Rev Stat §13-21-102(4) (1986).

[32] Ga Code Ann §51-12-5.1(E)(2) (1987).

be interpreted as the anguish and concern over the patient's physical and mental pain. Of course, each person has varying levels of tolerance of these emotions, and the portrayal of the plaintiff's actual or alleged pain and suffering is important to maximize the recovery.

A 1980 Utah court in *Judd v Rowley's Cherry Hill Orchards, Inc*[33] said:

> The pain and suffering for which damages are recoverable in a personal injury action included not only physical pain, but also mental pain or anguish, that is the mental reaction to that pain and to the possible consequences of the physical injury. Included in mental pain and suffering is the diminished enjoyment of life, as well as the humiliation and embarrassment resulting from permanent scars and disability.

Jurors can identify with the actual pain and suffering the plaintiff undergoes if the attorney properly and vigorously portrays such injury to them. One criticism of pain and suffering damages awards has been that the amount is directly related to the theatrics of the plaintiff's attorney.

There is, of course, no precise manner for calculating the amount of money which will provide salve for one's pain and suffering. The court in *Firestone Tire & Rubber v Pinyan*[34] said, "The law fixes no measure for pain and suffering except the enlightened conscience of impartial jurors."

Ordinarily, pain and suffering, being a general compensatory award, does not have to be specially pleaded. This type of damages naturally flows from the injury and is a direct and consequential part of the tortious act. It is also important to know that not only past pain and suffering but also future pain and suffering may be recoverable.

§1.29 —Pre- and Post-Judgment Interest

Historically, interest on judgments was not recoverable, but the modern era has seen not only post- but also pre-judgment interest awarded. Most jurisdictions have statutes governing this, and it would be most appropriate in the early stages of filing your lawsuit to see if such an unliquidated damages act or a pre-judgment interest statute exists.

Originally, a liquidated claim—i.e., one with a sum certain—was the only type of claim to allow pre-judgment interest. But now even unliquidated damages may be applicable for the interest. The reasons for an award of pre-judgment interest are:

1. Fairness to the parties [Since liability attaches at the time of the tort, it is felt only fair to allow the judgment to run from that date also]
2. To discourage delay [The defendant may have a certain financial incentive in delaying the suit if there is no fear of pre-judgment interest]

---

[33] 611 P2d 1216 (Utah 1980).
[34] 155 Ga App 343, 270 SE2d 883 (1980).

3. Equality of treatment amongst different plaintiffs [Two identical plaintiffs with identical injuries may receive different judgments because one brings the case to trial earlier than the other]
4. To encourage the settlement of cases [Probably the most important reason for the pre-judgment interest]

Post-judgment interest is provided for by every state, and the interest amount is usually also set by statute. The pure purpose of this doctrine is to allow the plaintiff to be compensated immediately for sums owed from a date certain. This idea encourages the defendant to promptly pay.

§1.30 Negligent Infliction of Emotional Distress

One must carefully understand the difference between intentional and negligent infliction of emotional distress to see to which cause of action the doctrine attaches. Negligent infliction of emotional distress can not only apply to the plaintiff/victim, but also to an innocent bystander. The 1968 case of *Dillon v Legg*[35] in California more fully discusses this aspect of emotional distress. The case involved the witnessing of a fatal automobile accident by the victim's mother and sister. They sought damages for emotional distress. The early rule of law required a satisfaction of a "zone of physical danger" for emotional distress to apply, but this seminal case discarded that rule and served as a model for other states to follow in defining this tort. Additionally, this case also argued that bystanders must have had a close relationship with the victim.

For the plaintiff to recover damages of negligent infliction of emotional distress, early law required an "impact rule" or a "zone of physical danger" to be present. Modern theory has replaced this requirement with the "zone of psychic danger." This doctrine requires that the plaintiff must be in a position to "foreseeably sustain mental distress." Obviously, this zone will also be present for the plaintiff/victim, and it is the plaintiff/bystander who must satisfy this requirement to prevail.

Alternatively, the tort of intentional infliction of emotional distress stands as a separate and distinct tort also known as the "tort of outrage." Here, no zones of physical or psychic danger are required since the direct and intentional infliction of the emotional distress is solely aimed at the plaintiff. While this tort may not be seen in the medical malpractice area, perhaps the most important thing to remember about it is that oftentimes insurance coverage will not be available for this tort.

---

[35] 68 Cal 2d 728, 441 P2d 912, 69 Cal Rptr 72 (1968).

§1.31 Collateral Source

The *Restatement (Second) of Torts* §920A (1977) says, "Payments made to or benefits conferred on the injured party from other sources are not credited against the tortfeasor's liability, although they cover all or part of the harm for which the tortfeasor is liable."

Alternatively, common law says that an injured party's recovery shall be limited to the actual damage suffered. Thus, although tension arises wherein a plaintiff recovers from an insurer full reimbursement yet seeks to recover the same amount from the alleged tortfeasor, the collateral source rule appears to abrogate the tension.

The tortfeasor should not benefit from the foresight of the plaintiff to have purchased insurance and, if the amount of premiums paid by the plaintiff to maintain the insurance are balanced against the amount which the insurance paid out, the benefits oftentimes may not cover the cost incurred.

The collateral source rule also functions as a rule of evidence, preventing any information involving insurance coverage to be given to the jury. Most jurisdictions will declare a mistrial if this information is revealed (*see* §1.42).

§1.32 Comparative Negligence

Under the harsh rule of contributory negligence, if a plaintiff contributed to any degree to the cause of the injury, he or she was barred from any recovery. Because this doctrine failed to consider apportionment of fault and thereby recovery, the comparative negligence system arose whereby a plaintiff is prevented from recovering only that amount of damages for which he or she is responsible. Most jurisdictions hold that if the plaintiff is either 49 per cent or 50 per cent responsible for the injury, no recovery is available.

A related issue is the "last clear chance" doctrine. Although it is now almost completely abolished, that doctrine provided that if the defendant could have avoided injury to the plaintiff even after the plaintiff's negligence occurred, the defendant was still liable.

§1.33 Assumption of the Risk

The defense doctrine of assumption of the risk is very complicated and this brief discussion will only superficially cover it. Basically, there are two types of assumption of the risk: expressed and implied. The expressed assumption of the risk is defined in *Restatement (Second) of Torts* §496B (1963) as follows: "A plaintiff who by contract or otherwise expressly agrees to accept a risk of harm arising from the defendant's negligent or reckless conduct cannot recover for such harm unless the agreement is invalid as contrary to public policy." Section 496C states that "a plaintiff who fully understands a risk of harm to himself . . . caused by the defendant's conduct . . . and he nevertheless voluntarily chooses to remain within the area of the risk is not entitled to recover for harm within that risk." While some jurisdictions have abolished the implied assumption of the risk, others have eliminated the need for any assumption of the risk prior to adopting the defense of comparative negligence. Georgia and others have retained assumption of the risk as a complete bar to recovery.

§1.34 Joint and Several Liability

This common law rule which allows a plaintiff to recover all or part of the proceeds from all or one of the defendants is available in most jurisdictions (*see* §1.46).

American Motorcycle Association v Superior Court of Los Angeles County[36] says:

> Adoption of comparative negligence to ameliorate the inevitable consequences of the contributory negligence rule does not warrant the abolition or contraction of the established Joint and Several Liability doctrine; each tortfeasor whose negligence is a proximate cause of an indivisible injury remains individually liable for all compensable damages attributable to that injury. The Joint and Several Liability doctrine continues to play an important and legitimate role in protecting the ability of a negligently injured person to obtain adequate compensation for his injuries from those tortfeasors who have negligently inflicted the harm.

§1.35 —Contribution

This is a doctrine whereby one tortfeasor who believes he or she has paid more than his or her fair share may recover from a joint tortfeasor those proceeds which were allocated to each tortfeasor's negligence. In other words, this is a reimbursement technique amongst tortfeasors to share the cost based on fault. Some jurisdictions define "contribution" as to comparative fault (i.e., an allocation), while others use the pro rata or equal shares method. As a corollary to contribution, it is also important to understand that a tortfeasor who has contributed less than his or her allocated share does not have a right of contribution from other tortfeasors.

It is most important for the reader to be aware of the Uniform Contribution among Tortfeasors Act which has been enacted in numerous jurisdictions. This act describes the rights of joint tortfeasors to obtain contribution and should be understood if applicable by each trial attorney.

§1.36 —Indemnity

This doctrine of joint tortfeasors involves the shifting of the burden of paying the entire amount of the recovery to one other joint tortfeasor. It is con-

---

[36] 28 Cal 3d 578, 578 P2d 899, 146 Cal Rptr 182 (1978).

trasted with contribution in that indemnification involves shifting the entire amount while contribution usually means sharing an allocated amount.

An exculpatory clause in a contract indemnifying a party is also known as a "hold harmless clause" and generally is looked on with disfavor by the courts and is very strictly construed.

It is important to realize that in medical malpractice cases a plaintiff may be put in the hands of the defendant doctor by an initial but separate negligent tortfeasor. Some courts call this situation one involving "successive tortfeasors," rather than joint tortfeasors, and allow indemnification for the original and initial tortfeasor.

If the negligence of the physician results in a separate and distinct injury, almost all jurisdictions which allow indemnification will apply it here. *Herrerro v Atkinson*,[37] a 1964 California case, concerned a motorist as the initial tortfeasor who was allowed to recover indemnity from the physicians who subsequently and negligently cared for the injured patient.

§1.37 Release

Since a release may be an important part of any personal injury case in which liability of a tortfeasor is avoided, a brief synopsis is necessary. Traditionally, the release is a contract between parties whereby one abandons any claim against the other. Unfortunately, the common law rule was that a release of one joint tortfeasor releases all the other joint tortfeasors. Since most jurisdictions recognize the harshness of the common law doctrine, efforts were made to ameliorate it, and statutory provisions as well as "covenants not to sue" were forthcoming. The covenant not to sue was a contract between the parties for the plaintiff not to sue that particular tortfeasor, and in exchange for that contract, the plaintiff received sums of money. This also allowed the plaintiff to continue the cause of action against other tortfeasors. It is important to understand that if the consideration received was greater than the total damage sustained by the plaintiff, the covenant not to sue may be considered to have the effect of releasing the other tortfeasors, also.

§1.38 Countersuits

As a reaction to what is perceived to be the filing of frivolous and ill-founded lawsuits against them, defendant physicians have been filing lawsuits against patients and plaintiffs' lawyers on the grounds that they were the subject of a malicious prosecution. Generally, these causes of action are unsuccessful. Inherent in any medical malpractice lawsuit is a requirement for the contemporaneous filing of an expert's affidavit, and, in view of this, courts are reluctant to find frivolous or malicious intent. In the seminal case

---

[37] 227 Cal App 2d 69, 38 Cal Rptr 490 (1964).

of *Berlin v Nathan*,[38] a 1978 Illinois case, the court held that where there was no showing of malice or improper motive, the physician suing the law firm for filing the suit against him did not have a cause of action for malicious prosecution.

Additionally, the 1981 Texas case of *Rodriquez v Carroll*[39] said that malicious prosecution suits by physicians to recover for injuries to personal and professional reputation, personal humiliation, mental anguish and distress, damages to professional practice, and increased insurance premiums do not trigger the special damages requirement of "interference with person or property" necessary for a suit for damages for malicious prosecution to lie in Texas.

Lest the beleaguered physician becomes distraught, let it be noted that in *Bull v McCuskey*,[40] a 1980 Nevada case wherein the attorney (1) failed to examine or obtain any medical records, (2) failed to confer with a doctor, (3) failed to submit the client's claim to a screening panel, (4) obtained no depositions from any doctor, and (5) did not obtain expert witnesses for the trial, the malicious prosecution judgment of $35,000 for compensatory damages and $50,000 for punitive damages was upheld in favor of the doctor.

§1.39 Peer Review

Peer review—i.e., the evaluation of one equal in rank—has become a buzzword in the healthcare field as it has been in other professions for many years. The military may be the best example of peer review performed to achieve advancement, but certainly all business corporations have utilized peer review for decades for the same purpose.

The healthcare profession has only recently (within the last 10 or 15 years) earnestly embraced the concept, and now peer review is not only considered a special doctrine, but the concept has spread to issues other than evaluation—e.g., credentialing, confidentiality, quality issues, utilization review, risk management, and expert witnesses in litigation, to name a few.

The reader needs to understand the peer review statutes of each jurisdiction. These statutes may provide plenary protection for the defendant or witnesses, but this shield may also be pierced under certain circumstances. The topic of protection of peer reviewers from liability is not pertinent here, and this discussion is confined to the confidentiality of those records and the ability or inability of the practitioner to gain access to the information.

It is important to understand that peer review records involve not only evaluation (i.e., credentialing, licensing, or critiquing) of the defendant physician, but also information which may be available from committee reports (utilization review, risk management, quality assurance) or other ad hoc dis-

---

[38] 64 Ill App 3d 940, 21 Ill Dec 682 (1978).
[39] 510 F Supp 547 (ND Tex 1981).
[40] 96 Nev 706, 615 P2d 957 (1980).

cussions concerning the defendant or issues in the case. This information may be the most desirable to obtain and on which one's case may turn.

Georgia provides in Ga Code Ann §31-7-143 (1983) that the proceedings and records of medical review committees shall not be subject to discovery or introduction into evidence in any civil action against a provider of professional health services arising out of the matters which are the subject of evaluation and review by such committees; and no person who is in attendance at a meeting of such committees shall be permitted or required to testify in any such civil action as to any evidence or other matters produced or presented during their proceedings of such committee.

In *Emory Clinic v Houston*,[41] the Georgia Supreme Court ruled that records of peer review groups and medical review committees are not discoverable or admissible in any civil action. In that case, Sargus Houston brought a medical malpractice action against Emory University and Clinic and Dr. Cavanagh after Dr. Cavanagh performed a corneal transplant on the wrong eye and then tried to conceal the mistake. Houston alleged fraud, deceit, and conspiracy and contended that Emory also undertook to cover up Dr. Cavanagh's mistake. Houston sought to compel production of the peer review/medical committee reports. The trial court denied the motion, and the Court of Appeals reversed in part, holding that the peer review/medical review privilege was waivable, and that a doctor who served on a committee could not be compelled to testify to information he or she received as a committee member. The Georgia Supreme Court reversed, holding that there was an "absolute embargo" on discovering the records of peer review/medical review committees and that the principle of waiver was not applicable.

In *Breddice v Doctors Hospital*,[42] a 1970 District of Columbia case which involved a plaintiff seeking records regarding a patient's death and the fact that the hospital committee minutes were in contradiction with the public's interest, the court stated: "Confidentiality is essential to effective functioning of the staff meetings, and these staff meetings are essential to the continued improvement in the care and treatment of patients.... [T]o subject these discussions and deliberations to the discovery process without a showing of exceptional necessity would result in terminating such deliberations."

However, in 1984, in *Chandra v Sprinke*,[43] the Missouri Superior Court refused to adopt a peer review privilege. The court found that the peer review system was designed to benefit the public, and that the public's interest lay with discoverability rather than confidentiality.

Finally, New Mexico may have the right idea. In *Southwest Community Health Services v Smith*,[44] the court said:

---

[41] 258 Ga 434, 369 SE2d 913 (1988).
[42] 50 FRD 249 (DC 1970).
[43] 678 SW2d 804 (Mo 1984).
[44] 107 NM 196, 755 P2d 40 (1988).

We hold that all data and information acquired by a review organization and the exercise of its duties and functions and opinions formed as a result of the review organization's hearing shall be governed by the peer review statute. When a party invokes the statute to immunize evidence from discovery, the burden rests with that party to prove that the data or information was generated exclusively as the result of peer review deliberations. If the evidence was neither generated nor formed exclusively for or as a result of peer review, it shall not be immune from discovery unless it is shown to be otherwise available by the exercise of reasonable diligence. The party seeking to compel discovery would have had the initial burden of proving relevance to the subject matter. The procedure will entail the trial court's in camera examination of the information and perhaps an evidentiary hearing to determine whether it properly falls within the parameters of the peer review statute.

We further hold that if the information is ruled to be confidential, the party seeking access must then satisfy the trial court that the information constitutes evidence which is critical to the cause of action or defense. If the trial court determines that the success or failure of a litigant's cause of action or defense would likely turn on the evidence adjudged to fall within the scope of the statute, then the trial court shall compel production of such evidence. It is the trial judge who will be interested with balancing the needs of litigants to discover evidence essential to the merits of their case.

While one could understandably perceive the conflict surrounding discoverability of peer review records as being between the public's right to know versus the ability of physicians to be critical of their peers without the fear of reprisal, an alternative direction is becoming apparent. It is true that physicians' uninhibited discourse relative to their peers will be chilled by the threat of discoverability, but without the prospect of disclosure of these peer review meetings, these effectively secret discussions only promote dialogues by those who would refuse to do so in any other setting. True peer review should be privileged from defamation actions, thereby encouraging forthright expressions, but the fact that the information discussed by doctors about their peers would be available for public scrutiny should not be a deterrent to such discussions. While it may be difficult to openly criticize one's peers knowing that this criticism will be available to anyone interested, this is what peer review should be—not such that it is done in a clandestine manner unavailable to others' analysis.

§1.40 Health Care Quality Improvement Act of 1986

It is important for the reader to be aware of the Health Care Quality Improvement Act of 1986. This federal act was mandated because of two main reasons: (1) the threat of treble money damage liability under federal antitrust law, which unreasonably discouraged physicians from participating in effective peer review despite a national need to provide protection for physicians engaging in such review; and (2) the national need to restrict the ability of incompetent physicians to move from state to state without disclosure or discovery of the physicians' previous damaging or incompetent performance.

The immunity for physicians participating in peer review is the topic for another text, and most of the act is devoted to that aspect, but Part B—Reporting of Information—is germane to this discussion.

The reported information will be sent to a national data bank to become operational in the summer of 1990. Unisys, an information system organization, has been awarded a five-year government contract to operate the bank. Information gathered will come from boards of medical examiners, healthcare entities, hospitals, and professional societies. Disciplinary actions, settlements or judgments in medical malpractice actions, and adverse actions regarding a physician's clinical privileges for over 30 days will be reported. Hospitals will be required to access the bank for any information on new or current staff physicians. Additionally, hospitals will be required to update information to the bank concerning their physicians.

Plaintiffs' attorneys may be able to access the information in certain limited situations, such as if a hospital has failed to obtain the data bank information on the practitioner, and only in cases involving litigation against the hospital.

§1.41 Tort Reform

This is a 1970s movement based on certain third parties' interests in modifying or changing the present tort system. The various factions include the medical profession, the legal profession, the insurance industry, consumer groups, and the government. The basic issue involves money awards, and it is the huge rise in settlements and jury awards which has really encouraged the total idea of tort reform. Other issues have arisen such as statute of limitations, expert witness, collateral source, etc., and all of these issues will be discussed in the remainder of this chapter.

One must also realize that tort reform affects not only medical malpractice, but also other torts—particularly products liability. Obviously, this brief discussion will confine itself to medical malpractice issues.

For whatever reason or on whatever basis, coalitions have been formed all over the country, concerned about their perspective of the issues. Most states have passed some form of tort reform, and it behooves the reader to carefully understand and be aware of his or her jurisdiction's statutes. Of course, lobbying efforts have been most successful to persuade either the public or legislators about a particular issue, and we must understand this in our focus on the topic.

Numerous task forces appointed by federal agencies and state governors have addressed the problem of tort reform, and their findings are all published and readily accessible. One of the most comprehensive sources of the issues in tort reform is the Tort Policy Working Group, a governmental agency which in March 1987 published its last work, *An Update on the Liability Crisis*. Its conclusions bear repeating:

> First, the crisis in insurance availability and affordability, while substantially ameliorated, continues to impose significant costs on most of the American economy. The effects of the crisis likely will be felt throughout the economy, particularly in certain sectors, for some time to come. Second, tort liability is a key underlying reason for the crisis in insurance availability and affordability. Its contribution to the crisis is two-fold: rapidly expanding liability including dramatically higher damage awards have substantially increased their cost of the tort liability system; and changing doctrinal standards have significantly heightened the uncertainty and unpredictability of the tort system, and thereby have exacerbated the already serious problems of the system. Third, legislative tort reforms are reasonable, legitimate and effective response to many of the deficiencies of tort law. Such legislation, however, is by no means the only answer to the problems of the tort system; much other responsibility for improvement remains with the courts. Fourth, rigorous and meaningful tort reforms can have a real impact on insurance availability and affordability, if given the opportunity and sufficient time to work. Fifth, the working group continues to believe that there is no justification or need for federal insurance regulation or the creation of federal insurance or indemnification programs. Sixth, there is an appropriate rule for federal tort reform legislation in those areas where there is a compelling federal interest. Such areas include product liability, the liability of federal government contractors, and the tort liability of the federal government and its employees. Seventh, the administration should continue to support and work actively with governors and state legislators to achieve reasonable and workable court reforms at the state level. Eighth, the working group continues to believe that the eight tort reforms recommended in its prior report represent the most sensible and effective potential reforms of the American civil justice system.

§1.42 —Collateral Source

As noted previously in §1.31, collateral source was a common law rule whereby the defendant was responsible to the plaintiff for any and all recovery. Only with the advent of insurance and especially insurance paid for by a third party (employers, governmental agencies) did offset of the collateral source become an issue. Many jurisdictions have included this offset in their collateral source modifications.

Thus, if a plaintiff has hospital insurance which has paid the entire bill, this amount will be deducted from the plaintiff's recovery. Of course, this raises the obvious question as to why the defendant should get the benefit of the plaintiff's insurance. If anything, the offset amount should go to the insurance company.

Other issues such as whether insurance paid for by a third party and not by the plaintiff should be the only collateral source offset have also been considered. The final enactment in most states is that the collateral source may be introduced as evidence to the jury for them decide as to any offset or not.

§1.43 —Attorney's Fees

The contingency fee has been a source of discontent from the insurance company and physician perspective. Strangely, clients are usually satisfied that whatever recovery they receive was on the basis of their attorney's efforts. It is the physicians and insurance companies who have raised the specter of higher transaction costs secondary to the enormous contingency fee system.

The contingency fee is that amount awarded to the attorney contingent upon prevailing in the case. Usually, this is from 33 per cent to 50 per cent of the total recovery. Frequently, this percentage is divided up, depending on the situation; i.e., if a referral attorney is involved, a certain percentage will go to him or her according to his or her participation in the case.

Opponents of the contingency fee say that since attorneys have a direct pecuniary interest in the case, they inflate claims and, in addition, such fees of hundreds of thousands of dollars are out of proportion to the amount of time spent on the case and that this is unconscionable.

Proponents of the contingency fee claim that this is the only way plaintiffs can afford attorneys and that the contingency fee demands that attorneys not file nonmeritorious claims.

Many jurisdictions have passed laws utilizing a sliding scale to compensate attorneys. While this ensures attorneys enough of a recovery to take smaller claims, it also decreases the huge windfall some attorneys get just because of the terrible damage incurred or "shock value" of a case.

Finally, the Federal Tort Claims Act as well as the Social Security Act and almost every state's workers' compensation laws have ceilings on the amount of attorney's fees allowable.

§1.44 —Limitation of Awards

Most jurisdictions have statutes imposing a ceiling for noneconomic damages (pain and suffering, mental anguish, loss of consortium), while some states have a flat ceiling on all recovery. This, perhaps more than any other issue, has been the one most often struck down by appellate courts.

California has been one of the few jurisdictions to uphold a "cap" on awards. *Jordan v Long Beach Community Hospital*[45] is a case involving the accidental removal of a patient's healthy left kidney instead of his cancerous right kidney. The jury awarded a total of $5,200,000 which the trial court reduced to $250,000 for the noneconomic damages. On appeal, the court upheld the California constitutionality of the statutory limitation on noneconomic damages.

Contrast that with *Smith v The Department of Insurance*,[46] in which the Florida Supreme Court invalidated a $450,000 cap on pain and suffering damages with the following: "If the legislature may constitutionally cap recovery at $450,000.00, there is no discernible reason why it could not cap recovery at some other figure, perhaps $50,000.00 or $1,000.00 or even $1.00."

In *Kansas Malpractice Victims Coalition v Bell*,[47] the Kansas Supreme Court held that the state's so-called Medical Malpractice Reform statute, imposing a comprehensive cap of one million dollars on the total amount of a victim's recoverable award and a sub-cap of $250,000 on the noneconomic damages and requiring payment of future damages through annuities, violates the state's constitutional right to trial by jury and remedy by due course of law.

An additional example is *Duren v Suburban Community Hospital*,[48] in which the court said, "Simply stated, the legislative scheme of shifting responsibility for loss from one of the most affluent segments of society to those who are most unable to sustain that burden—that is, horribly injured or maimed individuals—is not only inconceivable, but shocking to this court's conscience." The court refused to reduce the $1,000,000 pain and suffering component of the award to the $200,000 cap on general damages.

Finally, in *Carson v Maurer*,[49] the New Hampshire Supreme Court struck down a $250,000 cap on pain and suffering damages by saying: "It is simply unfair and unreasonable to impose the burden of supporting the medical care industry solely on those persons who are most severely injured and, therefore, most in need of compensation."

§1.45 —Statutes of Limitations

Traditionally, the time during which an action could have been filed against a tortfeasor is based on when the injury occurred. Statutes of limitations allow a certain period of time during which the action can be commenced or else forever be barred. In medical malpractice law, the "discovery doctrine" as adopted by most states is a less harsh concept wherein the cause of action accrues, and the statute on the time limitation commences to run, when the patient discovers or should have discovered the resultant injury.

---

[45] 201 Cal App 3d 1402, 248 Cal Rptr 651 (1988).
[46] 507 So 2d 1080 (Fla 1987).
[47] 243 Kan 333, 757 P2d 251 (1988).
[48] 24 Ohio Misc 2d 25, 482 NE2d 1358 (1985).
[49] 120 NH 925, 424 A2d 825 (1980).

The applicable statute of limitations varies from jurisdiction to jurisdiction and the practitioner must immediately focus his or her attention on this issue because of its importance. While there are numerous reasons for tolling the statute of limitations, it is absolutely important to be aware of the time frame and its consequences in any medical malpractice action.

The time of discovery rule has also created a problem in the medical malpractice insurance area. Policies are issued on an "occurrence" basis, meaning that the physician's conduct during a given year may be covered, even though a claim based on that conduct may not arise for many years. Additionally, insurance companies have a "claims made" policy which cover only claims filed against the physician in that year, regardless of when the act of malpractice occurred. Because of the "occurrence" type of malpractice policy, many insurance companies call for very high premiums, arguing that if state insurance commissioners would permit medical malpractice insurance to be issued on a "claims made" basis, premiums could be reduced.

Statutes of repose have also been enacted in most jurisdictions, and are based on the concept that there must be an absolute limit at some time, wherein a party is no longer responsible for past acts.

In the area of tort reform and statute of limitations, great concern has been voiced regarding the actions concerning minors. Here, most jurisdictions allowed for the statute of limitations to begin not from the time of discovery but at the age of majority. Hence, the time period during which a claim could be made could be over 20 years in some jurisdictions. Physicians complained about this harsh rule, and insurance companies said the actuarial calculations needed to determine insurance premiums would not only be impossible to calculate, but would also escalate the actual premiums.

Based on the insurance industry's theory that to shorten the statute of limitations for minors may indeed adjust the insurance premium physicians paid, many states have modified their statute of limitations regarding minors to a great extent. Once again, the important point is to ascertain your state's statute of limitation or statute of repose regarding your particular situation.

§1.46 —Joint and Several Liability

This common law doctrine, ignoring the concept of apportioning the payment of damages according to the proportion of liability caused by the defendant, has had the greatest impact in tort reform. Most jurisdictions have either abolished or modified this doctrine, and the most common legislative action is one which requires defendants to be held liable for only their pro rata share of the injury. Obviously, this concept equates with the comparative negligence rule. However, the reader must understand that there are still numerous jurisdictions which abide by the common law joint and several liability doctrine, and those jurisdictions which have modified the doctrine apply it more specifically to products liability lawsuits rather than medical malpractice actions.

§1.47 —Pre-Screening Panels and Arbitration

In an effort to unclog the court system and to allow sophisticated listeners to resolve complicated medical issues (rather than a jury of laypersons), pre-litigation screening panels were organized by statute in numerous states. These panels were mandatory but not binding, and the purpose was to screen out nonmeritorious claims.

The panels were to be composed of a physician, a lawyer, a layperson, and a judge, although some jurisdictions required that only healthcare providers be panelists.

While the proceedings of the panel varied from informal to that of a mini-trial with rules of evidence, witnesses, and opening and closing statements, most jurisdictions either allowed the findings of the panel to be subsequently introduced as evidence or a member of the panel was allowed to be brought into the inevitable trial, if the party did not abide by the panel's findings.

In spite of the possible threat from the adverse panel finding as a deterrent to a subsequent trial of the case, most pre-litigation screening panels proved unsuccessful.

One case which illustrates the panel's purpose is *Moss v Bjornson*.[50] Here, Verla Moss filed a medical malpractice action shortly before the two-year statute of limitations expired. After the statute expired, the patient then requested a pre-litigation screening panel as required by the Idaho statute. The defendants moved to dismiss the suit because, although the pre-litigation panel proceedings were to be "informal and nonbinding," they were, nevertheless, compulsory as a condition precedent to litigation. The trial court denied the motion, and the Idaho Supreme Court affirmed, concluding that filing with the screening panel was a condition precedent to proceeding with litigation, but was not a condition precedent to filing an action in order to toll the statute of limitations. Furthermore, the court ruled that the trial court should stay any further proceedings until the screening panel rendered an advisory opinion.

Arbitration is an activity that may be available in the reader's jurisdiction, but, if not, the practitioner should understand something of its composition.

First, arbitration is a mechanism for possible resolution of the dispute by an impartial third person or tribunal. To be effective, arbitration must be binding, and the parties must agree to forgo a "trial by a jury of their peers."

Depending on the jurisdiction, arbitration can be voluntary or mandatory, binding or nonbinding, and composed of a panel of professional arbitrators, physicians, lawyers, and laypersons. Some jurisdictions address all the arbitration issues by statute, and others allow the parties to agree and modify the rules.

Arbitration can exist by pre-claim agreement—i.e., all future claims will be submitted to binding arbitration—or by post-claim agreement. Issues involving notice, binding of third parties, the right of revocation, and constitutional challenges of equal protection and due process must all be consid-

---

[50] No 16894 (Idaho Dec 1988).

ered. It is best for the practitioner to be aware that arbitration policies may exist in one's own jurisdiction and, if so, it is important to become very familiar with all the rules.

Finally, other issues have been addressed in various states' tort reform activities. The role of the expert witness, modification of the standard of care and burden of proof, the ad damnum clause, structured settlements, patient compensation funds, and awarding costs are all issues which various jurisdictions have either enacted or modified. The interested reader is referred to those legislative activities in his or her state for further information regarding these issues.

§1.48 References

Health Care Quality Improvement Act of 1986, Pub Law No 99-660, §§401-432, 100 Stat 3784 (codified at 42 USC §§11101-11152).

Federal Tort Claims Act, 28 USC §2678 (1948).

Social Security Act, 42 Pub L No 89-97, §406, 80 Stat 67 (1965).

2

Opening the File

§2.01 Introduction
§2.02 Initial Interview
§2.03 Realistic Elements to Consider—Is There a Case?
§2.04 How Good Is the Plaintiff?
§2.05 How Good Is the Defendant?
§2.06 Getting an Expert
§2.07 Procedural Requirements
§2.08 —Jurisdiction
§2.09 —Venue
§2.10 —Forum Non Conveniens
§2.11 —Service of Process
§2.12 —Prior Dismissals
§2.13 Wrongful Death and Survival
§2.14 Derivative Actions
§2.15 Statute of Limitations—Generally
§2.16 —Torts
§2.17 —Tolling
§2.18 —Foreign Body
§2.19 Affirmative Defenses
§2.20 —Contributory Negligence
§2.21 —Last Clear Chance
§2.22 —Comparative Negligence
§2.23 —Assumption of the Risk
§2.24 Procedural Defenses
§2.25 Compromise and Settlement
§2.26 —Settlement Brochure
§2.27 —Types of Settlement
§2.28 References

§2.01 Introduction

Medical malpractice is one of the most difficult types of litigation for the trial attorney. All rules of the jurisdiction must be thoroughly understood prior to proceeding. This chapter is devoted not only to the procedural requirements generally applicable, but also to some of the practical and realistic points which will be of value to the reader. While nothing can replace the knowledge gained from the actual experience of getting involved in medical malpractice litigation, constant exposure to certain legal requirements will reinforce these issues to the trial attorney.

§2.02 Initial Interview

The initial interview is almost like the opening statement portion of the trial. This is where the attorney and client get the first impression of each other, where the issues are discussed, and where both the attorney and client make the decision about proceeding. Since the client will certainly be very anxious about this first meeting, it is incumbent on the attorney to recognize this and, in whichever way seems best, to approach the initial nervousness and resolve it.

Just as the patient going to the physician will understand and remember less than 50 per cent of what he or she is told, clients, too, will fail to remember what was discussed and, more importantly, will misinterpret what has been told to them. Almost everything of substantive value should be put in writing for future reference.

The initial interview should start out relaxed and informal, but in a professional atmosphere with time spent by both the client and attorney becoming comfortable with each other. Making small talk about mundane items will foster a generally relaxed dialogue. Take time to promote a good feeling about you as the client's champion and also be perceptive about your client regarding his or her intelligence, appearance, dress, hostility, etc. The image and perceptions from this interview will be lasting.

After the first few moments are spent in releasing some tension, get information as to the facts of the case. Perhaps the first item of utmost importance to ascertain is the date of the injury. This has many implications—most obvious, of course, is the statute of limitations. If time becomes extremely important vis-a-vis filing the action, this is the exact moment at which the attorney should spring into action to comply with the statute.

The date of the malpractice can also tell a lawyer a lot more. If the alleged injury occurred only 30 days prior to the interview, you should be rather skeptical about your client. Why does a client who sustains an injury only last month come running to a lawyer? True, some injuries are massive and obvious, but most of the time, clients will have faith in their physician and continue to work with him or her only to eventually come to the decision to seek legal counsel. The client who goes running to a lawyer the instant of a mishap may not be the type of client you want to represent.

Additionally, the client who tells you that the injury occurred two years ago (and the statute of limitations is now rapidly running out) may have lawyer-shopped and have been unable to get an attorney to represent him or her. Obviously, the client who has been to previous attorneys and not been able to get representation may pose more of a problem to you than one who finally decides to seek legal advice after careful consideration. This patient, in the last moments of the statute period, may actually have reflected long and hard prior to making the decision to go to an attorney. However, it is important to remember that an early question in the initial interview should concern whether the client has been to other attorneys and what was the result of that contact.

After hearing a brief outline of the issues, the attorney must make the important decision whether to take the case or not and, of course, the two most important facts to consider are liability and causation (*see* §2.03).

There are several ministerial activities that are absolute requirements, not the least of which is to have the client sign a contract for the legal services. The typical contract should include demographics of the client—i.e., name, home address, telephone number, age, occupation, and work address.

The fee arrangement should be abundantly clear in the contract. All medical malpractice actions are based on a contingency fee which can vary from one-third to one-half, and this must be discussed completely with the client. Also, the contract should disclose whether the fee arrangement is different if the case is settled, goes to trial, or is appealed.

Also in the contract should be a provision for the client to pay all costs such as filing and court fees, deposition and transcription fees, medical record fees, travel fees, and documentary evidence expenses.

Mainly, keep the contract simple and clear. Attorneys should understand, of all people, that this communication must be readily understood and agreeable to both parties.

§2.03 Realistic Elements to Consider—Is There a Case?

Of course, the legal requirements of duty, breach of duty, causation, and injury must be satisfied. These elements may be difficult to discern, and one should not jump to conclusions or immediately look to the injury sustained as the basis for taking the case. Of course, the bottom line in medical malpractice is the amount of money damages potentially recoverable, but it is most important not to jump to that issue first. Rather, it is incumbent on the attorney to objectively determine if the legal requirements are met.

The duty owed the patient is usually easy to determine in medical malpractice. Ordinarily, the patient seeks out the physician for the problem, and the physician usually responds appropriately. Once the patient/physician relationship has been established, although this duty can be terminated, the physician has a legal duty toward the patient. It is also important at this juncture to determine whether, in fact, the duty has been terminated between the physician and patient. This can be accomplished by either court order, proper withdrawal of the physician from the care of the patient, or revocation of that duty by the patient.

Breach of the duty is another question that needs to be answered. What is the breach, how did it occur, and what is the standard of care? Has a poor result (maloccurrence, as the physicians like to call it) occurred, or was it a departure from the standard of care? After some experience, many attorneys are able to judge this element quickly with some degree of success. Once the question is resolved, it is time to move on to the next element—injury.

It is good to recall the differences in the terms "injury," "damage," and "damages." Injury and damage are virtually synonymous, although a legal injury must be a violation of a legal right. In this context, an injury may be thought of as any wrong done to a person's property, reputation, rights, or body. Additionally, damage may be thought of as the loss caused by the negligence of one person to another. Lawyers use the word "damage" and "damages" interchangeably, and, in reality, damages means the money measurement of an injury, whereas damage means the injury itself.

It is important to determine whether the client has sustained some injury as a result of the physician's actions or omissions. Patients will have had some injury, temporary or permanent, physical or mental, total or partial, which is what brings them to the lawyer. The injury aspect of a case is usually the easiest to determine and, although of most importance to your client, probably the least important element for an attorney to consider in the decision whether or not to take the case. The old adage of "Clear liability but no damage" must always be kept in mind (*see* Chapter 1).

After the lawyer has decided that the duty, breach thereof, and injury have occurred, the next consideration should be proximate cause. This can be the thorniest of all decisions. A single act could give rise to a series of subsequent events which culminates in an injury to the patient. "But for" the original act, the subsequent events would not have occurred; however, "proximate cause" is a requirement, and the original act may have been the initiating circumstance but not the "proximate cause." The more complicated the medical issues, the more difficult it is to determine proximate cause. The patient's total health picture must be ascertained because, if the patient was not well to begin with, there may be alternative explanations of how the injury occurred.

Failure to timely diagnose a problem may not be the proximate cause of the injury. An example might involve a physician who performed a rectal digital exam on a patient and failed to detect prostate cancer. A few months later, a second physician performed the same examination and determined that advanced prostate cancer was present. The patient died soon after—clear liability on behalf of the first physician, but the question of proximate cause is more difficult. Was it the failure of the first physician to timely recognize and diagnose the prostate cancer which killed the patient, or was it the disease, already in advanced stages, which naturally progressed to the patient's demise? The attorney must determine whether the physician's negligent act was the proximate cause of the injury sustained.

Another factor to consider in proximate cause is the patient's contributory or comparative negligence. This legal issue is discussed in Chapter 1, and it is important for the attorney to determine whether the client had any degree of responsibility for the injury sustained. Whether the client failed to return for timely office visits or whether he or she failed to take medicine properly are questions that should be asked and answered.

And, now comes what we have all been waiting for—damages which potentially could be recovered. While I shall not address the altruistic issues of practicing law and/or medicine, the obvious reason attorneys take on cases is to recover money damages, both for the client and for him- or herself. No attorney should take on a case which would not justify an award large enough to satisfy the client and to compensate the attorney for time and energy expended.

The contingency fee basis requires very careful assessment of the elements involved prior to deciding to take on the case. Clear liability without significant money damages will limit the attorney's involvement because of the tremendous costs involved. Although total expenditures vary with the complexity of each case, even the simplest of cases will probably require $5,000 of out-of-pocket expenses, not including hours of work. Fees involving the court filing, medical records, expert opinions, depositions, travel, and trial preparation all consume large amounts of money. Although most jurisdictions require clients to ultimately be responsible for these expenses, realistically the attorney bears this burden. It is unusual for a client to be able to fund the expense of a medical malpractice lawsuit.

And, last but not least, any lawyer must always be prepared for a defendant's verdict. Better cases than yours have been lost!

§2.04   How Good Is the Plaintiff?

Evaluation of the client is another important decision in determining whether to take the case. Beware the client who is a felon. No matter what the injury is, when the plaintiff's criminal record is brought out—and it will be brought out—no jury will be sympathetic to his or her cause. The same can be said for a client's past history of alcoholism, drug abuse, or any past history that can make a client not the squeaky-clean, hard-working family man or woman who votes regularly. While almost no one can satisfy that description, the point is that if a client has unusual skeletons in the closet, the attorney should take those facts into consideration before accepting the case.

Try to determine if the client appears to distort or maximize the facts. Many times, perceptions of patients as to the reality of the situation is far different from actuality. This perception could be based on poor communication between the physician and the patient, inability of the client to intellectually understand his or her medical history, or a positive attempt by the client to intentionally distort the facts. Only a careful review of the records and gathering of as much information as possible will give the lawyer this insight.

Some patients go to a lawyer because they want to discipline their physicians. The client may believe that organized medicine's attempt and ability to discipline its members are dismal, and they are going to do it themselves—

with the attorney's help, of course. This type of plaintiff, even with a clear case, may be one to avoid. In spite of substantial settlement offers, this client may want to continue the fight to "punish" the physician. This client may even become hostile to the attorney if he or she does not believe the physician is being disciplined adequately.

Some plaintiffs go to an attorney when they are being badgered by their physicians to pay their bills. An attorney should not become the advocate for defending a bill collection claim under the guise of bringing a medical malpractice suit. Carefully examine each case, and always try to determine not only how much the bill was, but whether any balance is owed, and, even more importantly, who paid it!

Tort reform in many jurisdictions has mandated disclosure of a collateral source to the jury. If a client has had large medical bills, all of which were totally paid by insurance, it is very important for the lawyer to know the collateral source rule in the particular jurisdiction. This information should be a factor in deciding whether to accept the case or not. If the injury sustained is so significant that third-party payment will not affect money damages, divulging the collateral source will be a minimal problem.

Finally, beware the guilt-ridden plaintiff. This client is usually an injured child's parent or a decedent's spouse. Guilt and bereavement bring the client to the attorney, and by transferring the client's emotions to the treating physician, he or she relieves a burden of guilt. It is incumbent on the attorney to recognize this scenario in spite of whether negligence is present or not.

§2.05 How Good Is the Defendant?

Suing the only general surgeon in a rural South Georgia community, despite egregious conduct, is usually a losing battle. While this consideration may not be the most important aspect of a lawyer's decision whether or not to take a case, it is something to consider. Personal knowledge about the defendant-physician may not be available, so interrogatories may be a way to get this information. Among other queries regarding the facts of the case, the attorney should be sure to ask:

1. The defendant's education and training
2. His or her current hospital affiliations
3. Membership in professional societies
4. Any censure or disciplinary action against him or her
5. Any refusal of hospital privileges
6. Any previous malpractice actions—if so, write the attorneys involved for copies of previous depositions or interrogatories
7. Any articles or books written by the defendant

Of course, this is by no means a complete list of interrogatories, but to learn the reputation of the defendant-physician, these questions may be of some value.

§2.06 Getting an Expert

Almost all jurisdictions require an affidavit to be filed by an expert in conjunction with a lawsuit.[1] While this is of paramount importance, it is also extremely important at this stage for the attorney to be taught the medical issues by an expert in that field. It may even be worthwhile for the attorney to pay for a lesson in the medical issues by a physician who otherwise refuses to get involved in the litigation. Having an expert who will render an opinion and teach the lawyer the issues in the case is of inestimable value.

Also, it would be wise to consider using a computer-based literature search such as MedLine to get the current information on the issues. In other words, go to "mini-medical school." For purposes of any lawsuit, the attorney must be prepared to learn everything possible about the medicine involved and possibly know even more than the expert. This does not make the lawyer a physician—a belief some sophisticated medical malpractice attorneys hold—only a thorough and well-prepared attorney who knows the complexities of the particular lawsuit.

§2.07 Procedural Requirements

The following sections (§§2.08-2.12) consider requirements from a procedural prospective that must be met or at least considered when one prepares to file the action.

§2.08 —Jurisdiction

Medical malpractice actions rarely have a jurisdiction problem because the defendant-physician usually works and/or is domiciled in the same state as the plaintiff, and the court's jurisdiction over the defendant is usually apparent. There are instances wherein jurisdiction could prove to be a problem, so perhaps a few comments to refresh recollections about jurisdiction are important.

Jurisdiction is the authority by which courts take cognizance of and decide cases. It refers to power not only over the subject matter, but also over the person. Jurisdiction of the subject matter includes power to determine the justiciable issues, while jurisdiction of the person is the power of the court to subject the parties to the decisions made by it.

General jurisdiction is based on the relationship between the defendant and the forum—not the plaintiff, but the defendant. The three types of relationships sufficient to create general jurisdiction are: (1) defendant's consent to jurisdiction, (2) defendant's presence, and (3) defendant's domicile. If the relationship between the defendant and the forum is substantial and continuous, the court may have the power to adjudicate any controversy involving the defendant.

---

[1] Howard v Walker, 242 Ga 406, 249 SE2d 45 (1978).

Specific jurisdiction, on the other hand, involves only issues in the controversy when the defendant's contact with the state is insufficient to justify general jurisdiction.

General jurisdiction and specific jurisdiction are important if a healthcare facility or a healthcare provider is in one state providing services to a plaintiff from a bordering state. As the court said in *Cate v Gordon*,[2]

> That a fair number of out-of-state residents utilize a hospital located near a state border does not itself confer jurisdiction over the hospital in an out-of-state forum.
>
> Solicitation of nonresidents by a healthcare facility or provider, however, on a systematic and continuous basis will grant general jurisdiction powers to the foreign state.

In *Woodward v Keenan*,[3] the court said, "If Michigan residents are encouraged in a systematic or continuing basis to utilize professional facilities outside of Michigan, then those offering this encouragement will have purposefully availed themselves of the privilege of coordinating activities within Michigan and thereby having become amenable to the personal jurisdiction of our courts."

Physicians also are subject to general jurisdiction in the state of their principal place of business or in the state of their residence. Consider a physician who practices in State A and then moves to State B. He or she will be subject to jurisdiction in State A for all actions arising out of his or her activities in that state.

In *Ledford v Central Medical Pavilion, Inc*,[4] two Ohio physicians treated numerous Pennsylvania residents in Ohio. The Pennsylvania court dismissed the action against one physician, stating that merely treating the Pennsylvania residents in Ohio was not sufficient to subject the physician to the Pennsylvania court's jurisdiction; but, the court upheld jurisdiction over the other physician because he maintained an extensive business in Pennsylvania, appearing as an expert medical witness in Pennsylvania legal actions.

Compare this with *Kaileha v Hayes*,[5] where the Hawaiian Supreme Court rejected the lower court's jurisdiction over a Virginia physician who treated a Hawaii resident who was visiting Virginia.

Generally, however, the court's jurisdiction over the defendant-physician in most medical malpractice cases is of little concern. Also, while the subject matter jurisdiction of the courts in most states is readily available and of little significance in the medical malpractice action, the reader is cautioned to understand his or her state's civil practice act to determine which court is the appropriate forum for the action.

---

[2] 40 Conn Supp 15, 478 A2d 631 (1984).
[3] 79 Mich App 543, 261 NW2d 80 (1977).
[4] 531 F Supp 793 (WD Pa 1982).
[5] 556 Haw 306, 536 P2d 568 (1975).

While jurisdiction of the subject matter is conferred either by constitution or statute and cannot be waived by the parties, jurisdiction of the person may be waived by the appearance of the defendant.

The forum state's jurisdiction over a nonresident will only be satisfied when there is valid service of process or waiver thereof. As so nicely articulated in *Girard v Weiss:*[6]

> The plaintiff must have a legal cause of action against the nonresident which arises out of the nonresident activities within the forum, there must be a minimum contact between the nonresident and the forum, and the assumption of jurisdiction by the forum must be consonant with due process notions of "fair play and substantial justice."

Federal jurisdiction may be a consideration for the medical malpractice attorney. In general, there are two types of cases which may be brought in federal court by a plaintiff: (1) diversity of citizenship, if the amount in controversy exceeds $10,000; and (2) federal question cases, where no minimum dollar amount is needed and the cases are those arising under the Constitution, laws, or treaties of the United States.

To illustrate the complexities of jurisdiction and involvement between the state and federal courts, consider the case of *Jones v Griffith.*[7] John Jones died after undergoing an angiography performed by Dr. Harold Griffith. Carol Jones, the surviving spouse, began malpractice proceedings in conformity with Indiana's malpractice law by filing a proposed complaint with the State Commissioner of Insurance and with a medical review panel. In addition, as provided in the statute, she filed a motion for a preliminary determination, accompanied by her proposed complaint. Because the defendant moved from Indiana to California, Jones filed her motion in federal district court and sent copies of the motion to the insurance commissioner and the chair of the medical review panel. The defendant moved to dismiss for lack of complete diversity, contending that the plaintiff, the commissioner, and the chair were Indiana residents. The trial court denied the motion and proceeded to make the preliminary determinations, and the defendant appealed.

The appeals court agreed that there was no diversity problem since the insurance commissioner and the chair of the medical review panel were nominal parties, at most. However, the court held that because the federal district court lacked jurisdiction under Article III of the United States Constitution to render advisory opinions, the trial court erred in making a preliminary determination of issues based on a proposed complaint. Therefore, the trial court's ruling was vacated, and the case was remanded with instructions to dismiss for lack of subject matter jurisdiction.

---

[6] 160 Ga App 295, 287 SE2d 301 (1981).
[7] 870 F2d 1363 (7th Cir 1989).

§2.09 —Venue

Venue refers to the place where the lawsuit will be litigated. The general rule concerning venue is that all civil cases shall be tried in the county where the defendant resides. The purpose of venue is to protect the defendant from the risk that the plaintiff will select an unfair or inconvenient place for trial. Choosing proper venue can be part of tactics and strategy, but also can result in a dismissal if the attorney does not know the rules.

Jury verdicts are invariably higher in sophisticated metropolitan areas than verdicts in rural areas. Legal maneuverings may be required to get venue in a locality which the attorney perceives to be favorable to the client.

Joining a defendant may get the case to a better venue since suits against joint tortfeasors residing in different counties may be tried in either county. Georgia provides that the venue for a corporation is in the county where it has elected to have its agents for service and registered office. However, if a tort occurs in a county other than the county of the registered agent and office, then such county may also be a proper venue for such action, provided that the corporation not only has an office in that county, but also transacts business there.[8]

§2.10 —Forum Non Conveniens

This doctrine, usually invoked by the defendant, asserts the power of the court to exercise its ability to transfer the venue based on convenience to the litigants. The location of witnesses and parties and the familiarity of the forum with state law (in a case regarding federal venue) are factors to be considered.

Piper Aircraft Co v Reyno,[9] a 1981 case, concerned the venue issue. Here, Piper, the defendant and manufacturer of a plane which crashed in Scotland, moved for a dismissal of a wrongful death action filed against it in Pennsylvania by the decedent's representatives. Piper's motion was based on forum non conveniens, arguing that Scotland was a more appropriate site for the litigation because all the decedents were Scottish, all the witnesses were located in Scotland, and the plane's maintenance had been performed in Scotland. The plaintiff opposed because Scottish law, not recognizing strict liability and limiting items of damages, was much less favorable to her.

The United States Supreme Court, in finding for Piper, stressed that the essential purpose of forum non conveniens was to assure that the litigation take place in the most convenient forum and the "likelihood of an unfavorable change in law should not even be given substantial let alone conclusive weight in the forum nonconveniens decision."

---

[8] Ga Code Ann §9-10-31 (1983).
[9] 454 US 235 (1981).

§2.11 —Service of Process

Technically, this phrase means the manner in which the court compels the appearance of the defendant before it. Process includes writs, orders, rules, notices, and decisions. The service of it describes that act, by a court official, wherein the process is actually perfected on the defendant.

The purpose of service of process is to give the defendant notice of the lawsuit filed against him or her. The mere filing of the complaint without the service of process does not bind the defendant to the jurisdiction of the court. It is important for the attorney not to assume that the filing of the complaint automatically means the defendant gets served. The attorney must understand completely the jurisdiction's statutes concerning sufficiency of service, including personal, constructive, and substituted service.

Return of service, while showing that the service was actually accomplished, may not be legally conclusive, but since the return implies the service attached, the defendant has the burden of showing improper service.

§2.12 —Prior Dismissals

Georgia provides in Ga Code Ann §9-2-61 (1985), Renewal of Case after Dismissal:

> [W]hen any case has been commenced in either a state or federal court within the applicable statute of limitations and the plaintiff dismisses the same, it may be recommenced in a court of this state, either within the original applicable period of limitations or within six months after the dismissal, whichever is later—provided, however, if the dismissal occurs after the expiration of the applicable period of limitation this privilege of renewal shall be exercised only once.

One court has said: "It is important to realize that the applicable statute of limitations is not tolled during the pendency of a lawsuit, but the renewal of a case after a dismissal merely treats the renewed action as standing on the same footing as to limitations with the original case."[10]

The important point is that if the jurisdiction has a dismissal statute, it can be excellent strategy to be aware of it and use it judiciously. I am aware of one case which was dismissed in Georgia while the jury was deliberating because the plaintiff's attorney had "bad vibes" about how the case was going. The jury verdict was for the defendant, but the plaintiff's motion to dismiss was granted. Retrial of this case approximately one year later resulted in an award for the plaintiff of over $700,000. Thus, it is important for the attorney to understand all of the nuances of his or her jurisdiction's civil practice act which may come to fruition in the pursuit of any particular malpractice case.

---

[10] Stevens v FAA's Florist, Inc, 169 Ga App 189, 311 SE2d 856 (1983).

§2.13 Wrongful Death and Survival

It is essential to thoroughly understand these statutes in one's jurisdiction. Although a patient's death is not a common occurrence in urology as a result of negligence, attorneys may be called on to represent the family of a decedent, and the knowledge of these statutes is paramount.

At common law, the cause of action for personal injury abated with the death of the plaintiff or defendant. In response to this, each jurisdiction has now passed statutes allowing not only for the decedent (through a representative, of course) but also for the survivors to have a cause of action. Wrongful death statutes compensate the decedent's survivors for losses they sustained as a result of the death, whereas survival statutes allow the survival and thus continuation of suits which could have been brought by the decedent were he or she alive. Survival statutes compensate the decedent's estate for losses sustained by the decedent from the time of injury to the time of death.

The National Conference of Commissioners on Uniform State Laws proposed a Model Act applicable to both survival and wrongful death actions. The Model Act, in survival actions, provides for monetary damages recoverable for the injury causing death plus reasonable burial expenses. The wrongful death provision of the Model Act allows for medical expenses incident to the injury, value of support services, and financial contributions the decedent would have provided had he or she lived. Reasonable compensation for closely related survivors for the decedent's pain and suffering and their own mental anguish and loss of companionship are also provided for.

However, most jurisdictions' survival statutes allow recovery for the decedent's conscious pain and suffering and loss of earnings between the time of injury and the time of death. Since jurisdictions vary as to damages recoverable in both survival and wrongful death statutes, it is extremely important to thoroughly understand one's own statutes prior to commencing suit. Additionally, if a conflict of laws situation exists, the attorney should carefully evaluate each jurisdiction's statutes to determine which forum would be most favorable for the case.

Expert testimony in the form of employers, economists, or actuaries must be used to establish economic considerations such as loss of future economic contributions and support and earning capacity. This testimony presented to the jury will establish the potential monetary amount recoverable.

§2.14 Derivative Actions

Courts generally hold the family unit to be of the highest value and whose legal interests must be protected. All jurisdictions have statutory provisions for family members to have a cause of action against another family member's tortfeasor. These so-called derivative actions are important to consider in all negligence cases, and certainly those in which the patient was a spouse.

The husband and wife relationship is most valued to the courts, and all jurisdictions permit either spouse to sue for loss of consortium due to the negligence of a third party. While the injured spouse sustains physical damage, the other spouse may sustain mental damage and has the legal right to seek redress.

Consortium has been defined in numerous ways by numerous courts, but generally can be defined as the marital right of both husband and wife to "embrace services, society, companionship, sexual gratification and affection."[11] These rights are also known as "conjugal rights."

Death abates the loss of consortium claim, however, if the time between the injury and the death was virtually instantaneous or occurred within moments after the tortious injury. *Walden v Coleman*[12] is a case in which a surviving spouse was permitted to recover for loss of consortium when the time between the injury and the death was as little as two and one-fourth hours.

Just as spousal actions can be maintained for the loss of the other's consortium, a minor child may bring an action for the loss of an injured parent's support and society. This tort is relatively new, and most jurisdictions have not statutorily provided for it, but since *Ferriter v Daniel O'Connell's Sons, Inc*,[13] most jurisdictions have recognized a cause of action for loss of parental consortium.

In *Ferriter*, a case of first impression by any state's court of last resort, the children and wife of a seriously injured employee sued the employer for loss of consortium and society and to recover for mental anguish and impaired health from observing the employee's injuries. The Massachusetts Superior Judicial Court held:

> The children's claim for loss of employee's companionship and society caused by employer's negligence was a claim on which relief could be granted, and ... the facts indicated that the wife and children first saw the employee's injury in the hospital and ... applicable principles of proximity were satisfied so as to permit the maintenance of a cause of action for mental anguish and impaired health.

Of course, when a minor child is injured by a tortfeasor, the parent, as the guardian ad litem, is the proper party to bring suit to recover for medical expenses. Jurisdictions are divided, however, on the question of whether a parent can recover for loss of a child's consortium. It is most important for the reader to investigate case and statutory law in his or her own jurisdiction to determine if such a cause of action exists.

§2.15 Statute of Limitations—Generally

The primary purpose of a statute of limitations is to limit or ascertain the period of time of a right of action so that the defendant has an opportunity

---

[11] Nicholson v Hugh Chatham Memorial Hosp, 300 NC 295, 266 SE2d 818 (1980).
[12] 105 Ga App 242, 124 SE2d 313 (1962).
[13] 381 Mass 507, 413 NE2d 690 (1980).

to access and maintain any evidence in case he or she is sued. This time frame is one of expedience for the defendant. Each state legislates that period of time after which no claim may be brought, and in fact this procedural defense frequently releases the tortfeasor.

The next three sections discuss not only the beginning date of limitations, but also events which toll the statute, such as fraudulent concealment, the date of discovery, and incapacity.

§2.16 —Torts

While it is well known that statutes of limitation vary whether the cause of action arises in contract, tort, personal property, or real property, medical malpractice actions present a special problem. It is an absolute necessity for each attorney to clearly understand his or her state's provisions concerning limitations. While it would be easy to list each jurisdiction and limitation period, this would also be very misleading since issues of finding a foreign body, concealment, the date of discovery, and incapacity may all affect the stated period.

Generally speaking, however, most jurisdictions hold that the statute of limitation begins when the cause or right of action arises. In most instances, this is the date of the act which resulted in the plaintiff's injury. However, in some states, if a patient undergoes an operation which results in harm to the patient and the patient recognizes that harm at some later time, the statute runs for two years from that date. The date of discovery issue is discussed more fully in §§2.17 and 2.18.

The true test to determine when the cause of action arises is to determine when the plaintiff could have first maintained the action.

§2.17 —Tolling

This is the exciting part of statute of limitation discussions. While many great cases present themselves to a lawyer's office well within the limitation period, a great many marvelous cases will also appear where the statute has expired. Here, it is up to the adroitness of the plaintiff's attorney to try to remedy the situation.

Of course, the mere fact that the plaintiff has no knowledge of the statute and the right to sue does not toll the statute. *Mitchell v McGee*,[14] a Mississippi case, said, "Mere mistake, accident or ignorance of one not under a disability is not sufficient to suspend the operation of a statute of limitations."

The most common reason attorneys propose to toll the statute is the failure of the patient to discover the injury. In *Silva v Howe*,[15] the statute of limitation began to run at the time plaintiff's wife received a positive pregnancy test and plaintiff then knew his vasectomy was unsuccessful.

---

[14] 51 So 2d 198 (Miss 1951).
[15] 608 SW2d 840 (Tex Ct App 1980).

But consider *Lamar v Graham*,[16] a Texas case, wherein the plaintiff's illness was correctly diagnosed six and one-half years after the original misdiagnosis was made. The court held that the date of discovery rule only applies in cases of negligent treatment!

And, finally, *McKee v Williams*,[17] a 1985 Ohio case, most completely articulates the discovery rule:

> A cause of action arising for malpractice by a dentist accrues and the statute of limitations commences to run when the patient discovers or in the exercise of reasonable care and diligence should have discovered an injury which is the result of malpractice.
>
> In this action for malpractice against a dentist, what was to be discovered was a "legal injury" as opposed to a "physical injury."

The court said that the concept of a legal injury "contemplates that the plaintiff discovered that he had been injured by the defendant and this requires that there be a discovery of (a) the existence of a physical injury, (b) the reason for the physical injury and (c) the person responsible for the negligent act."

Incapacity is another reason for tolling the statute in most jurisdictions. Usually, infancy, insanity, and imprisonment are meant by incapacity. Infancy presents a special issue since all jurisdictions have passed laws regarding when the limitation period begins in the case of a minor. Tort reform has recently affected these statutes as new attempts to shorten the limitation period for minors in medical malpractice actions are occurring each year. This is especially applicable in cases of birth injuries or defects which are allegedly caused by negligent obstetrical care.

Concealment of the cause of action by the defendant tolls the statute in all jurisdictions. Fraudulent concealment may be difficult to show, however. A 1988 Georgia case, *Rowell v McCune*,[18] concerned a surgeon who operated on the patient's right hand in February of 1983. Because the pain persisted, the surgeon sent her to two other physicians who could not diagnose the problem. Another surgeon reoperated on the patient's hand in January of 1985, and told her that the original carpal tunnel release had not been performed.

The first surgeon testified that he had cut through the transverse carpal ligaments, and the court, in affirming dismissal of the complaint, said that there was no evidence of fraud by the original surgeon which would extend the limitation.

Yet, in a 1984 Florida case, *Phillips v Mease Hospital & Clinic*,[19] wherein an action was commenced against a hospital and physician alleging negligence in administering drugs which caused the plaintiff to suffer nerve and other injuries, the court found that the defendant had concealed the patient's

---

[16] 598 SW2d 729 (Tex Ct App 1980).

[17] 23 Ohio App 3d 187, 492 NE2d 461 (1985).

[18] 188 Ga App 528, 373 SE2d 243 (1988).

[19] 445 So 2d 1058 (Fla 1984).

problem and misrepresented to her that her problems were normal and not due to negligent care, and extended the two-year statute of limitation.

§2.18 —Foreign Body

Discovery of a foreign body may occur years after the standard statute of limitation has run, and therefore most jurisdictions accept this discovery date as the date which the right of action accrues. It is interesting that if the limitation after discovery of a foreign body is, for example, one year, and the regular period for medical negligence actions is two years, a right of action will fail if not brought within the one-year foreign body exception to the statute of limitation rule, even though the time period is less than the medical negligence limitation.

Sometimes determining what is a foreign body may be difficult. *Hall v Ervin*,[20] a 1982 Tennessee case, was an action alleging failure to discover an intrauterine device (which the defendants had not placed) after a normal delivery. The court found that the plaintiff knew of the existence of the IUD, that the defendants had not "negligently left" the IUD behind, and that they had not inadvertently installed the device. The court held that the suit was barred by the three-year statute of limitation, and that the foreign body exception to the statute was inapplicable.

Injections of silicone for breast augmentation have usually not been considered foreign bodies unless, as in a New York case, *Mateo v Rish*,[21] "food grade" type of silicone was injected rather than "medical grade."

§2.19 Affirmative Defenses

The defendant, in the answer to the complaint, may not only deny the charges, but also has the ability to espouse certain defenses. These affirmative defenses are so called because the defendant has not merely denied the charges, but is raising entirely new factual allegations. Affirmative defenses range from insanity, intoxication, and coercion in criminal cases to accord and satisfaction, arbitration and award, and discharge in bankruptcy and contract law. In negligence actions, such defenses as statute of limitation, contributory negligence, estoppel, res judicata, and assumption of the risk can be argued. Most jurisdictions require that affirmative defenses be set forth in responsive pleadings or be deemed waived.

§2.20 —Contributory Negligence

Contributory negligence may be asserted as a defense, but in medical malpractice actions may continue to focus part of the liability on the defendant.

---

[20] 642 SW2d 724 (Tenn 1982).
[21] 86 AD2d 736, 446 NYS2d 598 (1982).

Implicit in this defense is that even if the defendant is guilty of the negligence charged, the plaintiff by his or her own negligence contributed to the resulting injury.

Contributory negligence is defined by the *Restatement (Second) of Torts* §5 (1965) as "Conduct on the part of the plaintiff which falls below the standard to which he should conform for his own protection and which is a legally contributing cause cooperating with the negligence of the defendant in bringing about the plaintiff's harm."

South Carolina Insurance Co v James C Greene & Co[22] held: "If, in the exercise or ordinary care, the plaintiff might have avoided the consequences of the defendant's negligence, he is the author of his own injury in the eyes of the law."

Although the contributory negligence defense was born in the Industrial Revolution of England in the 1800s and applied throughout the nineteenth century, the twentieth century brought a new attitude toward this harsh, all-or-nothing rule. At the turn of the century, all jurisdictions held that if there was any evidence of the plaintiff's contributory negligence, he or she was barred from recovery. This severe totalitarian doctrine has almost completely been replaced by the comparative negligence doctrine.

The most common basis for contributory negligence as a defense by physicians is where the patient fails to return for follow-up visits. In *Grippe v Momtazee*,[23] the plaintiff's decedent failed to return to her physician for 19 months in spite of the fact that she had been told the lump in her breast "could be a problem," and she had read articles about this fact. Although there was evidence of negligence on the part of the physician, the decedent's actions constituted contributory negligence which contributed to the very "gist of the plaintiff's cause of action."

§2.21 —Last Clear Chance

The last clear chance doctrine is also known as "discovered peril," "humanitarian doctrine," or the "doctrine of subsequent negligence." Here, the one who has the "last clear chance" of avoiding injury to another, despite the negligent acts of that person, is accountable for actions or omissions if he or she is responsible for any injury to that person. Thus, in spite of the plaintiff's contributory negligence, if the defendant had a last clear chance of avoiding harm to the plaintiff, the defendant is liable.

§2.22 —Comparative Negligence

Because of the severity of the common law contributory negligence doctrine, many jurisdictions sought to modify or abrogate it. Jurisdictions have developed three major approaches to the comparative negligence doctrine.

---

[22] 290 SC 171, 348 SE2d 617 (1986).
[23] 705 SW2d 551 (Mo Ct App 1986).

The "pure" rule means that a plaintiff can recover despite any amount of his or her own negligence. In other words, even if 99 per cent responsible for his or her own injury, the plaintiff could potentially recover 1 per cent because of the defendant's actions.

The "modified" rule requires that the plaintiff's negligence be less than the defendant's for any recovery to occur. Thus, the plaintiff cannot be more than 49 per cent responsible for his or her own injury.

The "slight/gross" rule provides that, where the plaintiff's conduct was "slight" as compared to the "gross" conduct of the defendant, the plaintiff may recover. Of course, these jurisdictions are split on defining the terms "slight" and "gross."

Ordinarily, in medical malpractice actions, these doctrines are not applicable, but the reader can only benefit from awareness and refreshed recollection of this information.

§2.23 —Assumption of the Risk

Another affirmative defense which must be pleaded and proved by the defendant is assumption of the risk. This concept has great applicability in medical malpractice actions since it is based on the consent theory. The plaintiff who voluntarily assumes a risk of harm arising from the conduct of the defendant cannot recover for such harm. I have, however, left out the word "negligent" before the words "conduct of the defendant." This is what makes the medical malpractice cause of action different from other actions. Negligence and standard of care are much more critical in the context of medical malpractice actions, and need to be defined by an expert.

Assumption of the risk and contributory negligence must be distinguished if possible. Despite the previously mentioned bar of recovery for contributory negligence (see §2.20), assumption of the risk may not be such a harsh rule because of the standard of care which is articulated in medical malpractice actions.

Carr v Pacific Telephone Co[24] held: "Assumption of the risk is a narrow defense which should only be permitted in those rare cases where the injured person knowingly exposes himself to an obvious danger."

A number of jurisdictions have abandoned this defense, but almost all jurisdictions allow the trier of fact to determine whether the plaintiff did assume the risk. In medical malpractice actions, if the affirmative defense of assumption of the risk is used, the plaintiff then must establish that the defendant departed from the standard of care which contributed to the injury.

---

[24] 26 Cal App 3d 537, 103 Cal Rptr 120 (1972).

§2.24 Procedural Defenses

While this is not meant to be the last word on procedural defenses in one's answer to a complaint, a brief mention of some of the defenses available is necessary for completeness.

Most medical malpractice actions are well defined substantively and procedurally, and issues such as lack of jurisdiction, improper venue, or failure to state a claim usually are not available with any degree of success.

Denials in the answer usually should include specific denials to the plaintiff's averments rather than a general denial. Defenses such as jurisdiction over the person and subject are usually not of any significance in a medical malpractice action, but the following cases can illustrate the defense of insufficiency of service of process, another procedural defense.

In *Comforti v Beekman Downtown Hospital*,[25] the court held that, in accordance with the civil procedure act, there was personal service of summons on a doctor, although the service had been effected on his secretary who said she was authorized to accept service.

Contrast that with *Cohen v Miami*,[26] where service of process on a doctor by delivery of the papers to a secretary in his office was inadequate to meet the Fed R Civ P requirement 4(b)(1), that service must be made upon the defendant at his or her "dwellinghouse or usual place of abode."

Some of the more common defenses used, almost in a cookbook fashion, are:

1. Plaintiff's complaint fails to state a claim against the defendant on which relief can be granted
2. Defendant exercised that degree of care and skill which is ordinarily exercised by other physicians under the same or similar circumstances
3. Defendant is not an insurer or guarantor of the safety and well-being of persons committed to his or her care and, since he or she did not deviate from the standard of care, defendant is not liable in any respect
4. Defendant is without knowledge or information sufficient to form a belief as to the truth of the allegation in the plaintiff's complaint

While it may appear somewhat supercilious to include certain defenses in the answer, one must be very sure that all defenses should be averred in order not to waive them at some later date, either in the trial or in the appellate process.

Whitlock v Haj-Murad,[27] a Georgia medical malpractice action which was settled prior to trial, may exemplify one of the common procedural defenses. Here, a motion to dismiss was filed on the grounds that the pleading failed

---

[25] 79 AD2d 968, 435 NYS2d 284 (1981).
[26] 54 FRD 274 (1972).
[27] Civ Action No 87-1-1476-06 (Ga 1989).

to state a claim on which relief could be granted. In particular, the plaintiff failed to comply with the contemporaneous filing requirement of Ga Code Ann §9-11-9.1(A)(1987), which mandates the filing with the complaint of "an affidavit of an expert competent to testify, which affidavit shall set forth specifically at least one negligent act or omission claim to exist, and the factual basis for each such claim."

The complaints in this case were filed on July 14, 1987, seeking damages for alleged medical malpractice, but without an affidavit from an expert. The statute would have run on September 5, 1987, prior to the court ruling on this motion. In compliance with Georgia law, the plaintiff dismissed the case and immediately refiled it properly in state court with the appropriate affidavit attached to the complaint. This is an example of how an attorney, by not complying with the jurisdiction's requirement for filing complaints, could have had a case dismissed much to the detriment of the client.

§2.25 Compromise and Settlement

The law favors compromise and settlement to prevent litigation, and courts and will look very favorably on any agreement between the parties which may be construed as a compromise or settlement.

Rose v Pfister[28] said:

> In a medical malpractice action against a physician and a hospital wherein the hospital guaranteed minimum recovery of $75,000.00 to the plaintiff in exchange for a non-suit and this sum was to be reimbursed to the hospital from any monies recovered from the physician, such an agreement was a "settlement.

Although there are certain basic rules or requirements concerning settlement, realistically this term means negotiation. Obviously, some attorneys are better at negotiating than others and, because of their particular tactics, strategy, and personality, negotiation may be more successful for some than others who try. Some attorneys, a minority, consider settlement as an unwanted impediment toward an exciting and adrenalin-pumping trial, and pay little attention to settlement techniques. But, most attorneys believe in the interest of time, expense, emotional trauma, and trying to finalize the case that serious attempts and a serious commitment should be made toward settlement.

It is well known that most cases, medical malpractice or otherwise, get settled prior to trial, but this should not give the reader a false sense of security regarding a case. Preparedness is the absolute requirement for success, and for the attorney to believe the case will be settled and not go to trial will only create a situation of unpreparedness. The old adage that cases prepared for trial get settled and cases prepared for settlement get tried is quite

---

[28] 607 SW2d 587 (Tex Ct App 1980).

true. Thus, each case should be evaluated and prepared as though a jury will hear the merits, and, if settlement does occur, then the attorney can move on to the next case. This is quite a better feeling than if one depends on settlement to occur but none does, and then the trial date appears without enough time to properly prepare. This is what loses cases!

While the negotiating process may come more naturally to others, there are certain factors that both sides must consider which are always present in each case. Some of these issues are common to both the plaintiff and defense, but this discussion merely lists all factors, not necessarily in order of importance.

Of course, the plaintiff's attorney must totally evaluate the case before any settlement is even considered. Items to be included for this consideration are the amount of special damages incurred, the value of future loss of earnings, and future medical expenses. Additionally, the plaintiff's age, life expectancy, and social status must also be considered.

The strength of one's case—including the various witnesses, any outrageous conduct of the defendant, the nature of the injury, and the probability that the jury will identify with either the plaintiff or defendant—should also be considered. How much pain and suffering is or was present and the extent to which the injury was permanent or has been resolved are other factors. Also to be considered is the size of judgments generally in the area where the trial will be held. The cost of continued or even delayed litigation if the trial calendar is backlogged and any applicable derivative actions and prejudgment interests which may apply are also important. Not to forget, possibly most important of all, is the ability of the defendant to pay!

A brief word about formulas is in order. Many have heard that one way to evaluate the general damages is to treble (or higher) the specials. I mention this formula only to condemn it. Both sides, although the bottom line may be quite different, must properly evaluate their case, using some of the previously mentioned factors, and the final dollar amount should be realistic and based on sound reasoning rather than guesses or formulas.

It would be an easy world if everyone could go to the new car showroom and pay the sticker price of the vehicle, but, unfortunately, that rarely happens, and, as in all negotiating situations, the final figure is gradually reached.

While it would be marvelous for the plaintiff to ascertain the value of his or her case, present this figure to the defendant, and get a "yes" response, this probably never happens. Normally, the defendant takes that dollar figure as a high number and works downward from there. However, I must suggest that there is no small minority of respected plaintiffs' attorneys who have finally gained the reputation of dealing honestly and squarely in the negotiating arena so that the defense knows this dollar amount is not just a starting point, but THE point!

While this reputation may take years to attain, if the opposing counsel realizes that the plaintiff's attorney has properly evaluated and prepared the case and is prepared to show how the conclusions were reached, the bargaining process can be shortened.

One point to consider in this context is when one should start negogiations. Certainly, counsel should never put forth a demand figure until after fully, carefully, and thoroughly considering all the factors of the case. Interestingly enough, a complaint does not have to be filed before a demand can be made. It is common knowledge that cases are settled prior to filing suit if the plaintiff's attorney has done his or her homework. Of course, if the injury is such that future medicals or injury is a potential, early settlement demands would be foolhardy.

Of course, the client must be involved in all negotiating efforts. After all, whether the attorney is the sword or shield, it is the client whom the attorney represents and who must have not only some input into the settlement negotiations, but also the final word.

As a final note to this discussion, the issue of who should make the first move needs to be aired. While some experienced attorneys believe that to initiate negotiations is a sign of weakness, in fact, if the plaintiff is sure, competent, and thorough, the opening demand can (and should) be a show of strength.

If you are just at the beginning of your career in medical malpractice, it is most important to establish yourself as a no-nonsense, organized, and well-prepared professional. After you have thoroughly prepared and understood not only your case but also its value, then is the appropriate time to approach your adversary with a settlement proposal. But, do not use this tactic as a bluff, because not only will your reputation be tarnished, but you do a great disservice to your client.

Of course, it is of utmost importance to remember the client has the final word on any negotiating. In spite of the attorney's feelings about the settlement offer, if the client insists on accepting an offer that the attorney believes is inadequate, the attorney must acquiesce to the client's wishes. Of course, the attorney also has the obligation and responsibility to discuss with the client the reasons for disagreeing with him or her, but the final word is the client's.

§2.26 —Settlement Brochure

This negotiating tool is a package prepared by the plaintiff for presentation to the defendant. It can consist of video and/or written material, and includes a summary of the case, the issues involved, expert opinions, demonstrative evidence, and the settlement demand. If the settlement brochure is prepared with attention to detail which demonstrates the thorough preparation of the plaintiff's attorney, the defense counsel will only be impressed by the quality of the work. On the other hand, a poorly prepared settlement brochure may be the tipoff to the experienced defense attorney as to the level of competency of an opponent.

§2.27 —Types of Settlement

Simple

The most straightforward type of settlement is the simple cash payout and release. There is nothing arcane about this type of settlement other than for both sides to agree on the final sum. When that sum is paid to the plaintiff, a release is executed and the issue is over. Releases, however, can be very sophisticated, especially when several defendants are involved. The interested reader is referred to the numerous texts and form books for suggestions of releases.

Although tort reform legislation in most jurisdictions has probably modified the common law doctrine that release of one tortfeasor releases all, consider *Williams v Physicians & Surgeons Community Hospital*.[29] Here, the release of the original tortfeasor did not release the hospital as a successive tortfeasor unless: (a) the plaintiff had been fully compensated for the loss; or (b) the parties to the release intended to release the party claiming coverage under the release.

High/Low

An unusual type of settlement appearing throughout the country is known as "high/low." In these situations, the plaintiff is guaranteed a certain (low) dollar amount in return for an agreement not to accept more than a certain (high) amount should a jury award such a larger sum.

I am aware of one recent case wherein the plaintiff's attorney agreed to a $100,000 settlement if there was a defendant's verdict, but no more than $1,000,000 for a plaintiff's verdict. Both sides felt the weaknesses of their case, but each was willing to gamble. The defendant believed that the risk of a huge plaintiff's verdict could be diminished somewhat by the plaintiff agreeing to accept only $1,000,000 despite a larger jury award. For this forebearance by the plaintiff, the defense was willing to guarantee at least $100,000, even in the event of a defendant's verdict. Meanwhile, the plaintiff's attorney believed he could at least guarantee his client $100,000 and possibly $1,000,000, but, in the event of a huge jury verdict for his client, the plaintiff would only get $1,000,000. The trial ended in a defendant's verdict, but the plaintiff did win $100,000, according to the pretrial settlement agreement, yet the trial is on appeal, a right not given up by the plaintiff!

Structured

A structured settlement is any method to compensate the plaintiff with a lump sum payment plus a plan for a deferred and periodic payment schedule. This method of payment has become increasingly popular, particularly with larger verdicts forthcoming and with the more catastrophic injury sustained.

---

[29] 249 Ga 588, 299 SE2d 705 (1982).

The lump sum initial payment is to compensate the plaintiff for immediate pecuniary loss, such as medical bills and loss of income, while the deferred portion is to allow for any possible future need of medical services.

This type of settlement, although complicated and requiring the input of tax attorneys, accountants, financial advisers, and annuity experts, may have decided advantages for both plaintiff and defendant, and may be more of an impetus to settle for both sides than any other.

Although the feeling is that the defendant gains most from the structured settlement, indeed, considering all the ramifications of this type of settlement, it may be difficult to ascertain whether one side or the other has an advantage from the process. The plaintiff has the advantage of receiving a large initial lump sum, and then the security of knowing that future income is guaranteed without any burden of having to make investment decisions. Protection from inflation is available, and the entire settlement will be tax-free if the agreement is drafted to satisfy the Internal Revenue Service.

Although no lawyer should have the ability to make final financial decisions for clients, in the case of minors or unsophisticated clients faced with a windfall of money, the security of the guaranteed payments for a number of years, if not life, can hardly be measured.

Items such as a guaranteed number of payments to be made to the survivors even in the event of the plaintiff's death, as well as consideration for solvency of the carrier who has the obligation to make the payments, must all be considered.

Attorney's fees must also be carefully weighed. Some advocate the actual cost of the annuity to be the focus of the contingency fee basis while others suggest that the total amount paid to the plaintiff over the years be considered the basis for the contingency fee. However, in the latter case, attorney's fees are also being structured. Perhaps this is not such a bad idea for the same reason as advantages to the plaintiffs, although the attorney's fee will not be tax-free.

The basic advantage to the defendant or insurance company in the structured settlement is the lower cost to fund the final figure. Insurance companies can buy annuities at a lower figure than consumers which will return the full amount to the plaintiff, but at a much lower cost to the defendants. Additionally, the availability of monies not used in large lump-sum payouts may foster the earlier settlement of other actions.

A factor to be aware of and possibly avoid is the reversionary trust. Here, in the event of the plaintiff's death, the corpus of the trust would revert to the insurance company. Obviously, insurance companies love this type of trust, but plaintiffs' attorneys should be cautious about agreeing to such an arrangement.

§2.28 References

1 Am Jur 2d *Abatement, Survival and Revival* §§41, 48, 51-68 (1962)

61A Am Jur 2d *Pleadings* §149 (1981).

Restatement (Second) of Torts §463 (1963).

Unif, Model Survival and Death Act §4, ___ ULA ___ (1979).

Shrager, *Screening and Preparing the Medical Negligence Case,* Trial, Aug, 1988.

Trail & Maney, *Jurisdiction, Venue and Choice of Law in Medical Malpractice Litigation,* 7 No 4 J Legal Med 403 (1986).

3

Medical Records

§3.01 Function of the Records
§3.02 Hospital Records
§3.03 —Certified Copy
§3.04 —Patient Information Sheet
§3.05 —Admission Note, History, and Physical
§3.06 —Progress Notes
§3.07 —Doctor's Orders
§3.08 —Nurses' Notes
§3.09 —Laboratory Data
§3.10 —X-Ray Data
§3.11 —Operative Notes
§3.12 —Anesthesia Record
§3.13 —Recovery Room Record
§3.14 —Consultation Notes
§3.15 —Ancillary Records
§3.16 —Discharge Summary
§3.17 —Consent Form
§3.18 —Graphic Sheet
§3.19 —Circulating Nurse's Records (Operating Room Records)
§3.20 —Pathology Report
§3.21 —Medication Sheets
§3.22 —Emergency Room Records
§3.23 Abbreviations
§3.24 Office Records
§3.25 Lost or Altered Medical Records
Appendix 3-A Sample Forms

§3.01 Function of the Records

The medical record forms the absolute basis for the issues in most medical malpractice actions. Like the petroglyphs and the hieroglyphs of ancient Egypt, the medical records tell a marvelous story. Although omissions and commissions may occur, the astute reader, by utilizing all the components of the medical record (more commonly called the "chart"), can almost tell what was happening to the patient on an hourly basis.

The first and most important purpose of the medical record is to facilitate the rendering of proper care to patients. The medical record is the mechanism for communication between and amongst the healthcare team. The Joint Commission on Accreditation of Healthcare Organizations requires that a medical record serve "as a basis for planning patient care and for continuity in the evaluation of the patient's condition and treatment."

The medical record documents specific services received by the patient which third-party payors require prior to payment. The medical record is useful for quality assurance and risk management, as well as peer review and evaluation of physicians by licensing agencies. It provides evidence of patient care and allows physicians to recall events that may have taken place months or years prior. The medical record provides data for public health purposes, may be used by the government to evaluate threats to the public health, and is important for teaching and medical research.

This chapter includes discussions of the hospital and office record, as well as the emergency room record. There is also a brief glossary of accepted medical abbreviations which may assist one in interpreting the chart, and a short discussion concerning lost or altered medical records.

§3.02 Hospital Records

There are a few points in going over a chart which must immediately be appreciated. These general items may be a window into the plaintiff's case. The timeliness of the dictation of the admission history and physical, operative notes, and discharge summary is crucial. While the late dictation of any of the records may not be relevant to proximate cause, a great deal of damage can be done to the physician's credibility because he or she dictates notes late. Since charts rarely will be filed as complete by the medical records librarian without all of the components finalized, it would be unusual to get a medical record without, for example, a discharge summary. But the date that that discharge summary was dictated can be critical to the case and used for credibility and impeachment purposes.

One should examine the physician's progress notes carefully to determine the frequency of the physician visits. Ordinarily, the standard of care requires at least a daily visit to the patient, but certain instances may demand closer scrutiny by the physician. To be able to show that the defendant doctor only saw his or her critically ill patient every other day can be very helpful to the plaintiff.

The nurses' notes must be carefully read. These notes really detail the daily activity of the patient. While the physician progress notes are sometimes self-serving and noncommittal, invariably the nursing progress notes are extremely objective. This is not to say that the entire medical record must not be thoroughly read and understood, but the nurses' notes reflect the fact that the nurse spends a great deal of time with that particular patient and must be carefully evaluated for greater information.

Obviously, the admission history and physical, operative notes, and discharge summary also demand close scrutiny. Additionally, consultation notes, doctors' orders, and radiology reports should all be examined closely, and it would be difficult to prioritize the importance of one over another, but the nurses' notes reflect more of an objective appraisal of the situation rather than opinion evidence.

Lastly, remember to look through the laboratory data section carefully. While lawyers frequently will need a medical expert to assist in properly evaluating the case, the attorney should have some idea of the issues involved and whether appropriate lab testing has occurred.

In a nutshell, then, read the entire medical record. You will be astonished to find that even after numerous readings and re-readings of the chart, some new fact will surface which you never noticed before.

It is also important to understand the different types of hospitalizations. The inpatient hospitalization is what we ordinarily think of when we think of the medical record. Here, the patient goes to the hospital, is formally admitted into the hospital under the care of a specific physician, and spends at least 24 hours or much longer there. This hospital medical record will usually comprise most of what this chapter concerns.

The outpatient hospitalization is when the patient goes to the hospital for a procedure but then goes home the same day. *Same-day surgery* is another name for outpatient hospitalization. There is still a medical record available for each type of hospitalization, but, of course, it will be abbreviated. In fact, hospitals have certain rules which may allow a 24-hour or 48-hour hospital stay to be documented on a one-page, short form, rather than a separate history and physical, operative note, and discharge summary.

Another category is the *AM admit*. This ordinarily is reserved for patients who are to undergo surgery that day and who are admitted to the hospital prior to the surgery.

Of course, patients can also be admitted to the hospital directly from the emergency room or transferred from another facility. Invariably, there will be an emergency room record in addition to the usual hospital chart or, in the case of a transferral, there is ordinarily a transfer chart from the transferral facility.

Another factor to consider, particularly in this era of more than one physician treating a patient, is the difference between the admitting, attending, or consulting physician. This nomenclature has been an important factor in numerous lawsuits.

The *admitting physician* is one who actually accepts that patient under his or her care and admits the patient into the hospital. The *attending physician*, usually the admitting physician but not necessarily so, is the physician who is primarily responsible for the patient's care while in the hospital. For example, a urologist may admit a patient into the hospital under his or her care because the admitting diagnosis was a kidney stone, but, because the patient has complicated medical problems which must be resolved first, the urologist may consult with an internist who will not only be the consulting physician, but who will also be the attending physician until the patient is ready to be turned over to the care of the admitting urologist. The records may reflect some confusion in the care of the patient which could be the gravamen for the cause of the action.

§3.03 —Certified Copy

Finally, one must understand how to introduce the medical record as evidence. Many jurisdictions require a certified copy of the medical record to be filed with the pleadings. The certified copy of the medical records may be obtained by writing the medical records librarian and requesting same, with the proper consent form signed by the patient authorizing the record's release.

Additionally, while the certified copy of the medical records may be introduced as evidence, parts of the records will not be allowed in because of the hearsay rule. For example, unless the author of the consultation notes is available at trial, consultation notes will not be allowed in. Consultation notes render an opinion, as opposed to nurses' notes which merely are a factual narrative. An autopsy report will also probably not be allowed in because of the same reasoning. If the pathologist is brought into court to authenticate his or her autopsy report, then, of course, the autopsy report will be introduced.

Georgia Code Ann §24-7-8 (1985) provides that the term "medical records" means all written clinical information which relates to the treatment of individuals when such information is kept in an institution. Medical records or reproductions thereof, when duly certified by their custodians, need not be identified at the trial and may be used in any manner in which records identified at the trial by the custodian could be used.

Georgia Code Ann §24-10-71 (1985) relates to reproduction of records of an institution. Where it appears that medical records for which a subpoena or order for reproduction has been issued should be kept in an institution as reasonably necessary for the treatment of a patient, the court in which admission is sought shall order reproduction of the medical records. The reproduction, when duly certified, is admissible in place of the medical records.

The basic inpatient hospital records consist of approximately 18 different component parts. Because most hospitals are accredited by one accreditation agency, the Joint Commission on Accreditation of Healthcare Organizations (JCAHO), it is rather simple to go through any hospital record in any jurisdiction because they almost all look alike. Familiarizing oneself with the individual parts will make it easier to evaluate any hospital record. Additionally, the order in which I shall discuss each separate part is usually the order in which each chart is organized.

I cannot emphasize too highly, and will repeat this admonition more than once, that not to closely scrutinize the entire medical record, be they hospital or office, can flaw your case. These records tell a story, and it is in this story that victory or defeat dwells. The answer is there—it is up to the reader to find it.

§3.04 —Patient Information Sheet

This is the hospital's administrative record of information which, although it may be of a medical nature, is usually of a demographic format, and an example is included in this book as Sample Form 3-1. Items such as the patient's name, address, birthdate, insurance coverage, employment, date of admission, and discharge are noted here. Additionally, on this information sheet is the coded diagnosis of the patient, as well as the procedures performed during that hospital admission. Procedures as well as diagnoses are now computerized and given a numerical designation so that accurate statistics and biographics can be maintained. The CPT (Current Procedural Terminology) Manual is the source of all the procedures performed on a patient, and the ICD-9 (9th Revision of the International Classification of Diseases) Manual lists all of the different diagnoses. For example, cholecystitis (gallbladder disease) is 575.1; if there are stones in the bile duct, either the common or hepatic, the numeric code is 574.4. The patient information sheet must be signed by the attending physician before the record is considered complete.

The significance of this part of the record, other than the time and date of the patient's admission and discharge, is the exact discharge diagnosis which was given to the patient as well as the procedure performed. The procedures listed on the patient information sheet should have a corresponding operative note, anesthetic record, and other accompanying information concerning that procedure which can be reviewed prior to reading the entire record. There is also an area for complications to be listed on the "face sheet" (a synonym for patient information sheet). The medical record librarian will go through the chart to code out on the face sheet any complications which may not be listed or recognized as such by the dictating physician. Additionally, any blood transfusions given to the patient will be noted. Finally, but certainly not necessarily to be considered all-inclusive, the condition of the patient on discharge and the disposition of the patient (i.e., to home, transfer to another hospital or to a nursing home) are also noted.

§3.05 —Admission Note, History, and Physical

Most hospitals require not only that the admission history and physical be performed at the time of admission to the hospital, but also that an admission note be made in the physician progress notes as to why the patient was brought into the hospital.

The Joint Commission on Accreditation of Healthcare Organizations (JCAHO) requires that a documented current and thorough history and physical examination be on the chart prior to the performance of any surgery. If the history and physical are not on the chart, most operating rooms require at least a handwritten note concerning the examination of the heart and lungs, and will not allow a patient to go into the actual operating room suite until such a note is present.

The JCAHO is a private nonprofit organization which strives to improve the healthcare delivery system by standard-setting, survey, evaluation, accreditation, decisionmaking, and education. Since its founding in 1951, the JCAHO has become the principal standard-setter for hospitals, long-term care facilities, hospice programs, ambulatory centers, mental health, home care, and managed care organizations. Participation in the accreditation process is voluntary, but the JCAHO has become so powerful that if a facility does not have JCAHO approval, certain funds—i.e., governmental or private—may not be made available to it.

As mentioned in §3.02, the timely dictation of the history and physical is important and could serve as a basis for impeachment. There is a certain form for the history and physical which is as follows: The Chief Complaint (CC), which, in the patient's *own* words, is the current problem; the History of Present Illness (HPI), which states the chronological course of the patient's illness from its beginning to the present; the Past Medical History (PMH), which details previous surgery, any current medications, allergic history, or unusual medical problems; the Family History (FH), which divulges any unusual medical history in close family members; the Social History (SOC), which includes vocation, smoking and alcohol habits, marital status, or any other pertinent facts such as religious beliefs regarding blood transfusions; and the Review of Systems (ROS), which is a lengthy summary starting at the head and going to the feet, covering all of the body systems and related symptomatology.

The physical examination itself is a long and detailed evaluation of the patient which includes the vital signs (blood pressure, pulse, respirations, temperature) and a general description of the patient, utilizing such litany as "well-developed, well-nourished, white male" (WDWN W/M). Then a notation is made concerning every body part (head, skin, hair, etc.) as well as the body systems—e.g., respiratory (lungs are clear to percussion and auscultation), cardiovascular (the rate and rhythm of the heart), genitourinary (external genitalia and rectal exam), orthopedics (full range of motion of extremities), and neurological (patient is oriented to person, place, and time).

Another important part of the actual physical examination recordation is the final notation, "Impression," which is the conclusion that the physician has made at the termination of the history and physical exam. There may also be a list of differential diagnoses which are considered possible by the physician. Additionally, there will be a notation under "Disposition" which will ordinarily describe the physician's evaluation and treatment plan.

§3.06 —Progress Notes

This is the part of the chart that tells the reader what those directly concerned in the care of the patient are thinking. The physician usually makes "rounds" on the patient once a day (or more, depending upon the severity of the patient's illness) and documents his or her findings and thinking on the chart. Here, the physician usually describes the patient's current physical status in brief but succinct terms, and the problems which may be present. Additionally, the plan or course of management is usually described. It is the progress notes that provide a window into the treating physician's mind. The reasoning for decisions made about the patient should be detailed, but, unfortunately, and particularly in the malpractice area, the physician's progress notes are usually lacking in completeness. If a physician only sees the patient once a week, the progress notes will also reflect that.

There is a pattern in writing the progress notes. This is known as *SOAP:* Subjective (what the patient is complaining of or looks like); Objective (the actual facts such as pertinent lab data or vital signs of the patient); Assessment (the evaluation of the data and conclusions drawn); and Plan (the course of action to be taken). Since the SOAP pattern may not vary much on a day-to-day basis as in a convalescing surgical patient, there may be varying degrees of adherence to this type of note.

§3.07 —Doctor's Orders

The doctor's orders constitute that part of the chart which reflects what the physician wants to have done to or for his or her patient.

There is ordinarily a set pattern for the doctor's orders, although this may not be closely adhered to in all cases. A common mnemonic used to help neophyte physicians write their orders is *ADC Van Dissel:* A—Admit (to what room or floor), D—Diagnosis, C—Condition, V—Vitals (frequency of temperature, pulse, or respirations to be taken), A—Activity (out of bed, ambulate), N—Nursing (change dressings, enemas), D—Diet (regular, full liquid, etc.), I—In and Out (refers to all catheters, intravenous fluids), S—Specific drugs (antibiotics, cardiac drugs), S—Symptomatic drugs (laxative, sleep needs), E—Extras (electrocardiogram, x-ray), L—Lab (any orders for lab tests).

The orders should be signed and dated by the doctor, as well as signed and dated by the nurse who notes the orders and carries them out. Additionally, a physician may verbally give an order to the nurse, either over the telephone or personally, but these orders will have "T.O." (telephone order) or "V.O." (verbal order) by the physician's name. This is important because one would be able to ascertain whether or not a physician actually was in the hospital at the time that an order was given or whether he or she was at home telephoning orders.

§3.08 —Nurses' Notes

While it would be difficult to rank the importance of each segment of the medical record, certainly the nurses' notes must be regarded as one of the most important areas. Besides the fact that nurses have certain strict requirements to timely and appropriately document facts during their working shifts, nurses usually have no secondary gains involved in writing their notes. Physicians currently are very aware that all of their actions come under close scrutiny, and their notes may be less than objective or honest concerning the events as they occur. Nurses, alternatively, realize that they are rarely the object of a medical malpractice action, and their recordations usually reflect a more accurate picture of what is really occurring to that patient.

There is also a great deal of tension between physicians and nurses, in spite of what the medical profession attempts to portray. Physicians tend to be supercilious to nurses and address them in somewhat derogatory and sexist terms. Generally, physicians do not offer nurses the respect which their profession demands. Nurses' notes will frequently reflect controversies between the physician and nurse which rarely, if ever, are reflected in the progress notes. Such comments as "supervisor notified" may be insightful.

Additionally, the nurses' notes will reveal more detail about the patient in terms of activity, diet, general mental status, and cooperation. Nurses will describe dressing the wounds and catheters much more so than the visiting physician. Nurses' notes will describe how often and what time the physician visited the patient, as well as how many telephone calls were required to call the physician before he or she responded.

There is a wealth of information in the nurses' notes, and I cannot emphasize too highly that the reader carefully review them. The standard of care also requires that the prudent physician read the daily nurses' notes. Some physicians may not do this, and their progress notes may diametrically oppose what the nurse has written. This also will be very helpful to an inquisitive plaintiff's lawyer.

§3.09 —Laboratory Data

The portion of the chart concerning laboratory data is also in a certain chronological order. Once again, the timeliness of the ordering of the test as well as performing it should be noted. All laboratory tests ordered by the physician will have a laboratory slip reflecting that test in the chart. The time that the test was ordered and performed as well as the initials of the technician who did the actual determination in the laboratory will be reflected on the laboratory slip. It is important to note when the laboratory result was reported back to the chart. I recall one case where a urine culture and sensitivity was ordered on the 14th of the month and reported back on the 16th, yet treatment was not begun until the 18th! Bacteriological studies, blood transfusions and other body fluid testing will also be noted here.

Once again, important information could be gained if the doctor's orders reflect that a certain test was ordered yet never performed or, alternatively, if the test was never ordered at all.

§3.10 —X-Ray Data

This portion of the chart will reflect all of the x-rays performed on the patient as well as the time that each x-ray was performed and the report dictated. Radiologists usually are rather prompt in their dictation of the radiographic study, and this ordinarily does not present a problem. Procedures as routine as chest x-rays, kidney studies (intravenous pyelograms), and flat plates of the abdomen, or as sophisticated as computerized tomographic scans, magnetic resonance imaging, myelograms, arteriography, and other invasive and noninvasive imaging modalities will all be recorded here. A careful reading of each radiographic procedure is a must.

§3.11 —Operative Notes

The *operative note* is a dictated narrative by the operating surgeon concerning the details of the operative procedure performed on the patient. A standardized form is used which includes the name of the patient as well as the patient's hospital number, the date and time of surgery, the pre-operative and post-operative diagnosis, the type of the procedure performed, and the date of dictation of the operative note. Usually, a brief introductory paragraph is dictated, detailing the clinical course of the patient and the reason why the patient has come to the operating room.

The operative note should be descriptive in detail as to exactly what occurred during the operation. Ordinarily, these notes are not self-serving, and are accurately reported. However, it would be rather unusual for a physician to blatantly incriminate him- or herself in an operative note and, of course, this is quite understandable. Physicians tend to use terms such as "iatrogenic" or "inadvertent" rather than negligent or accidental.

A most important item to be noted in reviewing the operative note is the timeliness of the dictation. A delay in dictation has come to haunt more than one urologist over the years.

Obviously, the reading and understanding of an operative note require significant technical understanding. While anatomical and procedural terms may get very arcane, it behooves one to carefully read the note anyway because a general flow and idea can usually be derived as to what is being done. Certainly, the objective and candid surgeon will report in his or her note any untoward event, and this information needs to be carefully analyzed.

§3.12 —Anesthesia Record

If there is one part of the medical record that is confusing, it will certainly be the anesthesia record. Even experienced surgeons may have difficulty interpreting all the abbreviations and codes used on this form. Sample Form 3-2 is a nice blank example of an anesthesia record, but after it is all filled in, particularly in a more complicated case, it can indeed look like an Egyptian papyrus.

There is usually no explanation of the abbreviations and symbols, and frequently another anesthetist or anesthesiologist will be required to interpret all the jargon. However, the abbreviation section of this chapter (§3.23) may provide some assistance.

Let me digress briefly as to terms. An *anesthesiologist* refers to a physician with special training in anesthesia. An *anesthetist* means a specially trained nurse. CRNA refers to Certified Registered Nurse Anesthetist. To confuse you even more, there are a few areas in the country wherein nurse practitioners and physician assistants are also specially trained to provide anesthesia. However, most states, if not all, require the "direct supervision" of an anesthesiologist over the anesthetist, whether a CRNA or PA. It would be prudent, if the case involves an anesthetic issue, to know that particular jurisdiction's code as it applies to anesthesiologists.

Besides the written record which the anesthetist or anesthesiologist renders during the case, most operating rooms have SARA. *Systems for Anesthetic Respiratory Assessment (SARA)* is a computerized module with a printout of various vital signs and blood gases during the procedure. Most operating room procedures require the SARA record to be kept for at least one year, and this is an excellent source of valuable biochemical information.

SARA constantly monitors and displays the patient's oxygen saturation, anesthetic level, blood gases, pH, vital signs, etc. Of course, a written record of all this information is also being made at the same time.

Some of the more important aspects of the anesthetic part of the record would relate to length of the anesthetic and the surgery, blood pressure levels, estimated blood loss (EBL) and replaced, oxygen saturation levels, and types of fluids given intravenously.

§3.13 —Recovery Room Record

While at first glance the recovery room record (or PARR—post-anesthesia recovery room record) might appear to be a close cousin to the anesthetic record, careful scrutiny will reveal rather common sense information being recorded and not a mumbo jumbo of technical abbreviations. Sample Form 3-3 is an example of the PARR. Obviously, important information such as temperature, blood pressure, and respirations is recorded along with urine output and levels of consciousness. Observations regarding any wound or bleeding will also be made. Once again, the nurses' observations will be invaluable since these notes usually reflect an objective assessment of the patient.

One important item to look for is how long the patient stays in the recovery room. Usually, 30 to 40 minutes, even after significant anesthesia time, is the average length of stay in the recovery room. If any longer than this, be on the lookout for the reason.

§3.14 —Consultation Notes

The attending physician will formally put in a request in the doctor's orders to call in a consulting physician. The consultant will either write or dictate a note for placement on the chart.

The consultation note will contain information such as the name of the requesting and consultant physicians, the reason for the consultation, and the date and time of the request. The consultant is notified by the nurse or ward clerk of the request, and then sees the patient. The consultant will usually make a brief note in the doctor's progress notes and a more complete and separate consultation note.

Obviously, the importance of reviewing the consultation notes cannot be overemphasized. Here, significant information can be learned as to the reason for the referral, as well as to certain aspects of care concerning the patient. Frequently, observations made by the consultant physician will go unheeded by the attending physician and this may be very important during the lawsuit.

The role between the attending and consultant physician may frequently become blurred, and I am aware of a recent lawsuit wherein this factor played a great part in the downhill course and negligent death of the patient. The confusion and hostility between the two physicians were obvious from the records, and helped gain a significant plaintiff victory.

§3.15 —Ancillary Records

While most urology patients may not require ancillary services, a brief mention of these ancillary services provided by a hospital is in order. These services are: respiratory therapy, physical therapy, enterostomal therapy, speech therapy, occupational therapy, and dietary therapy.

Respiratory Therapy

Respiratory therapy means a treatment given to a patient to improve or enhance his or her respirations. Breathing exercises, cough production, humidifiers, and pulmonary drainage procedures would all be included in this. While patients with chronic pulmonary disease may definitely require respiratory therapy, almost all post-operative patients also would use this service. The use of "blow bottles" is a common procedure which involves the patient's requirement to deeply inhale and exhale to perform certain exercises which are aimed at expanding the lungs.

A *respiratory therapist* is a technician trained in the art to supply these services to the patient. There is usually a separate respiratory therapy sheet to document the visits and treatment by the technician. Information such as type and number of treatments, duration of the treatment, medication used, and the patient's response to the treatment will all be recorded.

Physical Therapy

Physical therapy is also commonly used in the hospital. The physical therapy technician can provide whirlpool exercise machines, both active and passive, as well as gait-training for patients with ambulation problems. The physical therapist's records also will reflect those types of treatment, duration and number of treatments, as well as patient response.

Enterostomal Therapy

Enterostomal therapy is another ancillary service provided by a hospital. The *enterostomal therapist* is an individual who advises, educates, and monitors a patient with a stoma. *Stoma* refers to an artificially created (i.e., by a surgeon) opening between the skin and an interior organ. A urological type of stoma would be an *ileal conduit*. Here, the ureters are detached from the bladder and then connected to an isolated segment of the ileum, the one end of which is sewed closed and the other is attached to the skin. Urine, then, comes down the kidney via the ureters, into the ileum, and out the stoma into a collecting bag. The enterostomal therapist would be asked to see a patient with an ileal conduit to give advice on how to wear the collecting bag, as well as clean and prepare the skin around the stoma.

While no formal section of the record will be devoted specifically for this service, the therapist will usually make a note in the doctor's progress notes as to the visits with the patient.

Speech Therapy

The *speech pathologist* is a specially trained individual who provides programs to improve communication skills in patients with language and speech impairments. Hearing-impaired and stroke patients utilize these services primarily. Once again, there may be no formal hospital document detailing the speech pathologist's recordation, but frequently a note will be made somewhere in the record, either on a separate consultation note or in the doctor's progress notes as to the speech pathologist's efforts.

Occupational Therapy

The *occupational therapist* is one who can train patients in skills which will restore their social and economic independence. The therapist will develop skills in self-care, work, and play with the physically and emotionally disabled. Here, again, no formal document may be in the record, but the therapist will certainly make some recordation of activities performed by the patient.

Dietary Therapy

A hospital-based dietitian plays a significant role in patient care. Dietitians are mandated by the Joint Commission for Accreditation of Healthcare Organizations (JCAHO) and hospital regulations to monitor the level of dietary activity on each patient—whether the patient is NPO (nothing by mouth), on surgical liquid, full liquid, regular, or special diet. Dietitians will also help compose the contents of parenteral nutrition, either peripheral or central. In an issue involving nutritional status, this information may be vital.

§3.16 —Discharge Summary

This formal part of the record should be the most revealing aspect of the patient's clinical course. Hospital bylaws require that this recordation be completed within 30 days of the patient's discharge from the hospital. This is mainly for insurance payment purposes, since insurance companies rarely will pay the bill until the discharge summary is dictated and on the chart. Of course, the obvious thing to look for, as in all components of the record, is the timeliness of the dictation as well as the accuracy of the facts. While patients sometimes get discharged and the physician is not able at that time to dictate the note, most prudent physicians will dictate the discharge summary at the time that the patient is actually discharged. Obviously, the longer the period of time between the patient's discharge and the dictation of the discharge summary, the less accurate the facts on the summary will be. Although laboratory data and operative notes will be on the chart to refresh the physician's recollection as the discharge summary is dictated, most of the daily activities of the patient will be forgotten.

A form is usually followed for the discharge summary. The note should reflect the reason for the patient's admission, along with a brief recapitulation of the physical examination. The laboratory data are usually presented next, followed by the clinical course, and ending the note with the discharge instructions to the patient, including prescriptions given, diet, physical activities, when to return to the doctor's office, and the like. The final diagnosis and operative procedures performed are also a part of the discharge summary.

Frequently, comments made in the discharge summary may not be supported by observations made in the daily recordation in the chart, and this may be an area to be explored during the litigation.

§3.17 —Consent Form

The consent form (*see* Sample Form 3-4) is that part of the medical record wherein the patient signs a piece of paper with various descriptions of either invasive diagnostic techniques or operations, and agrees to the performance of such procedures. Usually, the name of the physician who will be performing the procedure will also be noted. This is important, in that frequently the patient will believe one physician is performing the procedure when, in fact, the records may show that another physician actually carried out the procedure. Frequently, an addendum to the consent form will also be found in the chart. A physician will instruct the nurse to have the patient sign a consent form for a particular procedure and, for one reason or another, prior to performing that procedure, the physician may want to do an additional or different procedure, and the nurse will have an addendum signed. This usually will occur in the operating room suite. An addendum is also used when it is apparent that a different procedure was performed than the one to which the patient consented. This certainly can be of significant interest if there is a negligence claim.

Informed consent is a legal doctrine wherein the physician must explain certain risks, complications, alternative modes of therapy, and the like to the patient, and this may or may not be part of the hospital consent form. Basically, the hospital consent form is merely one to avoid the charge of assault.

§3.18 —Graphic Sheet

The graphic sheet (*see* Sample Form 3-5) is a recordation of the patient's vital signs. Even more than this, it is a summary of the numerical data of the patient. Whereas the nurses' notes will reflect in a handwritten statement the daily activities, complaints, and occurrences surrounding the patient, the graphic sheet is more numerically oriented. For example, the daily recordation of the patient's temperature, usually every eight hours unless ordered more frequently by the physician, will be plotted on a graph by connecting dots which reflect the daily temperature readings. A single glance will easily allow one to note trends in elevated or normal temperatures during the day or over a period of time. This graph makes up the largest portion of the graphic sheet.

Significant information is also on the graphic sheet, such as ambulatory activity, number and type of daily body excretory functions, how the patient tolerated a diet, the amount of fluids taken in and put out, and other vital signs, such as respiration, pulse, and blood pressure readings. The letters "IRRG" refer to irrigating fluid quantity if used on the patient. "NG/Eme" refers to a nasogastric tube placed in a patient's nose and down the esophagus into the stomach. This tube is frequently used in a post-operative patient whose bowel motility has been anesthetized and has not returned to normal, to suck out any of the gastric secretions which accumulate in the stomach. Patients who have significant nausea and vomiting (emesis) will also get much relief if a nasogastric tube is inserted. The amount of fluids aspirated is recorded on the graphic sheet.

Of course, it goes without saying that a patient's graphic sheet, as all the examples of charts and forms shown, may be modified and very different, depending on the hospital and who designed the particular form.

§3.19 —Circulating Nurse's Records (Operating Room Records)

Before describing the circulating nurse's records (*see* Sample Form 3-6), it is important to understand the role the circulating nurse plays in the operating room.

In every operating room (suite, or theater—all are synonyms), the team consists of the anesthesia personnel, the surgeons, and the nurses. The nursing team consists of a *scrub nurse* (usually an operating room technician and not a nurse in the usual sense), as well as a registered nurse. The operating room technician (or scrub nurse) is trained specifically to understand the type of surgical instruments used, as well as the technique of assisting the surgeon during the operation. The *circulating nurse* is usually a registered nurse who has more training and responsibility in the operating room. For example, all instruments and sponges must be counted before and after an operative procedure. The operating room technician must count these in front of the circulating nurse as part of the operating room rules and regulations. The operating room technician cannot just count these instruments unilaterally nor in front of the anesthesia personnel, but must indeed corroborate the count with the circulating nurse.

This form is a great source of information because of the data disclosed. Particularly important on this form is the count of the lap (i.e., laparotomy) sponges, needles, instruments, etc., both pre- and post-operation. The nurses' notes made during the procedure may be most revealing. Types of prostheses used, whether specimens were sent to the laboratory and the number of drains, tubes, or catheters left in the patient will all be documented. I well recall a particular case wherein a certain urological stenting catheter was left in a patient for five years without her physician's recollection of it, yet the operating room record clearly revealed that the stent had been inserted.

Even names of persons in the room at the time of the surgery will be documented, a fact which may or may not incriminate your client.

§3.20 —Pathology Report

There are several different types of pathology reports. Besides the laboratory data—i.e., blood counts, biochemical profiles, urinalyses—there are bacteriology reports—i.e., sputum and urine cultures, wound and blood cultures, and blood bank reports for blood typing. There are also pathology reports concerning biopsy specimens which may or may not have been obtained in the operating room. In addition, almost every tissue or foreign object (e.g., bullet) retrieved from a patient must go to the pathologist for identification. Some hospital regulations will allow the physician to make a decision whether or not to submit a particular tissue for examination (e.g., most hospitals do not require the submission of a prepuce from a neonatal circumcision to be sent to the pathologist for identification), but most state laws require almost all tissue to be submitted.

The pathology report concerning tissue or specimens received from the operating room will be extremely detailed, describing not only the gross appearance of the tissue in terms of weight, dimensions, color, etc., but a very specific microscopic description culminating in the final diagnosis of the tissue submitted.

The importance of this cannot be overlooked. Hospitals have a tissue committee, and if a particular surgeon submits a significant number of *normal* appendices as part of his operative specimens, this activity will be closely examined by his or her peers.

I have often seen the following scenario as a common issue in urological malpractice actions. Urologists will frequently perform a transrectal or transperineal prostatic biopsy to help make a diagnosis of prostatic cancer. It is not unusual for the tissue specimen to be described as "Colonic and skeletal muscle seen, but no prostate tissue is identified." In other words, the surgeon's needle did not penetrate the prostate. This, in and of itself, is not particularly a departure from the standard of care; so-called blind or closed biopsies may be technically difficult to perform, but to not follow up and repeat the biopsy after such a pathology report is submitted is most definitely a departure from the standard of care.

§3.21 —Medication Sheets

Nurses have certain policies and procedures which they must follow, and record-keeping plays a large part in their job.

In today's highly specialized medical treatment of patients, there may be numerous physicians involved in the treatment of any one patient. With all these doctors writing orders in the chart, confusion may and does occur regarding which medications and dosages a patient is to receive. The medication sheet (*see* Sample Form 3-7) is used to clarify the medication picture and to serve as the single source documenting when and how much of a particular drug is given to a patient.

This information may also be found in other parts of the chart, such as the nurses' progress notes, graphic sheet, operating room record, and recovery room nurses' notes, but the total picture can always be found on the medication sheet.

Again, there is nothing magic about the information on these records, and most hospitals even have a "stop order" as part of these regulations—i.e., certain narcotics and antibiotics, even though ordered by the physician to be given to the patient without a specific period of time when the drug should be terminated, will be automatically terminated by the nurse unless another written order is placed in the chart.

§3.22 —Emergency Room Records

The emergency room can be visualized as a mini-hospital. When a patient presents to the emergency room, a patient information sheet as well as a chart is made out for him or her. If laboratory data or x-rays are a part of that visit, all of this information is compiled and kept together. If the patient is subsequently admitted to the hospital, this information will be assimilated into the hospital record, but if the patient is sent home, the emergency room record, including all its components, is tabulated and kept in the medical records library.

Careful reading of the emergency room record is just as important as any other part of the chart. Significant information can always be obtained from this record which may be very pivotal to a malpractice case. Referral to a specialist, whether the physician responded in a timely fashion, vital signs, stability of the patient, orders sent home with the patient, lab tests ordered, etc., may have an impact on the potential cause of action.

§3.23 Abbreviations

No medical record can be properly understood without a guide to the abbreviations noted. There is an inner world in most hospitals wherein abbreviations used can be very arcane. Every hospital has a list of approved abbreviations which may be used on the record. Although the approved abbreviations may be used within the chart, they may not be used in recording the final diagnosis, either on the front sheet or in the discharge summary. While there are certain urological abbreviations that are very specific to urology, I am going to list a general number of abbreviations which may be found in any hospital record. Additionally, this list is not to be considered exhaustive, and one may find an unusual abbreviation in any hospital record which may defy definition.

Abbreviations

abd.	abdomen
ABG	arterial blood gases
a.c.	before meals
ad. lib.	at pleasure
AgNO$_3$	silver nitrate
AIDS	acquired immunodeficiency syndrome
AJ	ankle jerk
AK	above the knee (amputation)
alb.	albumin
alk. phos.	alkaline phosphatase
ant. ax. line	anterior axillary line
aort. regur.	aortic regurgitation
aort. sten.	aortic stenosis
AP	anteroposterior
ARC	AIDS-related complex
AS	left ear
ASCVD	arteriosclerotic cardiovascular disease
ASHD	arteriosclerotic heart disease
AU	both ears

aur. fib.	auricular fibrillation
AV	arteriovenous
bands	banded neutrophils
baso	basophils
BCP	biochemical profile
BE	barium enema
b.i.d.	twice a day
BK	below the knee (amputation)
bl. cult.	blood culture
BM	bowel movement
BOW	bag of waters
BP	blood pressure
BPH	benign prostatic hypertrophy
BR $\bar{c}$ BRP	bedrest with bathroom privileges
br. sounds	breath sounds
BS	bowel sounds
BUN	blood urea nitrogen
bx.	biopsy
$\bar{c}$	with
CA	carcinoma
C&S	culture and sensitivity
cap.	capsule
cath.	catheter
CBC	complete blood count
CC	chief complaint
CHD	congenital heart disease
CHF	congestive heart failure
chol.	cholesterol
circ.	circumcision
cm.	centimeter (2.5 cm. = 1 inch)
CNS	central nervous system
CPK	creatinine phosphokinase
C/O	complains of
CO	carbon dioxide
CPR	cardiopulmonary resuscitation
CRIF	closed reduction internal fixation
C/S	cesarean section
CSF	cerebrospinal fluid
CT scan/CAT scan	computerized axial tomography
CSR	central supply room
CVA	cerebrovascular accident
CVP	central venous pressure
CXR	chest x-ray
D1, D2, etc.	1st, 2nd dorsal vertebra, etc.
D&C	dilatation and curettage
d/c	discontinue

D/C	discharge
DIC	diffuse intravascular coagulation
dil.	dilated, dilatation
DIP joint	distal interphalangeal joint
DOA	dead on arrival
DVT	deep vein thrombosis
D/W	distilled water
dx.	diagnosis
EBL	estimated blood loss
EDC	expected date of confinement
EEG	electroencephalogram
EKG or ECG	electrocardiogram
EMG	electromyography
ER	emergency room
ERCP	endoscopic retrograde cholangio-pancreatography
ESR	erythrocyte sedimentation rate
ET	endotracheal
F	Fahrenheit temperature
FB	foreign body
FBS	fasting blood sugar
FFP	fresh frozen plasma
FH	family history
FHM	fetal heart monitor
FHT	fetal heart tones
FTSG	full thickness skin graft
FUO	fever of unknown origin
fx.	fracture
GBS	gallbladder series
GC	gonorrhea
GI	gastrointestinal
gm.	gram
gr.	grain
Grav. I, etc.	pregnancy times one, etc.
GTT	glucose tolerance test
gtt.	drops
GU	genitourinary
gyn.	gynecology
H&H	hemoglobin and hematocrit
H_2O	water
H O	peroxide
hct.	hematocrit
HCVD	hypertensive cardiovascular disease
hgb.	hemoglobin
HIV	human immunodeficiency virus
HNP	herniated nucleus pulposus

hpf.	high power field
HR	heart rate
hs.	at bedtime
ht.	height
hx.	history
I&D	incision and drainage
ID	identification
IM	intramuscular
IMP	impression
I&O	intake and output
IPPB	intermittent positive pressure breathing
IV	intravenous
K	potassium
KJ	knee jerk
KUB	kidney, ureter, bladder (x-ray)
kg.	kilogram
KVO	keep vein open
L&D	labor and delivery
L1, L2, etc.	1st, 2nd lumbar vertebra, etc.
L or lt.	left
lab.	laboratory
lat.	lateral
lb.	pound
LDH	lactic dehydrogenase
LE prep.	lupus erythematosus prep
LLL	left lower lobe
LLQ	left lower quadrant
LMP	last menstrual period
LOA	left occiput anterior
LOP	left occiput posterior
LP	lumbar puncture
lpf.	low power field
LTL	laparoscopic tubal ligation
LUL	left upper lobe
LUQ	left upper quadrant
lymphs	lymphocytes
M	murmur
med.	medicine
mEq/l	milliequivalents per liter
mg.	milligram
mg.%	milligrams per 100 milliliters
MI	myocardial infarction
min.	minute
ml.	milliliter
mm.	millimeter
mono.	monocyte

MRI	magnetic resonance imaging
myr.	myringotomy
NA	not applicable
Na	sodium
NEC	necrotizing enterocolitis
NG	nasogastric tube
NIDDM	non-insulin-dependent diabetes mellitus
NKA	no known allergies
n.p.o.	nothing by mouth
noct.	nocturnal
NSR	normal sinus rhythm
O_2	oxygen
O_2 cap.	oxygen capacity
O_2 sat.	oxygen saturation
OB	obstetrics
OBS	organic brain syndrome
O.C.	oral contraceptive
O.D.	right eye
OM	otitis media
oob	out of bed
OR	operating room
ORIF	open reduction internal fixation
ortho.	orthopedics
O.S.	left eye
OT	occupational therapy
O.U.	both eyes
P_2I2	pulmonic second heart sound
P	pulse
PA	postero-anterior
PAC	premature atrial contraction
PACU	post-anesthesia care unit
P&A	percussion and auscultation
Para I	one pregnancy
PC	packed cells
pc.	after meals
PCN	penicillin
pCO_2	partial pressure carbon dioxide
PCV	packed cell volume
PDA	patent ductus arteriosus
PE	physical examination
ped.	pediatric
peri-care	perineal care
peri-pad	perineal pad
periph.	peripheral
PERRLA	pupils equal, round, reactive to light and accommodation

PH	past history
pH	hydrogen ion concentration
PI	present illness
PID	pelvic inflammatory disease
PIP	proximal interphalangeal joint
PKU	phenylketonuria
PMI	point of maximal impulse
p.o.	by mouth
pO$_2$	partial pressure oxygen
polys	polymorphonuclear leukocytes
PP	post-partum
premie	premature
prep.	preparation
p.r.n.	when necessary
prot.	protein
protime	prothrombin time
pt.	patient
P.T.	physical therapy
P.T.T.	partial thromboplatin time
PUD	peptic ulcer disease
PVC	premature ventricular contractions
q.	every
q. AM	every morning
q.d.	every day
q.h.s.	at bedtime only
q.i.d.	four times daily
q.n.	every night
q.s.	quantity sufficient
q.n.s.	quantity not sufficient
q.o.d.	every other day
q.2 h.	every two hours
quant.	quantity
R or rt.	right
RBC	red blood cells
RDS	respiratory distress syndrome
RLL	right lower lobe (lung)
RLQ	right lower quadrant (abdomen)
R/O	rule out
ROA	right occiput anterior
ROM	range of motion
ROS	review of systems
RPG	retrograde pyelogram
RUL	right upper lobe (lung)
RUQ	right upper quadrant
Rx	treatment, therapy, prescription
s	without

sed. rate	erythrocyte sedimentation rate
segs.	segmented neutrophils
SGOT	serum glutamic oxaloacetic transaminase
SGPT	serum glutamic pyruvic transaminase
SH	social history
SMR	submucous resection
S&O	salpingo-oophorectomy
SOB	short of breath
sp. gr.	specific gravity
SSE	soapsuds enema
sta.	station
Staph.	Staphylococcus
stat	immediately
Strep.	Streptococcus
STSG	split-thickness skin graft
surg.	surgery, surgical
SVD	spontaneous vaginal delivery
T	temperature
T1, T2, etc.	1st, 2nd thoracic vertebra, etc.
tab.	tablet
TAH	total abdominal hysterectomy
T&A	tonsilloadenoidectomy
t.b.	tuberculosis
tbsp.	tablespoon
TEDS	thromboembolic disease stockings
t.i.d.	three times a day
T&X	type and cross-match
TMJ	temporomandibular joint
t.o.	telephone order
TPN	total parenteral nutrition
TPR	temperature, pulse, respiration
tsp.	teaspoon
TUR	transurethral resection
TURBN	transurethral resection bladder neck
TURP	transurethral resection prostate
TVH	total vaginal hysterectomy
Tx	treatment
U/A	urinalysis
UGI	upper gastrointestinal
umb.	umbilical
ung.	ointment
up ad. lib.	out of bed as desires
UPJ	ureteropelvic junction
URI	upper respiratory infection
urol.	urology
US	ultrasound

UTI	urinary tract infection
UVJ	ureterovesical junction
vag.	vaginal
VD	venereal disease
vit.	vitamin (followed by letter)
v.o.	verbal order
VS	vital signs
WB	whole blood
WBC	white blood count
WD	well-developed
WN	well-nourished
WNL	within normal limits
wt.	weight
YO	year old

§3.24 Office Records

The office medical record is the official business record of the doctor. The medical record describes the care and treatment of the patient, and may be released only if the patient or the patient's personal representative expressly consents to its release. However, a subpoena requiring the production of documents may be used to obtain the records. A valid subpoena requires a response, which may be the production of documents requested or a motion requesting the court to excuse the recipient of the subpoena from complying. Failure to respond to the subpoena may lead to contempt proceedings, jail, or fines! Georgia Code Ann §24-9-40 (1985) states: "Any physician releasing information under written authorization . . . or pursuant to any law, statute or lawful regulation or under court order or subpoena shall not be liable to the patient or any other person." The patient generally signs an authorization form describing all records to be released.

To be admissible in court, the medical records must be properly authenticated. This means that the physician must have signed all entries and it means that the custodian of the medical records—either the doctor or the office manager—must testify or certify as to the records' identity. The medical record is a legal document that may not be altered. Not only is the record essential for the plaintiff attempting to prove a case, but it is also essential to the physician in proving that the treatment of the patient did not deviate from the required standard of care.

§3.25 Lost or Altered Medical Records

Spoliation of evidence constitutes a grave offense. Medical records, and particularly office records, allow for the greatest of ease in spoliation. The physician usually receives the request for records and has the opportunity (and possibly the motive) to either alter or destroy portions of those records. Some clues to spoliation may be the use of different color ink, notations out of chronological order, crowded writing, misaligned typing, erasures, changes in handwriting techniques, or the use of forms not available at the time of the entry.

The comparison with insurance records, FAA physical examinations, and outside radiology or laboratory reports may also reveal clues to alteration of the medical records.

Additionally, there are now scientific methods which can be utilized if the suspicion is great. These methods include chemical analysis, ultraviolet and infrared exam, chromotography, and spectrophotography.

Some jurisdictions allow the jury to infer negligence if there is proof of suppression of evidence or of spoliation, while other jurisdictions in the case of lost or missing medical records allow the creation of a rebuttable presumption of negligence.

Additionally, while omission of the recordation of an act in the records may not be as serious as spoliation, the failure to record what should have been recorded certainly infers that that act was not performed. I recall one case wherein neither the urologist nor general surgeon, seeing a gunshot victim in the emergency room, recorded whether a rectal examination was done. At trial, each said he thought the other did the rectal exam, setting up a fertile field for the plaintiff's attorney.

Finally, even though bodily harm may not occur, if conduct is extreme and results in severe distress, spoliation of the hospital medical record may support a claim for intentional infliction of emotional distress.

Appendix 3-A Sample Forms

Sample Form 3-1

Appendix 3-A 91

Sample Form 3-2

Sample Form 3-3

_____ HOSPITAL

POST-ANESTHESIA RECOVERY ROOM RECORD

DATE	ADMISSION TIME AM/PM	DISCHARGE TIME AM/PM	SURGEON
ANESTHESIA			ANESTHESIOLOGIST/CRNA

OPERATION

SPECIAL CONSIDERATIONS:
ASA #

ALLERGIES:

CODE	B/P	PULSE •	RESP. ○

PRE-OP V.S.	B/P		
T	P	R	

PARR SCORE	ADM	30'	1°	D/C
Activity				
Respiration				
Circulation				
Consciousness				
Color				
TOTAL				

AIRWAY MANAGEMENT

On Adm.		D/C Time	
Oral			
Nasal			
ETT/NTT			
Mandibular Sup.			
O₂ Mist	%		

DRAINS/PACKS

OR.	INTAKE	P.A.R.

NURSES SIGNATURE	INIT.

NURSING OBSERVATIONS TREATMENTS	INIT.

TIME	MEDICATION	DOSE	ROUTE	SITE	INIT.

TOTAL

OR.	OUTPUT	P.A.R.

TOTAL

TIME	INFUSION	VOLUME	D/CD	ADDITIVES	INIT.
O.R.					

TOTAL OR + PARR	
INTAKE	OUTPUT

TEMPERATURE	AXILLARY
	ORALLY

TIME RECEIVED ON UNIT
AM   PM

B/P	P	R

IV STATUS @ D/C

ANESTHESIOLOGIST SIGNATURE AT D/C	FAMILY NOTIFIED OF EXTENDED STAY TIME:	FLOOR NURSES SIGNATURE

CMS 347 (REV. 6/83)

P.A.R.R. RECORD

Appendix 3-A 93

Sample Form 3-4

FORM CMS 348

_____ **HOSPITAL**

WRITE PATIENT NAME OR IMPRINT PATIENT CARD HERE

AUTHORIZATION FOR TREATMENT

I hereby authorize and consent to such treatments including, but not limited to, surgical operations, anesthesia and x-ray examination or treatment as may be ordered by Dr. _____ and assistants of his choice in the case of

_____
(Name of Patient)

In connection with or relating to the following described operations or procedures to be performed:

_____
_____
_____

I authorize any additional operations or procedures as are considered therapeutically necessary on the basis of findings during the course of said operation.

I consent to the disposal of tissues or parts removed in accordance with routine hospital practice.

I hereby certify that I have read and fully understand the above authorization for surgical treatment, the reasons why the above described surgery is necessary, and the risks in surgical operations and in the use of anesthetics. I accept and assume all such risks and consequences. I also certify that no guarantee or assurance has been made as to the results that may be obtained.

I hereby certify that I am signing this consent form in the following capacity:

Initial
( ) An adult consenting for himself or herself
( ) A parent consenting for his or her minor child
( ) A married person consenting for his or her spouse
( ) A minor married person consenting for himself or herself
( ) A guardian consenting for his or her ward
( ) A person temporarily standing in loco parentis, whether formally serving or not, consenting for the minor under his or her care.
( ) A minor (under 18) consenting for himself or herself
( ) A female, regardless of age or marital status, consenting for herself in connection with pregnancy or childbirth
( ) An adult, in the absence of the parent, consenting for his or her minor brother or sister
( ) A grandparent, in the absence of a parent, consenting for his or her minor grandchild

DATE:_____ SIGNATURE OF PERSON SIGNING:_____

SIGNATURE OF WITNESS:_____

Sample Form 3-5

____________________ HOSPITAL

GRAPHIC SHEET

DATE																														
P.O. DATE																														
	A.M.			P.M.			A.M.			P.M.			A.M.			P.M.			A.M.			P.M.			A.M.			P.M.		
Hour	12	4	8	12	4	8	12	4	8	12	4	8	12	4	8	12	4	8	12	4	8	12	4	8	12	4	8	12	4	8
TEMPERATURE 105°																														
104°																														
103°																														
102°																														
101°																														
100°																														
99°																														
NORMAL																														
98°																														
97°																														
96°																														
PULSE																														
RESP.																														
BLOOD PRESSURE																														

ADMISSION HT.	WT.			WT.			WT.			WT.			WT.		
INTAKE	PO	IV and IV Piggy Backs	IRRG	PO	IV and IV Piggy Backs	IRRG	PO	IV and IV Piggy Backs	IRRG	PO	IV and IV Piggy Backs	IRRG	PO	IV and IV Piggy Backs	IRRG
11-7															
7-3															
3-11															
24-HOUR TOTALS															
OUTPUT	Urine	NG/ Eme.	Misc.	Urine	NG/ Eme.	Misc.	Urine	NG/ Eme.	Misc.	Urine	NG/ Eme.	Misc.	Urine	NG/ Eme.	Misc.
11-7															
7-3															
3-11															
24-HOUR TOTALS															
BOWEL MOVEMENT	11-7	7-3	3-11	11-7	7-3	3-11	11-7	7-3	3-11	11-7	7-3	3-11	11-7	7-3	3-11

CMS-357 (Rev. 4/80)

Appendix 3-A 95

Sample Form 3-6

HOSPITAL
OPERATING ROOM RECORD

GEN ☐	C-SECT ☐	NEURO ☐	VASCULAR ☐
GYN ☐	ORTHO ☐	GU ☐	THORACIC ☐
ENT ☐	PLASTIC ☐	PACEMAKER ☐	
EYE ☐	DENTAL ☐	☐	☐

DATE OF OPERATION: | O.R. ROOM NO.: | SURGEON:

FIRST ASSISTANT: | ANESTHESIOLOGIST/ANESTHETIST:

SURGICAL NURSE: | CIRCULATING NURSE:

| TIME IN | A.M. P.M. | TIME OUT | A.M. P.M. | INCISION TIME | A.M. P.M. | CLOSING TIME | A.M. P.M. | ANESTHETIC & TYPE: GEN. ☐ SP ☐ LOC* ☐ |

PRE-OPERATIVE DIAGNOSIS:

POST-OPERATIVE DIAGNOSIS:

OPERATION:

CONSENT (SIGNED ON CHART): YES ☐ NO ☐ | ARRIVAL TO O.R.: ASLEEP ☐ AWAKE ☐ CONSCIOUS ☐ UNRESPONSIVE ☐ | PATIENT IDENTIFIED: VERBAL ☐ CHART ☐ ID ☐ | TUBES ☐ DRAINS ☐ CATHETER ☐ PRE-OP: | PATIENT POSITION: SUPINE ☐ PRONE ☐ LITHOTOMY ☐ LATERAL ☐ JACKKNIFE ☐ OTHER:

PREP: | CLASSIFICATION:
SOL USED | BY | I II III IV
GROUND DEVICE SITE: | TOURNIQUET: WHERE _____ PRESSURE _____
| UP _____ DOWN _____
| BOVIE USED NUMBER

	LAP SPONGES	SPONGES-RAYTEC	NEEDLES	INSTRUMENTS	BLADES	OTHER
TOTALS						

CORRECT COUNTS: PRE COUNT YES ☐ NO ☐ COUNT 1 YES ☐ NO ☐ COUNT 2 YES ☐ NO ☐ COUNT 3 YES ☐ NO ☐

SIGNATURES:

SPECIMEN:
TO LABORATORY YES ☐ NO ☐
CULTURES: YES ☐ NO ☐ SITE _____

PROSTHESIS: | TYPE | SERIAL #

DRAINS, TUBES, PACK (LOCATION):

NURSE'S NOTES DURING SURGERY: | MEDICATIONS USED OTHER THAN FOR ANESTHESIA:
| DRUG | AMOUNT | HOW GIVEN

PATIENT DISCHARGED TO:
ICU ☐ CCU ☐ RR ☐ ROOM ☐ OTHER ☐ BY

O.R. NURSE'S SIGNATURE

FORM CMS-309 (REV. 1/83)

CHART COPY

Sample Form 3-7

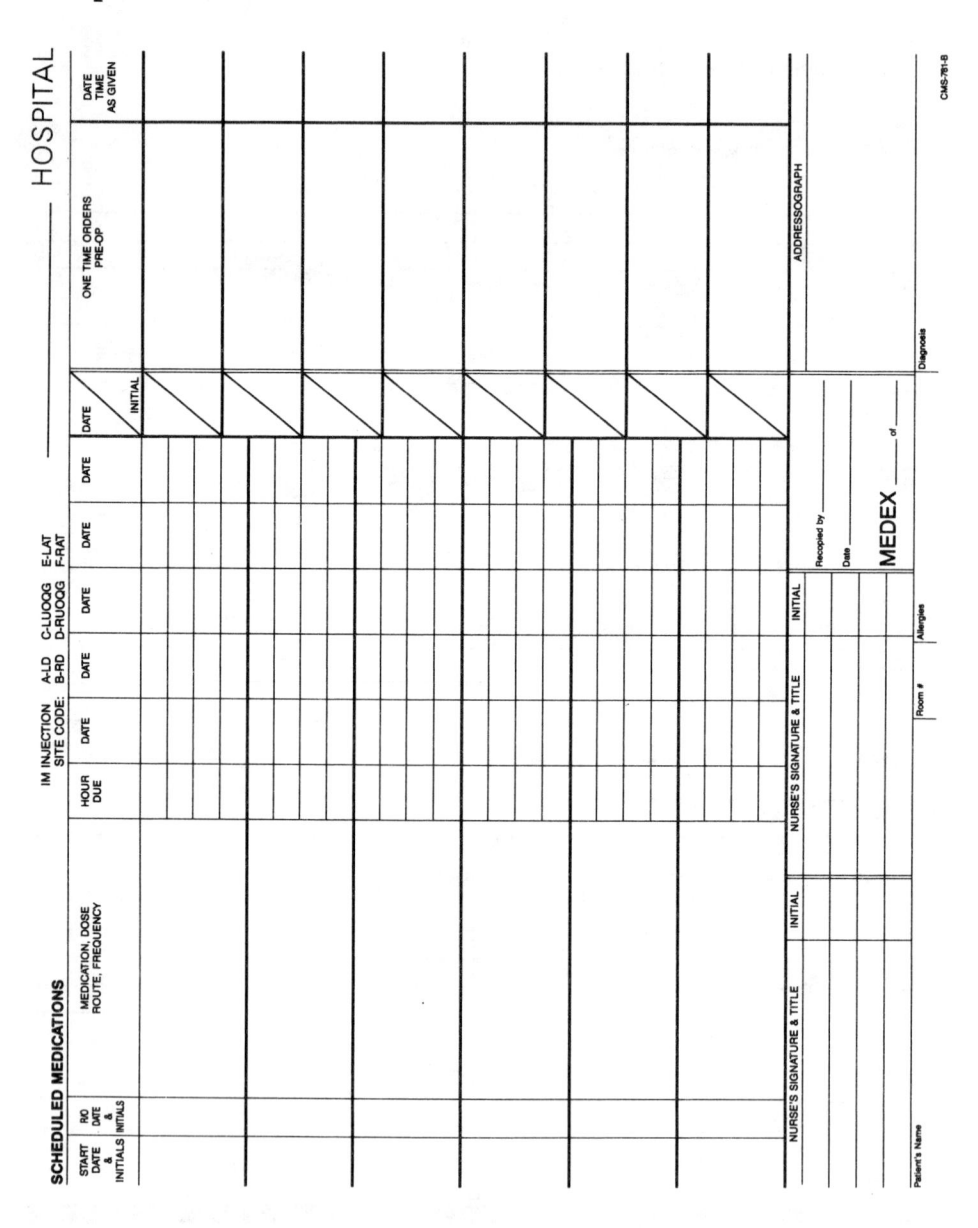

Sample Form 3-8

_____ **HOSPITAL**

PREADMISSION PATIENT QUESTIONNAIRE

I AGREE TO HAVE NOTHING BY MOUTH AFTER MIDNIGHT THE NIGHT BEFORE MY SURGERY UNLESS INSTRUCTED TO DO SO.

PATIENT COMPLETE

- YES ___ NO ___ Is this your first anesthetic?
- YES ___ NO ___ Have you had any problems with prior anesthesia? Specify: _____
- YES ___ NO ___ If female, are you having your period?
- YES ___ NO ___ A. Wearing a tampon?
- YES ___ NO ___ B. Are you or could you be pregnant?
- YES ___ NO ___ Have members of your family had problems with anesthesia? Specify: _____

DO YOU HAVE OR HAVE YOU HAD:

- YES ___ NO ___ A. Heart disease
- YES ___ NO ___ B. High blood pressure
- YES ___ NO ___ C. Lung disease
- YES ___ NO ___ D. Asthma
- YES ___ NO ___ E. Kidney disease Specify: _____ Difficulty Voiding? YES ___ NO ___
- YES ___ NO ___ F. Liver disease
- YES ___ NO ___ G. Jaundice (yellow color of skin/eyes)? Specify: _____
- YES ___ NO ___ H. Diabetes
- YES ___ NO ___ I. Epilepsy/Seizures/Neurological problems
- YES ___ NO ___ J. Thyroid or goiter problems
- YES ___ NO ___ K. Bowel/colon disease or problem? Specify: _____
- YES ___ NO ___ A. Chest pain
- YES ___ NO ___ B. Shortness of breath
- YES ___ NO ___ C. Chronic cough
- YES ___ NO ___ D. Back trouble Specify: _____
- YES ___ NO ___ E. Neck trouble Specify: _____
- YES ___ NO ___ F. Muscle weakness
- YES ___ NO ___ G. Past/present possible carrier of a contagious disease Specify: _____
- YES ___ NO ___ H. Bleeding or clotting abnormalities Specify: _____
- YES ___ NO ___ Have you had broken bones in your face, back or had nose surgery? Specify: _____

- YES ___ NO ___ Have you had blood transfusions
- YES ___ NO ___ Do you smoke or ever smoked? Amount per day: _____
- YES ___ NO ___ Are you on a special diet at home? Specify: _____
- YES ___ NO ___ Are you currently taking any daily medications? Specify: _____

- YES ___ NO ___ Have you taken medicine such as cortisone or steriods during the past year
- YES ___ NO ___ Do you use eye drops Specify: _____
- YES ___ NO ___ A. Do you have glaucoma
  DO YOU HAVE ANY OF THE FOLLOWING:
- YES ___ NO ___ A. Dentures ___   B. Partial Plate ___   Bridgework-permanent ___   C. caps ___
  ARE YOU WEARING ANY OF THE FOLLOWING:
- YES ___ NO ___ A. Contact lenses ___   B. False eyelashes ___   C. Wig/hair piece ___   D. Hearing Aid ___
- YES ___ NO ___ Have you ever had an abnormal chest x-ray
- YES ___ NO ___ Have you ever had an abnormal EKG
- YES ___ NO ___ Any exposure to communicable diseases in the past 3 weeks? Explain: _____
- YES ___ NO ___ Recent weight loss? Amount lost _____

What is your height _____ Weight _____ Age _____

PLEASE COMPLETE THIS AREA: List medical/surgical problems or history of past surgeries:
_____
_____
_____

PATIENT SIGNATURE _____ NEXT OF KIN IF MINOR _____ RELATIONSHIP _____

CMS-1540-A REV. 4/88

Sample Form 3-9

_____ **HOSPITAL**

CLINICAL JUSTIFICATION FOR USE OF
BLOOD AND BLOOD PRODUCTS

Physician who ordered blood:

_____

Stamp Plate

PACKED RBC's _____ UNIT(S).

___Restore oxygen-carrying capacity and correct hypovolemia secondary to surgery, trauma, bleeding.
___Symptomatic chronic anemia (due to chronic disease or neoplasm) with Hgb < 8 gm or Hct < 24%.
___Symptomatic chronic anemia plus documentation of coronary artery disease, chronic pulmonary disease, or cerebrovascular disease.
___Necessary for general anesthesia, as determined by Anesthesiologist.

WHOLE BLOOD _____ UNIT(S).

___Brisk active bleeding with loss of 25% or more of total blood volume.
___Active bleeding after receiving at least 4 units of packed RBC's.
___Neonatal exchange.

*PRETRANSFUSION HEMOGLOBIN/HEMATOCRIT: _____ (Hbg) _____ (Hct)

*POST-TRANSFUSION HEMOGLOBIN/HEMATOCRIT: _____ (Hgb) _____ (Hct)

*OTHER JUSTIFICATION (WHOLE BLOOD OR PACKED CELLS) EXPLAIN: _____

_____

PLATELET CONCENTRATION _____ UNIT(S).

___Dangerously low platelet count (e.g., < 30,000).
___Scheduled for surgery within 12 hours and platelet count < 50,000.
___Platelet dysfunction (thrombasthenia).

*PRETRANSFUSION PLATELET COUNT: _____

*POSTRANSFUSION PLATELET COUNT: _____ (within 18 hours of platelet transfusion)

_____

FRESH FROZEN PLASMA _____ UNIT(S).   CRYOPRECIPITATE _____ UNIT(S).

___Coagulation defect documented by prolonged PT and/or PTT.   ___Hemophilia A
___Given in massive transfusion to help restore or maintain coagulability.   ___Von Willebrand's Disease.
___Von Willebrand's disease.   ___Fibrinogen deficiency (below 200).

*PRETRANSFUSION PT: _____ PTT: _____

*POSTRANSFUSION PT: _____ PTT: _____
  (Within 4 hours of transfusion with FFP or CRYO)

_____ M.D.
Signature

CMS-833

4

Urology as a Specialty

§4.01 Historical Background
§4.02 Glossary
§4.03 The Making of a Urologist
§4.04 Licensure
§4.05 Board Certification
§4.06 —Recertification
§4.07 Demographics and Socioeconomics
§4.08 Subspecialization
§4.09 Standard Texts and Journals
§4.10 Urological Societies

§4.01 Historical Background

It is important to understand the specialty of urology, how it came to be, what a urologist is, and some of the accoutrements of a urologist in order to better understand the urological issues or the defendant physician. Additionally, information in this chapter may be important as resources for background material. This will become more evident as we proceed.

First of all, a brief history of urology is in order. Since libraries are filled with tomes about the history of urology starting from prehistoric times until the present, I can do only a little justice to a marvelously complex and exciting story.

Possibly, the most ancient object of urological interest is a bladder stone approximately 7,000 years old, discovered in an Egyptian prehistoric tomb in 1901. It was found among the pelvic bones of a teenage boy. Illustrations of circumcisions can be easily seen in Egyptian hieroglyphics, and Babylonian cuneiforms mention the practice of uroscopy (diagnosing illnesses by looking at urine) as early as 4000 B.C. Oriental writings as early as 3000 B.C. discuss kidneys, urine, and the idea that spermatic fluid was produced in the brain. Venereal diseases were also mentioned. Moses, in about 1500 B.C., decreed, "When any man hath a running issue out of his flesh, because of his issue, he is unclean" (*Leviticus* 15:2). This has been thought to describe gonorrhea.

Greece is not only the cradle and birthplace of medicine, but also of Aesculapius, the Greek God of Healing. His sword and staff, the Caduceus, came to be the logo for medicine today. Hippocrates was born in 460 B.C., and the Hippocratic Oath is taken by every medical graduate today. Strangely, the Oath says, "I will not cut persons laboring under the stone, but will leave this to be done by practitioners of this work."

The Roman era also produced urological essays, and the artifacts found at Pompeii near Naples include catheters as well as remarkable illustrations of diseased and normal genitalia (I refer the interested reader to the House of the Vetii in downtown Pompeii).

Galen's writings about the kidney are quite clear, and his work (although inaccurate) cast considerable influence for over 1200 years. After the fall of the Roman Empire, however, little progress was made in medicine until the Italian Renaissance.

Surgeons were originally itinerant, and looked down upon by "physicians." Even though there was no anesthesia, lithotomists operated on patients for stones in the bladder and kidney, and, in spite of a significantly high mortality rate, they flourished. It was not until the 1600s that surgeons were accepted as professionals. In 1731, the Academy of Surgery was founded by De La Peyronie (a very important name in urology), and the barber surgeons were forbidden to practice any more.

The greatest anatomist of all was Vesalius, born in Brussels in 1514. His marvelous life is one of the brightest gifts given to mankind, and his rather accurate anatomical descriptions changed the course of medicine until the English anatomist, John Hunter, in the mid-1700s.

Ambrose Paré, the Father of Modern Surgery, worked in the sixteenth century and published numerous treatises on urinary retention and its relief. In the seventeenth and eighteenth centuries, urinary catheters, cutting for stone, treating venereal diseases, and uroscopy flourished.

The first attempt to see inside the bladder was carried out in 1806 by Philippe Bozzini, but it was not until Edison invented the incandescent lamp in 1880 that real progress was made regarding endoscopy. The modern cystoscope was invented by Max Nietze in 1877.

Of course, it is the twentieth century that has given us the modern concept of urology as a specialty, and a discipline devoted to certain anatomical and physiological areas.

While various physicians were performing surgery on kidneys, bladders, prostates, etc., the very first planned nephrectomy was carried out in 1869 by Gustav Simon in Germany.

The first "open" prostatectomy was accomplished in 1891 by George Goodfellow in Tombstone, Arizona, and the first "closed" (transurethral) prostatectomy, claimed by many, was probably carried out in 1913 in France by Georges Luys. But, it was not until the Stern-McCarthy resectoscope (still in use, and the most popular of all resectoscopes) was invented in 1932 that the transurethral approach became popular.

It is also important to note that general anesthesia was not used until 1842, when Crawford W. Long of Georgia claimed its benefit, although a dentist, W. T. G. Morton of Boston, also claimed to be the first to use ether.

The twentieth century additionally brought gigantic leaps, not only in the technological knowledge, but also in the broader parameters of urology. Innovative surgical procedures were attempted and perfected, and investigative work was begun in such areas as infertility, impotency, stone disease, and congenital urological problems.

New urological armamentaria were made available, such as those involved in diagnosis—i.e., intravenous pyelography, ultrasound, and computerized tomography—and therapeutics, including lithotripsy, dialysis, transplantation, and prostheses.

The discussion could go on and on, but for the purposes of this chapter, the reader now should have a brief and better idea of the background and growth of urology in order to better understand the issues involved in urological medical malpractice today.

§4.02 Glossary

This section is included as a brief commentary on common urological phraseology. While not meant as a complete compendium of urological terminology, this reference may give the reader some insight into what may look like triple gobbledygook.

An example of a most difficult word is "ureteroneo cystostomy." Breaking this word down into segments—ureter, new, bladder, opening—clearly defines ureteroneo cystoscomy to be the name of an operation whereby a new opening into the bladder is made for the ureter. This technique can make it simple to decipher complex terms.

To really make it easy, it is important to learn very common and frequently used prefixes and suffixes. The following list is by no means complete, but it includes the most common ones used in urology. Read these over, think about each syllable of the urological term, and your ability to understand each word should improve markedly.

Prefixes

Cyst (or vesico)—bladder
Cystitis: inflammation of the bladder; vesicostomy: an opening into the bladder

Hemato—blood
Hematospermia: blood in the semen

Hydro—water
Hydrocele: a collection of fluid around the testicle

Litho—stone
Lithotomy: cutting out of the stone

Lipo—fat
Lipoma: fatty tumor

Myo—muscle
Myositis: inflammation of the muscle

Nephro—kidney
Nephrectomy: removal of the kidney

Pyelo—pelvis
Pyelitis: inflammation of the pelvis of the kidney

Pyo—pus
Pyospermia: pus in the semen

Orchio (or test)—testicle
Orchiectomy: removal of the testicle

Prostato—prostate
Prostatitis: inflammation of the prostate

Uretero—ureter
Ureterolithotomy: cutting a stone out of the ureter

Urethro—urethra
Urethritis: inflammation of the urethra

Vesico (cyst)—bladder
Vesicovaginal fistula: opening between the bladder and the vagina

Test—testicle
Testalgia: pain in the testicle

Suffixes

-algia—pain
Orchialgia: pain in the testicle

-coele (-cele)—swelling
Varicocele: a swelling of veins around the testicle

-ectasia—dilation
Ureterectasia: dilation of the ureter

-ectomy—to cut out
Prostatectomy: to cut out the prostate

-emia—in the blood
Bacteremia: bacteria in the blood

-ism—the condition of having
Prostatism: condition of having a prostate condition

-itis—inflammation of
Nephritis: inflammation of the kidney

-oid—looks like
Spheroid: looks like a sphere

-oma—tumor
Lipoma: fatty tumor

-oscopy—looking into
Cystoscopy: looking into the bladder

-ostomy—making an opening into
Nephrostomy: making an opening into the kidney

-otomy—incision
Ureterotomy: making an incision into the ureter

-pex—to suture
Orchiopexy: to suture the testicle into the scrotum

-rrhaphy—to sew up
Nephrorrhaphy: to sew up the kidney

-rrhea—discharge
Prostatorrhea: discharge from the prostate

-uria—in the urine
Glycosuria: sugar in the urine

Now, let us look at some of the more common terminology of urological procedures so that we can better interpret and understand the phrases by using our knowledge of the common prefixes and suffixes.

Pyelolithotomy: Removing a stone from the renal pelvis

Nephrolithotomy: Removing a stone from the kidney

Nephrostomy: Making an opening into the kidney

Heminephrectomy: Removing half of the kidney

Nephropexy: To suture the kidney so as to support it (an archaic operation)

Ureterolithotomy: Removing a stone from the ureter

Ureterostomy: Making an opening into the ureter

Ureterectomy: Removing the ureter

Cystolithotomy: Removing a stone from the bladder

Cystostomy: Making an opening into the bladder

Cystorrhaphy: Suturing up the bladder

Cystectomy: Removing the bladder

Prostatectomy: Removing the prostate

Spermatocelectomy: Removing a spermatocele (which is a collection of sperm in a small cyst at or near the testicle)

By no means is this list complete, but when confusing and technical jargon is used in any urological record, remembering the commonly used prefixes and suffixes will enable the reader to better understand the type of procedure identified and to have a better grasp at interpreting the terminology.

§4.03 The Making of a Urologist

Every medical student, when he or she matures in medical education and knowledge, makes the decision about which discipline in medicine most appeals to him or her. In the early years of medical education in this country, most graduates became general practitioners, but the 1940s, 1950s, and 1960s brought a tremendous impetus for specialization. Although this trend has continued, there is also a significant return of young physicians to the primary care specialties, such as family practice and emergency medicine.

Every individual who decides to be a urologist goes through the same thinking process prior to finalizing his or her decision. Urology is a surgical subspecialty, and that attracts many. The specialty deals with every age group and with both sexes. There are significant diagnostic procedures available to allow for proper investigative techniques. The hours are good, emergencies are rare, and the pay is great!

Urologists make up only about 10 per cent of the total physician work force, and this probably assures every urologist a good job.

The training program for urologists is supervised and derived from actions of the Liaison Committee on Medical Education (LCME), the American College of Surgeons (ACS), the American Board of Urology (ABU), the American Urological Association (AUA), the Council of Medical Specialty Society (CMSS), and the Accreditation Council for Graduate Medical Education (ACGME). Out of all these organizations comes the final decision regarding the requirements for urological training and Board eligibility.

The current requirements are graduation from an acceptable medical school or school of osteopathy, two years of nonurological training (preferably in surgery) in an acceptable program, and, finally, three years of additional urological training in a program approved by the Accreditation Council for Graduate Medical Education. Over 60 per cent of the current residency programs now add another year of training to include research experience or electives such as dialysis.

Thus, after college, the student has four years of medical school plus five to six additional years of training before being able to "hang out a shingle"—a popular medical expression for "open his or her office."

The internship year was the first year out of medical school and usually was a year devoted to a brief exposure to all of the disciplines of medicine such as surgery, obstetrics, psychiatry, ophthalmology, etc. This was called a rotating internship, implying that the intern would rotate for a month or more through the various departments in the hospital.

Straight internships became popular in the 1960s, wherein a budding surgeon would only study surgery or one of the subspecialties for the internship year, rather than rotating through all the areas of medicine. It is popular now not to use the word "internship" since all training after medical school graduation is referred to as postgraduate training or postgraduate year one, two, etc., (PGY-1, PGY-2, etc.).

Even the connotation of a "resident" in a residency program has been changed to include the nomenclature of postgraduate year training. In past decades, the first-year resident was called the junior assistant resident (JAR), who then moved up to the assistant resident (AR), and then the senior assistant resident (SAR), and finally the resident (or chief). This nomenclature is currently not in vogue.

While fellowship programs are common in other postgraduate training programs, this is not the case in urology. Although fellowships are available in pediatric urology, most residency programs are concerned only with the general training of urologists. More about subspecialization appears in §4.08.

The Executive Committee of the American Urological Association in 1987 promulgated the essentials of urology residency training. Those areas to be covered by an individual in his or her training are:

1. Pediatric urology
2. Stone disease, endourology, and lithotripsy
3. Urologic oncology
4. Andrology/infertility/impotency
5. Renal transplantation and renovascular disease
6. Urodynamics
7. Female urology
8. Infectious disease
9. Trauma

When a physician finishes exposure to all these areas, he or she is felt to be ready for the practice of urology.

As of 1986, according to data compiled by the American Medical Association's Physician Master File concerning physician characteristics and distribution in the United States,[1] there were 110 female urologists (including those in postgraduate training programs) in the United States. This represents 1 per cent of the total female physician/surgeon population of 10,547.

While we are dealing with numbers, consider the following: In 1986, there were 569,160 physicians in the United States; 86,670 of these were women, and 123,090 were foreign medical graduates.[2]

This chapter, by the way, contains a certain amount of statistics and data, and most of the information that I have gleaned from my research was compiled around 1986. In certain instances, if more than one reference is used, some of the statistics do not exactly correlate. However, the general statistics are valid for presenting an overall picture.

---

[1] Socioeconomic Fact Book for Surgery (P. Politser & E. Cunico eds 1988).

[2] Ansell, *Trends in Urological Manpower in the United States in 1986*, 138 J Urol 473 (1987).

§4.04 Licensure

This topic is of great importance to the attorney in a medical malpractice case. Of course, any suspension, revocation, or denial of any physician's license is obviously an area that must be thoroughly investigated.

By licensure is meant the ability of each state to define the necessary credentials and approve the applicant for the practice of medicine (which includes the practice of surgery). There are three ways to gain state licensure. One is to take the examination provided by the state, another is for the state to recognize other states' licenses (reciprocity), and the third is for the state to recognize the applicant's passage of either the National Board of Medical Examiners (NBME) or the Federation Licensing Examination (FLEX).

National Board of Medical Examiners

The NBME is a three-part exam, the first two parts of which are given in medical school, and the third part after postgraduate year one (PGY-1). The successful completion of this exam is recognized by most states as a substitute for taking the individual state licensing examination. This has not always been so, however, and, in years past, physicians who successfully passed the NBME would, in certain states, still have to take that state's examination.

Federation Licensing Examination

The FLEX is given to those foreign medical graduates (FMGs) who have not been allowed to take the National Board of Medical Examiners. The FLEX examination does not have the reputation of the NBME, and certain states do not allow the passage of this to automatically gain state licensure. Since many states, however, do recognize FLEX, currently, if a United States medical student fails the National Boards, he or she can take the FLEX and possibly gain state licensure.

Educational Council for Foreign Medical Graduates (ECFMG)

The ECFMG is an exam which must be taken by the foreign medical graduate in order to attest and certify as to his or her qualifications. Every state and postgraduate training program requires this examination to be taken by every foreign medical graduate before that physician is allowed either to take a licensing exam or to take part in a residency program. The purpose of the ECFMG is to certify that no matter what medical school the applicant attended, his or her knowledge is equivalent to that of a graduating student from a United States medical school.

There is great controversy about the NBME, the FLEX, and the ECFMG. Graduates of United States medical schools feel that foreign medical graduates attend medical schools outside the United States either because they were not good enough to attend a United States medical school or because the curriculum in a foreign medical school is less demanding than in the

United States and would be easier to attend and pass. There is a great deal of competition for postgraduate training programs, and the huge influx of foreign medical graduates has increased tension between the two groups of graduates. Alternatively, there is some concern regarding what may be a discriminatory attitude toward foreign medical graduates in not allowing them to take the same examination (NBME) as the United States graduates.

A plan to create a single licensure examination for United States physicians is developing and gaining support from groups such as the Federation of State Medical Boards and the National Board of Medical Examiners. This plan, under consideration by the American Medical Association, would merge the FLEX and the NBME.

§4.05 Board Certification

Being certified by a single national body after completing certain requirements is what is meant by being "Board-certified." Board eligibility merely means that the physician has satisfied all of the requirements prior to taking the examination and is now eligible for the Board exam.

Because of the large number of residency programs in the United States and the natural diversity of teaching material and instruction, a single system of certification has evolved. After the candidate has satisfied all of the requirements and passed the examination, he or she is recognized as a subspecialist and certified by the American Board of Urology.

The American Board of Urology was founded in 1935 and, as of 1989, has certified over 9,000 physicians. The number of certificates issued annually by the American Board of Urology has decreased by 18 per cent from 332 in 1980 to 237 in 1986. There are 133 urology residency programs in the United States with 1,068 positions that graduate approximately 260 urologists each year.

While not all urologists who are Board-eligible become Board-certified, the need to become Board-certified is becoming more apparent. All hospital staffs now require Board eligibility for active staff privileges, and some even require Board certification. Certain job positions require Board certification, and some third-party payors also demand this.

An impeachable item for an expert witness would be if he or she is only Board-eligible and not Board-certified.

§4.06 —Recertification

There is no requirement as of this writing for recertification process for urologists. Once one is Board-certified, he or she is not required to recertify. Additionally, there is no requirement for mandatory continuing medical education (CME) for urologists. Only a few states require CME for physicians—a tragic oversight. While the merits of attending a CME course at some posh resort may be debated, at least some measure of continuing education must be mandated to require physicians to keep their professional knowledge up-to-date.

The American Board of Medical Specialities was first established in 1933, and currently there are 23 member boards. This organization is concerned with establishing, maintaining, and elevating standards for education and qualification of physicians recognized as specialists. This board also conducts research on physician performance/assessment and on the evaluation of medical skills.

§4.07 Demographics and Socioeconomics

There are approximately 8,500 practicing urologists in the United States today, not including those in postgraduate training programs. A 1988 survey of urological practices of 2,500 urologists revealed that the 1987 before-tax mean net income of a urologist in practice less than five years was $117,000, and was $200,000 if he or she had been in practice anywhere from five to twenty-four years.[3]

There is some concern about urological manpower and whether the specialty is getting overcrowded. Various studies have shown that almost 300 urologists a year will stop practicing, which correlates with the approximately 300 per year of new urologists entering the total pool. The ideal urologist: population ratio is 1:30,000, according to the Graduate Medical Education National Advisory Committee. However, one could ask why this ratio is significant other than keeping the income levels of urologists high. Additionally, how and why the ratio was determined would be of some interest to know. I wonder what would happen to urologists' incomes if more training programs were available and suddenly we had one urologist for every 15,000 people.

Another interesting set of statistics involves the average number of procedures performed by urologists in 1983. These ranged from 43 transurethral resections of the prostate to 11 circumcisions to 6 orchiectomies to 4 nephrectomies to 3 varicocelectomies.

Once again, all figures can be interpreted and reported in strange and wonderful ways. So, patient age, population, geographical location, type of hospital, and personality of the urologist all certainly can skew the statistics.

§4.08 Subspecialization

Subspecialization within urology is another area that is growing yearly, even though the American Board of Urology does not issue any subspecialty certificates. A recent survey in the *Journal of Urology* revealed that 16 per cent of all urologists consider themselves subspecialists in such areas as pediatric urology, urological oncology, transplantation, andrology, neurourology, urological gynecology, and calculus disease. Most of these physicians practice their subspecialty less than 25 per cent of the time.

---

[3] B. Wilson, *Survey of Urology Practice,* Urology Times, Sept, 1988.

§4.09 Standard Texts and Journals

This section is probably the most dynamic in terms of changing resources. While the reader should be familiar with the standard texts and journals involving urology, there is a wealth of written material available, some of which may not yet be published at the time of this textbook's publication.

While reading the textbooks may serve as a basis for the generalized approach to the topic, the most up-to-date and current information is obtained from the urological journals. Obviously, even this material may be a year old. Introducing texts or journals as authoritative evidence may be difficult, depending upon the admissibility of treatises, but it still is important for the attorney involved in a urological medical malpractice case to read and research as much of the topic as possible to stay informed.

Medical libraries are filled with hundreds of textbooks, ranging from general urology to superspecialized texts on infertility. Some of the classic texts and their publishers are mentioned here only as a starting point, and by no means should this list be considered complete.

The classic textbook of urology which has taught urologists for years is Campbell's three-volume textbook, *Urology* (1978), now past its Fourth Edition. Additionally, there are the following well-known texts:

1. E. Tanagho & J. McAninch, *Smith's General Urology* (12th ed 1988)
2. E.D. Whitehead, *Current Operative Urology* (1984)
3. Weiss & Mills, *Atlas of Genitourinary Tract Disorders* (1988)
4. B. Stewart, *Operative Urology* (1982)
5. J. Gillenwater, *Adult and Pediatric Urology* (1987)

The official journal of the American Urological Association is the *Journal of Urology*, first published in 1917. However, the past 10 or 15 years have seen a dramatic rise in the number of urological journals including:

1. *Urology*
2. *Contemporary Urology*
3. *Monographs in Urology*
4. *International Urogynecological Journal*

There are numerous audiotapes which pharmaceutical companies produce and mail to all urologists, usually as a public service, such as "Medical Portfolio for Urologists" (The Cortland Group, Inc., New York), as well as numerous newsletters, such as *AUA Today*, the official house organ of the American Urological Association, *Urology Times*, and *Urological Financial News*.

VideoUrology is a video journal for urologists published four times a year (VideoUrology, New York City). The American Urological Association Office of Education also produces numerous videotapes available for rental or purchase.

Yearbook Publishers publishes an annual *The Yearbook of Urology*, as well as a new innovative annual publication entitled *Advances in Urology*.

Finally, just as Veralex and Lexis-Nexis are available to attorneys, Medline, a computer-assisted search of the medical literature, is also available and is probably the most efficient and comprehensive manner in which one may find all of the available information on a certain topic.

The National Library of Medicine's computerized Medical Literature Analysis and Retrieval System (MEDLARS) was established in 1964. MEDLARS On-line (Medline) first became available for computer on-line searching from remote locations in 1971. Now, more than 6,000,000 entries from over 3,500 journal titles are available and retrievable through this system. By using specific text words, standardized subject headings, author, or title, an extract of the paper can be obtained with one's computer and modem. Further information can be obtained from the National Library of Medicine in Bethesda, Maryland.

Finally, the exact titles of all these texts, journals, videos, etc. are not as important as the knowledge that there are all sorts of available sources of information concerning the topic. One must carefully ask the urologist defendant or expert witness in the case what journals or textbooks he or she reads, what he or she has relied on to base his or her opinion, and what he or she considers to be authoritative. Frequently, this information can be valuable for impeachment purposes.

§4.10 Urological Societies

It is important to determine if the defendant is Board-certified in urology or a member of any professional societies. This speaks to the physician's desire to be involved professionally with urology, and theoretically means he or she is interested in keeping up with current urological thinking.

The most important urological society is the American Urological Association, founded in 1902, and comprising over 5,000 members, all of whom have been certified by the American Board of Urology.

The American Urological Association meets annually in various cities around the nation for educational and socioeconomic purposes. For one week, daily activities range from subspecialty society meetings (such as the Society of University Residents, the Pediatric Urological Society, and the Society for Urology in Engineering) to presentation of papers, awards, and videotapes, to instructional courses and social events. There is so much activity that a bound volume of over 600 pages is prepared to assist the attendee. The American Urological Association, of course, has numerous committees, as in any large organization, and is the voice of organized urology.

According to the Executive Committee minutes of January 1986, the American Urological Association's definition of urology states: "Urology is the branch of medicine and surgery which especially concerns itself with diseases of the adrenal gland, the urinary tract and the genital tract in patients of any age and of either sex." Although this may be the official definition of urology according to the American Urological Association, in fact urologists generally do not deal with diseases of the adrenal gland, as this usually falls into the category of the general surgeon. Additionally, most urologists will not handle diseases of the genital tract in females, leaving this to the gynecologist. I believe most urologists would be very surprised at this definition of urology.

Additionally, the American Urological Association defines a urologist as: "A physician and surgeon who is especially trained for the diagnosis and treatment of diseases of the adrenal gland, the urinary tract and the genital tract in patients of any age and of either sex." This definition, too, may be slightly at variance with what the urologist in clinical practice believes. The training of urologists may include the diagnosis and treatment of adrenal gland diseases, but, as stated previously, the treatment of these problems usually is in the area of a general surgeon. Again, most urological training programs do not involve treatment of diseases of the genital tract of the female.

I mention these two definitions and the current status of a urologist merely to suggest that the standard of care of urologists probably does not involve the treatment of the adrenal gland, and certainly does not involve the treatment of female genital diseases.

In addition to the American Urological Association, geographical regions of the United States have developed their own sections, such as the Southeastern Section, the Northeastern Section, etc., all of whom have their own annual meetings—a miniature of the national annual meeting.

There are also numerous state urological societies, subspecialty societies (pediatric urology, urodynamics, infertility, etc.), and even a socioeconomicopolitical organization called the American Association of Clinical Urologists, particularly concerned with legislative issues as they pertain to urology.

Last but not least is the Urology Lawyers Council. This neophyte organization, composed of only six urologists/lawyers, has begun to have a presence collectively at the national level. These six meet semi-annually to discuss health care issues, medical malpractice, peer review, risk management, and legislative concerns as related to urology. The goal of the council is to make the urologist aware of medicolegal issues which may affect the profession and, by identifying these issues, more properly prepare the urologist to comprehend them.

Finally, one can find a urological meeting in all corners of the world (from Australia to Saudi Arabia to Big Sky, Montana) virtually every week. While some of these meetings may have a heavy social schedule, most of the meetings are oriented to a professional program of continued medical education. The interested reader is referred to the headquarters of the American Urological Association in Baltimore, Maryland for further information.

5

Urologic Anatomy, Physiology, and Common Laboratory Tests

Robert M. Frank, M.D., J.D.

Anatomy
§5.01　Introduction
§5.02　The Retroperitoneum
§5.03　The Adrenal Glands
§5.04　The Kidneys
§5.05　—Internal Anatomy of the Kidneys
§5.06　—External Anatomy of the Kidneys
§5.07　The Urinary Transport System
§5.08　—The Ureter
§5.09　The Urinary Storage System
§5.10　—The Urethra
§5.11　The Prostate Gland
§5.12　The Penis
§5.13　The Testicular and Spermatic Cord Structures
§5.14　The Seminal Vesicles
Physiology
§5.15　Nephrology and Urology
§5.16　The Formation of Urine
§5.17　Urine Transport and Micturition
§5.18　—Transporting the Urine
§5.19　—The Bladder
§5.20　—Voiding the Urine
§5.21　The Male Reproductive System
§5.22　Sexual Dysfunction Generally
§5.23　Impotency
§5.24　—Psychological Causes

§5.25 —Physical Causes
§5.26 —Drugs
§5.27 Other Sexual Dysfunction
Common Laboratory Tests
§5.28 Overview
§5.29 Urinalysis
§5.30 Hemogram
§5.31 —Chemical Analysis of the Blood
References
§5.32 References
Appendix 5-A Illustrations

Anatomy

§5.01 Introduction

Any discussion of anatomy, almost by definition, is apt to be a monotonous litany. But coupled with the sciences of physiology and pathology, there is formed a foundational triad without which the practice of medicine would not be possible. Anatomy is a descriptive discipline, a means by which one physician chronicles his or her observations such that any other health professional can continue treatment of the case with an accurate understanding of the patient's problems and progress.

Thus, it is the language of medicine. It has much of its origin in the descriptive nouns of Latin or Greek. As with any foreign language, there seems to be an endless list of information that must be memorized by rote. Only repeated usage makes it become part of medical discipline.

This should seem obvious, but it has not always been so. About 30 years ago an explosion in medical knowledge occurred. Educators in our medical schools began to downplay the study of anatomy. There was just too much to teach in too short a time. The time-honored practice of introducing the student to the dissection laboratory on the first day of school was dropped. The hours of anatomy instruction were moved into the second or third year and markedly curtailed. Some institutions actually discontinued it completely as a compulsory course of instruction. The anatomy laboratory was made available as an elective to those who thought they might have an interest in general surgery or the surgical subspecialties.

The experiment did not work. What should have been obvious initially rapidly became apparent. Could an internist accurately relate findings to another without proper anatomical description? Could a radiologist interpret x-rays or other imaging modalities without the necessary language? Would the referring physician understand the report? Once again anatomy became in vogue. The necessary foundation had to be present upon which all the remaining disciplines would be built.

Certain ground rules are in order. As in any descriptive subject where interrelationships are important, a frame of reference must be established. Therefore where terms such as *above* or *below* are used, the reference is to the subject's habitus: above being towards his or her head, below being towards his or her feet. Similarly, *anterior* and *posterior* refer to the abdominal wall and back, respectively. *Medial* means toward the midline, *lateral* means away from it. *Right* and *left* are that of the subject and not the observer. This terminology is universally accepted and will be used here.

Anatomy, an academic science unto itself, is important to the physician as a means of understanding the disease process. To the operating surgeon, it is a road map. Sections **5.02** to **5.14** stress the relationships between the various anatomical structures and the practical practice of medicine and surgery.

§5.02 The Retroperitoneum

The term, as so much of the medical descriptive language, has its roots in Latin. *Retro* comes from the Latin word meaning "back" or "behind." But, behind what? To understand the retroperitoneum, one must first have an understanding of the peritoneum.

The *peritoneum* is the serous membrane lining the interior of the abdominal cavity and surrounding those viscera that are contained therein. It is the largest serous membrane in the body, which in the male is a completely closed sac. In the female this is not so; the ends of the uterine tubes open directly into the peritoneal cavity. The opening is minute, usually not larger than one millimeter, but this is sufficient for the fimbriated end of this structure to fulfill its function of capturing the extruded ovum at ovulation. Its patency and connection to the peritoneal cavity is easily demonstrated by using appropriate radio-opaque media. This procedure (*salpingography*) is done as part of a fertility workup.

That portion of the membrane lining the abdominal wall both anteriorly and posteriorly, as well as along both sides, is called the *parietal* peritoneum. That portion that invests the contained viscera appropriately is named the *visceral* peritoneum. If one reflects for a moment, it is obvious that everything is retroperitoneal. Those viscera that are described as within the peritoneal cavity are in reality not physically within this intraperitoneal space. It is analogous to pushing your finger into an inflated balloon from the side. Though the tip of the finger appears to be within the balloon, it is completely covered by the balloon's rubber membrane and physically is outside the balloon cavity. The only thing that is truly intraperitoneal is a small amount of serous fluid that provides lubrication so that the "contained" organs may glide against each other and the parietal peritoneal wall with a minimum of friction.

The retroperitoneum, then, is by convention alone that area that is behind the parietal peritoneum lining the back edge of the abdominal cavity. It is this area that contains the paired structures of the urinary tract: the adrenal glands, the kidneys, and ureters. In the pelvis it refers to that area occupied by the bladder and its associated anatomy. The physical location of these paired organs, located deep behind the peritoneum, protected by the spinal column and its musculature, makes surgical approach to these structures a formidable procedure. An absolute familiarity with both the anatomy of the urological organs and their relationships with the immediately adjacent nonurological structures is mandatory.

§5.03 The Adrenal Glands

The *adrenal glands,* also known as the *suprarenal glands,* are paired structures lying, as their name would suggest, above the kidneys. They average in size from 3 to 5 cm. in length, slightly smaller in width, and about 0.5 cm. thick. The average weight is between 3.5 and 5 grams each.

The right adrenal gland is usually triangular in shape, having an appearance that has been suggested to mimic a three-cornered hat. Its medial edge may lie partially behind the inferior vena cava stretching laterally almost coming in contact with the right lobe of the liver. At this point it is usually devoid of any peritoneal attachments. The base of the gland rests upon the medial and anterior surfaces of the right kidney. Its posterior surface, at its upper end, reaches from the diaphragmatic musculature to the upper pole of the right kidney.

There is usually only one main vein draining the right adrenal gland. Emerging medially from the gland near its midpoint, this vein runs directly into the inferior vena cava.

The left suprarenal gland is usually somewhat larger than the right, tending to be more flattened, splaying over the medial anterior surface of the left kidney. Its upper end may reach the cardiac end of the stomach. Its inferior borders are closely adjacent to the tail of the pancreas and the vascular supply to the spleen.

The left adrenal gland also usually has only one vein. It tends to emerge more inferiorly than the vein does on the right side. It drains directly downward to the left renal vein. Occasionally there is alternative drainage into the left phrenic vein.

The arterial supplies of the adrenal glands are mirror images of each other. Each gland has three distinct sources which freely anastomose with each other as they reach the gland:

1. The *superior suprarenal artery,* a branch from the ipsilateral inferior phrenic artery which arises directly from the aorta just above the celiac axis

2. The *middle suprarenal artery,* which runs directly from the side of the aorta at the level of the superior mesenteric artery

3. The *inferior suprarenal artery,* which arises from the ipsilateral renal artery directly below it.

The nerve supplies of the adrenal glands are numerous filaments from the celiac and their respective renal plexuses.

The above description is a highly stylized representation, for tremendous variability exists both in size and location of these glands. Many accessory adrenal glands have been reported in the connective tissue around the upper poles of both kidneys.

The microscopic anatomy of the adrenal glands is closely tied to their physiological function. Arising from different embryonic structures, there are two distinct areas identifiable in each gland. The *cortex* (outer portion) completely envelops a central area, the *medulla*. The cortex is mesodermal in origin and has a characteristic deep golden-yellow hue. Its cellular structure is very complex, having three distinct identifiable zones. The central medulla of each gland is significantly more vascular and appears dark brownish red. It is ectodermal in origin, containing principally chromaffin cells, so named because of their characteristic brown-like staining when treated with a potassium bichromate solution. Chromaffin material is also found in association with other parts of the sympathetic nervous system.

Both segments of the adrenal glands function by secreting directly into the blood stream. This classifies them as *endocrine* glands, to be distinguished from the *exocrine* glands that secrete directly onto an epithelial surface.

The anatomical location of the adrenal glands does not lend itself to an easy surgical approach. Their locations above and behind some of the most vital structures in human anatomy have tested surgical ingenuity to its limit. When there is significant adrenal enlargement, often the thoraco-abdominal approach is the only means of achieving adequate visualization. For many years there were those who advocated approaching the adrenal structures through the back of the patient to avoid working behind the body's major vascular structures. This proved to be most limiting in exposure. Today most surgeons prefer to use the transabdominal or thoraco-abdominal approach. Improvements in vascular surgical technique have eliminated many of the risks that the posterior approach carried in years past.

§5.04 The Kidneys

The *kidneys*, like the adrenals, are paired structures in the retroperitoneum. Though rarely thought of as "glands" by the average physician, they are so classified by anatomists for they function by excreting an effluent (urine).

The kidneys vary widely in their size and weight. They range from 9 to 12.5 cm. in length and 4.5 to 6.5 cm. in width. Their normal thickness measures from 2.5 to 3.5 cm. They weigh from 110 to 160 grams each. The left kidney characteristically is slightly longer but narrower than the right.

The kidneys are usually mirror images of each other, placed in the retroperitoneal space with their long axes directed downward and slightly away from the midline. The transverse axis of each bends slightly backward and again laterally. Situated one on each side of the vertebral column, they are embedded in a mass of fat and loose areolar tissue. The perirenal fat is enclosed by a definitively more condensed layer of connective tissue known as the *fascia of Gerota* or *Zuckerkandl*. This fascial layer fully encircles the entire renal structure fusing into a cylindrical sheath which surrounds the ureter as it commences its downward course towards the bladder. Gerota's fascia is significantly more dense on the posterior surface of the kidney. On the anterior surface, especially towards the midline, it is more tenuous, but adherent to the parietal peritoneum. There is not a urological surgeon who has not at one time or another found himself or herself within the abdominal cavity when his or her intent was to stay in the retroperitoneal space. Years ago this misadventure carried an ominous prognosis. Today with antibiotics removing the dread of peritonitis, it no longer carries such threats. This does not mean that the surgeon can be cavalier and ignore the unintended entry. It must be recognized and dealt with appropriately.

The kidney moves rather freely within this fascial envelope as the diaphragm contracts and relaxes with respiration. Absence of this normal movement is a significant finding, suggestive of phrenic nerve paralysis or an ongoing disease process in the perirenal space. Fluoroscopy is rarely done these days. Unless the physician suspects a "fixed" kidney and orders films to check for kidney motion, this diagnosis is apt to be missed.

Each kidney is invested with a tough fibrous *capsule*. Once its integrity is broken, it strips easily from the underlying surface. If this occurs during renal surgery, the perforating arteries to the capsule may tear. Renal tissue is exceedingly difficult to suture without destroying healthy functioning cortex. At best it is analogous to trying to sew warm butter. Hemostasis should be achieved using the needle electrocautery on as "low" a setting as possible. Hoping the oozing will stop is foolhardy. A post-operative perirenal hematoma with secondary infection can be a troublesome complication.

The blood supply to the kidney is about 18 to 20 times greater than to any other organ in the body. It is estimated that 25 per cent of the cardiac output peruses the kidneys. Each renal artery arises laterally from the aorta immediately below the takeoff of the superior mesenteric artery about the level of the intervertebral disk between the first and second lumbar vertebra. They leave the aorta at right angles running directly to the hilum of their respective kidney. The *left renal artery,* shorter than the right (the aorta is to the left of the midline of the body), runs behind the left renal vein, the body of the pancreas, and the splenic vein. The *right renal artery* mimics the left, running behind the head of the pancreas, the second portion of the duodenum, and the inferior vena cava.

Both renal arteries divide into a larger, lower, anterior branch that supplies better than half the kidney, and a smaller one placed more posteriorly. These two arteries effectively "sandwich" the renal pelvis as all three structures enter the renal mass at the hilum.

Variations in the renal arterial supply are exceedingly common. Estimates vary, but some writers claim that as high as 30 per cent of the general population have an accessory artery to one kidney or the other, the left side being involved more frequently than the right. About half of those with accessory arteries will have the artery enter the renal mass directly at one of the poles of the kidney. This may become a serious problem for an operating surgeon should the procedure require more mobility of the kidney than this accessory artery will allow.

Arterial division within the renal substance is quite extensive. However, there is no anastomosis between these various branches, unlike what is seen in the arterial supply of many other organs. Injury or embolization of one of these smaller arterial branches causes immediate anoxia to the renal tissue it supplies. If the condition persists there is permanent loss of that section of functioning cortex.

Another interesting variant from usual anatomical rules is the venous system of the kidney. In most organs of the body, arteries and veins run side by side. Not so in the kidney. As the venous tree builds from the small venules in the cortex towards the main renal vein, the venous system draining the posterior half of the kidney crosses over the neck of the minor calyces to join similar veins on the anterior side. Thus only one *renal vein* emerges from the hilum of each kidney. There is no significant venous drainage on the posterior aspect of the renal pelvis.

Unlike the arterial tree, there is extensive anastomotic connection with other venous systems: adrenal, lumbar, and spermatic or ovarian. This may afford significant collateral channels should there be interference with the main venous drainage from the kidney.

§5.05 —Internal Anatomy of the Kidneys

Being mirror images of each other, a single description of the internal anatomy of the kidney is sufficient. External gross anatomy is another matter. As the relationship to immediately adjacent structures is quite different for the right and left kidneys, special attention will be given to the risks and problems an unwary diagnostician or operating surgeon may face.

The functional unit of the kidney is the *nephron,* sometimes called the *renal tubule.* This structure begins in the cortical portion of the kidney and runs a circuitous course finally ending at the apices of the renal pyramids where the urine is passed first into the calyceal system, then on through their infundibula into the renal pelvis. It has been estimated there are greater than 4,000,000 nephron units, although not all of them function at any given moment.

At the head of the nephron unit is the *glomerulus*. This term is derived from the diminutive form of the Latin word *globus* meaning "a ball." It is a network-like tuft of nonanastomosing capillaries which invest a double-walled, single-layer epithelial sac. These structures are named *Bowman's capsules* or the *Malpighian corpuscles* after the men who first described their microscopic anatomy. Malpighi is credited with discovering the capillary tufts, describing them as "apples hanging from a tree limb." Bowman is credited with the description of the drainage capsule. The terms, however, are used interchangeably.

That portion of the epithelial sac that covers these capillary loops acts as a filtering membrane. At this initial stage in the formation of urine the content of the filtrate is determined solely by the concentration and molecular size of the solutes in the blood. The filtrate collects in the space between the two layers of epithelium which is continuous with the *proximal convoluted tubule*. This is the first of several distinct tubular structures which make up the nephron unit.

These convolutions disappear as the tubule begins to enter the medullary portion of the kidney. There it assumes a straight course and abruptly decreases in caliber. Making a 180° turn, it becomes thicker and larger in caliber as it follows itself back up into the renal cortex. These are the descending and ascending limbs of the *loop of Henle*. Once back in the cortex the tubule further dilates and becomes tortuous: the *distal convoluted tubule*. In turn this drains into a *collecting tubule*. Joining with other collecting tubules, the diameter of the drainage system progressively increases, terminating on the summit of one of the renal papillae as the stoma of a single short tube (the *duct of Bellini*). These are readily visible to the naked eye. There the urine is discharged into a calyx which drains into the renal pelvis.

Between individuals there exists extreme variability both as to the number of calyces in a kidney and their physical relationship to each other. Some are large, others are small. Some may be spindle-shaped, others are capacious. Though vastly different between individuals, there is a remarkable mirror-like identity of the calyceal pattern in any one individual's right and left kidney.

It is not unusual to see duplication of structures in the urinary tract. This can be as complete as two distinctly separate renal masses arising on the same side, each with its own ureter, or it can be a partial duplication with one distal ureter draining two ureters, each from a separate system "fused" into one kidney. The possibilities are endless. Over 12 per cent of the general population has sufficient bifurcation of the draining structures to be called a "duplication." Though usually bilateral, it sometimes occurs unilaterally—an exception to the mirror-image rule. This writer has personally seen five ureters in one patient, three on one side, two on the other, opening into a total of four distinct ureteral orifices, two on each side.

Embryological development almost invariably plays a "trick" on the unsuspecting when there is complete duplication of the ureter on one side. Contrary to what would be expected, the ureter draining the *upper* segment of the kidney will enter the bladder *closer* to the bladder neck, *more distally*, than the ureter draining the lower portion of that kidney. As these two ureters must physically cross each other, it may present a surgical problem if they share a common sheath as they transverse the bladder wall.

§5.06 —External Anatomy of the Kidneys

As mentioned in §5.05, the two kidneys are vastly different in their gross anatomic relationships. The *right kidney* is usually about one centimeter lower than the left. It lies immediately lateral to the *inferior vena cava*. Directly anterior to the inferior vena cava and frequently adherent to the most medial aspect of the right kidney is the second portion of the *duodenum*. The attachment between these structures is usually loose areolar tissue. For surgery, this must be carefully "taken down" to establish a safe surgical plane. Its importance is its recognition. Technically the dissection is easy to perform. However, inadvertent duodenal fistulae are notoriously difficult to treat.

The *right adrenal gland,* as described in §5.03, rests on the anterior superior surface of the right kidney near its upper pole. Again, recognition is the key to avoid surgical misadventure. Its vascular structures are small and quite easily torn. The *right adrenal vein* drains directly into the inferior vena cava. This junction may be very close to the origin of the renal vein. During nephrectomy, if the adrenal gland is to be saved, it is advisable to ligate the branches of the renal vein individually rather than the vein itself. If the right renal vein is short and wide, the torsion of gathering this mass of tissue in one suture ligature may unintentionally include the adrenal vein junction. Thus, the surgeon should stay as far from the inferior vena cava as possible consistent with good operating technique.

The lower pole of the right kidney is often hidden under the *right* or *ascending colon.* At this level the large bowel is both intraperitoneal and extraperitoneal. The parietal peritoneum meets this segment of large bowel about midway between its anterior and posterior surface. It then reflects anteriorly over the colon to the lateral abdominal wall. Because its vascular supply runs in its mesentery medially, there is relative safety in reflecting the colon if the parietal peritoneum is incised in the lateral gutter. Then pushing the bowel medially, the kidney will be fully exposed.

Although the right kidney lies partially beneath the right lobe of the *liver,* this rarely interferes with surgical exposure. Even when employing an intraperitoneal approach, correct positioning of the patient on the operating table will cause the liver to fall away from the operative field. Only in those cases where the kidney is abnormally large (tumor or polycystic disease) may exposure be limited.

The posterior surface of the right kidney is relatively free from important adjacent structures. Here Gerota's fascia (*see* §5.04) lies upon the musculature arising from the vertebral column: the *quadratus lumborum* and *psoas* muscles. If a planned operative procedure, such as reconstruction of the ureteropelvic junction, does not require immediate control of the renal artery and vein, this is the area of maximum safety for surgical approach.

The *pleura* usually is not much cause of concern in the surgical approach to the right kidney for only occasionally does its reflection reach as low as the twelfth rib. But in those cases where additional exposure is necessary, it is imperative that the surgeon identify the structure and gently push the pleural reflection cephalad. Inadvertent opening into the pleural space becomes a problem only if it is not recognized.

The *left kidney* has its own assemblage of important structures which concern the surgeon. Anteriorly, much of the upper lateral aspect of the kidney may be covered by the reflection of the parietal peritoneum. Directly behind the peritoneum is the *spleen,* a highly vascular organ. Frequently a metal retractor is used in this area by the surgical assistant. Careful attention to the placement of these instruments is in order, as more splenic injuries occur from retraction than the operative procedure itself.

The tail of the *pancreas* lies immediately adjacent to the mid-anterior surface of the left kidney. It rarely interferes with renal surgery, but should be identified. Injury to the pancreas releases proteolytic enzymes into the retroperitoneal space.

The *left adrenal gland* presents the same problems as discussed with the right kidney. The gland here is usually broader and more closely adherent to the upper medial portion of the renal capsule. Its venous drainage runs inferiorly to the left renal vein rather than medially to the inferior vena cava as on the right side. If a surgeon wishes not to sacrifice the left adrenal gland while removing the kidney, the left renal vein must be ligated distal to this junction. At times this is relatively close to the hilum of the kidney.

The lower pole of the left kidney also may be hidden under bowel. Here it is the *left* or *descending colon* that must be reflected away from the operative field. There is a similar lateral avascular plane as on the right side. Again the posterior surface of the kidney is the safest approach if immediate vascular control is not an issue.

Because the left kidney is slightly more cephalad than the right, its upper pole is closer to the reflection of the *pleura*. Most urologists agree that inadvertent entry into the pleural space occurs more frequently on the left than on the right.

§5.07 The Urinary Transport System

The structures which move the urine from within the kidney to its temporary storage site, the bladder, have a common embryological source. Though appearing to be distinct entities, they all have common anatomical characteristics: a serosal outer coat, thin layers of muscle which actively propel the urine, and a continuous inner lining of transitional cell epithelium that is relatively impervious to those chemical compounds normally found in urine.

This transport system begins with the *minor calyces*, which are cup-shaped structures located deep within the renal parenchyma. Each minor calyx has one or two renal papillae invaginating into it. It is from the crests of these papillae that the ducts of Bellini (*see* §5.05) first pass urine into the system. Groups of these minor calyces, usually four in number but sometimes as many as ten, coalesce to form the *major calyces*. Each major calyx, usually two or three in each kidney, runs through a narrower tubelike structure, the *infundibulum*, to the *renal pelvis*. Real time imaging systems have shown that all these structures actively move the urine by coordinated muscular contractions: *peristalsis*. At its medial inferior edge the renal pelvis is continuous with the *ureter*.

The renal pelvis is probably the most highly variable anatomical structure in the urinary system. At one extreme it can be entirely *intrarenal*—i.e., surrounded by renal substance. In such a case, the ureter runs directly into the kidney. At the other extreme the renal pelvis may be entirely *extrarenal*.

Here it is outside the functioning kidney connected only by large infundibula to the major calyces. These cases may have been included in the 12 per cent of the population having duplication of the upper urinary tract.

The more the renal pelvis is extrarenal the more distensible it is. Without the resistance of the parenchyma to confine it, the capacity of an extrarenal pelvis can become alarmingly large. This is often the result of a chronically obstructive narrow *ureteropelvic junction.* When the pelvis has been stretched to its limit by the increase in hydrostatic pressure, the proximal collecting structures begin to dilate. This condition, *hydronephrosis,* is one of the more common anomalies presenting as a palpable mass in young pediatric patients.

§5.08 —The Ureter

The *ureter* extends from the renal pelvis to the urinary bladder. Its length is dependent upon the height of the individual. Because the right kidney is slightly lower than the left, its ureter is about one cm. shorter than the contralateral one. The exact location of the ureteropelvic junction often is difficult to determine. Its gross appearance is a funnel-like continuum from a capacious pelvis to a relatively uniform narrow tube. Even when the junction is functionally obstructive, it is difficult to see exactly where it occurs. Fortunately, corrective operative procedures for this problem have not been dependent on the exact location of the transition. Most urologists remove the "area" of the ureteropelvic junction during reconstructive surgery.

Today the availability of more sophisticated endoscopic instrumentation prompts management of this problem without open operation. Reports are now appearing in the literature of successful dilation and/or the "cutting" of one wall of the strictured area to relieve the obstruction. It is too early to know if the long-term follow-up will yield comparable results to proven reconstructive surgical techniques.

The ureter describes a slightly reversed S-shaped curve between the kidney and the bladder. As it leaves the renal pelvis it runs medially and slightly downward over the "belly" of the psoas muscle. At times when this muscle is well developed, the ureter must climb anteriorly up the lateral muscle wall before continuing its downward course. This presents a characteristic concentration of the radio-opaque dye used in routine x-ray imaging to outline the ureter. Though a normal anatomical variant, it has often been confused with ureteral pathology.

The ureter then passes behind the spermatic or ovarian vasculature, becoming loosely adherent to the parietal peritoneum. Any surgeon, working in the peritoneal cavity, should identify the ureter before blindly sweeping a needle through the peritoneal layer. Unfortunately all too often the ureter is either directly caught within the ligature itself or "tented" into a fold of peritoneum that has been suture ligated. In either case the sequelae can be disastrous.

The ureter then crosses *over* the iliac vessels at the level of the sacroiliac joint. Immediately it takes a broad outward, downward course closely following the hypogastric artery and vein. At the level of the ischial spine, it turns back towards the bladder in a sweeping curve staying anterior to all the vasculature except the uterine and bladder vessels. It enters the urinary bladder obliquely through its muscular wall ending at the *ureteral orifice*. This structure appears as a slit-like opening on the interureteric ridge of the bladder at the lateral edge of the trigone.

Knowledge of the ureteral anatomy is equally important to the diagnostician as to the operating surgeon. There are three definitively narrowed areas:

(1) The *ureteropelvic junction* is the first point where an obstructing foreign body may cause symptoms. A foreign body is anything which normally is not present within the urinary drainage system. This is usually a calculus, but a sloughed renal papilla seen in diabetic patients, or a blood clot, can be equally obstructive. The usual caliber of the ureteropelvic junction is 7 to 10 French (2⅓ to 3⅓ mm.).

(2) The ureter as it crosses the iliac vessels, though not significantly narrowed, is usually more densely bound to the surrounding structures causing acute angulation. This sharp curve is apt to impede the passage of any obstructing matter.

(3) The narrowest region of the ureter is the *ureterovesical junction*. Its usual caliber is 4 to 6 French (1½ to 2 mm.). Many tiny calculi will hang up at this site but pass spontaneously within a relatively short time. Often "skillful neglect" is the treatment of choice. The physician is sorely tested when a patient, continuing to have severe colic in spite of the narcotics, pleads, "Doctor, please do something!"

There are subtle differences in the symptoms secondary to obstruction at these sites. Stones impacted at the ureteropelvic junction produce a characteristic dull ache in the flank which is unrelenting. Changes in position have no effect upon its intensity. There may be occasional twinges of pain that radiate along the course of the ureter down into the testicle or labia.

Stones which become obstructive within the ureter have the same constant ache secondary to swelling of the collecting system. They also exhibit *renal colic*. This is intense, unrelenting pain probably secondary to spasm of the ureteral musculature. Its quality is decidedly different from the usual discomfort of a "renal" stone.

Stones impacted in the distal ureter may cause both types of pain *plus* urinary frequency. Apparently the distention of the intramural ureter increases the irritability of the bladder musculature, sending neural impulses which are interpreted as a "full" bladder.

Most anatomy texts do not mention any relationship between the ureter and the vermiform appendix. The appendix is a worm-shaped tubular structure joining the cecum near the iliocecal junction. Highly variable in length (2 to 20 cm.), it may be found within the peritoneal cavity relatively far removed from the ureter. Though this is the classic description, one large series (10,000) found the appendix to be postcecal or retrocolic 65 per cent of the time. Here the ureter may be quite close to the appendix without a protective layer of peritoneum between them. I have personally seen two cases of acute appendicitis mimic obstructive ureteral pathology when the inflamed appendix was retrocecal.

The blood supply of the ureter is multiple in origin with free anastomosis between the systems. Its upper third receives branches from the renal artery. The middle third is supplied both directly from the aorta and from branches of the inferior mesenteric and iliac arteries. The most distal portion receives its vascular supply from the vesical arteries. These vessels run in the adventitial coverings of the ureter. If sufficient tissue remains with the ureter when dissecting it from its peritoneal attachments, viability can be assured, even if it has been transected at one of the ends. There is a bonus! The innervation of the ureter is mainly autonomic with ganglion cells sprinkled throughout its adventitia. However, if the ureter has been "stripped," dilation and atony will occur.

§5.09 The Urinary Storage System

The *bladder* is the principal reservoir of the urinary tract. It is a musculomembranous sac, whose position, size, and relationship to other structures is dependent upon the quantity of fluid contained within it. Its general position is in the midline, resting on the pelvic floor behind the pubic bone (*ossia pubis*). In this area the male bladder is tightly bound to the prostate. Strong fibrous bands, the *puboprostatic ligaments,* run from the prostatic capsule to the under surface of the pubes. In the female this area of the bladder and urethra has only filmy attachments. In both sexes the dome of the bladder is fixed to the *urachus* (the "true" umbilical ligament) and the *obliterated hypogastric vessels* (the "false" ligaments). The bladder's most posterior surface lies directly above the *rectum*. There are ligamentous attachments between these two structures variously named: the *rectovesical ligaments* or the *rectovesicales,* as often they contain smooth muscle fibers.

The posterior-superior surface of the bladder is intimately bound to the parietal peritoneum which continues up over the apex and appears to cover much of the anterior surface when the bladder is empty. As the viscus begins to fill, the anterior surface moves anteriorly and cephalad rolling this reflection of the peritoneum ahead of itself, in effect further enlarging the *space of Retzius*. The bladder is then free anteriorly from peritoneal covering and easily accessible to the surgeon.

Classic teaching has been that the bladder is an abdominal organ in the child but becomes a pelvic structure in adulthood. This is a play on semantics. It is true that its relative position appears to be more cephalad in infancy than in adult life, but it is a pelvic organ nevertheless. At birth, only one-third of the bladder lies above the upper anatomical limit of the pelvis. It is more easily palpable in the infant as the bony pelvis is less angulated than in the adult.

The interior of the bladder is lined by a loosely attached transitional cell epithelium. When the bladder is empty, this surface is thrown into folds. As the bladder fills, it irons out and has a smooth and glistening appearance. The mucosa is firmly fixed to the vesicle musculature at a triangular shaped area near the bladder neck, the *trigone*. Its appearance does not change during bladder filling. The *ureteral orifices*, usually about 2.5 cm. apart, are located at the posterolateral corners of the trigone atop the *interureteric ridge*. As the bladder fills to capacity, this distance increases slightly.

The apex of the trigone is at the most dependent portion of the bladder, the *internal urethral orifice*. In the male, this is the entrance into the *prostatic urethra*. In the female, the urethra merely extends for another 4 cm. until it opens into the vaginal vestibule at the *external urethral orifice*.

Although described as a "meshwork" with fibers running at right angles to each other, the bladder musculature functions effectively and is able to generate substantial pressure. Chronic outlet obstruction from prostatic hypertrophy or bladder-neck contracture will cause hypertrophy of these muscles, presenting a classic configuration to the examining endoscopist: *trabeculation*. Graded on a scale of 0 to 4, the magnitude of these changes is a rough guide to the physiologic severity of the obstruction.

The blood supply of the bladder is derived from branches of the hypogastric arteries. The *superior vesical artery* supplies the upper section, occasionally dividing into a smaller *middle vesical* branch. The inferior portion of the bladder is supplied by the *inferior vesical artery* which also supplies the seminal vesicles, the prostate, and the vas deferens. In the female, small branches run along the proximate urethra.

§5.10 —The Urethra

The *urethra* is continuous with the bladder outlet. It is the tube through which urine is discharged out of the body. As the sexual differences are profound, the male and female urethra will be described individually.

The female urethra is a relatively short, tubular structure which runs a direct course from the bladder neck to the *external urethral orifice* in the vestibule of the vagina. Located immediately behind the anterior wall of the vagina, it passes directly beneath the *symphysis pubis*. Throughout its length there are many small paraurethral glands opening into its lumen. The urethral wall has three distinct layers: a *mucous, submucous,* and *muscular* coat. Though continuous with the bladder epithelium, the mucous layer abruptly changes at the bladder neck from transitional cell to stratified squamous epithelium which persists throughout its length.

The submucous layer is highly vascularized, containing a plexus of large veins. This is surrounded by the muscular coat which is continuous with the bladder musculature. During micturition, its contraction shortens urethral length.

The female urethra, a relatively fragile structure, is easily traumatized during childbirth or transvaginal surgery. If tears are not promptly recognized and repaired, a urethrovaginal fistula may develop. The patient then may be continuously "wet," a most distressing symptom. Almost invariably this complication will require repeat operative intervention.

The male urethra is 22 to 24 cm. long. Besides serving as an outlet for urine, it functions as a conduit for the products of the reproductive system. The anatomist splits the urethra into an *anterior* and *posterior* segment.

The anterior urethra is further divided into three sections: the *glandular, pendulous,* and *bulbous.* The glandular urethra is that portion that runs through the distal end of the *corpus spongiosum* which forms the *glans penis.* It exits at the *urethral meatus.* This is a vertical slit-like opening near the summit of the glans about 6 mm. in diameter.

Immediately proximal to the urethral orifice, running the length of the glans, is a fusiform enlargement of the urethra, the *fossa navicularis.* This is substantially larger than the meatus, usually about 10 to 11 mm. in diameter. The distal end of this urethral segment is lined with squamous epithelium, rather than the stratified columnar epithelium found elsewhere in the urethra.

The *pendulous* portion of the urethra runs through the course of the corpus spongiosum. About 14 to 16 cm. in length and slightly narrower than the fossa navicularis (9 to 10 mm. in diameter), it extends from the level of the corona of the glans to the point where the suspensory ligament of the penis attaches. Along this segment are the small mucous secreting *glands of Littré* which open directly into the urethral lumen.

The *bulbous* urethra, the most proximal portion of the anterior urethral segment, is the widest section of the entire male urethra, 11 to 13 mm. in diameter. Extending distally from the attachment of the suspensory ligament to the entrance into the urogenital diaphragm, it carries the dubious distinction of being that area most often traumatized by urethral instrumentation. The ducts of the *bulbourethral* or *Cowper's glands* open into the urethra at this level.

The *posterior urethra* is subdivided into two segments, the membranous and prostatic. The *membranous urethra* is the most fixed portion of the urethral channel as it runs through the *urogenital diaphragm.* Here the urethra is surrounded by the fibers of the *urethral sphincter.* Strictures in this area are particularly difficult to treat without causing damage to urinary control.

The remaining part of the posterior segment is the *prostatic urethra,* extending through the length of the prostate gland. Near its distal end is a narrow, slightly elevated, longitudinal ridge ending in a mound-like structure, the *verumontanum.* Immediately beneath are the terminal ends of the *ejaculatory ducts* which exit into the urethra on the distal edge of verumontanum. The ducts from the prostatic lobe enter the urethra at this level, some in the midline closer to the bladder neck, others laterally on either side of the verumontanum.

The verumontanum is a clinically significant landmark used as a reference point by the operating urologist. When performing a transurethral resection of the prostate (TUR), if the operator removes tissue up to but no further than the verumontanum, injury to the external sphincter can be avoided. Though some surgeons have advocated resection of the verumontanum during a TUR ("After all—it is routinely removed as part of the prostate in open prostatectomy!"), most resectionists prefer the peace of mind that an intact "veru" provides at the end of the endoscopic surgical procedure.

§5.11 The Prostate Gland

Authors have described the *prostate gland* as a horseshoe-shaped chestnut or a truncated cone. Neither of these two descriptions is accurate as its shape is highly variable and ultimately depends upon the symmetry and degree of adenomatous enlargement. It is the accompanying symptoms of obstruction and bladder irritability that bring the patient to the urologist.

Whatever its three-dimensional configuration may be, the benign gland feels quite firm with a characteristic elasticity. Anatomically, it is situated at the bladder neck, immediately distal to the internal urethral orifice. There are four principal lobes, a *right* and *left lateral*, a *posterior*, and an *anterior* lobe (usually of little consequence). It is the posterior lobe that is easily palpable by digital rectal exam. The examining finger will give only a rough estimate of the gland's enlargement, but is quite accurate in detecting prostatic pathology. Studies have shown only a 10 per cent rate of "silent malignancy," where the tumor was *not* palpable at the initial examination.

Occasionally the prostate will project beneath the bladder neck, producing a *subtrigonal* lobe. This may be massive enough to markedly elevate the floor of the bladder and distort the usual anatomical relationships. The ureteral orifices are apt to be quite close to the incision needed to remove the adenoma. In such a case it is wise for the surgeon to take extra caution and have the anesthetist give indigo carmine, a dye rapidly excreted by the kidneys, which colors the ureteral efflux dark blue. Some surgeons also will place ureteral catheters *before* enucleation of the adenoma. This assures identification of the orifices when suturing to effect hemostasis.

The prostate is fixed in place by heavy fascial layers: the *puboprostatic ligaments* anteriorly, *Denonvilliers' fascia* posteriorly. This tough, pearly-white sheet of fibroconnective tissue encases the gland *immediately anterior* to the rectum. During perineal surgery, again, recognition is the keynote. A *rectourethral fistula* is a disastrous complication.

The arterial supply of the prostate is primarily from branches of the *inferior vesical artery*. These pierce the capsule near the bladder neck below and lateral to the midline. Additional supply occasionally arises from the *middle hemorrhoidal* and *internal pudendal arteries*.

The venous drainage of the prostate is quite extensive. Encased in the prostatic capsule are numerous venous sinuses. These drain into large channels which join with veins draining the anterior surface of the penis to form the *plexus of Santorini*. This complex nest of veins lies just anterior to the prostatic capsule and should be carefully controlled during a retropubic approach to the prostate or other structures.

§5.12 The Penis

The Latin word *penis* means "tail." The anatomy of this structure in the human organism suggests no correlation with its Latin root other than perhaps the visual image of an affixed appendage.

The penis is almost cylindrical. It is attached and suspended at three points: (1) to the *urogenital diaphragm* by *Buck's fascia;* (2) to the *pubic rami* by the *crura* of the *corpora cavernosa;* and (3) to the *linea alba* by the *suspensory ligament.* It consists of three cavernous masses of erectile tissue: the two lateral *corpora cavernosa,* and the midline *corpus spongiosum* containing the anterior urethral segment. All these structures are encased within a very dense layer of fascia (*Buck's fascia*). Between this fascia and the skin is *nonfatty* connective tissue in which lie the superficial blood vessels and nerves. The penile skin is much thinner than that elsewhere. It is devoid of hair follicles except at the base of the penile shaft where it is continuous with skin covering the pubis, perineum, and scrotum. Just proximal to the corona of the glans, the skin is folded back upon itself forming the *foreskin* or *prepuce.* It is this structure which is removed during circumcision.

The distal three-fourths of the corpora cavernosa are bound together having a common septum. This makes up the bulk of the shaft of the penis. At the level of the pubic symphysis, the proximal one-fourth of these two structures diverge laterally downward becoming smaller tapered masses, the *crura.* At the ramus of each ischium, each crus is enclosed by the fibers of the *ischiocavernosus muscle.* Contraction of these muscles aids in erection by compression of the cavernous bodies.

The corpus spongiosum rests in a ventral groove formed at the junction of the two corpora cavernosa. Its expanded proximal segment, the *bulb,* is firmly attached to the lowest layer of the urogenital diaphragm. It is at this point that the urethra passes through the urogenital diaphragm to become the prostatic urethra. The corpus spongiosum expands at its distal end creating the *glans* (Latin meaning "acorn"), which forms a cap over the two corpora cavernosa. At the glans' proximal edge there is a rounded border, the *corona* (Latin meaning "crown") which is significantly larger in diameter than the rest of the penis.

The *bulbocavernosus muscle,* also known as the *ejaculator urinae,* is located in the midline. It arises from both the central tendinous point of the perineum posteriorly and the median raphé anteriorly. Its fibers diverge on both sides encircling the corpora cavernosa. During most of micturition its fibers are completely relaxed, only contracting under voluntary control to aid in the evacuation of the urethra.

The arterial supply of the penis is principally from the *internal pudendal artery.* As it enters the penis it quickly splits into the paired *bulbourethral, dorsal,* and *cavernous arteries.* The bulbourethral artery supplies both the corpora spongiosum and urethra, anastomosing with terminal twigs of the dorsal artery at the level of the glans. The dorsal artery runs in the subcutaneous space between Buck's fascia and the skin. Besides supplying the glans penis, it sends numerous perforating branches through the fascia to the erectile tissue. The cavernous arteries, which are the main vascular supply to the corpora cavernosa, enter the structures at the junction of the crura. The penis also receives arterial supply from the *external pudendal* and the *superficial perineal arteries*.

The venous drainage is split into two groups. The small superficial veins drain into the subcutaneous *superficial dorsal vein*. This in turn drains into the *saphenous* or *femoral venous system*. It may also join with the *deep dorsal vein* of the penis. The deep system begins at the level of the glans and receives branches from all the erectile bodies. It exits at the base of the penis joining with veins from the prostate to form the complex *plexus of Santorini*.

The nerve supply of the penis mimics the arterial supply. Arising from the *perineal nerve*, the *dorsal nerve* of the penis accompanies the internal pudendal artery. The erectile tissue receives its sympathetic innervation from fibers accompanying its arterial supply. They originate in the hypogastric and prostatic plexuses. The latter also sends nervous filaments to the seminal vesicles, urethra, the corpora cavernosa, and a few fibers which join the dorsal nerve of the penis.

§5.13 The Testicular and Spermatic Cord Structures

The *testes*, the left usually slightly lower than the right, are paired ovoid structures each suspended within the scrotum by the elements of its respective *spermatic cord*. Closely adherent to each testis is a long, narrow, slightly flattened structure, the *epididymis*, containing a mass of tightly coiled tubules. The testis is attached to the lower end of the scrotum by a band of fibrous tissue, the remnants of the foetal *gubernaculum testis*, a structure thought to play a role in testicular descent.

The testis and epididymis hang together within the *tunica vaginalis*, a normally closed epithelial sac containing a small amount of fluid. The sac is formed by the descent of the testis into the scrotum. During foetal life, the testis migrates from its original position deep within the pelvic portion of the abdominal cavity up to the internal ring, through the inguinal canal, and down into the scrotum. As this occurs, a layer of parietal peritoneum is pushed ahead by the migrating testis. The trailing peritoneal channel, the *processus vaginalis*, then fuses leaving the testis and its associated structures within a closed epithelial envelope. If complete fusion does not occur, there remains a potential connection to the abdominal cavity. This is the *hernial sac* into which abdominal structures may migrate establishing a clinical diagnosis of an *inguinal hernia*. Actually, the hernial defect was there all along as the patent processus vaginalis. No symptoms develop until something bulges within the sac and/or becomes incarcerated.

The testes are about 4 to 5 cm. in length, 2.5 to 3 cm. in breadth, and about 3 cm. in their anteroposterior diameter. The weight is highly variable, from 10 to 20 grams.

Each testis is covered by an extremely thick, fibrous, bluish-white membrane, the *tunica albuginea*. Within the testis, this is continuous with septa which form the basic framework upon which the *seminiferous tubules* lie.

It is in these tubules that spermatogenesis occurs. These structures when uncoiled are up to three feet in length. As each testis may possess as many as 1,200 seminiferous tubules, their combined length approaches one mile.

Groups of these tubules form lobules which unite with each other near the testicular upper pole, forming the *rete testis*. Where the head of the epididymis lies against the tunica albuginea, the rete testis has coalesced into 15 to 20 muscular ducts, the *ductuli efferentes,* which perforate the tunica albuginea and carry the spermatozoa to the epididymis.

The epididymis lies along the long axis of the testis on its posterolateral surface. It is variably separated from the testis by a pouch-like structure, the *sinus of the epididymis.*

Anatomists divide the epididymis into three sections: the head (*globus major*), body (*corpus*), and the tail (*globus minor*). The head of the epididymis is tightly fixed to the upper pole of the testis by the ductuli efferentes. The entering ductuli become the *coni vasculosi* of the epididymis. These structures make up the bulk of the globus major emptying into a densely coiled canal lined by ciliated epithelium. This constitutes the body of the epididymis. The ciliation is thought to play a significant role in spermatozoan transport to the *vas deferens*. Although the epididymis measures only 4 to 5 cm. in length, this canal, if uncoiled, can reach 20 feet. At the tail of the epididymis it enlarges becoming continuous with the vas deferens.

There are important embryonic remnants within the tunica vaginalis that may have clinical significance. One, the *appendix testis (nonpedunculated hydatid of Morgagni)*, is a vestige of the Müllerian ducts. It is a tiny structure fixed to the tunica albuginea at the upper pole of the testis. Although anatomically described as sessile, it frequently has its own small pedicle containing a tiny artery and vein. A second vestigial remnant is the *appendix of the epididymis (pedunculated hydatid of Morgagni)*. This arises from the head of the epididymis also having its own vascular pedicle. Either of these structures may twist upon itself mimicking torsion of the testis, a surgical emergency. Occasionally present is the *organ of Giraldes* or *paradidymis*. This remnant of the embryonic Wolffian body arises anteriorly at the lower end of the spermatic cord immediately above the globus major of the epididymis.

The *spermatic cord* is a name for a collection of structures that both nurture and support the testis within the scrotum: the *vas deferens,* vascular elements, lymph channels, nerve filaments from both the spermatic and pelvic plexuses, and the *cremaster*. This is a thin muscular layer arising from the middle of the inguinal ligament inserting at the crest of the pubis. Between these two points, bundles (*fasiculi*) of muscle fibers form loops extending down the cord as far as the testis itself. Between these loops is the *cremasteric fascia,* an extension of fascial coverings of the internal oblique muscle. Innervation of the cremaster muscle is by the *external spermatic branch* of the *genitofemoral nerve*. Contraction shortens the length of the spermatic cord drawing the testicular structures upward towards the external inguinal ring.

The vas deferens is a firm cylindrical tube, most easily palpable in the scrotum, having the characteristic feel of uncooked spaghetti. It is about 35 cm. long in the adult, extending from the tail of the epididymis to the prostate where it joins the efferent duct of its ipsilateral seminal vesicle to form the *ejaculatory duct*.

As it leaves the tail of the epididymis, it runs directly cephalad entering the inguinal canal at the external ring. It transverses the inguinal area leaving through the internal ring *lateral* to any hernial sac. It then runs down along the parietal layer of the peritoneum towards the prostate, passing *anterior* to the iliac vessels. Crossing in front of the ureter and partially encircling it, it runs *beneath* the bladder and prostate to join with the duct of the seminal vesicle.

The vas deferens has an outer fibrous sheath throughout most of its length: absent at its epididymal origin, partially developed in the inguinal area, but complete in the retroperitoneum. All the arteries, veins, and nerve elements course through it. Between the sheath and the lumen are three distinct muscle layers: two longitudinal with a circular layer between. Spermatozoa, though motile as they enter the vas deferens, progress mainly by peristalsis, as the lumen of the vas has nonciliated columnar epithelium except at its epididymal origin.

The arterial supply running with the vas deferens is threefold: the *internal spermatic, external spermatic,* and *deferential arteries*. The internal spermatic artery arises from the aorta immediately below the renal artery, sends one branch to the ureter as it crosses it, and then continues with the spermatic cord to the epididymis and testis. The external spermatic, also called the *cremasteric artery*, arises from the *epigastric artery*, joins the other structures in the spermatic cord sheath, and continues down to both testis and epididymis. The third artery, the deferential, is a branch of the inferior vesical artery, running parallel with the others. Even in the adult these structures are very small, demanding great care during surgical manipulation. All three are not essential for organ survival, but the loss of any two severely limits viability.

The venous drainage is dual. A *deep system*, alternatively known as the *primary system*, consists of the *internal* and *external spermatic veins*, as well as those veins directly draining the vas deferens. These veins coalesce with each other until one single vein remains, usually at the level of the internal ring. This *internal spermatic vein* drains directly into the inferior vena cava on the right and into the left renal vein on the left. The other more *superficial system* contains the *epigastric veins*, the *superficial internal circumflex*, and veins of both the internal and external pudendal plexus. These drain into the iliac venous system and prostatic venous plexus.

The lymphatic drainage of the testicular structures also runs in the sheath of the cord. It drains primarily to the lymph nodes adjacent to the renal hilum, not to the inguinal or pelvic areas as topographical anatomy might suggest. This has significant clinical importance when "staging" the extent of malignant disease of the testis or epididymis.

§5.14 The Seminal Vesicles

The *seminal vesicles* are lobulated structures lying between the rectum and the base of the urinary bladder. Anteriorly, they are in direct contact with the serosa of the bladder. Posteriorly, however, an extension of Denonvilliers' fascia separates them from the anterior surface of the rectum. They are membranous pyramidal pouches which are directed backward, cephalad, and somewhat laterally following the course of the ureters. Each vesicle consists of a separate tube coiled not unlike that seen in the epididymis. Though the vesicle rarely measures more than 5 or 6 cm. in length, if fully uncoiled, its length may approach 15 cm. Its distal end becomes more constricted into a straight narrow duct that joins with the corresponding ampulla of the vas deferens to form the *ejaculatory duct*. The seminal vesicles, being extremely thin-walled, are more susceptible to injury than their size would suggest. When "packing off" or retracting to develop surgical exposure, gentleness is more a virtue than speed.

The arterial supply to the seminal vesicles arises mainly from the *deferential artery* described in §5.13. There are a few minor branches from the *inferior vesical artery* as well as the *superior* and *middle hemorrhoidal* system. The venous drainage is into the plexus of veins lying on the lateral surface of the prostate. Nervous innervation is both sympathetic and parasympathetic, arising from the hypogastric and pelvic plexuses respectively.

Physiology

§5.15 Nephrology and Urology

The subspecialities of nephrology and urology supposedly meet at Bowman's capsule within the kidney. The nephrologist, an internist with special training in renal physiology and disease, is responsible for treating problems in urine formation. The urologist, a surgeon with specialty training in the treatment of nonmedical problems of the kidney, has his or her purview confined to the transport system of that urine. Such a sharp demarcation is more verbal academics than realistic practice. The renal glomerulus is merely where the *start* of urine formation occurs. The physiological process is not complete until somewhere near the end of the distal convoluted tubule. There is also a practical consideration that any surgical endeavor on the "uphill" side of a minor calyx within the kidney will involve microsurgical techniques yet to be developed.

Though the urologist is well skilled in using biopsy needles to obtain tissue from the prostate and other organs, generally it is the nephrologist who biopsies the kidney. If a patient presents with an acute renal infection secondary to an obstructing calculus, though the nephrologist routinely treats pyelonephritis, it is the urologist who will choose the antibiotic and regulate its dosage while deciding if and when the stone should be treated. These gray areas become mutual problems in renal transplantation cases. Here the two subspecialties work as a team. It is thus imperative that each have an understanding of both the medical and surgical physiology of the urinary system.

§5.16 The Formation of Urine

The principal function of the urinary system is the maintenance of homeostasis within the body. The formation of urine, besides effectively removing waste products, helps regulate electrolyte concentrations and the pH of the blood. This in turn directly affects blood pressure and other fluid dynamics.

The formation of urine is the end result of three processes: *filtration, reabsorption,* and *secretion.*

Filtration is a passive process occurring across a semipermeable membrane when there exists a differential hydrostatic and/or oncotic pressure between the two sides. Such conditions exist in the renal glomerulus. The epithelial membrane forming Bowman's capsule is semipermeable, having intracellular interstices of such size that water and electrolytes freely pass out of the blood plasma, but larger molecules (*albumin* and other proteins) do not. This *glomerular filtrate,* when measured against time, is a valid test of one aspect of renal function. The *glomerular filtration rate* (GFR) for an average adult male is about 125 ml. per minute.

The GFR can be affected by factors other than the pressure gradient alone. Edema within the kidney can change the permeability of Bowman's membrane. The rate of renal blood flow, closely tied to systemic blood pressure, also will affect filtration. It has been shown that the capillary pressure within the glomerulus is significantly higher than capillary pressure elsewhere in the body. This is believed to be due to the high resistance of the efferent arterioles at the outlet of the glomerulus. The net effect is an increase in the pressure gradient. The filtration process, which by definition should be passive, acquires an active "push." Physiologists have named this process *ultrafiltration.*

Resorption first begins to occur within the proximate convoluted tubule, continuing throughout much of the rest of the nephron. This is a very efficient system, reabsorbing about *99 per cent* of the 180 liters of glomerular filtrate produced daily in the average adult. Resorption is mainly a process requiring active cellular metabolism. Some passive transport occurs secondary to osmosis, the result of differential oncotic pressures existing on each side of the membrane. But this is of minor import. Besides water, there is active resorption of electrolytes, proteins, and amino acids. Waste products, however, such as phenols, sulfates, phosphates, uric acid, and urea are less efficiently reabsorbed across these tubular membranes. They are excreted with what water remains.

Secretion occurs in both the proximal and distal convoluted tubules and to a much lesser extent in the most proximal portion of the collecting ducts. Again, this is an active process requiring cellular energy. Creatinine is mainly excreted in the proximal tubule, uric acid at the other end of Henle's loop, in the distal convoluted tubule. Potassium and hydrogen ions, important factors in maintaining homeostasis, also are secreted in this portion of the nephron.

The kidney also plays a role in blood pressure control. When systolic pressure falls, there is reflex vasoconstriction in the splanchnic circulation reducing both renal blood flow and the glomerular filtration rate. This causes a release of *renin* from an area of highly specialized cells in the wall of the proximal convoluted tubule, the *juxtaglomerular apparatus*. Renin is a kidney protein which when released into the systemic circulation combines with a globulin to produce *angiotensin,* a very powerful vasoconstrictor. The increase in peripheral resistance causes a prompt pressor response.

Occasionally, a patient will have a partial blockage in one or both renal arteries. Again renin will be released. This time, however, the patient will have an elevation in blood pressure. This form of *renal hypertension* was first described by Dr. Harry Goldblatt and bears his name.

§5.17 Urine Transport and Micturition

Micturition, the act of voiding urine, is the result of a complex but coordinated relationship between the structures of the urinary tract. Before dissecting the physiological components of these relationships, it would be wise to outline some basic concepts.

Though control of one's urine may be a perplexing problem, common sense can frequently cut through the confusing physiology and direct the diagnostician to a plausible solution. Basically, urinary control is a delicate balance between conflicting forces. On one hand is the force generated by the contracting bladder musculature with or without increased intraabdominal pressure (the *Valsalva maneuver*—holding one's breath and bearing down). On the other is the inherent resistance of the external urinary sphincter plus any obstruction impeding urinary flow. When the force to empty the bladder is *always* greater than the resistance, there is continual flow. When the contrary is true, the patient is unable to urinate. Between these two extremes of *incontinence* and *retention* there is urinary control. It is the inability to balance these forces that quickly brings a patient to see the physician.

Another simple concept often overlooked is the bladder's *functional capacity* as distinct from its *anatomical capacity*. The latter value is the volume of urine that the bladder can physically hold. The former is the measured maximum quantity of urine that the individual can void at any one time. For example, a patient with an obstructing prostate often cannot completely empty his bladder. He will void frequently, perhaps as much as 150 cc. (5 ounces). If the *residual urine* is immediately measured, you may find there is still remaining another 240 cc. (8 ounces). Although his bladder may hold 13 ounces, functionally it is a 5-ounce bladder. When this quantity of urine has been generated, he says he is "full" and must void.

§5.18 —Transporting the Urine

How then is the urine transported from its formation in the renal tubules to its temporary storage site, the bladder? As has been described in the anatomy sections (§§5.01 to 5.14), the calyceal system, the renal pelvis, and the ureter all have muscular layers. One would expect concordant contractions of these muscular layers so that the urine will be moved progressively from the calyces to the renal pelvis, then on into the ureter. This has been extensively studied by real time radiographic imaging. The system is not perfectly coordinated. Occasional retrograde pyelocalyceal "backwash" occurs. But there is a general overall effectiveness that clears urine from the kidney.

The renal pelvis has rhythmic contractions that tend to shorten and straighten its length (*systole*), as it empties the bolus of urine into the ureter. It then relaxes until its capacity is reached (*diastole*), when the cycle repeats. This system is relatively low pressure, only 5 to 10 cm. of water existing in the absence of obstruction.

The ureter has powerful muscular coats to propel the urine through its lumen and into the bladder, going from a relatively low pressure system within the ureter, into a high pressure system that may exist when the bladder is full. In diastole, the intraureteral pressure is almost as low as within the renal pelvis. Therefore its muscular coat must have sufficient strength to keep the more proximal ureter functionally isolated as the bolus of urine is ejected into the higher pressure bladder lumen. Though gravity plays a role, it is a relatively minor one as urine is moved efficiently from the kidney to the bladder even with the patient's head lower than the feet.

The ureteral contraction moves from above downward. It is not a continuous event as a wave moving towards the shore. Rather, the ureter is divided into functional segments that individually contract and expand shoving the bolus of urine ahead. Thus, ureteral radiography will rarely show the entire ureter in any one film. Where a ureteral segment is in complete contraction, its lumen is occluded and contains no radio-opaque medium to cast a shadow. When no external compression has been used by a radiologist to better "see" the ureter, if the radiograph demonstrates the entire ureteral length, it is pathognomonic of obstruction at its distal end, unless there is associated ureteral pathology.

When obstruction exists within the ureter, the pressure may reach abnormally high levels. Spasm of the ureteral musculature has been associated with degrees of the most intense pain known to humans (*ureteral colic*). Some investigators have dissociated pain from these ureteral contractions fixing its source as the acute distention of the immediately proximal muscular wall. This does not explain the intense colic seen in those patients in whom obstruction has raised the intrarenal pressure sufficiently to reduce kidney function, delaying radiographic visualization of the upper urinary tract *without* any demonstrable stretching of the proximal ureteral wall or renal pelvis (*hydroureter* or *hydronephrosis*). Dilation of the renal collecting system, which includes stretching of the musculature within its walls, *can* produce severe discomfort. However, patients report a distinct difference in the quality and intensity of this type of pain as compared to classic ureteral colic.

Although ureteral peristalsis operates independently of bladder muscular activity, it is well documented that an overly distended bladder will reduce the frequency of ureteral contractions, at times completely stopping them for several minutes. Also, the normally appearing, supposedly competent *vesicoureteral junction* (the ureteral orifice) may be rendered incompetent and allow *reflux* if intravesical pressures are raised over a critical level. Usually ureteral peristalsis and the angulation of the ureter through the bladder wall will prevent reflux from occurring, but almost any ureteral orifice can become incompetent if bladder pressures are raised high enough.

Vesicoureteral reflux is the condition when urine within the bladder flows retrograde *up* the ureter during an elevation of intravesical pressure. This is especially clinically significant, if it occurs with only minimal elevation of bladder pressure. The upper urinary tract may be inoculated with infected bladder content and does not tolerate well constant high intralumenal pressures. Urine, as any other fluid, is relatively incompressible. When severe reflux exists, there may be a continuous column of urine from the bladder into the kidney. The intrarenal pressure may rise to many times normal. If this condition chronically persists, the renal collecting system gradually dilates. The muscular layer begins to atrophy. As the pressure gradient within the kidney continues to drop, renal function decreases. Eventually the kidney will be destroyed.

§5.19 —The Bladder

The physiology of the bladder has been studied extensively, perhaps more so in recent years than any other component of the urinary system. Undoubtedly this has been prompted by the tremendous number of patients presenting with urinary control difficulties. Most often these are not life-endangering situations, or even demonstrable infections. But disturbances with urinary control are so socially unacceptable that these problems have become a major part of urological practice.

Anatomists have described the bladder as a typical hollow viscous organ in the body having an outer serous coat, a middle muscular coat, and an inner *mucous membrane.* This innermost layer is not a true "mucosa," for it is an epithelium consisting of transitional cells that have no secretory activity. It is relatively impervious to the normal contents of urine. Sodium, potassium, hydrogen, and urea are in urinary concentrations significantly different from those present in the interstices directly beneath the epithelium. One would expect the oncotic pressures to equalize but there is no appreciable transfer. The efficient removal of waste products is maintained. The differential also is responsible for urinary pH (usually acidic) being independent of blood pH.

The mechanisms of bladder contraction and evacuation of its contents are intimately tied with the neuroanatomy of the bladder. There are three main sources of innervation: the *hypogastric sympathetic nerves,* the *pelvic parasympathetic nerves,* and branches from the *pudendal nerves.*

The hypogastric sympathetic nerves arise from the first four lumbar sympathetic ganglia. They collect together as the *superior hypogastric plexus* (presacral nerve). Fibers run from this plexus to the bilateral *hypogastric ganglia* lateral to the rectum. These ganglia also receive sympathetic fibers from the third and fourth sacral paravertebral chains, conducting both pain and proprioception.

The parasympathetic nerves arise at the sacral level, send filaments via the hypogastric ganglia to all layers of the bladder. They control bladder muscular contraction, as well as conveying proprioceptive and pain sensations.

The pudendal nerve is a somatic nerve. It sends a *perineal* branch to supply the external sphincter and supplies branches to the bladder itself including the bladder neck.

Much of the physician's armamentarium to control bladder function is focused on counteracting or assisting the neurophysiology at nerve endings or the neural synapse. When sympathetic nerves are stimulated, *norepinephrine* is released. Tofranil, a trade name for *imipramine,* has been found useful in the treatment of *enuresis* (bed wetting) in children. Though its mechanism of action is not definitely known, it is hypothesized that its clinical effect is due to the potentiation of sympathetic synapses by blocking the uptake of norepinephrine at the nerve endings. The child does not sleep as deeply as before and is more apt to be awakened by the sensation of a full bladder.

Stimulation of the parasympathetic nerves causes release of *acetylcholine.* This substance exhibits strong *muscarinic* effects, so named after an extremely poisonous alkaloid found in certain mushrooms. Muscarine causes severe bronchospasm, coronary artery vasoconstriction, and smooth muscle contraction. Cholinergic drugs such as Urecholine, *bethanechol,* are used to increase bladder muscle contractility. It directly mimics the stimulation of the parasympathetic nervous system. If exogenous acetylcholine is administered, it is rapidly hydrolyzed by *cholinesterase.* Urecholine is refractory to this enzyme and thus achieves prolonged therapeutic results. However, the practitioner must be careful not to use this drug in the presence of mechanical obstruction of the bladder outlet or intestinal tract. The effect of an irresistible force against an immovable object achieves nothing but disastrous results.

For those patients who have an "irritable" bladder and experience inappropriate contractions causing bouts of incontinence, physicians have been successful using Ditropan, *oxybutynin.* This drug inhibits the muscarine effect of acetylcholine. It exerts a direct antispasmodic effect upon smooth muscle. As above, if these symptoms are due to an obstruction, the therapy is contraindicated. Ditropan will "put the bladder to sleep." The patient may be cured of incontinence, but the resultant acute retention has substituted a more severe problem for the original complaint.

§5.20 —Voiding the Urine

The process of emptying the urinary bladder is more than a simple reflex response to excitation of stretch receptors within the detrusor of the bladder. It is a highly complex, well-integrated system of contraction and relaxation of the involved muscular groups. Much of this coordination occurs within a *sacral micturition center* located principally in the third and fourth segments. It is here that sensations of pain and proprioception arrive from the bladder to be acted upon and/or relayed up the central nervous system. Columns of nerve fibers run from this "voiding center" cephalad to terminate in the midbrain and medulla. In these higher centers are specific areas which control the constriction and relaxation of both bladder and urethral musculature. Neuroanatomists have also identified the returning descending pathways.

Part of micturition is reflexive. Infants obviously void at demand of a full bladder. But children can be taught to empty their bladders voluntarily long before our social mores play a significant role in their behavior. This does not negate the presence of reflex arcs independent of higher central nervous system control. The bladder detrusor has been shown to contract in response to a variety of stimuli ranging from cold, electrical shock, to physical manipulation of the anal canal.

There are synergistic relationships between the muscle bundles of the urinary structures. As the detrusor of the bladder begins to contract, there is concomitant contraction of extensions of the ureteral musculature which have formed the interureteric ridge. This fixes and slightly shortens the trigone facilitating bladder evacuation. There is also prompt relaxation of the external sphincter. Once voiding has begun, it is possible to stop the urinary stream by *voluntary* contraction of this sphincter.

There has been extensive research in the study of urodynamics. Today there is available sophisticated instrumentation which can quite accurately quantify urinary flow, pressure relationships, and in some cases delineate the site of obstruction. This is a quantum leap forward from where our knowledge stood less than 30 years ago.

§5.21 The Male Reproductive System

The *testicle* has a dual role in reproductive physiology: the manufacture of *spermatozoa* and the maintenance of hormone levels which are necessary for sexual activity to achieve successful intromission and ejaculation.

Spermatogenesis begins in the germinal epithelium of the seminiferous tubules. It is not an active process until the onset of puberty, when *follicle stimulating hormone* (FSH) from the pituitary gland causes an increase in the number of *spermatogonia*, the primitive male germ cells lining the tubules. There also occurs a marked increase in mitotic activity. This is followed by progressive maturation of the daughter cells through the spermatocyte and spermatid cell types ending with juvenile *spermatozoa*. This final form is a free nonmotile cell that has a well-formed head and tail. It carries the male's genetic code to be integrated with the female counterpart at the time of fertilization. These young sperm cells are passed into the epididymis. There, further maturation occurs, including the ability to be self-propelled. This characteristic, so vital to the human process of fertilization, is further enhanced when the spermatozoa come in contact with the chemical secretions of the prostate gland and seminal vesicles.

The adult spermatozoa are carried through the vas deferens to its distal end where they are temporarily stored in the ampulla. At ejaculation, they are emptied into the urethra simultaneously with discharge of prostatic fluid. The seminal vesicles secondarily empty their contents accounting for most of the volume of the semen. About 75 per cent of the sperm discharged are found in the leading third of the ejaculate. The remaining aliquots are rich in sugars, particularly fructose, a simple sugar easily metabolized by the spermatozoa. Apparently, adequate concentration of sugars is necessary for maximum motility.

Today fertility problems occupy a larger percentage of the urologist's practice than occurred a generation ago. With the better understanding of testicular physiology and the sperm transport system, an infertile couple now has hope if the apparent cause of the husband's *oligospermia* (low sperm count) or *aspermia* (no sperm) appears to be reversible. In the latter case, microsurgical techniques such as vasovasostomy or epididymovasostomy have successfully restored viable sperm to the semen, achieving pregnancy. Oligospermia rarely is secondary to obstruction. The response to medical therapy has not been as successful.

Spermatogenesis is a fragile process. Unless conditions are above threshold levels, the production of healthy viable sperm may be markedly decreased. At times sperm production may cease completely. The process is exquisitely sensitive to temperature variation. Intrascrotal temperature is normally about 5° F. below body temperature. When a testis is congenitally intraabdominal (*cryptorchidism*), spermatogenesis is absent. Laboratory experiments with mammalian models show a prompt regression of spermatogenic activity if the testis is placed back within the abdominal cavity or otherwise subjected to temperature elevation. Normal sperm production may resume when the testis is returned to its normal environment, most often after considerable delay.

Although there are a few reports of "regeneration" of spermatogenic activity in an adult patient following exposure to ionizing radiation, the seminiferous tubules are generally considered to be extremely radiosensitive. Minimal doses of radiation produce prompt loss of the germinal epithelium. Unless the exposure has been less than 350 rads, the resultant sterility is probably irreversible.

Spermatogenesis can be suppressed by a variety of exogenous agents, normal sperm cell generation resuming when the drug is discontinued. The nitrofurantoins (Furadantin, Macrodantin) and estrogens are among those drugs most frequently implicated. Exogenous testosterone also reduces sperm production. This is a direct result of the inverse hormonal relationship between the testis and the pituitary gland. High serum levels of circulating testosterone inhibit the pituitary output of gonadotropins. Clinicians were quick to utilize this in their practice. For a while it was fashionable to give oligospermic patients suppressive doses of testosterone until their sperm count dropped near zero. The "rebound" with discontinuance of the drug supposedly achieved acceptable levels of spermatozoa. Not being uniformedly reproducible, the therapy has since fallen into disrepute.

Located in the interstitial tissue between the seminiferous tubules of the testis are the *Leydig cells*. These produce *testosterone,* an androgenic hormone necessary for masculine pubescence and maintenance of both sexual interest and performance. Leydig cells respond directly to the pituitary's secretion of gonadotrophic hormone. This "hormone push" has been shown to be essential in testosterone synthesis, for destruction of the pituitary results in prompt cessation of all testicular androgen production.

These cells are not sensitive to heat as are the germinal layers. Thus a patient with bilateral *cryptorchidism* will have normal secondary sexual development and function, but be *azospermic.* Although originally thought not to be relatively sensitive to radiation, recent work in mammalian models has shown a significant decrease in Leydig cell steroid production after external beam radiation at levels far below that originally believed necessary.

The ejaculate consists of the spermatozoa, some minimal secretions from small accessory paraurethral glands (Cowper's and Littré's), 25 per cent of the volume from prostatic secretion, and the rest from the seminal vesicles. The seminal vesicle portion is rich in fructose, a sugar that is closely tied with sperm cell motility. The prostatic contribution is high in zinc, a fact that has prompted clinicians to use zinc preparations in the treatment of prostatic disorders if the patient's serum zinc level is low. Results at best have been marginal. There is still much conjecture about the role zinc plays in prostatic physiology.

§5.22 Sexual Dysfunction Generally

The subject of sexual performance, impotency, and male sterility no longer is confined to the doctor's consultation room. Our Puritan heritage once helped codify laws forbidding writings of this nature to be sent through the mail or openly displayed in book stores. It was not until well after World War II that publications containing articles on these subjects were received in other than plain brown wrappers. Today these subjects are featured in magazines, debated on radio, and sensationalized on the afternoon television talk shows. Advertisements for the treatment of impotency now appear in the newspapers and other media. Whether he or she has been specially trained or not, the physician, by default, has become the local expert. Fortunately this liberalization of our society has prompted research in these areas. The urologist now is armed with factual answers where once he or she was as poorly equipped as his or her nonmedical colleagues.

Thus the treatment of sexual dysfunction is becoming a significant part of the practice of urology. If it were not for this history of our society's mores, the sudden increase in the number of patients seeking help would be called an epidemic. Misinformation available to the general public, coupled with the psychological overlay associated with sexuality, makes diagnosis and treatment as challenging as any problem presented to the urologist.

§5.23 Impotency

The term *impotency* comes from the Latin *impotentia* (lack of power). In a society where by tradition the male is dominant, it is a source of intense emotional difficulty. It has come to encompass any problem where the ability "to perform" does not reach the patient's expectations. Frequency of intercourse, "staying" power, and the quality of partner satisfaction have all become indices of masculinity. Though part may be psychiatric in origin, it is the urologist who first sees the patient and who must separate the wheat from the chaff.

Before intromission can be successfully achieved, there must be sufficient rigidity of the penis. The mechanism of *penile erection* has been carefully studied. Though not in absolute agreement on all aspects, most investigators have general acceptance of the following:

1. Erection is achieved by an increase of arterial flow into the corpora with an accompanying decrease in the cavernosal vascular resistance. At the onset of erection, though systemic blood pressure is relatively unchanged, a significant increase in arterial flow into the penile erectile tissue occurs. This can only result from a decrease in terminal resistance—i.e., *dilation* of the distal penile arterioles and sinusoids.
2. Simultaneously there must be a mechanism that prevents this increased arterial flow from immediately leaving the sinusoids within the corpora. The anatomists describe numerous *venules* draining the corpora cavernosa. They run between these sinusoids and the tunica albuginea for a short distance before piercing the latter to emerge as the *emissary veins*. When the penis is flaccid and the sinusoids relatively empty, these venules are free to drain the minimal arterial blood supplied for normal penile cellular nutrition. As the penis fills and the intracavernous pressure rises, they are compressed between the sinusoid wall and the tunica albuginea effectively limiting venous outflow. When intracavernous pressure has peaked, the emissary veins are "pinched off" by the tightened fascial sheath reducing veinous drainage to a minimum.
3. The fascial coverings of the corpora cavernosa are relatively inelastic. Once the cavernous spaces are filled, the pressure within rises rapidly and approaches that of the mean arterial pressure. If this small differential is sustained, the erection becomes functional.
4. The *ischiocavernosus* muscle contracts, raising the intracavernous pressure even higher to above systemic systolic levels. If maintained, the penis has sufficient rigidity for successful intromission. This muscle, innervated by the perineal branch of the pudendal nerve, proba-

bly responds reflexively (the bulbocarvernous reflex) when the penis is stimulated.

5. *Ejaculation* is a reflex phenomenon. As semen is first extruded into the urethra from the ejaculatory ducts, the pudendal nerve carries impulses to the sacral plexuses and back to the perineal musculature causing synchronous rhythmic contractions which completely empty the urethra.

6. *Detumescence* occurs after ejaculation. It is the result of sympathetic neural discharge contracting arteriolar smooth muscle which reduces arterial inflow. The venous channels then reopen and flaccidity returns. Painful stimuli, especially to the penis, may also initiate detumescence.

Sexual dysfunction may be the result of interference with one or any combination of the physiological reactions in the above scenario. Therefore the clinician should systematically run through a checklist to rule in or out all possible causes.

§5.24 —Psychological Causes

First on the checklist of possible causes of impotency must be an evaluation of psychological factors. Though conscious volition is not needed in all parts of the sexual act (ejaculation is reflexive and cannot be inhibited once begun), it is the single element which *starts* the process of penile erection.

Determining the cause of impotency is easier than it was only 8 to 10 years ago, but it is far from a foolproof inquiry. The normal adult male has spontaneous erections during sleep. This may be measured by a variety of devices. There are strain gauges (expensive) to the simple circumferential strip of postage stamps (economical) which can be applied to the patient's penis before he retires for the night. In the latter case, if the strip continuity has been interrupted during the night, there is the presumption that an erection occurred, ruling out physiological causes. But there is no way of determining its completeness or duration. May not a patient have *both* physical and emotional problems?

With the patient in a sleep laboratory, a strain gauge attached to his penis, and an electroencephalograph (EEG) running continuously, the above dilemma is more easily solved. But this is inordinately expensive and not readily available except in large medical centers.

In recent years, a test has been developed which does away with both the expense of the sleep laboratory and the uncertainty of the perforated stamps. Thirty milligrams of papaverine, a nonspecific smooth muscle relaxant, is injected directly into the corpora cavernosa. If there is a prompt full erection lasting more than 25 minutes or so, the clinician can be quite certain that the patient has normally responsive vascular elements. If his history is accurate, his impotence *must* be psychological in origin.

§5.25 —Physical Causes

The physical causes of impotency fall into three general categories: (1) interference with the transmission of neural impulses to the penis; (2) insufficient arterial inflow; and (3) the presence of venous "leaks."

Interference with neural transmission is frequently seen after trauma which injures or transects the sacral parasympathetic outflow to the penis (the *nervi erigentes*). Gunshot wounds, fractures of the pelvis, and other crushing injuries are common causes. Extensive pelvic surgery, both general and urological, may produce similar interference. The recent introduction of a "nerve sparing" radical retropubic prostatectomy looks promising anatomically. Whether the operation is one which takes wide enough margins to "cure" malignancy is an issue yet to be decided. Transurethral resection of the prostate (TUR) has also been implicated as a cause of impotency. Many urologists disagree, but if it does in fact occur, it may be due to thermal injury of the electrical current by cutting too close to the nerves as they run near the bladder neck.

There is also continuing debate whether diabetes mellitus has a neural component causing impotency. Investigators have found a correlation between the presence of peripheral neuropathy and sexual dysfunction. These symptomatic patients have microscopic changes in peripheral nerve structure not present in sexually potent diabetics. What these changes mean to nerve function is unknown.

The problem of insufficient arterial blood flow into the penis is difficult to quantify. Patients who have widespread atherosclerosis may have a similar narrowing of the penile arteries. A simple noninvasive screening test is the use of Doppler ultrasound. It is relatively inexpensive and adaptable to office practice. Critics point to the fact that measurements made on the flaccid penis are not necessarily indicative of blood flow during erection.

Can we then demonstrate anatomical changes in the arteries which would preclude erection? At a few specialized medical centers, selective radiographic imaging of the penile arterial vasculature has been done. And yes, arterial stenosis and other changes have been described in impotent patients. But is it functionally significant? Because this is an invasive procedure carrying a significant risk of severe complications, it has not been used to study normal, sexually functional males. Do they also have areas of stenosis?

Evaluating the venous side of the equation carries much less risk, but the tests still are invasive. Radio-opaque media must be injected directly into the corpora. Although this is in the flaccid or passively dilated penis, if a vasoactive agent (*papaverine*) is used in concert with these venous studies, the technique becomes one that is reasonably accurate for evaluating vasculogenic impotency. Full tumescence is not required. Even with a partial erection, these studies may demonstrate graphically the site and magnitude of the venous "leak."

Papaverine is not without some problems, but they are few and relatively infrequent. Patients with known susceptibility to vasoactive drugs naturally should not be subjects of such investigation. If there were a significant venous "leak," the drug might be disseminated rapidly with possible serious consequences. Occasionally a patient will have a sustained erection lasting more than eight or nine hours. Almost invariably this is reversible by intracavernous lavage using dilute solutions of *phenylephrine* (Neo-Synephrine). This drug does not exhibit the cardiac stimulation characteristic of other adrenergic compounds. In the rare case of lavage failure, surgical correction (corporoglandular shunting) may be necessary.[1]

§5.26 —Drugs

Drug associated sexual dysfunction is not a newcomer to the impotency scene. It may be fashionable to point to the 1960s as the emergence of social acceptance of drugs, but humans have been ingesting "drugs" in one form or another as long as they have been social animals, perhaps even before. Many of these compounds directly or indirectly affect sexual ability.

Alcohol is probably the most commonly ingested substance which may cause sexual dysfunction. Such direct relationship was well recognized even in sixteenth century England. Shakespeare has the Porter answer MacDuff's question about the effects of alcohol:

> Lechery, sir, it provokes and unprovokes: it provides the desire, but takes away the performance. Therefore much drink may be said to be an equivocator with lechery: it makes him and mars him; it sets him on and takes him off; it persuades him, and disheartens him; makes him stand to and not stand to . . . .[2]

Alcohol's depressant effect on the central nervous system is well established, ultimately taking priority over an initial loss of inhibition. The effects of chronic alcoholism are also well documented. It is unclear whether this is due to changes in peripheral nerve ability to transmit impulses or a high serum estrogen level secondary to alcoholic cirrhosis. Such an estrogen level, if high enough, will reduce testicular endocrine function decreasing both sexual desire and performance.

Antihypertensive drugs have been almost universally associated with sexual dysfunction. Again this is not new. In India, *Rauwolfia Serpentina,* a snakeroot shrub, has been used for centuries to calm agitation. Its secondary characteristic of reducing libido was well known. Today the rauwolfia alkaloids or their derivatives are an important part of the physician's armamen-

---

[1] Papaverine has been used extensively as a therapeutic agent. Most patients easily learn how to inject themselves. But reports of significant sequelae to its chronic use have precluded the Federal Drug Administration's approval for the treatment of impotence. Nor has it ever been formally approved for diagnostic purposes. Therefore, before *any* use of intracavernous papaverine, it is incumbent upon the physician to obtain a full informed consent and properly signed release.

[2] Macbeth: Act II, Sc. 3.

tarium against hypertension. Other antihypertensives—the diuretics, the sympatholytic compounds, and the alpha or beta adrenergic drugs—have all been reported as causing impotence or ejaculatory failure. Other classes of therapeutic compounds used to treat depression or heart failure have been implicated in sexual dysfunction. It behooves the physician to question carefully the drug history of any patient complaining of sexual problems.

§5.27 Other Sexual Dysfunction

Priapism, from Greek mythology (Priapos—the God of male sexuality), is the persistence of an erection, initially pleasurable but ultimately painful, without sexual desire. Patients rarely seek medical help until the condition has existed for an extended length of time, frequently 12 hours or more. By this time blood in the corpora is thick, appearing partially deoxygenated, often described as sludge. Treatment consists principally of corporal lavage or the establishment of a corporoglandular shunt. Unfortunately many of these patients subsequently will be impotent.

Priapism is seen occasionally in patients who have sickle cell disease. It has also been reported secondary to local extension of malignant tumors originating in the prostate gland or penis. However, most cases are neurological in origin. Those that occur during a spinal anesthetic are recognized immediately and respond favorably without operative intervention. These cases rarely are impotent afterwards.

Peyronie's disease is the presence of localized areas of fibrous infiltration (*plaques*) in the intercavernous septum of the penis. Investigators theorize that this is secondary to a localized inflammation of the terminal arterioles. During erection there is an unequal expansion of the two corpora causing the penis to curve towards the involved side. It may be painful or entirely asymptomatic. Sexual intercourse becomes difficult if the angulation is severe.

Treatment has been exceedingly varied. These patients have been subjected to x-ray irradiation, ultrasound, and direct injection of the plaques with steroid or Vitamin E. All have had a notable lack of success. One investigator wrote a series of glowing reports using large doses of POTABA (potassium aminobenzoate). This writer has been unable to duplicate his results and knows of no other urologist who has. Part of the difficulty in evaluating therapy is the fact that Peyronie's disease often will be self-limiting. The symptoms of painful erection and curvature may spontaneously improve over the course of several months. Is the improvement the result of therapy, or merely "tincture of time?" For those cases that ultimately require treatment, the plaques may be surgically removed and/or penile implantation done.

Common Laboratory Tests

§5.28 Overview

The medical laboratory has always played a role in the practice of medicine. In classical Greece, physicians described the color and taste of urine. Today medical students are still taught to observe, but the chemical analysis of the urine has replaced our taste buds. We have learned to quantify as well as describe. Where once the "lab" was merely an adjunct to diagnosis, it has become increasingly an important component of the physician's armamentarium.

For those of us who spend time teaching medical students, interns, and resident physicians, it has been fascinating to watch these young doctors rely more and more on the "readout" from a computer terminal at the nursing station rather than what their observations have told them. The infallibility of the computer is part of this generation's socialization. They forget that there are other human beings, as prone to error as themselves, who entered the data. But we live in an electronic age and the machine *is* slowly replacing the art of the practice of medicine. At times it is difficult to convince a surgical resident that the computer should not, cannot, and must not make the decision to operate.

However, we still need the laboratory. There are diagnoses which by definition exist only with specific findings. The following is a brief overview of the more common tests done in urology. It is far from complete. I have merely chosen those that most urologists use in their everyday practice.

§5.29 Urinalysis

Urinalysis is probably one of the first clinical tests taught in medical training. It plays an integral part in urologic diagnosis and many other non-urologic problems. It is part of the admission workup of every hospitalized patient. Most physicians merely check the "lab report" in the chart rather than look at the urine. This is unfortunate as much can be learned by individually inspecting the specimen itself. Urine undergoes significant changes if allowed to stand at room temperature for extended periods of time. Bacteria multiply. The pH becomes more alkaline which may destroy cellular elements originally identifiable in the fresh specimen. Special attention should be paid to the following factors.

Clarity

Urine generally is clear enough to see through. However, the presence of cloudy urine does not mean necessarily that it is loaded with cellular debris or pus. Urine with a high concentration of phosphates (*phosphaturia*) may appear opaque. If it is then centrifuged, as much as one-sixth of the tube may have a packed white powder at the bottom. The uninitiated are quite amazed when it disappears upon the addition of a few drops of acetic acid. Phosphate salts are vastly more soluble in acidic than alkaline urine.

However, a cloudy urine may be clinically significant and should not be ignored. The fresh unspun urine, or the residue of the spun specimen, must be examined under a microscope. Observations are recorded as the number of cells or casts seen per high power field. This is dependent upon the degree of magnification. There are no set rules, but customarily a x400 lens is used.

Normal urine may contain a few white cells (*WBC*) and an occasional red cell (*RBC*) per high power field. Again because there is little or no standardization of the rate or for what length of time a urine specimen is centrifuged, laboratory slips tend to be meaningless. As impractical as it seems to be in a hospital setting, the physician should try to do the microscopic urinalysis on his or her own patients. If it is done the same way each time, the number of cells or casts seen in each high power field will begin to have meaningful correlation with patients' signs and symptoms.

Pyuria, the presence of white cells in the urine, is perceived as a response to an infection within the urinary tract. Some investigators claim to be skillful enough to pinpoint the focus of infection, differentiating the upper from the lower urinary tract by the presence of distinctive granules seen within the white cells' cytoplasm. However, others have shown these same changes to be present in inflammatory disease of the prostate.

The presence of *casts* is a more reliable finding. These packed aggregates of precipitated protein, cellular debris, and white or red cells are so named for they assume the shape of the distal collecting tubules of the kidney, where presumably they were formed. They are pathognomonic of intrarenal pathology, often seen long before the patient is symptomatic.

Urine may have a cloudy milky appearance. This is due to the presence of fat globules (*chyluria*), a condition diagnostic of lymphatic obstruction with fistulization into the urinary collecting system.

Color

The color of urine is directly dependent upon the concentration of solutes and foreign matter suspended within it. It normally varies from light yellow to a soft amber, but all gradations of the spectrum have been described. Changes in hue are not necessarily indicative of pathology. Indigo carmine or methylene blue is promptly excreted by the kidneys, imparting a bluish-green color to the urine. Urologists use this as a rough test of kidney function during endoscopy procedures. College fraternities have been known to mix this chemical in their pledges' food during "hazing week."

Red urine usually means the presence of blood. But in certain individuals, a breakdown product of beets may stain urates a characteristic reddish color. Dark red urine, port wine in color, is seen in *porphyrinuria*, which is a relatively rare congenital condition involving the ability to metabolize porphyrins, a class of pigments distributed widely throughout the food chain.

Brown urine may indicate "old" blood—i.e., bleeding into the urinary tract that has ceased hours, perhaps days before. This often is confused with the discoloration caused by bile pigments, *urobilinogenuria,* seen in patients with liver disease and/or biliary obstruction with secondary cholangitis

Pseudomonas aeruginosa, a gram negative aerobic bacillus, produces two water soluble pigments: greenish-yellow *flourescein* and bluish-green *pyocyanine.* If the concentration of the infecting organism is high enough, the urine will have a greenish fluorescent luster.

Microscopic Analysis

The examination of the urinary sediment goes beyond the notation of cellular elements and casts. Larger bacteria can be seen as thin rods with characteristic Brownian movement. If the specimen is fresh and was collected in such manner that there was little likelihood of contamination, this presence of bacteria is clinically significant.

Cultures of urine are done routinely not only to identify the infecting organism, but also to determine to which antibiotic it is sensitive. The presence of bacteria is reported quantitatively. Concentrations below 10^3 per cc. are considered a contaminant. At or above 10^5 per cc., indicative of active infection, sensitivity studies are done. For any of these tests to be valid, it is imperative that the urine be collected in as sterile a manner as is practical. In children this may necessitate needle aspiration directly from the bladder. For adults, a midstream aliquot caught in a sterile container is sufficient. Specimens should never be taken from a drainage bottle or leg bag.

pH

pH is chemical shorthand for "potential of electricity for positive hydrogen ions." Mathematically, this is the logarithm of the reciprocal of hydrogen ion concentration. At one time this measurement was cumbersome and expensive. It necessitated comparing the voltage in two batteries, one with known chemical composition, the other containing the unknown solution. Today we have chemically treated strips of paper (*dip sticks*) which turn a characteristic color dependent upon the solution's acidity or alkalinity.

Hydrogen ion concentration directly affects chemical solubility. Patients with gout and certain types of leukemia may have *hyperuricemia,* an elevated serum uric acid. They excrete excessive uric acid in their urine. As the solubility of uric acid increases dramatically in less acid urine, stone formation can be controlled by maintaining a urinary pH above 6.5. This is readily achieved through diet control plus sodium bicarbonate or similar alkali.

Urinary pH may facilitate the growth of an infecting organism. If infected urine is alkaline, the causative agent is apt to be *Proteus vulgaris* or another urea-splitter. These bacteria generate an enzyme, *urease,* which separates ammonia from urea giving urine its pungent odor. If the urine is acidic, the infection is apt to be *Escherichia coli.* This ubiquitous bacteria, living symbiotically in the intestinal tract of humans, is the most common microorganism isolated in urinary tract infections.

Specific Gravity

The unmodified glomerular filtrate is an ultrafiltrate of blood plasma and has a specific gravity of 1.010. The normal specific gravity of urine varies from 1.006 to 1.025. In severe dehydration, levels as high as 1.030 have been reported. These values are directly related to the concentration of urinary solutes. If the renal tubules have lost their ability to resorb water, as in the diuretic phase of a lower nephron nephrosis, the urine specific gravity will be approximately that of the plasma, 1.010. A high specific gravity, 1.020 or more, in a protein-free specimen, is evidence of good renal function. Likewise, a urine specific gravity *below* 1.010 is indicative that cellular energy has been expended in active resorption of electrolytes. Excessively high values of specific gravity are suggestive of other dissolved compounds such as glucose or protein.

Chemical Analysis

Concentrations of protein in the urine are normally too small to be detected by other than sophisticated chemical analysis. If there is acute or chronic renal disease, the integrity of the surface of the capillary loops in the glomerulus is damaged. Proteins such as *albumin* (molecular weight about 69,000) easily filter through the widened interstices. Though there is some resorption in the tubules, enough passes through the collecting system to be detectable. Dip sticks are available for a gross estimation of the degree of *proteinuria* present.

Included on many of these dip sticks are chemically treated areas to detect reducible sugars and acetone. The presence of sugar in the urine (*glycosuria*) usually indicates a metabolic defect in carbohydrate metabolism, occurring when the kidney tubules cannot *completely* resorb the glucose present in the glomerular filtrate. In normal individuals this "threshold" occurs at a blood glucose level of 140 to 160 mg. per ml. Glycosuria is found in a variety of pathologic states, principally diabetes mellitus, but it also is detectable in about 10 per cent of pregnant women and in other normal healthy individuals after rigorous exercise. A common error is that a patient is brought to an emergency room, an intravenous infusion of glucose started, and *then* the urinalysis ordered. Most normal patients will exhibit a transient glycosuria.

Acetonuria is a general term for the "ketone bodies" found in the urine. Acetone, acetoacetic acid, and B-oxybutyric acid are such compounds, occurring naturally in tiny amounts. When the urine level becomes detectable on the dip stick, the physician should be alerted to a more serious defect in carbohydrate metabolism. Acetonuria is seen in diabetic acidosis, some acute febrile states, and in patients with intractable vomiting.

§5.30 Hemogram

Laboratory analysis of the blood is part of the initial evaluation of every hospitalized patient. It should include examination of its potential oxygenation, an actual count of the cellular elements, and an appraisal of the their morphology. It is the one laboratory examination that directly affects *all* specialties in the practice of medicine.

The following values are reported: hemoglobin, hematocrit, white cell count (including the differential), red cell count, and the corpuscular indices (MCV, MCH, and MCHC).

Hemoglobin, abbreviated *Hb,* is the respiratory pigment of red blood cells. It has the unique capability of combining with and releasing oxygen. Most laboratories report the value as a percentage (*grams*). This is a misnomer as there is a wide variation of normal values. What actually has been measured is the quantity of hemoglobin in 100 ml. of blood. Normal values for adult men are: 16 ± 2 gm per 100 ml. For women, the range is: 14 ± 2 gm per 100 ml.

Hematocrit, abbreviated *Hct,* expresses the volume per cent of packed red cells. The test is simple to do and reliably reproducible. The normal range in males is: 47.0 ± 7.0 per cent; for females: 42.0 ± 5.0 per cent.

The *red cell count* is always reported as part of the hematologic workup. The normal average value varies within a narrow range of 5×10^6 per ml. Laboratories once counted red cells by diluting an aliquot of venous blood with an anticoagulent, then introducing a minute amount of this solution into the counting chamber of a *hemocytometer.* The technician then used a microscope to physically count the number of cells seen within a prescribed lined area of the hemocytometer. The total count was adjusted for the dilution factors to arrive at the actual number of red cells per milliliter. Though great care would be taken to measure both the aliquot and diluent accurately, studies have shown that the variation in counts on the *same* blood sample could reach ± 5 per cent.

Today the computer coupled with laboratory automation has eliminated these sources of error. But medical customs die hard. Physicians still rarely employ the red cell count as an index of a patient's status. The terms hemoglobin and hematocrit are preferably used when writing progress notes or discussing the case with another physician.

However, the red cell count is used to calculate two blood indices: *mean corpuscular volume* (MCV) and *mean corpuscular hemoglobin* (MCH). The third index, *mean corpuscular hemoglobin concentration* (MCHC), is derived from the hemoglobin and the hematocrit. These indices play an important role in the differentiation of various types of anemia.

The *MCV* is calculated by dividing the red cell count into the hematocrit (x10). The resultant quotient is expressed in cubic microns (μ^3). For a healthy normal adult this figure is about $90\mu^3$. When a patient loses blood slowly and continuously for an extended length of time, as occurs with carcincoma of the large bowel, the patient will develop a hypochromic anemia characterized by small, pale, red blood cells. A hemogram on such a patient will dramatically demonstrate this microcytosis, the MCV dropping to as low as $60\mu^3$.

The *MCH* is calculated by dividing the red cell count into the hemoglobin (x10). This quotient is expressed in micromicrograms per cell ($\mu\mu g$ or 10^{-12}

gm. per cell). A normal individual has an MCH about $30\mu\mu g$. The hypochromic microcytic patient's cellular hemoglobin may be exceptionally low: $15\mu\mu g$. This 50 per cent loss is due to the cumulative effect of reduced corpuscle size (MCV) as well as the overall reduction of hemoglobin. The macrocytosis seen in pernicious anemia, sprue, and other intestinal disorders can push the indices in the other direction. Values of MCV as high as $150\mu^3$ have been reported and MCH levels have reached $50\mu\mu g$.

The *MCHC* is calculated from the hemoglobin and hematocrit values alone. The computer prints it on the laboratory slip along with the other two, but having limited application, it is the least used of the three indices.

Another basic laboratory test done on all patients is the *white cell count*. Normal values range from 4,000 to 10,000 per ml. Most physicians do not regard an elevation of the white cell count (*leucocytosis*) to be significant until that upper limit has been surpassed.

The counting procedure is similar to the red cell count, except for the diluent which is one that will hemolyze red cells but not destroy the leucocytes. As the magnitude of this dilution is quantitatively less, the percentage potential error is proportionally much smaller. Physicians have intuitively recognized this and pay close attention to changes in the white count.

The laboratory also will do a *differential* count. This is a percentage breakdown of white cells, according to their morphological types. Diagnostically this may be more important than the absolute number.

The white cells are classified primarily into three groups: *granulocytes, lymphocytes,* and *monocytes*. The granulocytes can be thought of as the "infection fighters." In a normal adult they comprise about 65 to 70 per cent of the leucocyte count. Acute bacterial infection is frequently associated with this form of a leucocytosis. The granulocyte division is further broken down into *neutrophils, eosinophils,* and *basophils,* identifiable by their staining characteristics when prepared for microscopic examination. Neutrophils, which constitute the bulk of the granulocyte percentage, are also called *polymorphonucleocytes* (PMN). *Eosinophilia,* an increase in the percentage of eosinophils above the usual 3 to 5 per cent, is seen in patients with allergies, parasitic diseases, and certain toxic bacterial infections such as scarlet fever. The lymphocytes usually comprise about 25 to 30 per cent of the white cell count. Viral infections such as the common cold may produce a rise in this percentage without any significant elevation in the overall count.

Platelets, also called *thrombocytes,* are another cellular form reported on the hematology slip. They often are not counted unless specifically ordered. Usually the report reads "adequate" or "sufficient." These cells function as a "glue" to assist blood clot formation. *Thrombocytopenia,* the condition of too few platelets, can transform a minor surgical procedure into a major event. If the surgeon is forewarned, such problems can be averted by judicious preoperative transfusion of fresh platelet preparations.

§5.31 —Chemical Analysis of the Blood

The medical laboratory today is capable of running a plethora of chemical analyses. At admission to most hospitals it has become *routine* to order an extensive battery of tests, though many are not clinically indicated. The physician merely orders: "Routine lab" or "SMA." Some medical centers have automated the procedure and run as many as 14 different chemical analyses. It is expensive and at times unnecessarily invasive, but the ogre of medical malpractice coupled with the rationalization that it is in the patient's best interest has made it the standard of care at most hospitals in the United States.

The common tests ordered routinely which have urological significance are: *blood urea nitrogen, creatinine,* and the *creatinine clearance.*

Urea is the major nonprotein nitrogenous component in the blood. This *blood urea nitrogen* (BUN) can be a measure of renal function, as it is principally excreted by the kidneys. But nitrogen in the blood will also be dependent upon dietary intake. Because the amount of protein ingested daily may be highly variable, there is no one value accepted as "normal." Rather, a wide range exists, from 7 to 17 mg. per 100 ml. of blood. Again medicine has been sloppy in its verbalization and refers to BUN values as "x milligrams per cent."

As the BUN is a measure of the quantity of urea nitrogen in a liquid medium, any reduction in the amount of the liquid will raise the measured concentration. This is well demonstrated medically. A patient who is dehydrated from profuse sweating (marathon runner), chronic diarrhea (dysentery), or persistent vomiting (food poisoning etc.), may have an increased BUN though renal function is perfectly normal.

An elevated BUN often is observed in patients with chronic bleeding from gastric ulcers or other lesions in the intestinal tract. This results from reabsorption of nitrogenous components from the hemolyzed red cells.

In a healthy adult with normal renal function, the BUN will not rise until about two-thirds of the nephrons have ceased functioning. Charting a patient's BUN against the percentage of remaining viable renal tissue produces a graph that is almost flat abruptly changing at a sharp "knee." Once that point is reached, BUN levels begin to rise very rapidly. Therefore, any dehydration or other condition of insufficient magnitude to raise the BUN level in a patient without kidney disease will do so in dramatic fashion if the patient's renal function already is marginal.

Creatinine is an anhydride of creatine, an organic compound essential to the anaerobic phase of muscular contraction. Creatinine itself serves no biological function in the body and is excreted entirely by the kidneys. Thus, the production of creatinine will be proportional to the muscle creatine in the body. With normal renal function, because both muscle mass and daily activity are relatively unchanging, the blood creatinine level of any one individual remains constant. The normal range again is quite wide: 0.5 to 1.0 mg. per 100 ml. Not reflecting dietary intake, it has a distinct advantage over the BUN when evaluating renal insufficiency.

The *creatinine clearance test* is an offshoot of routine creatinine determinations. The test is easy to perform, reproducible, and reasonably accurate. The laboratory measures the number of grams of creatinine present in the patient's urine collected over a 24-hour period. This figure is divided by the serum creatinine concentration (expressed as grams per liter). The resultant quotient is a close approximation of the glomerular filtration rate. For a normal individual, this averages between 150 and 170 liters per 24 hours. As slight changes in renal function are easily detected, this is one of the more meaningful tests available to the clinician.

The *serum acid phosphatase* is a determination not in a routine hospital laboratory workup. As the enzyme is found principally in prostatic tissue, the test is ordered for all male patients with a prostatic nodule or outlet obstruction symptoms. Usually, serum contains no more than very small amounts of acid phosphatase. This is so even with massive benign prostatic hypertrophy. Elevations above normal are found *only* in cases where carcinoma of the prostate has extended *beyond the surgical capsule of the gland.* This would seem to be the perfect test of a patient's suitability for radical prostatectomy and "cure." But this is not so. A significant percentage of patients have demonstrable disseminated disease *without* elevation of the acid phosphatase. A normal serum value does not assure the surgeon that a planned "cancer operation" will totally remove all malignant tissue. This is the classic false negative.

There is an additional caveat. The digital prostatic exam itself may raise serum acid phosphatase levels into the abnormal range for a period of several hours. If the test is to be reliable, it must be done *before* rectal exam or after sufficient length of time has passed.

If a patient is known to have carcinoma of the prostate with spread beyond the confines of the gland, the acid phosphatase can be a rough guide to the efficacy of the treatment protocol. If treatment is successful, levels should fall to within normal parameters. I have omitted actual numbers as the "normal range" is dependent upon the particular system of chemical analysis used in each laboratory.

In 1979, the *human prostatic-specific antigen* (PSA) was first identified. It is a glycoprotein produced *only* by prostatic cells and not found in any other body tissue. If a patient has a proven malignant prostatic nodule with no demonstrable metastases, in theory, the complete removal of all prostatic tissue, as in radical prostatectomy, should reduce PSA to zero. Then if the antigen still can be measured, in all probability there is distant metastatic disease, yet to be detected.

As acid phosphatase has its problems with false negatives, prostatic-specific antigen has an equal problem with false positives. A substantial percentage of patients with benign prostatic hypertrophy will have an elevation of their PSA level. There has been shown to be, however, a more significant increase of the antigen, often by a factor of two or three, measured in those patients who have prostatic malignancy. In many of these carcinoma patients, PSA is the *only* marker which is elevated.

Thus prostatic-specific antigen becomes useful in the evaluation of a patient with known prostatic cancer. As the antigen levels increase with advancing clinical stage and correlate well with the estimated tumor volume, the test is emerging as one of the best tools available for this purpose. A recent report showed that PSA levels had become undetectable after definitive radiation therapy three years previously. At the time of this study, these patients were clinically free of disease. Longer term, larger series are yet to be done to determine if this marker can be equally effective for measuring the presence and magnitude of recurrent disease.

§5.32 References

Consolidated Omnibus Reconciliation Act (COBRA), Pub L No 99-272, 49 Stat 648 (1985).

Curran, *A Further Solution to the Malpractice Problem: Corporate Liability and Risk Management in Hospitals,* 310 New Eng J Med 704 (1984).

Hospital Corporate Liability: An Effective Solution to Controlling Private Physician Incompetence?, 32 Rutgers L Rev 342, 360 (1979).

Peters, *Hospital Malpractice: Eleven Theories of Direct Liability,* 52 Trial 82 (Nov 1988).

Restatement (Second) of Agency §1 (1957).

Appendix 5-A Illustrations

Figure 5-1

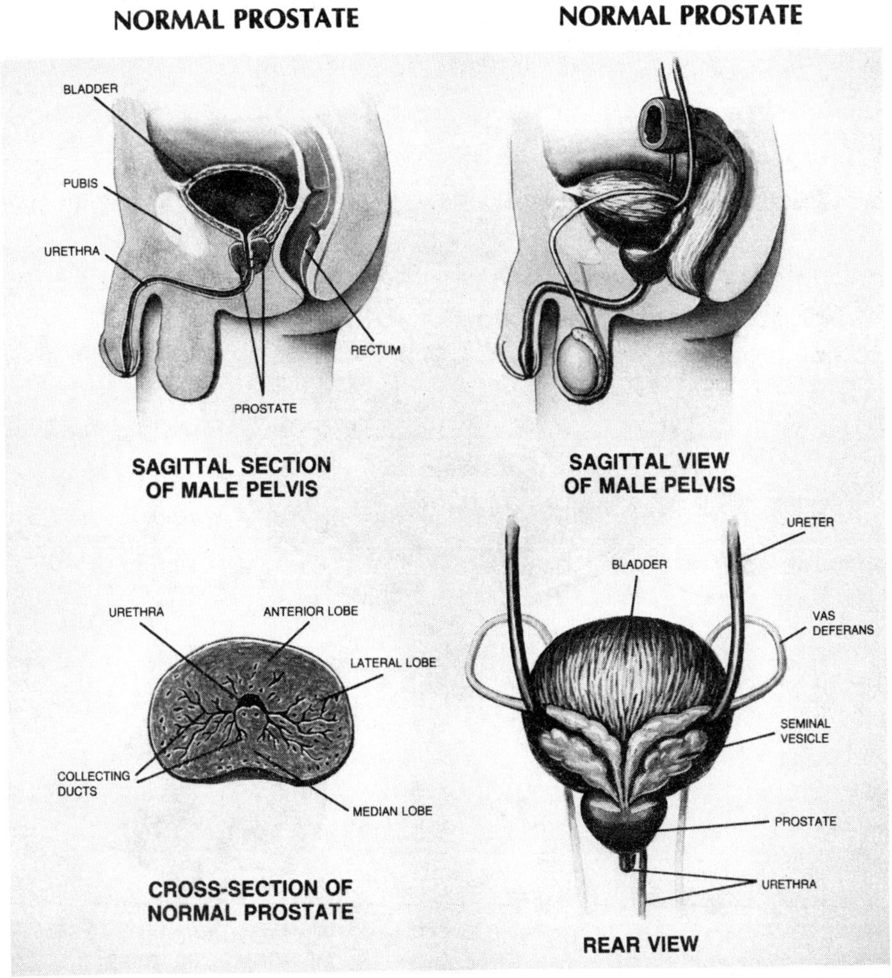

Illustrations reproduced from *Illustrated Guide to Normal and Diseased Areas of the Urinary Tract* (1984). Reproduced with permission of Burroughs Wellcome Co.

156   Anatomy, Physiology, & Tests

Figure 5-2

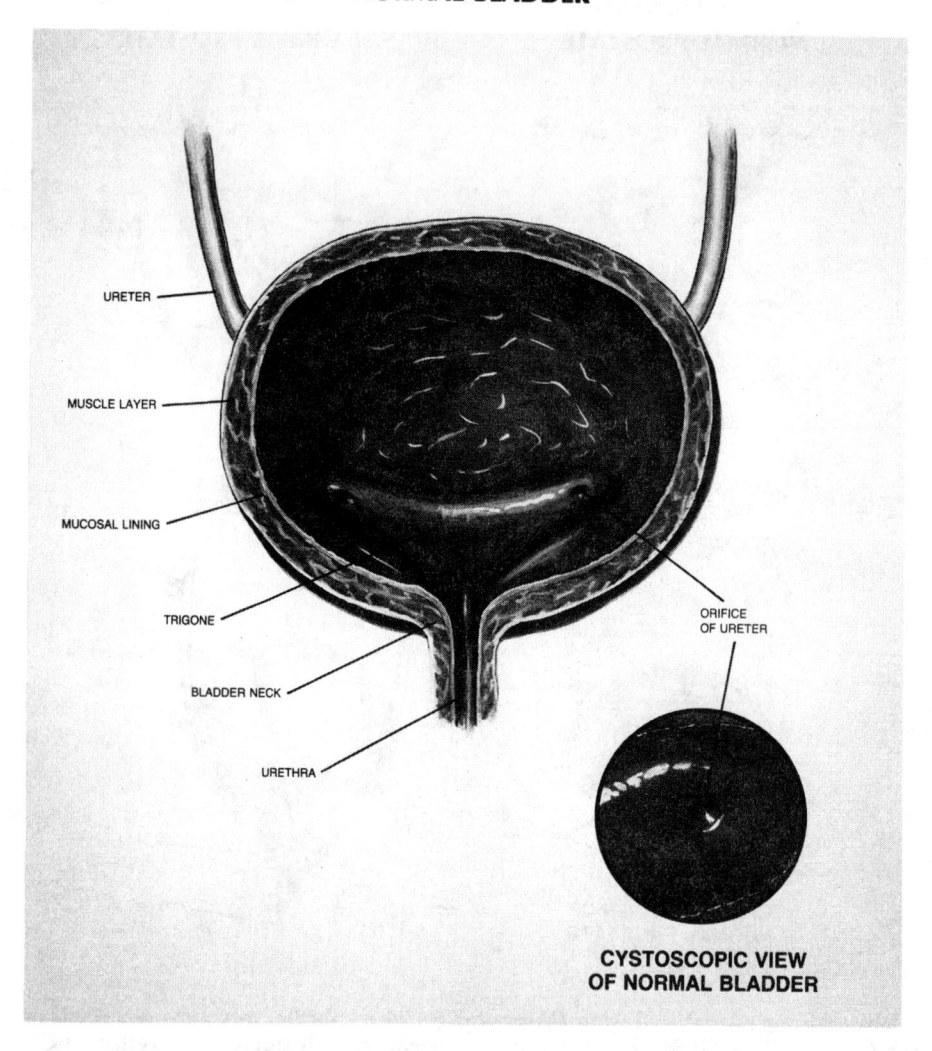

NORMAL BLADDER

CYSTOSCOPIC VIEW OF NORMAL BLADDER

Illustrations reproduced from *Illustrated Guide to Normal and Diseased Areas of the Urinary Tract* (1984). Reproduced with permission of Burroughs Wellcome Co.

Figure 5-3

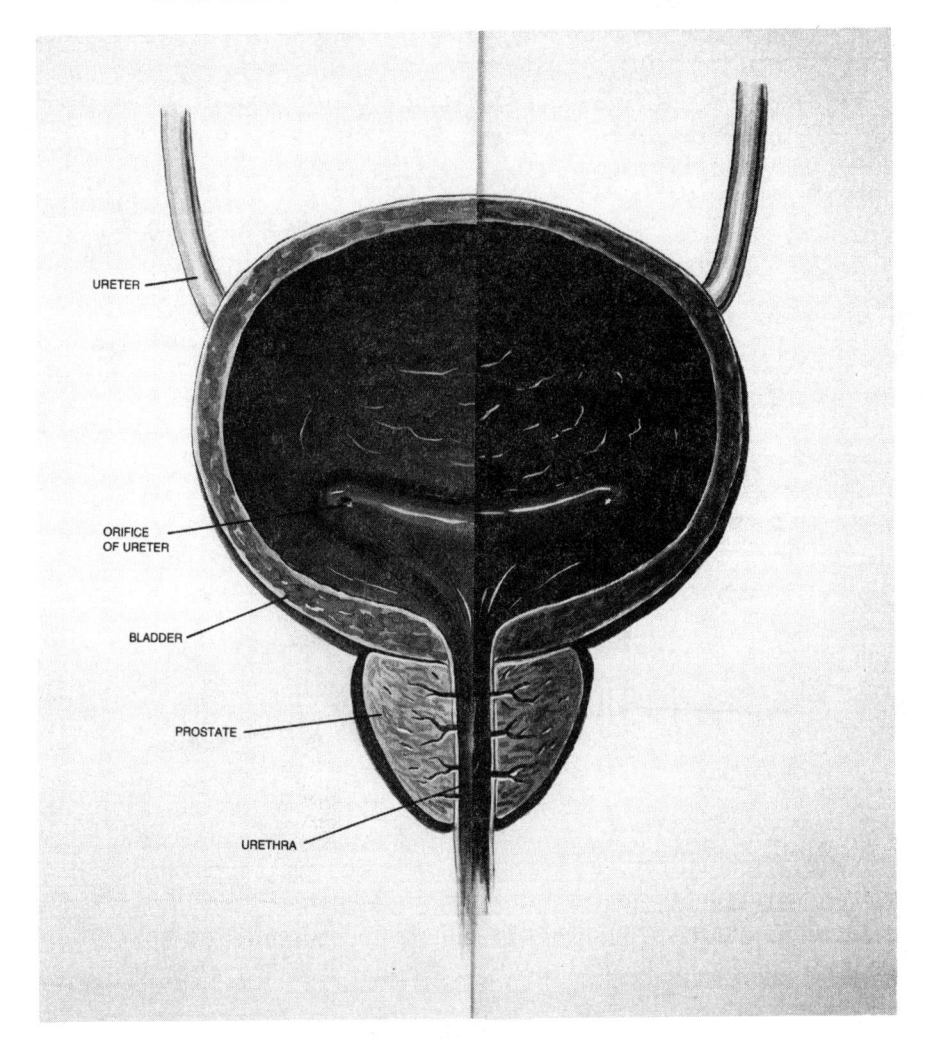

NORMAL BLADDER AND PROSTATE   **NORMAL BLADDER AND PROSTATE**

Illustrations reproduced from *Illustrated Guide to Normal and Diseased Areas of the Urinary Tract* (1984). Reproduced with permission of Burroughs Wellcome Co.

158   Anatomy, Physiology, & Tests

Figure 5-4

NORMAL KIDNEY

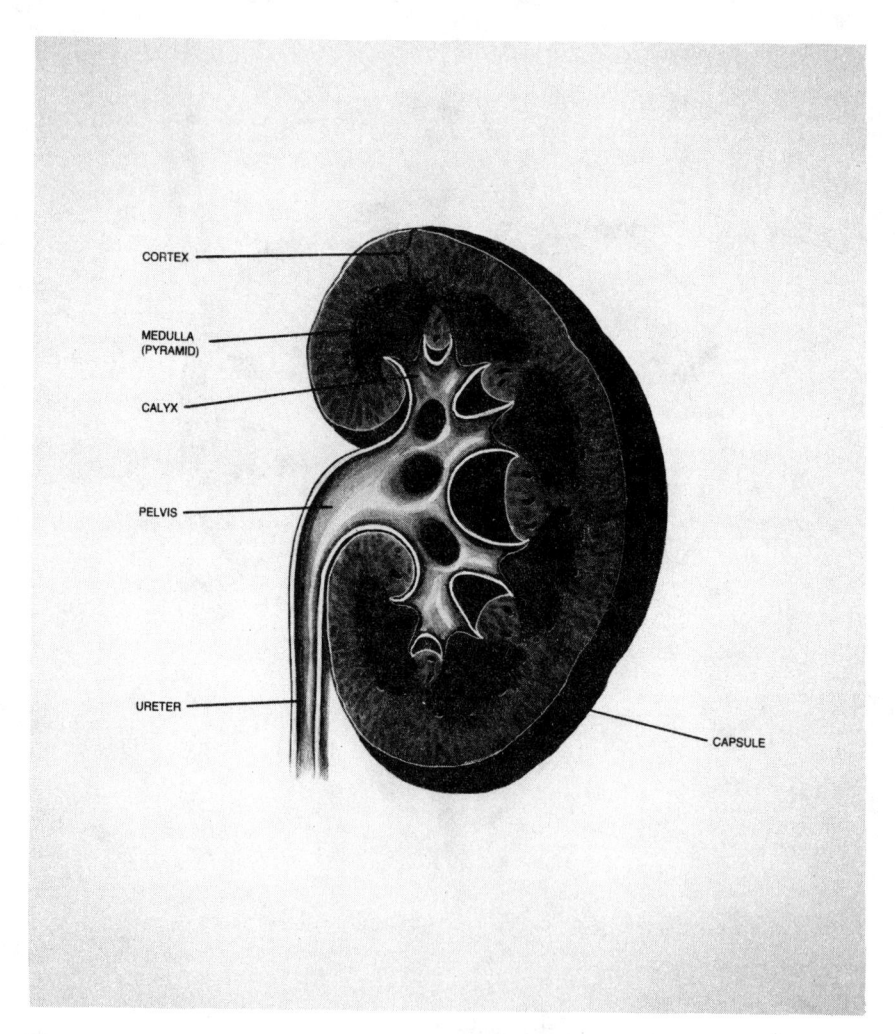

Illustrations reproduced from *Illustrated Guide to Normal and Diseased Areas of the Urinary Tract* (1984). Reproduced with permission of Burroughs Wellcome Co.

§5.32 References 159

Figure 5-5

NORMAL MALE URINARY TRACT

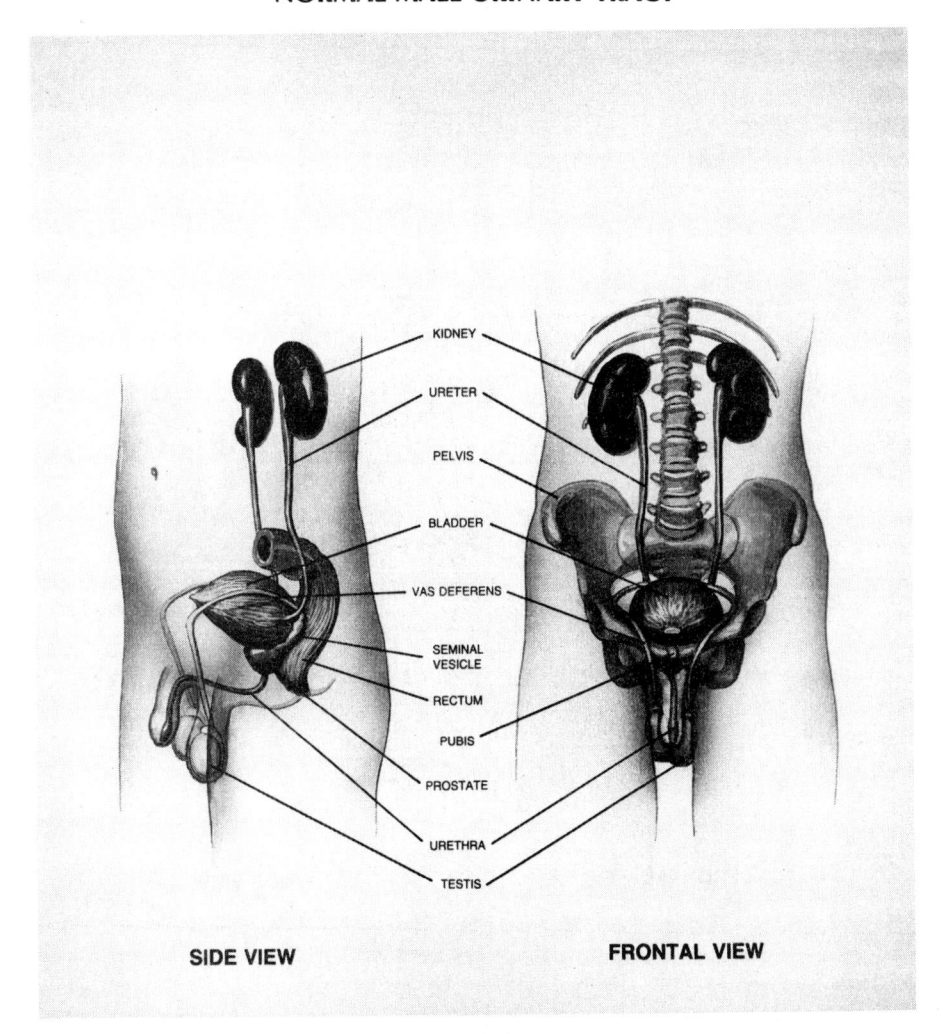

Illustrations reproduced from *Illustrated Guide to Normal and Diseased Areas of the Urinary Tract* (1984). Reproduced with permission of Burroughs Wellcome Co.

Figure 5-6

NORMAL FEMALE URINARY TRACT

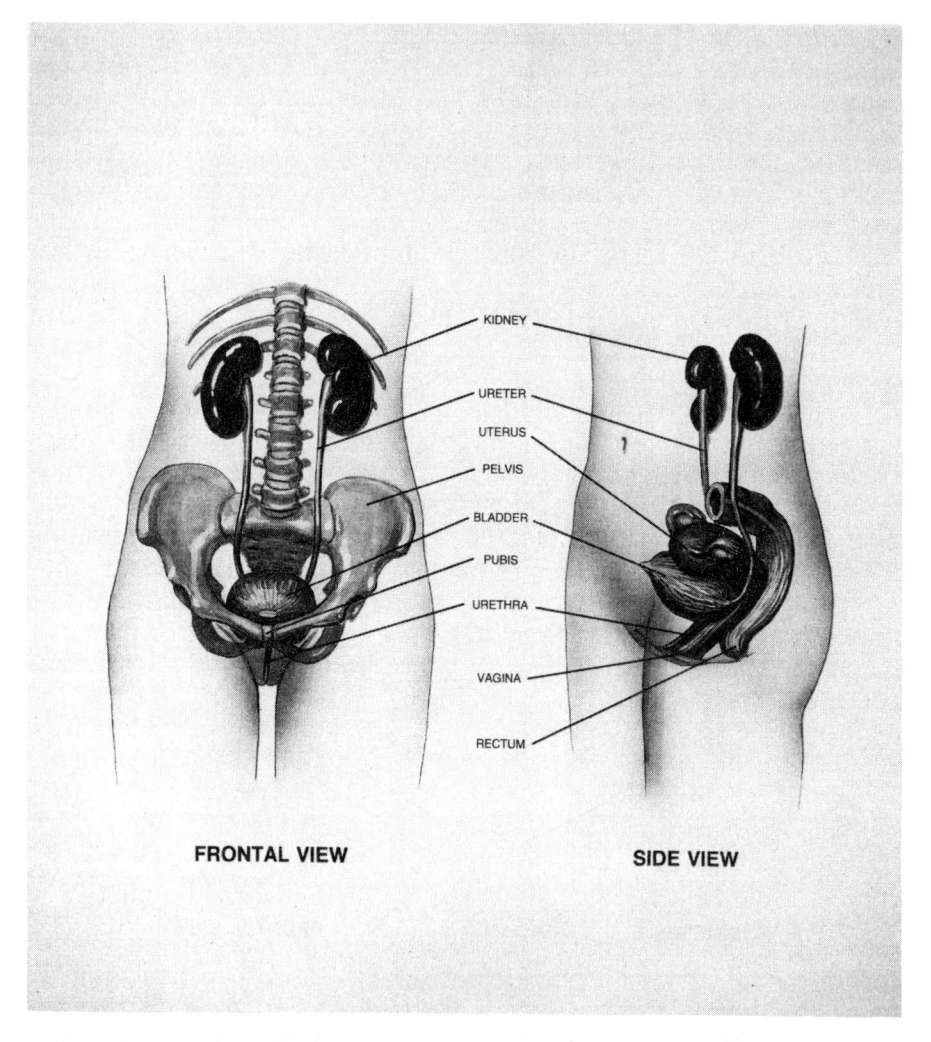

Illustrations reproduced from *Illustrated Guide to Normal and Diseased Areas of the Urinary Tract* (1984). Reproduced with permission of Burroughs Wellcome Co.

6

The Use of Instruments and Devices in Diagnosis, Evaluation, and Treatment of the Urogenital Tract

David G. McLeod, M.D., J.D., F.A.C.S.

§6.01 Introduction
§6.02 Urethral Catheters
§6.03 Ureteral Catheters
§6.04 Urethral Sounds
§6.05 Cystoscopic Instruments
§6.06 Resectoscope
§6.07 Lithotrite
§6.08 Urethrotome
§6.09 Stone Baskets and Ureteroscopes
§6.10 Biopsy Instruments
§6.11 Penile Prosthesis
Appendix 6-A   Illustrations

§6.01 Introduction

This chapter is intended to familiarize the reader with the armamentarium of instruments used by urologists in all aspects of patient care. The urologist has a vast array of instruments that he or she uses in the practice of the specialty of urology. This fact is in contradistinction to the dichotomy one often sees with reference to the practices of general surgery and gastroenterology. Not infrequently the internist (gastroenterologist) makes a diagnosis and may treat through special instruments while the general surgeon performs surgery based, in no small part, on the diagnosis having first been made by the former. The urologist, on the other hand, has retained practically all the instruments of the specialty and is actually expanding the field, both from a diagnostic and a therapeutic standpoint.

Most urological instruments are graduated according to the French (Fr.) system whereby one-third millimeter equals one French size, e.g., a number 18 Fr. catheter has a diameter of 6mm. There is a plethora of companies that manufacture urologic instruments. Bard Urological Division of C.R. Bard, Inc. has allowed us to publish a chart of an array of catheters and some other instruments (Appendix 6-A, Figure 6-1). I shall refer to numbers on the chart at times to illustrate a particular catheter or instrument.

§6.02 Urethral Catheters

The urologist is recognized as an expert in the insertion and care of urethral catheters. Catheterization is usually performed in a clinical setting with the catheter being inserted into the urethra after first being lubricated with a sterile surgical lubricant such as Surgilube[R]. In a patient who is difficult to catheterize—e.g., a male with a large prostate and/or scarred (strictured) urethra—an anesthetic jelly with xylocaine, namely Lidocaine[R], is often used if the patient has no allergic history to xylocaine. The glans penis in the male or the vestibule of the vagina and the labia in the female are first cleansed. Using a sterile technique the catheter is slowly inserted into the urethra until urine is returned from the bladder. When the catheter is not to remain in the bladder, a straight catheter (Robinson) is used for in-and-out catheterization (Figure 6-1, 0560, 0561).

If a catheter is to be left in the bladder (indwelling), a self-retaining Foley catheter (balloon catheter) is employed. Several types are shown in Figure 6-1, 0123RV, 0118V, 0165V, and 0166V. In addition to the lumen seen in a Robinson catheter, there is a smaller lumen that is filled through an external side arm on the catheter allowing the collapsed balloon to be inflated at the tip that is retained in the bladder. This type of catheter is used when the bladder has to be continually drained because of obstruction (primarily prostatic obstruction), when there is a need to monitor the urine as is the case in a number of surgical procedures, and following an operation upon the prostate such as transurethral resection of the prostate (TUR-P) or an open prostatectomy. The balloon sizes are either 5 or 30 cc., but the balloons will hold more fluid than their stated amounts. Other specialized balloon catheters are three-way irrigation catheters (Figure 6-1, 0119V, 0167V, and 0134V). These catheters have a triple lumen and can be used to irrigate the bladder continuously through a second side-arm which is attached to a container of irrigation solution by special tubing. The aforementioned catheters sometimes are manufactured with a curved tip (Coude) (Figure 6-1, 0102V, 0101), and at times this type of catheter is easier to pass by an obstructing prostate. The drainage ports of most catheters may be singular or multiple and vary in their placement at their tips, depending on the manufacturer's design.

In difficult catheterizations, the catheter may be aided in passing with the use of one or more filiform guides (Figure 6-1, 0219, 0221). These guides are made with various curved shapes at their tip to transverse urethral pockets, folds, false passages, and/or an enlarged prostate. Once one of the filiforms is felt to be within the bladder, graduated Phillips followers (Figure 6-1, 0215) are screwed into the protruding tip one at a time. Usually each can serially be passed into the obstructed urethra. The urethra is enlarged enough to ultimately allow a Foley catheter to be placed after removing the filiform with its last follower. There is a specialized Foley catheter called a Councill catheter which has a hole in the tip (Figure 6-1, 0196V). It may be placed over a filiform or over a guidewire (Figure 6-1, top left column) or else over a threaded metal stylet (Figure 6-1, 00437). The filiform, guidewire, or stylet is removed once the catheter has been advanced into the bladder. This catheter also has a Foley balloon to retain it in the bladder.

An unthreaded metal stylet or guide (Figure 6-1, 04026) is another instrument that is first sterilely lubricated. Next a Foley catheter is placed over it to give the catheter rigidity. After the catheter is placed in the bladder, the stylet is removed. This instrument is curved to fit the urethra and may be used in difficult catheterizations, but because it is metal the urologist must be careful not to push it outside the urethra (perforation). It should be noted that in the vast majority of patients it is usually the male urethra that is compromised by obstructive conditions.

The catheterization technique the urologist uses is based on his or her experience and assessment of the situation, but on occasion it may be impossible to traverse the urethra. The urologist may then resort to a suprapubic cystostomy. After injecting a local anesthetic and making a small skin incision, a trocar (Figure 6-1, 0488) may be pushed through the subcutaneous tissue and underlying muscles into the bladder. A small Foley catheter is passed through the sheath after removing the obturator. Newer suprapubic catheters with a smaller metal trocar within them have been developed—e.g., 10 Fr. Once the bladder is entered, the catheter is pushed forward as the stylet is removed. The balloon is inflated and the catheter is usually sewed to the skin. A suprapubic tube is usually a temporary measure, but occasionally there is a need for long-term or permanent urinary diversion. If a larger catheter—e.g., 22 Fr.—is needed, the tract from the bladder to the skin may be serially dilated at intervals of several days by placing the next larger size catheter in the tract. A straight stylet (Figure 6-1, 600431) may be employed to put a Malecot or Pezzer catheter in place (Figure 6-1 0640, 6090, 0650, and 0920). These catheters have special shapes, not balloons, that help them to be retained in the bladder.

Not infrequently the urologist is called upon to irrigate a urethral catheter. A Toomey syringe is a specialized syringe that fits into the external tip of the catheter (Figure 6-1, 0412). Sterile solution (usually saline) can be flushed into the bladder to dislodge and evacuate blood clots and/or tissue debris that has obstructed the outflow of urine.

§6.03 Ureteral Catheters

Small specialized catheters may be used to collect urine from one or both kidneys or to obtain a retrograde pyelogram (*see* Chapter 7). These catheters are manufactured in sizes from 4 to 8 Fr. For instance, when a stone (calculus) is lodged in a ureter, a ureteral catheter may be used to help delineate the stone. In recent years, several specialized ureteral catheters—e.g., double or single J catheters—have been developed. These catheters at the time of cystoscopy can be inserted up a ureter over a small guidewire which is subsequently removed. This placement results in the double J or pigtail configuration (Figure 6-1, 080) allowing the catheter to be retained in the kidney—one end of the double J or pigtail. The catheter thus traverses the length of the ureter with the other end remaining curled in the bladder—the second end of the double J or pigtail. With the single J catheter the straight end protrudes into the bladder. There are several different configurations that hold the catheter in place such as the "Figure Four" catheter or stent (Figure 6-1, 1884). These catheters are of different lengths, and one of these specialized catheters can be left in place in a ureter when there is obstruction secondary to stones. Not infrequently a ureteral catheter is placed when a ureter is obstructed secondary to disease, usually cancer.

Frequently in an obstructed situation when the ureteral catheter cannot be placed through the bladder, the catheter will be placed through the skin (percutaneous route) into the collecting system of the kidney. If possible it will be pushed down the ureter over a guidewire that has been manipulated under fluoroscopy down the obstructed ureter. The advantage of an indwelling ureteral catheter, whether passed percutaneously down the ureter or up the ureter through the bladder, is that a patient will not have to have the urine collected in an external bag. These specialized ureteral catheters are called stents since they are actually stenting the ureter. In this context, a ureteral stent is synonymous with an indwelling ureteral catheter.

On occasion it is not possible to traverse the ureter with a guidewire, and the catheter is left in the pelvis of the kidney called a nephrostomy "tube." Today with better localization from advanced fluoroscopy, a nephrostomy can usually be performed under fluoroscopy by the percutaneous route. In the past, nephrostomy was performed by open surgery. Before the advent of percutaneous tubes, the Malecot or Pezzer catheters (*see* §6.02) in larger French sizes were used as nephrostomy tubes. Most of these catheters are straight, although some are manufactured in a right angle configuration (Figure 6-1, 0920). Malecot catheters have flanged tips that help them be retained in the kidney. At the present time, these catheters in smaller sizes (usually in the range 10 to 22 Fr.) are used in operations on kidneys where drainage is required following some type of renal surgery—e.g., repair of drainage problems (pyeloplasty) or removal of large stones (nephrotomy). The nephrostomy tube is then attached to a connecting tube and a collecting bag which drains and collects the urine from that kidney.

Ureteral catheters have different tips, and some types are graduated in centimeters so that during insertion the urologist can gauge the distance from the ureteral opening (orifice) to the ureteral lesion in question. In general, the catheters are made with either a cone, whistle, olive, or round tip. Some examples are Figure 6-1, 1380, 0374, 0365, and 0363. There is also a Braasch Bulb ureteral catheter that is occasionally used to calibrate the size of a ureter (Figure 6-1, 6037, 0376).

Ureteral catheters, if left indwelling in a ureter, will extend from the urethral meatus alongside a urethral catheter. This technique allows quantification of urine from the stented ureter. The urethral catheter is necessary to alleviate the need of the patient to void.

§6.04 Urethral Sounds

"Sounds" are metal instruments which are also graduated according to the French system. These instruments are manufactured in sizes from 10 Fr. to 40 Fr. All sounds, especially the smaller ones which are more pointed, have the potential for tearing or perforating the urethra. Very seldom are pediatric sounds used, and the overall use of sounds is diminishing. In the past, patients with scarring of the urethra (strictures), not infrequently resulting from gonorrhea, would have their urethras dilated on a regularly scheduled basis.

The sounds, as mentioned above, have to be carefully inserted, usually starting with one in the 16 to 18 Fr. range and increasing to around 24 Fr. in size. Chronic urethral strictures are not as common today since the advent of better surgical and endoscopic treatment of strictures, and due to more effective antibiotic therapy for gonorrhea.

The most common metal sounds are Van Buren urethral sounds. An example of a similar sound by Bard is shown on the chart (Appendix 6-A, Figure 6-1, 6049). There are also specialized LeFort sounds which are threaded allowing them to be screwed onto the end of filiforms (*see* §6.02) used to dilate a narrowed/scarred urethra. Shorter graduated urethral sounds are used for dilation of the female urethra—e.g., Wather and McCray models, the latter seen in Figure 6-1, 6042.

There is also an instrument called Bougies-A-Boules, which is a special type of sound that has graduated acorn-tipped ends (Figure 6-1, 0485). This instrument can be used to estimate the size of the urethral opening (meatus), especially in the female urethra. In the recent past, this type of sound was frequently used to test for urethral narrowing (stenosis), but the use of this instrument has diminished since not much credence is being given to the term "urethral stenosis" especially in female children. The Bougies-A-Boules may still be used to calibrate the size of the urethra during open surgical repair of a stricture.

§6.05 Cystoscopic Instruments

Cystoscopy is performed for diagnosis and treatment of diseases of the bladder. Urethroscopy (examination of the urethra) is also carried out at the same time, and cystourethroscopy is the more correct term. Most patients easily tolerate a diagnostic examination with a cystoscope using only an anesthetic jelly, although some patients require sedation. Others may require general or spinal anesthesia, especially when an operative procedure is to be undertaken.

Cystourethroscope

Of all instruments used in urology, the cystoscope is the one that epitomizes the field of urology. It is this instrument that enables the urologist to examine and treat lesions of the urethra and bladder. The ureter, and even some lesions of the kidney, can be examined with specialized instruments passed through the cystoscope. However, the cystoscope is used primarily to examine the lower tract—bladder and urethra.

The three basic components of the cystoscope are a sheath with obturator (several sizes), a bridge (different styles), and a telescope (variety of viewing angles) with a light source (Appendix 6-A, Figures 6-2 and 6-3). Older cystoscopes were the Brown-Bruger and Wappler models, but the McCarthy Panendoscope is the standard instrument where different angled lenses are used to examine the bladder (Figure 6-4). Cystoscopes are manufactured by several companies. The leading companies are American Cystoscope Manufacturers Inc., Olympus, and Wolfe. All these instruments are basically the same, but all have some minor though unique features.

There are usually two irrigation ports on the sheath which will allow fluid (sterile saline or water) to enter and distend the bladder. This distention allows the urologist to view the bladder using the different angled lenses. In males, the urethra is usually visualized as the instrument is inserted into the bladder. In the female, the sheath is usually passed with the obturator in it. The obturator is subsequently removed and the bladder is examined with the telescope within the sheath (Figure 6-4). As the urologist removes the cystoscope, the urethra is visualized. The bridge connects the telescope to the sheath and has one or two ports through which various instruments may be inserted. It is through these ports that urethral catheters are passed by direct vision up the ureters.

Biopsies of the bladder may be performed using either "cold cup" or "alligator" forceps (Figure 6-5, D, F). The former's name is derived from the cup-like configuration of the forceps. "Cold" refers to the fact that an electrical current is not used as in a resection of the prostate. "Alligator" refers to the jaw-like configuration of that type of biopsy forceps. These biopsies can usually be performed with the patient awake. Occasionally anesthetic jelly may be instilled into the bladder, and the biopsy can be made under this "local anesthesia." Other specialized instruments (Figure 6-5, A, B, C, E) may be used through the cystoscope.

In the past several years, a flexible cystoscope has been developed and refined (Figures 6-6 and 6-7). This type of cystoscope is being used more as urologists gain experience with it, especially in a routine cystoscopic procedure where the patient does not undergo general or spinal anesthesia. The standard metal cystourethroscope is still the instrument most widely used by the practicing urologist today. Various instruments may also be passed through the flexible cystoscope.

§6.06 Resectoscope

The more correct term for this instrument might be the electroresectoscope because of the loop-shaped electrode made of fine wire—usually tungsten. As with other instruments, various manufacturers make modifications of the instrument although all have a measure of similarity. One type of resectoscope is seen in Appendix 6-A, Figure 6-8.

The sheath for the instrument is made of either an insulating material (Bakelite) or metal. The metal sheaths have a Teflon coating which helps prevent transfer of high frequency current induced by the cutting loop. Sheaths are available in three sizes—20, 24, and 28 Fr. The external end, as in the panendoscope, has a port for irrigation and also a mechanism for locking the electrode into the instrument. All sheaths have an obturator which allows the sheath to be passed through the urethra. The obturator can be straight or hinged at the bladder end. Unless a specialized viewing obturator is used, the surgeon first examines the bladder and urethra with a cystoscope to make sure no lesion is present in either area. The resectoscope also consists of a telescope and a cutting loop control mechanism. It is with the latter that the cutting loop is projected and withdrawn removing a portion of prostate called a "chip" (Figure 6-9). Prostatic chips are irrigated out of the bladder through the sheath either by a Toomey syringe or another specialized instrument known as an Ellik evacuator. Also, after resection of one or more bladder tumors (transurethral resection of bladder tumor—TUR-BT), the tissue is removed as in a TUR-P. There is also a fiber-optic light source for the resectoscope as with the cystoscope. On both instruments, this light source receptacle is on the telescope. Finally, there is a diathermy unit located on the cutting loop control mechanism. Both cutting and coagulation are carried out with the cutting loop. Less current is used in TUR-BTs due to the possibility of cutting through the bladder wall. Biopsies can be made with the cutting loop of areas of the bladder that are suspicious for cancer.

§6.07 Lithotrite

This older instrument was used to crush stones (calculi) in the bladder. For all practical purposes, it has been discarded due to the ability to perform litholapaxy (fragmentation of calculi by electrohydrolic pressure waves, ultrasound, or laser). This instrument has a jaw-like device for crushing a calculus in the bladder (Appendix 6-A, Figure 6-10). After insertion through the urethra, the instrument was moved in the bladder until it was felt to touch the calculus. A later version employed a telescope for visualization. The fragmented calculus was then washed out with a Toomey syringe or Ellik evacuator.

§6.08 Urethrotome

A urethrotome is an instrument which is used to incise the urethra. It is usually used for treatment of stricture disease, and there are two types. The first, an Otis Urethrotome, is placed in the urethra with a filiform tip attached. Once the instrument is proximal to the strictured area, a dial on the handle is turned to the desired French setting, and a rounded blade that has been elevated to the desired setting is pulled through the strictured areas. The second type is a direct vision urethrotome. The strictures can be visualized through the telescope and then incised under direct vision. After incision of the strictures, a Foley catheter is left indwelling for a period of time which varies with the urologist.

§6.09 Stone Baskets and Ureteroscopes

These instruments when closed are similar in size to urethral catheters. The handle allows metal filaments to open and to snare stones. Several examples are shown in Appendix 6-A, Figure 6-1, two of which are seen in numbers 039040 and 039045. These baskets can be passed blindly, but it is preferable to watch them go up a ureter with fluoroscopy. Once the closed basket is above the calculus it is opened by its handle and slowly withdrawn until it hopefully snares the calculus (Figures 6-11, 6-12 and 6-13). These instruments are only effective on smaller calculi—usually less than one centimeter. It is usually more advantageous to pass a ureteroscope up the ureter so that the stone can be manipulated under direct vision. For large calculi, special instruments can be placed up the ureter inside the ureteroscope to fragment a calculus. Prior to passing the rigid instruments, it is necessary to dilate the opening of the ureter into the bladder—the intramural portion and meatus with a special balloon (Figure 6-1, top right column). There are two specialized probes that can be used to fragment calculi in the ureter. The first is an ultrasonic one which fragments the calculus by vibrations when the probe is placed on the calculus. An electrohydraulic probe can also be used, but it is felt that this instrument might damage the ureter, and it is not generally used. This probe is used mainly for fragmenting bladder calculi.

Ureteroscopes are either rigid or flexible. Although vision is not as great an advantage of the flexible scope, there is less likelihood to push through the ureter (perforation). The rigid ureteroscope is manufactured in sizes 9, 11, and 13 French while the flexible scope is approximately 8.5 Fr. The flexible ureteroscope looks like a minature flexible cystoscope (Figure 6-14). Laser filiments are also being used to fragment ureteral calculi and may be passed up either of these ureteroscopes.

§6.10 Biopsy Instruments

With the high incidence of prostate cancer, the urologist frequently biopsies the prostate. When on digital examination of the prostate a suspicious area is discerned, a needle is inserted into the gland guided either through the anus by the index finger to the suspicious area (transrectal) or below the scrotum (transperineal) where the needle is inserted into the prostate and felt to be within the gland by a finger in the rectum. There are proponents of both routes.

The transrectal approach is felt to be somewhat more accurate for smaller lesions, but it carries a higher risk of infection than the transperineal route. The latter route is usually performed under a local anesthetic. Although implantation of tumor cells has been reported with the transperineal route, this implantation is rare. A core of tissue is removed (16 G needle). Several cores may be taken and some slight bleeding (hematuria) is a common finding following a biopsy by either route. If bleeding is severe, urinary retention due to clots forming in the bladder may be seen. An enema should be given prior to biopsy, and an antimicrobial drug is usually administered, especially if the urologist utilizes the transrectal route.

Another technique frequently used in Europe which has gained some proponents in this country is the fine needle aspiration biopsy. A very fine needle is used to suck (aspirate) cells from the prostate. This technique is usually devoid of complications, but the main drawback is that it takes a very well-trained person (cytologist) in prostatic aspirations to make a reliable diagnosis.

More frequently, especially with the advent of rectal ultrasonography, a spring-loaded "gun" is utilized. This automatic Biopty[R] instrument is made by Bard and now by several other manufacturers. Due to its rapid removal of the core of tissue (less traumatic) and the smaller size of the needle (18 G), the complication rate is lower even though most of these biopsies are performed transrectally. An oral antimicrobial is recommended prior to biopsy. More and more urologists are using the Biopty[R] instrument, and it seems to be rapidly replacing the larger needle biopsy. The Biopty[R] instrument is frequently used without ultrasound in those cases where the lesion seems obvious on digital rectal examination.

§6.11 Penile Prosthesis

A penile prosthesis is a paired, surgically implanted device that allows an impotent man to have an erection sufficient for sexual intercourse. Penile prostheses have evolved over the past 50 years once suitable biocompatible materials were developed, and the devices were paired and were made rigid enough for penetration. Numerous types of prostheses have been designed. There are three basic types at the present time: (1) the semi-rigid rod (remember that a given prosthesis is actually paired—one rod/cylinder in each corpus cavernosum); (2) the inflatable penile prosthesis; and (3) the self-contained prosthesis.

The semi-rigid prosthesis produces a permanent erection that can be positioned up or down so that it is not very noticeable. This type is the easiest to implant and has no mechanical component to malfunction. The names of the different types and the manufacturers are as follows: Small-Carrion,

Mentor Malleable, Flexirod[R], and Flexirod II[R] (Surgitek); Jonas[R] (Bard); Omniphase[R] and Duraphase[R] (Dacomed); and AMS Malleable 600[R] (American Medical Systems) (Appendix 6-A, Figures 6-15 and 6-16).

The inflatable prosthesis consists of either two or three parts connected by tubing. In the three-part prosthesis, there are the following: a spherical reservoir, a pair of cylinders, and a pump. The reservoir is surgically placed under the muscles of the lower abdomen, each cylinder is placed in each corpus cavernosum, and the pump is placed in the scrotum. In a two-piece inflatable prosthesis, the reservoir and pump have been combined into the "resipump," which is placed in the scrotum. The two-piece prosthesis is, in reality, "one-piece" since the components are connected at the factory.

The AMS 700 CX[R] prosthesis (Figures 6-17 and 6-18) and the Mentor Inflatable prosthesis are two types of the three-component prostheses. Mentor also makes a two-component model (GFS[R]), as does Surgitek (Uniflate[R]). The inflatable prosthesis is able to expand the girth of the penis and becomes rigid, but when deflated gives a more natural flaccid prosthesis.

The self-contained prosthesis consists of two cylinders, each with its own reservoir and pump. The cylinders are inserted into the shaft of the penis as is the semi-rigid type. The two types are the AMS Hydroflex (Figures 6-18 and 6-20) and the Flexi-Flate[R] (Surgitek). This type of prosthesis is an attempt to combine the simplicity of insertion of the semi-rigid prosthesis with the more natural appearance of the inflatable prosthesis.

All prostheses require surgery to be implanted. There is always the risk of a mechanical malfunction, although all prostheses are becoming more reliable. Most are made of silicone, although the Mentor inflatable prosthesis is made of bioflex polyurethane, which is another type of biocompatible material.

A relatively new device is the vaccuum constrictor system consisting of a cylinder which is placed over the penis, a vacuum pump which is used to draw air out of the cylinder, and a constriction band which is used to hold blood within the penis (Figure 6-21). The constricting band is placed over the cylinder, which is then placed over the flaccid (resting) penis. Upon operation of the pump, air is drawn out of the cylinder causing blood to flow into the penis.

When sufficient blood has entered the penis, engorgement and rigidity will result. At this point, the constriction band is guided from the cylinder to encircle the base of the penis, the vacuum is released and the cylinder is removed. An erection-like state, adequate for vaginal penetration, should be maintained as long as a properly fitted constriction band is in place. This device is another example of the ongoing development of newer instruments and devices in the field of urology.

A practicing urologist must have a working knowledge of all the instruments discussed in this chapter. If the urologist is confining his or her practice to only a segment of urology, then his or her expertise with those specialized instruments will naturally be greater in that area.

Appendix 6-A Illustrations

The author wishes to thank the following manufacturers for permission to publish pictures of their products.

Figure 6-1—Courtesy of Bard Urological Division of C.R. Bard, Inc., Covington, Georgia.

Figures 6-2 to 6-14—American ACMI Division of American Hospital Supply Corporation, Stamford, Connecticut.

Figures 6-15 to 6-20—Courtesy of American Medical Systems, Inc., Minnetonka, Minnesota. Medical illustrations by Michael Schenk.

Figure 6-21—Courtesy of Smith-Collins Pharmaceutical Inc., West Chester, Pennsylvania.

172   Instruments & Devices

Figure 6-1

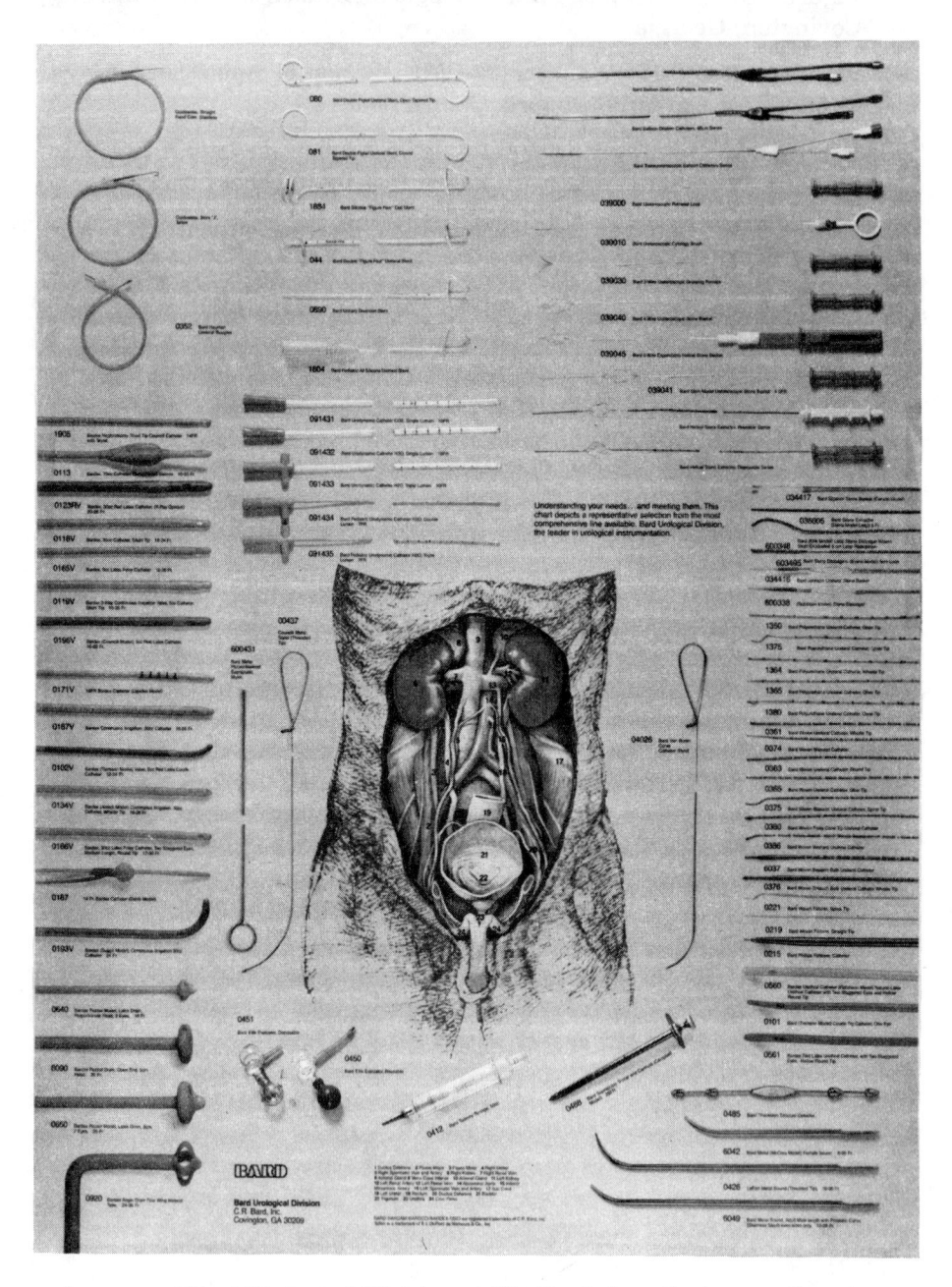

Courtesy of Bard Urological Division of C.R. Bard, Inc., Covington, Georgia.

Figure 6-2

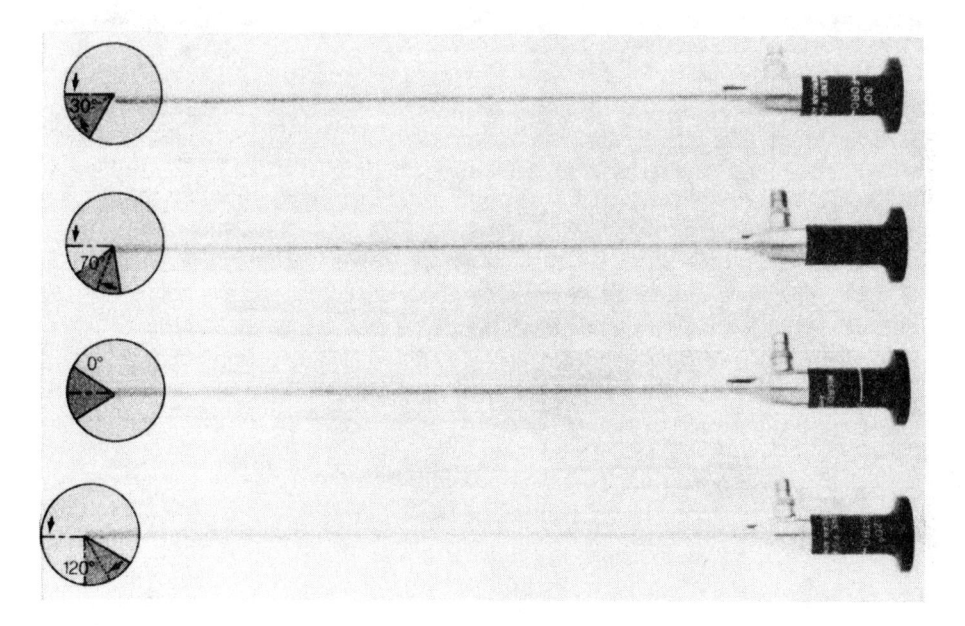

Courtesy of American ACMI Division of American Hospital Supply Corporation, Stamford, Connecticut.

174   Instruments & Devices

Figure 6-3

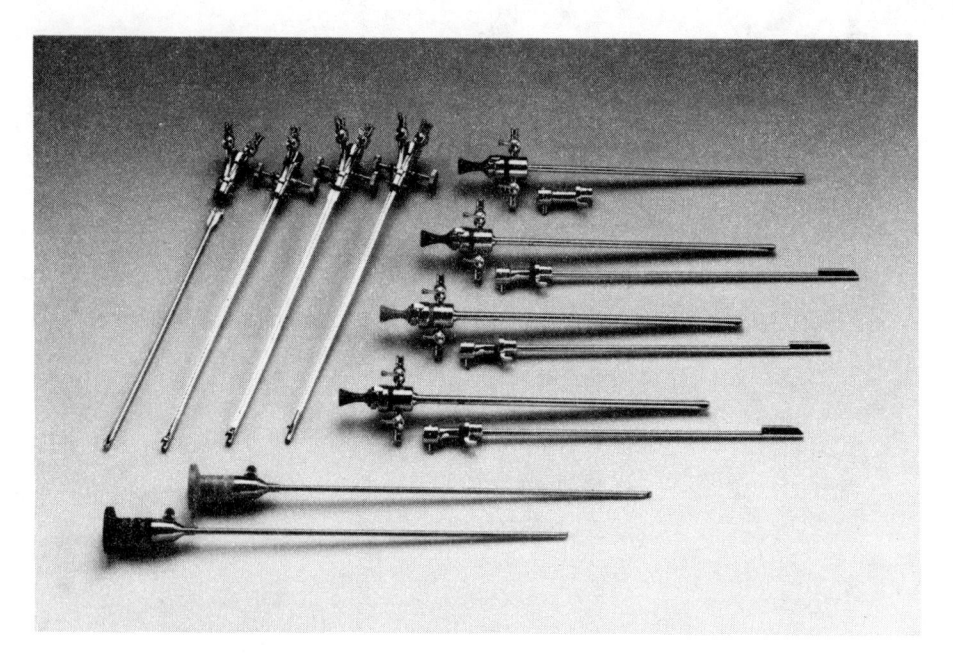

Courtesy of American ACMI Division of American Hospital Supply Corporation, Stamford, Connecticut.

Figure 6-4

Courtesy of American ACMI Division of American Hospital Supply Corporation, Stamford, Connecticut.

176   Instruments & Devices

Figure 6-5

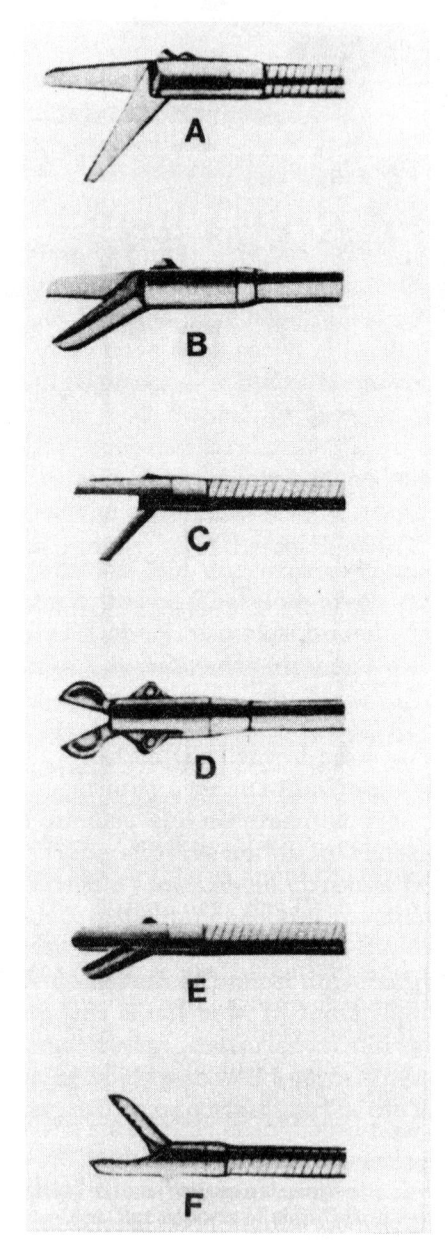

Courtesy of American ACMI Division of American Hospital Supply Corporation, Stamford, Connecticut.

Figure 6-6

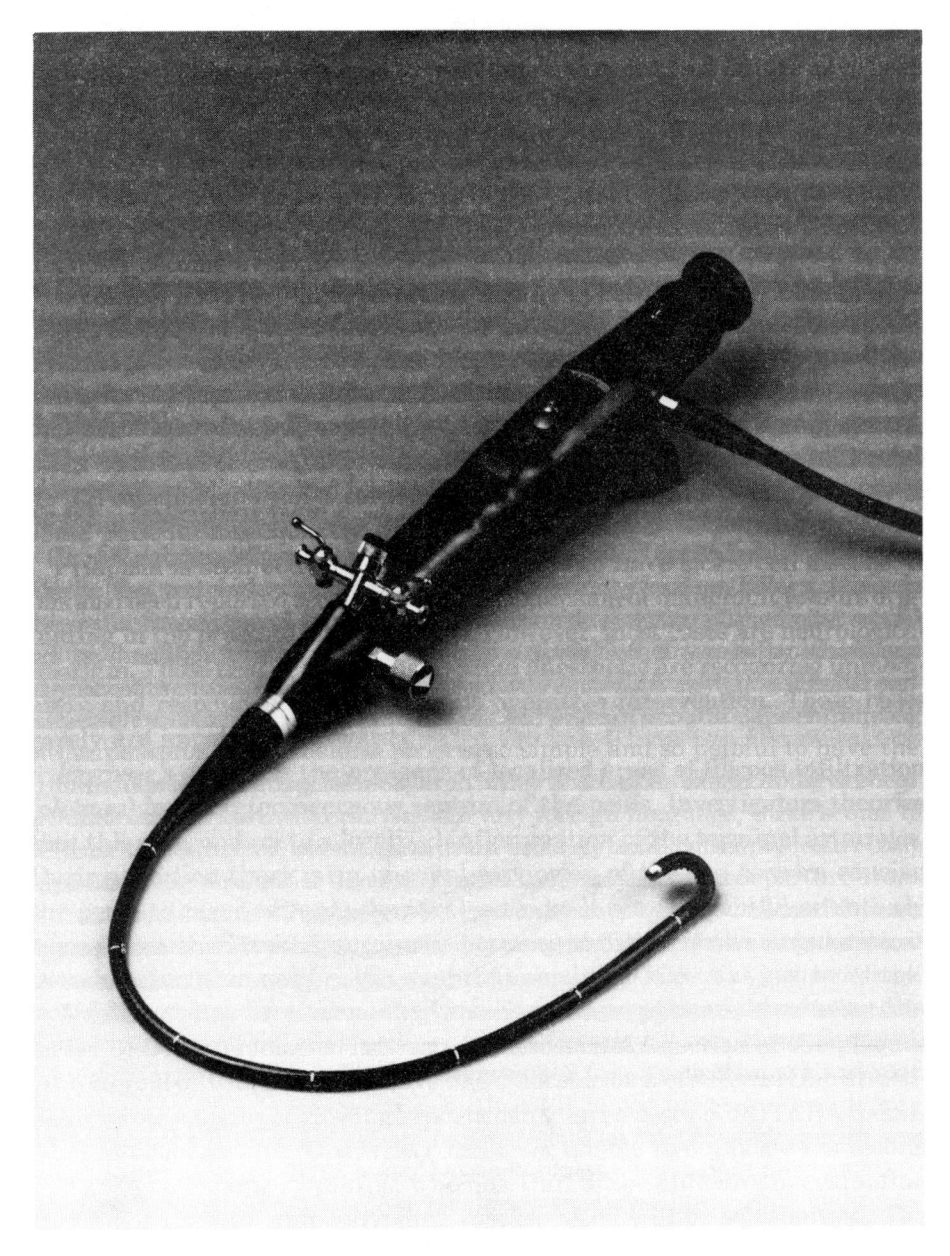

Courtesy of American ACMI Division of American Hospital Supply Corporation, Stamford, Connecticut.

178   *Instruments & Devices*

Figure 6-7

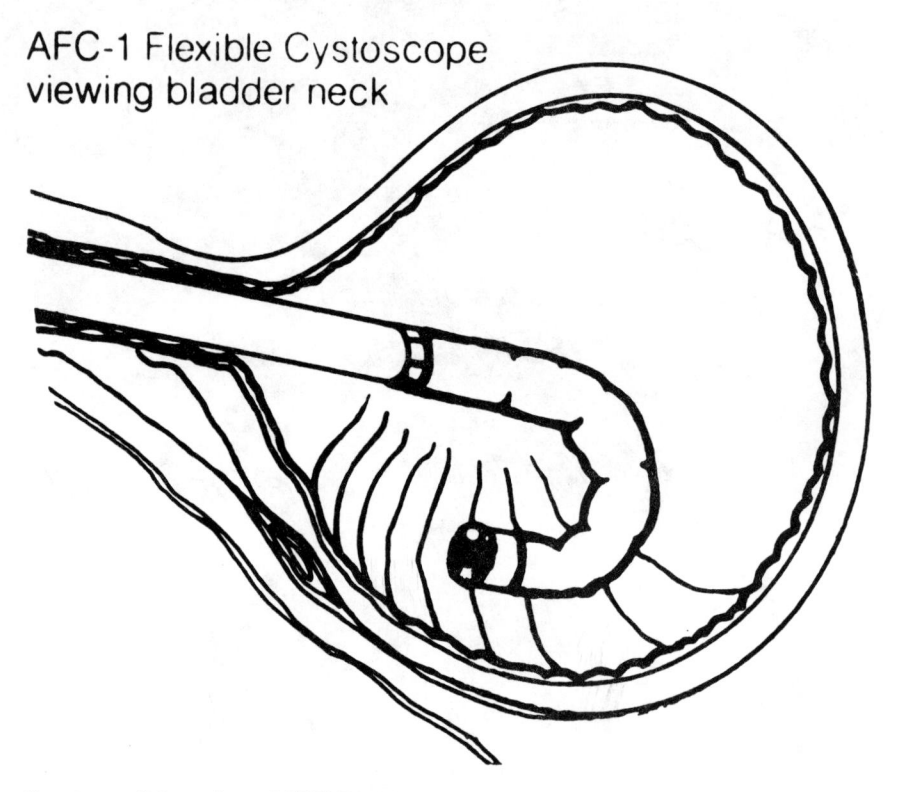

AFC-1 Flexible Cystoscope viewing bladder neck

Courtesy of American ACMI Division of American Hospital Supply Corporation, Stamford, Connecticut.

Appendix 6-A 179

Figure 6-8

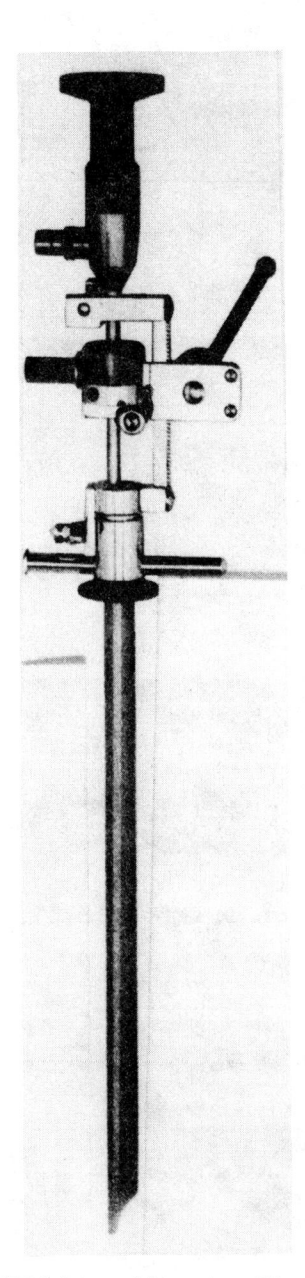

Courtesy of American ACMI Division of American Hospital Supply Corporation, Stamford, Connecticut.

180   Instruments & Devices

Figure 6-9

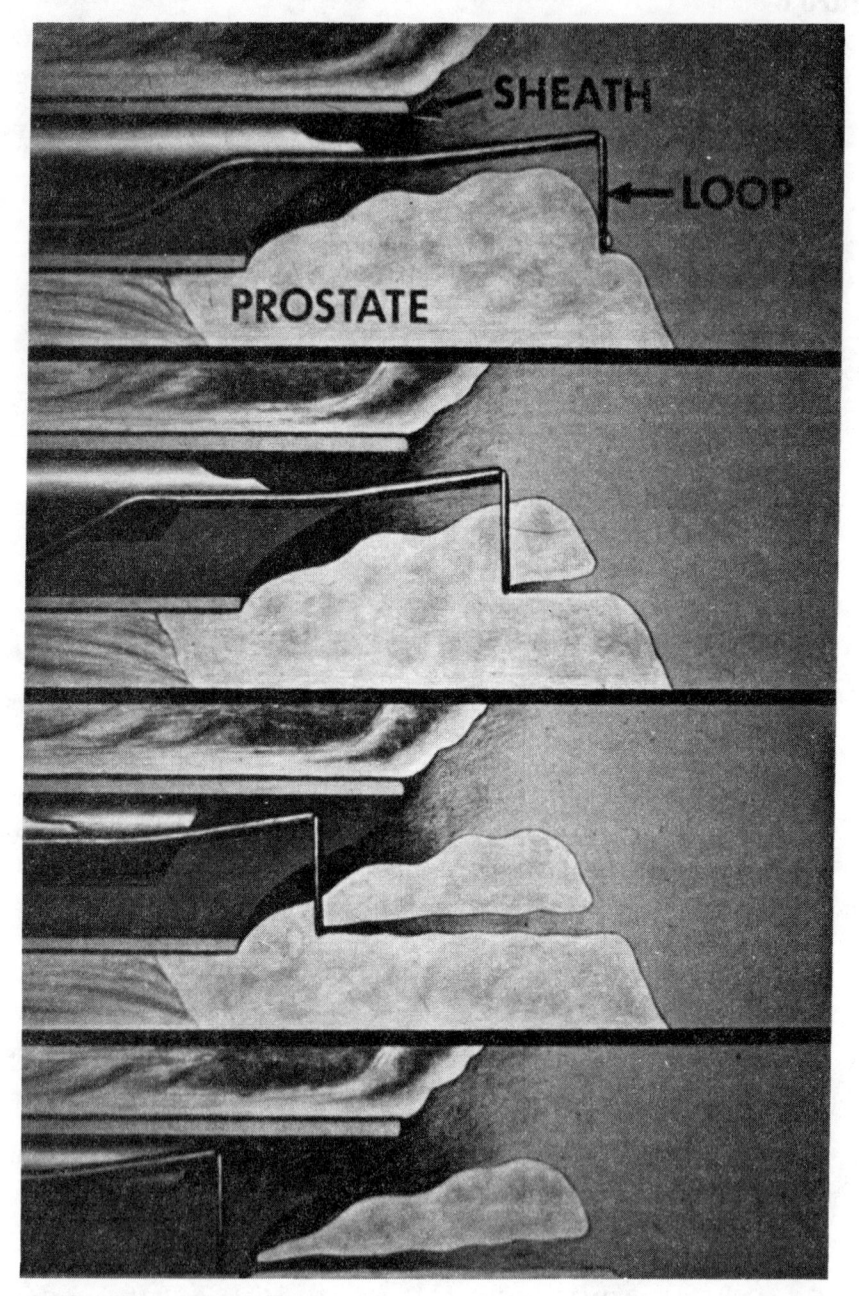

Courtesy of American ACMI Division of American Hospital Supply Corporation, Stamford, Connecticut.

Appendix 6-A   181

Figure 6-10

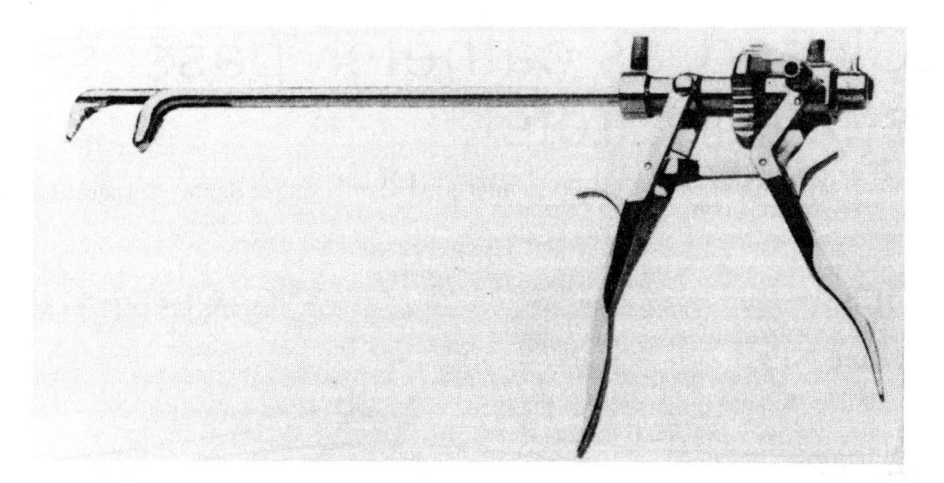

Courtesy of American ACMI Division of American Hospital Supply Corporation, Stamford, Connecticut.

Figure 6-11

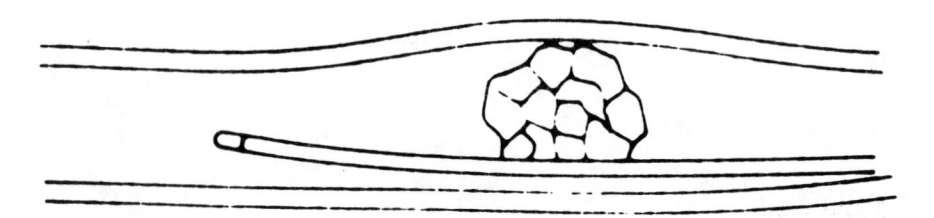

Closed, as catheter, passes stone in ureter;

Courtesy of American ACMI Division of American Hospital Supply Corporation, Stamford, Connecticut.

Figure 6-12

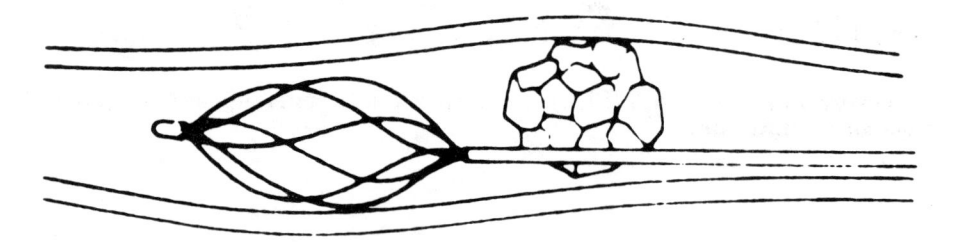

Basket is opened;

Courtesy of American ACMI Division of American Hospital Supply Corporation, Stamford, Connecticut.

Figure 6-13

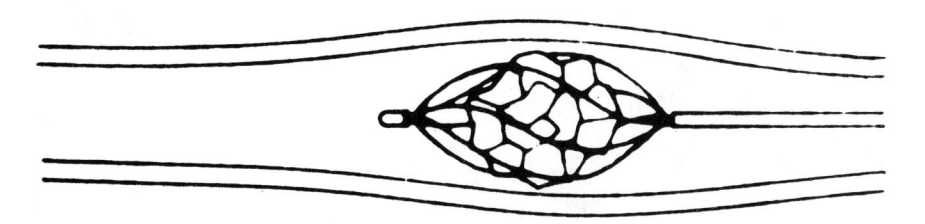

Basket is simultaneously rotated and withdrawn, entrapping stone.

Courtesy of American ACMI Division of American Hospital Supply Corporation, Stamford, Connecticut.

184   *Instruments & Devices*

Figure 6-14

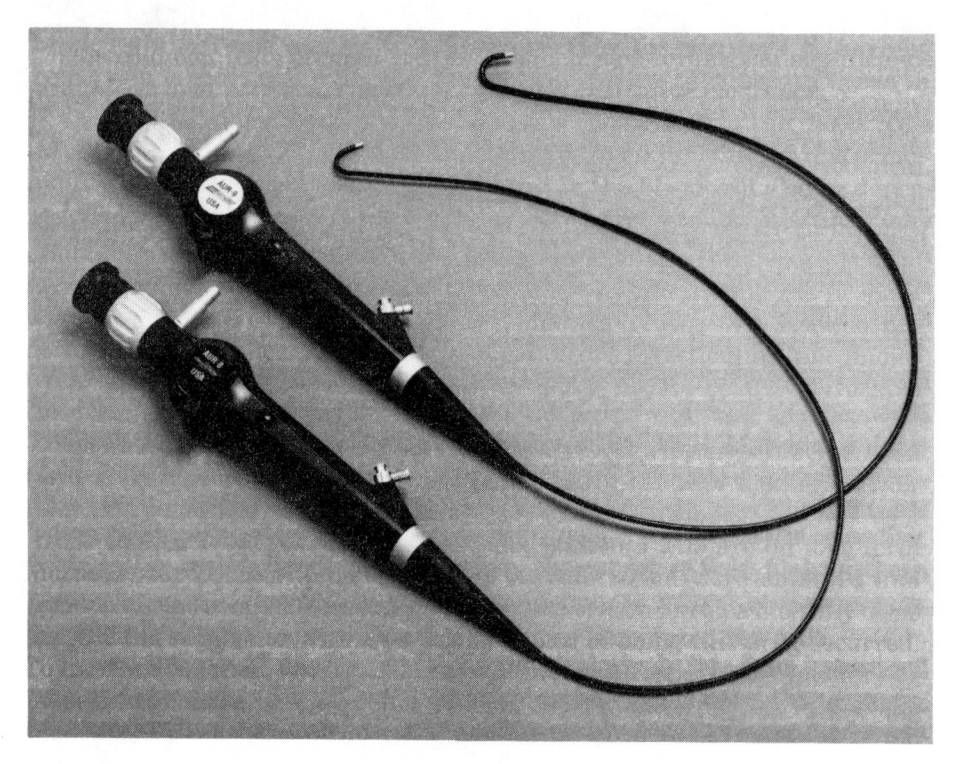

Courtesy of American ACMI Division of American Hospital Supply Corporation, Stamford, Connecticut.

Appendix 6-A 185

Figure 6-15

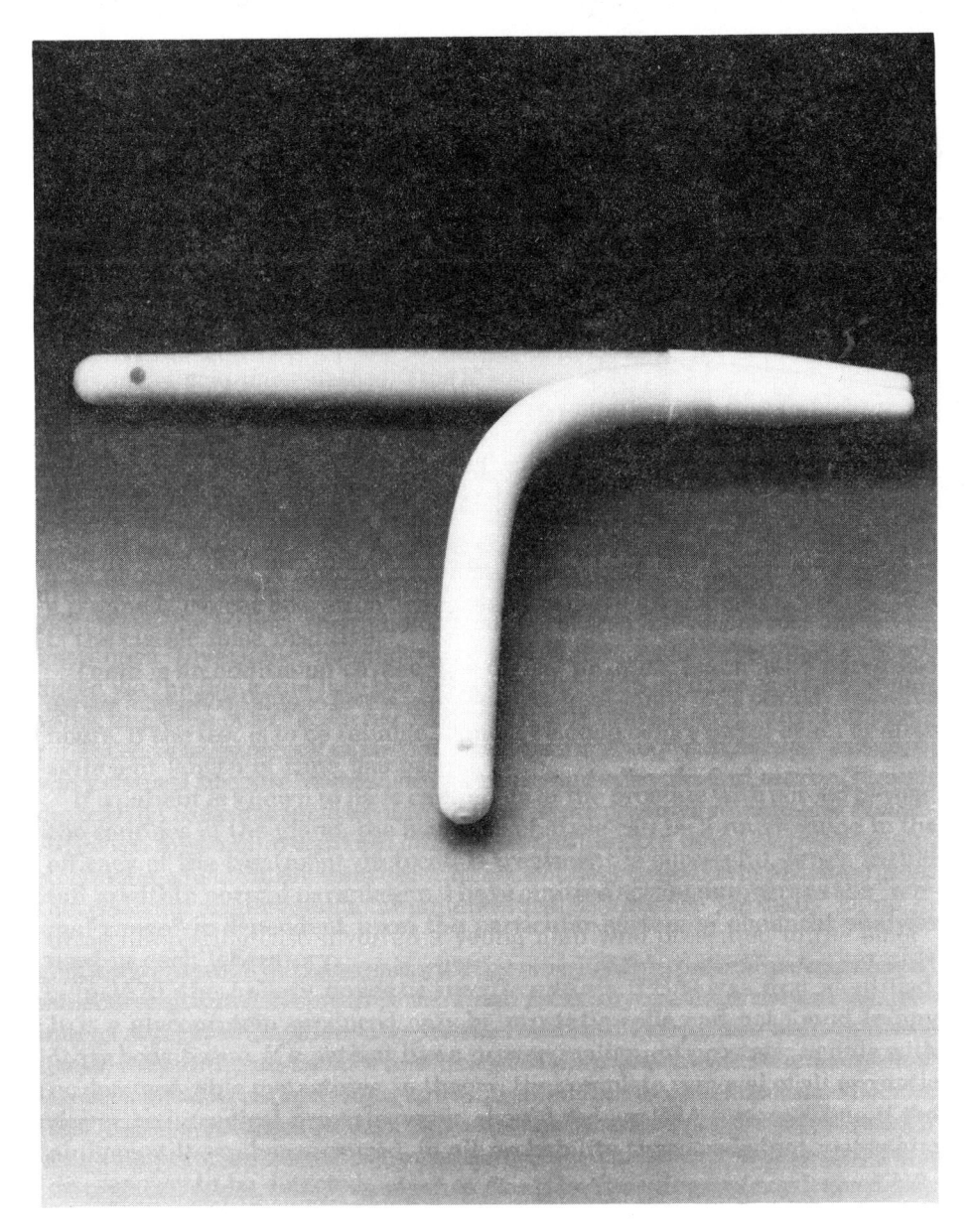

Courtesy of American Medical Systems, Inc., Minnetonka, Minnesota. Medical illustrations by Michael Schenk.

Figure 6-16

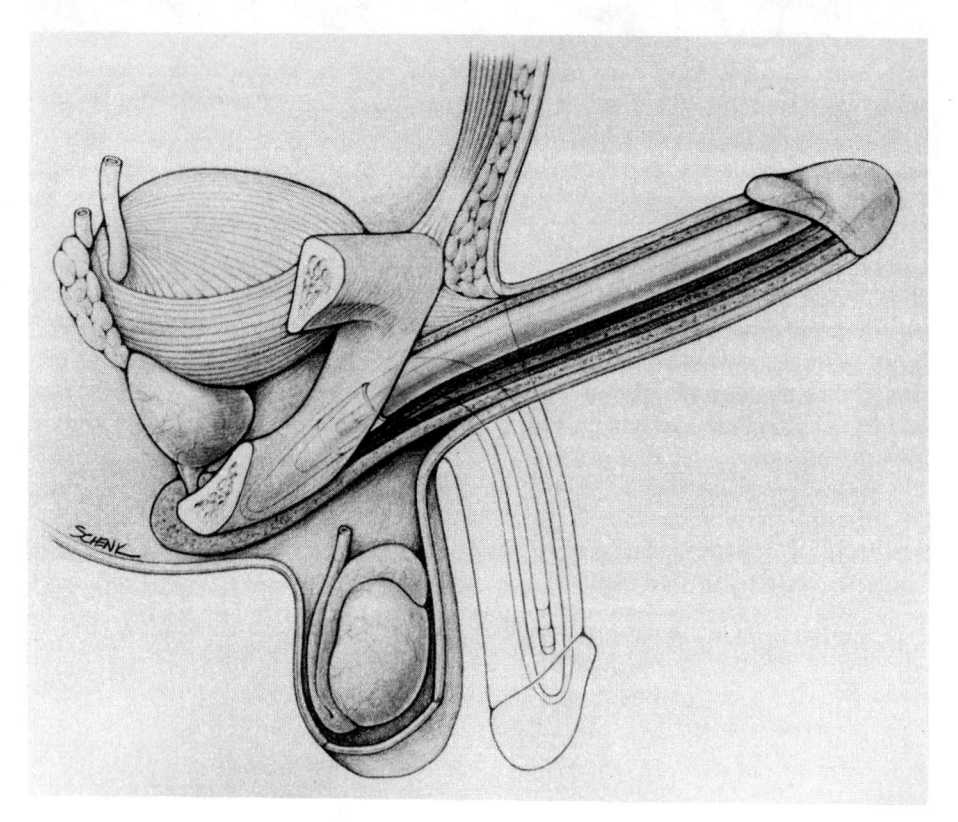

Courtesy of American Medical Systems, Inc., Minnetonka, Minnesota. **Medical illustrations by Michael Schenk.**

Appendix 6-A 187

Figure 6-17

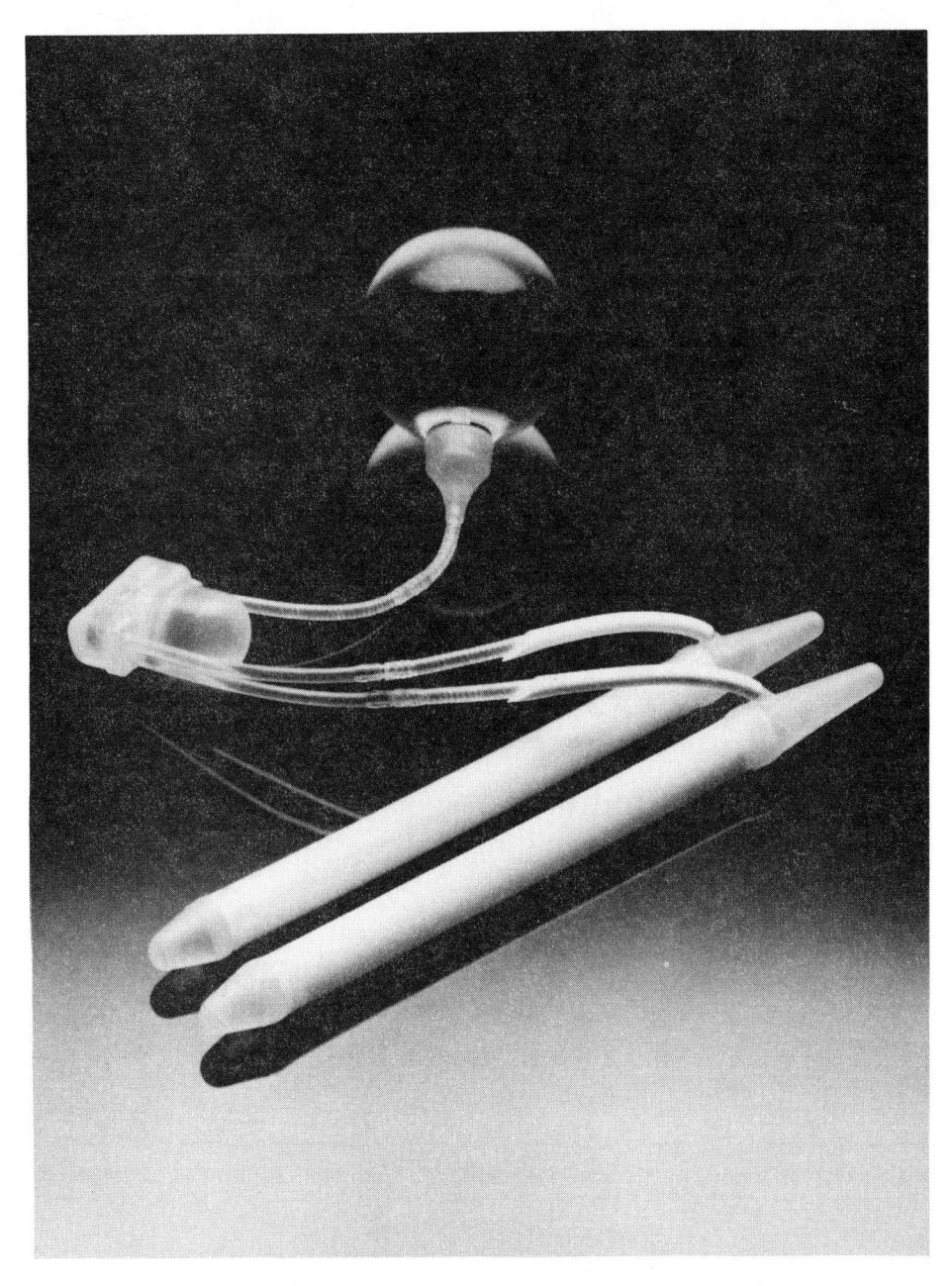

Courtesy of American Medical Systems, Inc., Minnetonka, Minnesota. Medical illustrations by Michael Schenk.

Figure 6-18

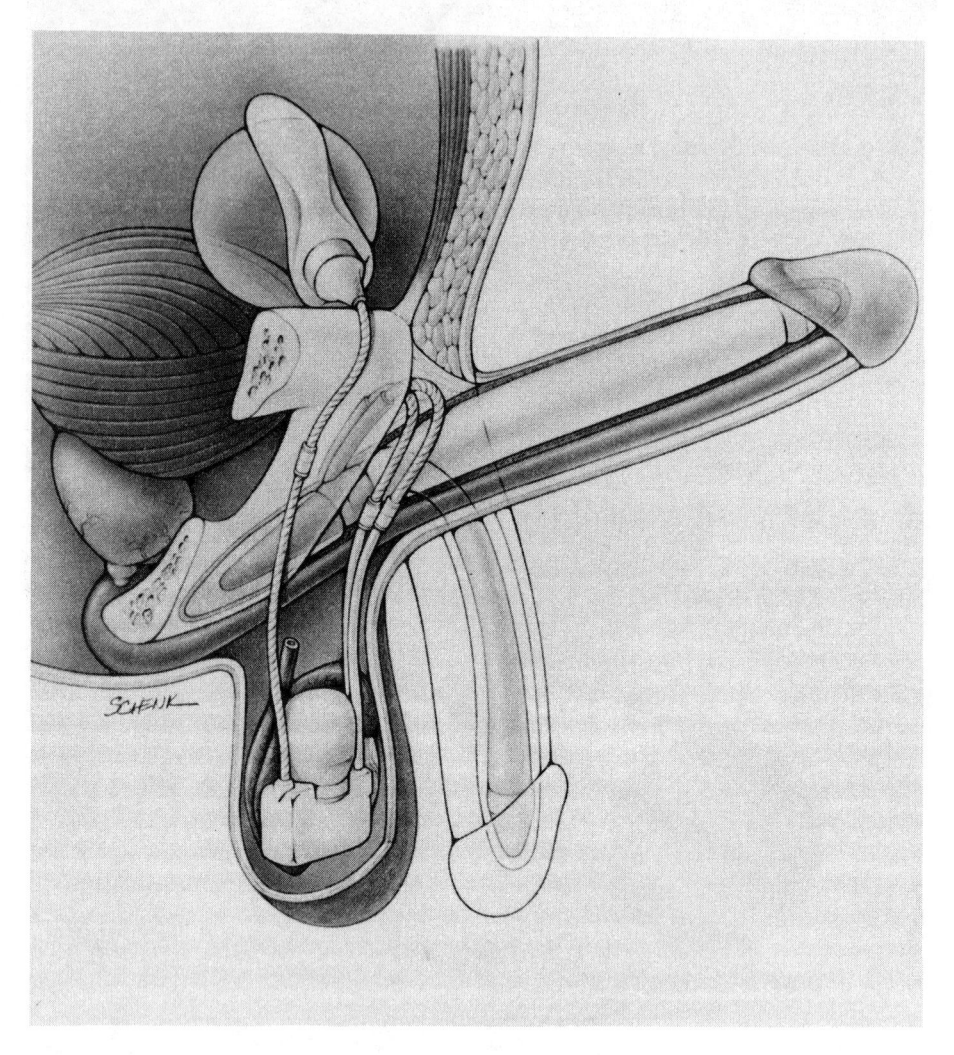

Courtesy of American Medical Systems, Inc., Minnetonka, Minnesota. Medical illustrations by Michael Schenk.

Figure 6-19

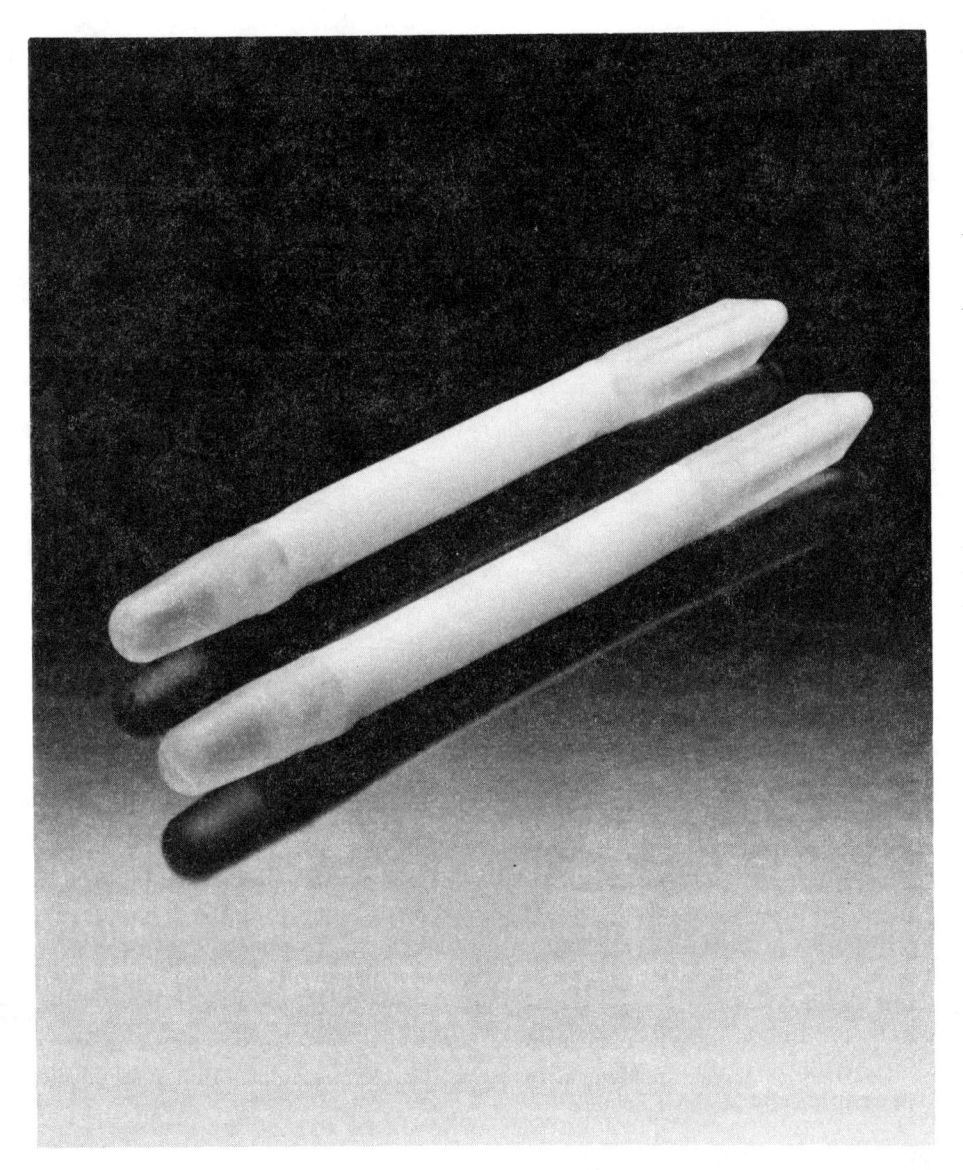

Courtesy of American Medical Systems, Inc., Minnetonka, Minnesota. Medical illustrations by Michael Schenk.

190 Instruments & Devices

Figure 6-20

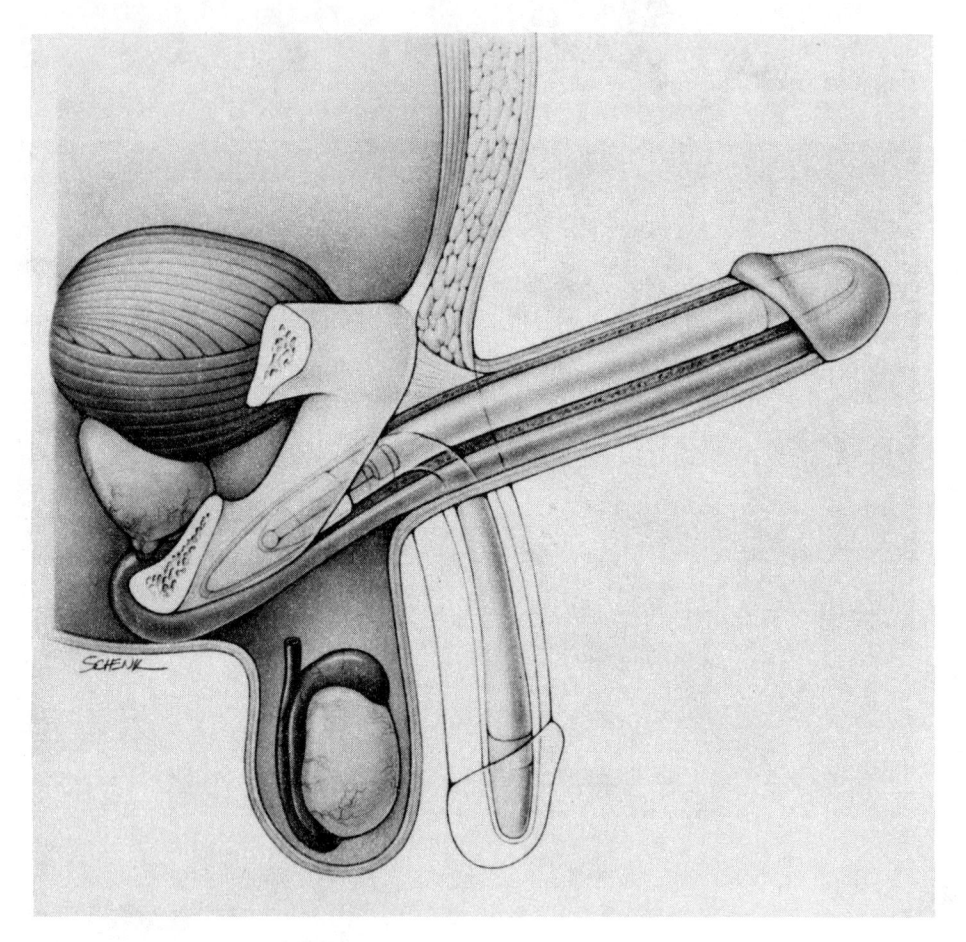

Courtesy of American Medical Systems, Inc., Minnetonka, Minnesota. Medical illustrations by Michael Schenk.

Figure 6-21

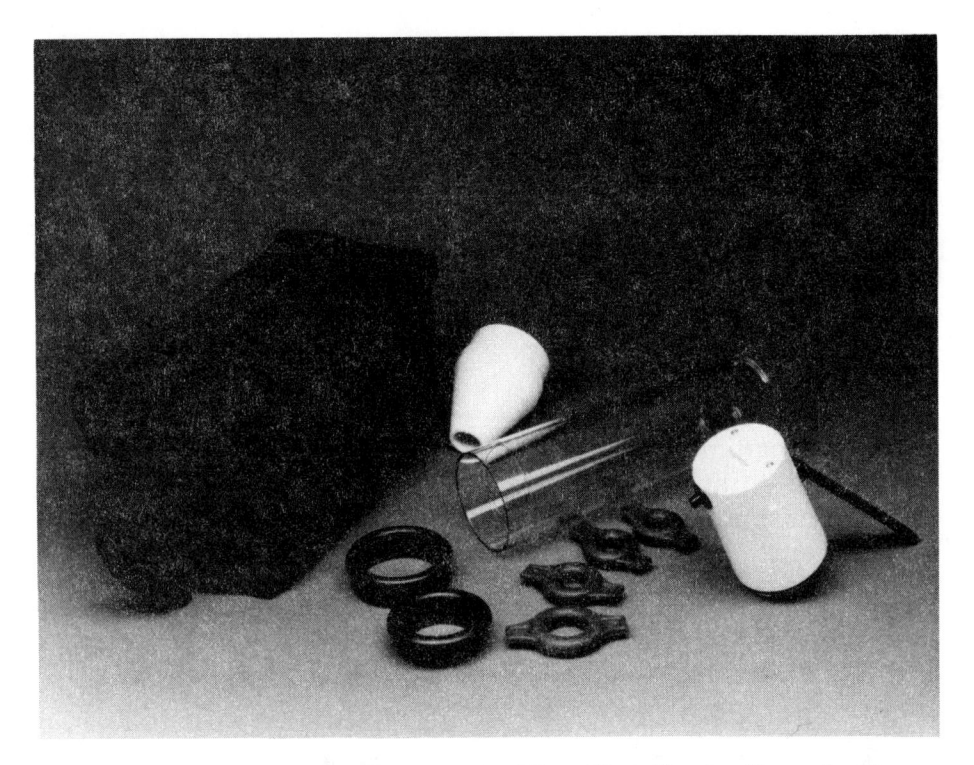

Courtesy of Smith-Collins Pharmaceutical Inc., West Chester, Pennsylvania.

7

Radiology of the Urinary Tract

§7.01 Introduction
§7.02 Excretory Urography
§7.03 Tomography
§7.04 Retrograde Pyelography
§7.05 Antegrade Pyelography
§7.06 Cystography
§7.07 Loopogram
§7.08 Urethrography
§7.09 Vasogram
§7.10 Angiography
§7.11 Radionuclides
§7.12 Renal Ultrasound
§7.13 Computerized Tomography
Appendix 7-A Sample Radiological Procedures

§7.01 Introduction

This is a "nuts-and-bolts" chapter to introduce the reader to some sophisticated urological radiographic procedures and terminology. There are no case cites in this chapter, only a description of the radiographic procedures available to urologists and a discussion concerning the indications and potential complications of each.

The specialty of urology is heavily endowed with the ability to make a proper diagnosis prior to any surgical intervention or treatment modality. Urology is one of the few disciplines of medicine with so many different investigative techniques, both invasive and noninvasive. While amazing technological advances have swept medicine generally, urology has been the fortunate recipient of most of the advances. Obviously, internal organs with which urologists are mainly concerned can only be visualized or palpated at open surgery, but, with contrast-enhanced radiographic techniques, function and anatomy of the organs can be perceived without surgical exploration.

As each technique is discussed, I will also describe a brief clinical scenario which is applicable.

§7.02 Excretory Urography

This radiological technique involves injecting a medicine—"dye" or "contrast material"—into the patient's vein which is selectively excreted by the kidneys in such a concentration that an outline of the collecting system of the kidneys and the ureters is clearly visible on the x-ray plate. This technique is called an *intravenous pyelogram* (IVP).

The IVP is the heart and soul of urology. For years, this valuable tool was used on a daily basis by every urologist to give information concerning the patient's renal anatomy and renal function. Other newer techniques are now being utilized, so that the IVP is becoming slightly dated, but it is still a valuable and important investigative technique used by all urologists.

Because some patients have an allergic reaction to the contrast medium which is injected into them as part of the procedure, the IVP is also a great source of urological medical malpractice actions. A typical cause of action involving an allergic reaction to the IVP dye is discussed more fully in Chapter 9.

The contrast material, a solution containing iodine, is the basis for the potential reaction. All patients are questioned—or at least should be questioned—very carefully prior to the injection of the iodinated solution, but reactions do occur. Fortunately, most reactions are nonfatal and involve itching, some nausea, or slight respiratory distress, but a rapid total cardiovascular and respiratory collapse is not all that rare. While most IVPs are performed in a hospital environment, in the emergency room or radiology department, physicians also perform IVPs in their offices. It is the standard of care for any physician performing IVPs in the office not only to carefully question the patient about any potential reaction to the dye, but also to have oxygen, adrenalin, and other life-support measures available in the event of a reaction. This is a key point that any attorney handling an office-related IVP allergic reaction case should know.

While numerous articles have been written about the allergic reaction to the IVP dye, this chapter is concerned more with exposing the reader to the radiology of the genitourinary tract, and will leave the complete discussion of these allergic reactions to other texts. Suffice it to say that informed consent with disclosure of the risks as well as taking the proper history and having survival equipment handy are all important factors to understand in the event the reader is asked to evaluate a "reaction" case.

It is important in understanding the value of the IVP to understand the anatomy of the kidney and ureters. Please refer to Chapter 5 for a complete discussion as well as diagrams of the anatomy. As stated earlier, the IVP outlines the *collecting* system of the kidneys—i.e., the calyces and the renal pelvis—and the ureters. The main reason for performing an IVP is to demonstrate whether any obstruction is present. If a patient has a stone somewhere in the kidney or ureter, that stone will impede the outflow of urine (and contrast material), and it is the difference of the excretion of the dye between the two kidneys which suggests the diagnosis of stone disease.

Of course, IVPs can be used to evaluate renal cysts, filling defects in the ureter or renal pelvis, and abnormal calyceal anatomy suggesting renal cancer, etc., but the big reason most IVPs are performed is for urinary stone disease. Since I am not trying to make a urographer out of each reader, but only giving the "big picture" about all these techniques, I refer the reader to the three films in Figure 7-1 of Appendix 7-A. The first two films show a normal IVP and the third shows a large mid-ureteral calculus obstructing the right ureter.

§7.03 Tomography

An adjunctive part of doing some intravenous pyelograms (IVPs) is a procedure known as a *tomogram* (or *laminogram*). This is a technique wherein the focal point of the x-ray is adjusted so that different levels of the kidney can be better visualized. The patient lies still on the x-ray table, but the x-ray tube takes pictures at various depths of the patient by adjusting the distance of the tube from the patient. A dense nephrogram is obtained which clearly outlines the kidney and most of the structures within it. *Nephrogram* is a term of art indicating an exaggerated denseness to the renal shadow. While a nephrogram is usually indicative of a distal obstruction because the dye is backed up and cannot get out of the kidney, in tomography the nephrogram occurs because of the level of depth of the radiogram and the higher concentration of the contrast material at that level.

Tomograms are indicated to sharply define structures within the kidney and to help delineate cysts from tumors (*see* Appendix 7-A, Figure 7-2).

§7.04 Retrograde Pyelography

When dye is injected from within the bladder up the ureters to outline the collecting system, it is called a *retrograde pyelogram* (RPG) as opposed to dye injected intravenously or even percutaneously (*see* §7.05). Obviously, the RPG is always done as part of a cystoscopic procedure, wherein a small catheter is passed through the cystoscope and inserted into each ureteral opening (the orifice) in the bladder. Contrast material is then injected retrograde up the ureters. This procedure is done when a better picture is needed of the ureter or parts of the upper tract. The catheter can be advanced up the ureter and the dye injected to selectively obtain an enhanced image of a specific area.

In addition, when a patient has a history of allergy to the iodinated contrast material, doing an RPG is a safe and accepted method of delineating the collecting system.

The natural question is why the patient does not get an allergic reaction to the dye when it is injected retrograde as opposed to getting a reaction to the dye when it is given intravenously. Allergic reactions only occur when the agent is absorbed into the patient's system; the ureters and collecting system must be understood as a "tube" or "conduit" within the body, but not connected to the physiological system of the body. Injecting the dye retrograde does not bear the risk of an allergic reaction because it never really gets into the body.

Finally, another indication for the RPG is when patients are in renal failure and the kidney does not have the ability to excrete the contrast material. The kidney must have a relatively normal functioning ability to receive the dye, concentrate it, and then excrete it. If damage to the kidney is such that renal failure is present, the dye will not be concentrated enough to show up on x-ray (*see* Appendix 7-A, Figure 7-3).

§7.05 Antegrade Pyelography

While an intravenous pyelogram (IVP) is technically an antegrade procedure, urologists use that particular term when any radiogram is performed on a patient who has some percutaneous access to the kidney.

A nephrostomy tube was a common urological instrument for decades and is merely a catheter which is placed through the flank of the body directly into the kidney. With the advances in endourology (that area of urology dealing with catheters, stents, guidewires, etc. placed into the collecting system), it is not uncommon nor particularly difficult to place a small polyethylene tube from the outside flank through the muscles and into the kidney—all done using the fluoroscopy machine. Injecting contrast material down one of the catheters is known as *antegrade pyelography*.

The percutaneous approach to the kidney (perc) has numerous applications ranging from removing a kidney or ureteral stone to bypassing an obstruction in the ureter to draining the kidney because of a blockage. The field of endourology is relatively new, and great advances are being made every year in new techniques and treatment modalities.

§7.06 Cystography

While an intravenous pyelogram (IVP) does give a certain amount of information concerning the bladder when the dye goes down the ureters and starts filling the bladder, a cystogram is a specific radiographic examination of the bladder itself.

A small catheter is inserted through the urethra directly into the bladder, and contrast material (the familiar iodinated material) is injected via the catheter into the bladder. As with retrograde pyelography, since no contrast material is absorbed through the bladder wall into the body, patients do not get allergic reactions to the contrast medium in a cystogram.

The urologist is specifically looking for any abnormal bladder contour or "filling defects" (areas where the dye appears to "not be") in the bladder.

There is one condition which should be of interest to the reader known as *vesicoureteral reflux* which is also perfectly delineated by the cystogram.

Vesicoureteral reflux is serious, and most commonly found in young (prepubertal) females, although both sexes and all age groups can be afflicted. Vesicoureteral reflux does arise as an issue in the medical malpractice area because the surgical treatment for reflux is technically complex, and injuries do occur to patients who undergo this surgery.

Vesicoureteral reflux is a condition wherein urine which flows down the ureters from the kidney to the bladder is regurgitated back up the ureters when the patient voids. Figure 7-5 in Appendix 7-A is an example of a cystogram showing vesicoureteral reflux. Notice that it can look like an IVP, but, here, no dye has been injected intravenously, only intravesically. A normal cystogram without evidence of vesicoureteral reflux is shown as Figure 7-4 in Appendix 7-A and a cystogram with a large filling defect in it which later proved to be a large bladder cancer is shown in Figure 7-6 in Appendix 7-A.

The actual cystogram is performed by gradually filling the bladder until the patient complains of discomfort, and then, as the patient voids, using cinefluoroscopy (motion picture fluoroscopy) for recording the image. Thus, an evaluation can also be made of the urethra and particularly the bladder neck at the same time.

§7.07 Loopogram

Patients who have had the bladder removed for cancer or who have a neurogenic bladder which does not function properly will have a new bladder made for them out of a loop of bowel. The ureters are cut off from the bladder and attached to an isolated segment of bowel (the loop), one end of which is sutured closed and the other end of which is sewn to the skin. Thus, urine goes down the ureters, into the loop, and out the opening (stoma) in the skin, where it is collected into a urinary drainage bag. This is not the most pleasant situation in the world, but, with new glue and collecting bags being developed, patients can live a normal life, even go swimming, and take part in most other physical activities.

The loopogram is very similar to a cystogram in that dye is injected via a catheter placed in the loop through the stoma. However, here, the urologist is looking for reflux of dye up the ureters which, in the case of a cystogram, would be abnormal, but in the case of a loopogram is normal. Although there are new antirefluxing techniques to implant the ureters into the loop, reflux is supposed to be present when ureters are attached to a loop of bowel.

Indications for a loopogram are the same as for a retrograde pyelogram, and most commonly are performed to:

1. Follow a patient with a cystectomy and urinary diversion ("ileal loop")
2. Search for any urinary leaks in the early post-operative period
3. Rule out upper-tract obstruction

§7.08 Urethrography

Actually, radiographic examination of the urethra is only done in males and is called a *retrograde urethrogram* (RUG). This procedure is performed by injecting iodinated contrast material into the meatus of the penis, thus outlining the entire urethra. While a voiding cystogram does give a good picture of the urethra, the best technique for outlining the urethra is the RUG.

Virtually the only reason to perform an RUG is to delineate or diagnose a urethral stricture. I recently was involved as an expert witness in a urological medical malpractice case involving urethral stricture disease wherein numerous retrograde urethrograms were an important part of the demonstrative evidence. Figure 7-7 in Appendix 7-A shows a normal retrograde urethrogram, but a very narrow stricture of the bladder neck.

§7.09 Vasogram

The significance of a vasogram may not be of the highest legal priority, but the vasogram is a commonly used technique which may be of interest to the reader.

Dye is injected into each vas—with the patient under anesthesia—by inserting a small needle directly into the vas through a scrotal skin incision. This technique nicely outlines and identifies the vas as it courses from the testis up the scrotum into the pelvis around the ureter and then down behind the bladder to enter into the prostatic urethra at the ejaculatory ducts.

The indication for a vasogram is narrow and only involves a situation wherein infertility evaluation of a male reveals complete absence of sperm—azospermia. One of the reasons for azospermia is blockage of the vas; therefore, a vasogram is the mechanism whereby patency of the vas can be proven (Appendix 7-A, Figure 7-8).

§7.10 Angiography

Strictly defined, this is a radiologic examination of any blood vessel, but, as related to urology, angiography really refers to the renal angiogram or arteriogram.

This is a specific examination whereby a tiny catheter is introduced via the femoral artery (in the groin) up the aorta to the area of the renal artery. Contrast material is then injected very rapidly. This is an extremely specific test to differentiate malignant renal neoplasm from a benign cyst of the kidney. With the advent of the computerized axial tomography (*see* **§7.13**) arteriography has become slightly outdated, but the examination is still done quite frequently throughout the United States.

Another important reason to perform renal arteriography is in cases involving trauma. If there is a question of a renal injury, arteriography can rapidly help make the proper diagnosis of whether a laceration to the kidney has occurred. A normal intravenous pyelogram (IVP) in a trauma situation does not necessarily rule out severe renal damage, but the arteriogram can definitively make the diagnosis.

Figure 7-9, in Appendix 7-A illustrates a normal renal arteriogram, and Figure 7-10 reveals a large renal tumor with the neovascularity or "puddling" so characteristic of cancer.

§7.11 Radionuclides

This term refers to a method of using radiographically tagged agents which can be injected into the body, and by using a gamma scintillation camera, an external image can be obtained which graphically determines either physiology or anatomy of the organs being studied. That is as simple as I can put it!

While attorneys generally will not have the need to deeply understand the meaning of a measurement of a I^{131} xenon, there are a few commonly used radionuclide studies of which the reader should be aware.

The renal scan is probably the most commonly used study wherein the radio-tagged agent (and it is not important to remember whether hippuran, iodine, xenon, or technetium is being used) is injected intravenously, and the scanning camera is placed over the kidneys. The resultant picture gives some idea of the function of the renal unit (Appendix 7-A, Figure 7-11).

The renogram (Appendix 7-A, Figure 7-12) is really radionuclide angiography, and measures the blood flow through the kidney. It is a useful test to evaluate both kidneys when one is concerned about renovascular hypertension.

Scans can also be used in renal trauma to see if there is any leakage of the radiopharmaceutical agent out of the kidney. Also, if an x-ray reveals what looks like a small nonfunctioning kidney on an intravenous pyelogram (IVP), a renal scan will give a better idea of what the actual function of that kidney is.

All of these radiographic techniques, whether an IVP, scan, retrograde urethrogram (RUG), or retrograde pyelogram (RPG), are to be used in conjunction with as much information about the patient as can be had; to depend upon any one test alone can be foolhardy and is not the standard of care in the practice of urology.

§7.12 Renal Ultrasound

Ultrasound consists of brief electrical impulses which are converted to sound waves and then directed into the object examined. When the ultrasound waves strike tissues of different densities, an "echo" is produced which is converted to an image on a screen.

The use of renal ultrasound has become accepted as a means of differentiating between solid and cystic renal masses (Appendix 7-A, Figure 7-13). Ultrasonography is also used for needle-placement guidance into the kidney.

Testicular ultrasound (Appendix 7-A, Figure 7-14), is an excellent technique for diagnosing solid masses, and, using the Doppler wave ultrasound, differentiation of torsion versus epididymitis is now available. (See Chapter 9 for urological causes of actions regarding torsion of the testicle.)

The most recent and popular application of ultrasonography in urology involves the prostate. By this noninvasive and inexpensive technique, extremely early prostate cancer may be detected. In the past, the digital examination of the prostate was the best means to diagnose prostate cancer, but usually, by that time, it was too late to effectuate a cure. With the arrival of the prostate ultrasonographic technology, early cases of prostate cancer have been found and successfully treated (Appendix 7-A, Figure 7-15).

§7.13 Computerized Tomography

This is probably the most exciting and technologically advanced modality to invade urology in decades. Known also as the computerized axial tomogram (CAT), the computerized tomography (CT) scan is a sophisticated means (too technical for this text) of acquiring information from a number of angles within a single cross-sectional plane, and the computation of these data is then presented in a single recognizable image.

Renal CT is a marvelous tool for all sorts of diagnostic challenges, and has almost made the intravenous pyelogram (IVP), scan, and arteriogram obsolete. The pictorial definition is so detailed that densities of fat, blood, and renal tissue can all be visualized (*see* Appendix 7-A, Figure 7-16). While the reader is not expected to be able to interpret the CT scan if one is found on the chart, at least you will know what CT or CAT is, when confronted with the radiographic report.

Appendix 7-A Sample Radiological Procedures

Figure 7-1(1)

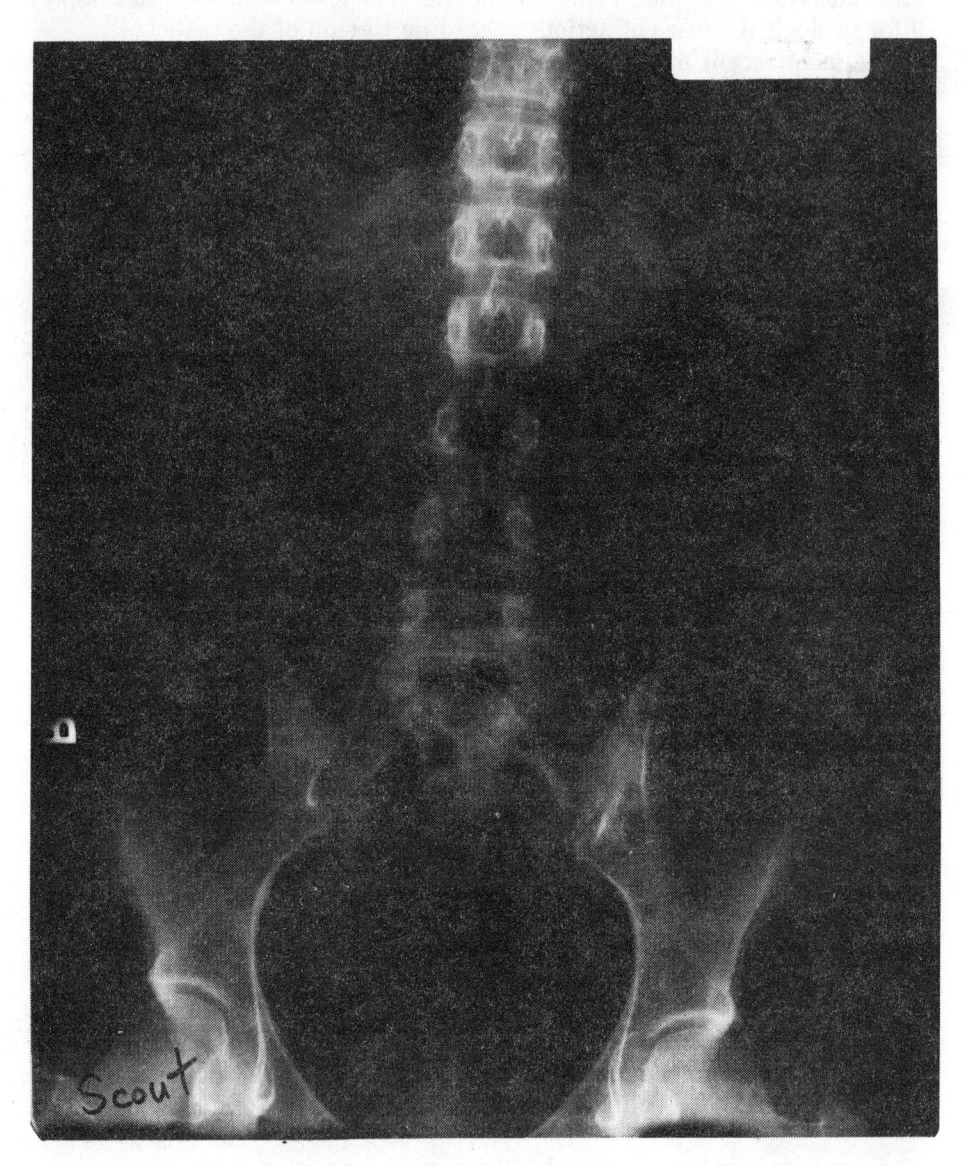

Intravenous pyelogram: The first film of the intravenous pyelogram (IVP) is known as a scout film or the flat plate of the abdomen or a KUB (kidneys/ureter/bladder). This IVP reveals a normal KUB and a normal 15-minute film, outlining both kidneys and ureters. Ordinarily, there may be five or six films taken during the entire process of the IVP, but for purposes of this text, only these two films are being shown. The third picture of this series shows an obstructed right kidney with a large (lima bean size) stone on the right side overlying the right transverse process of the sacral vertebra.

Figure 7-1(2)

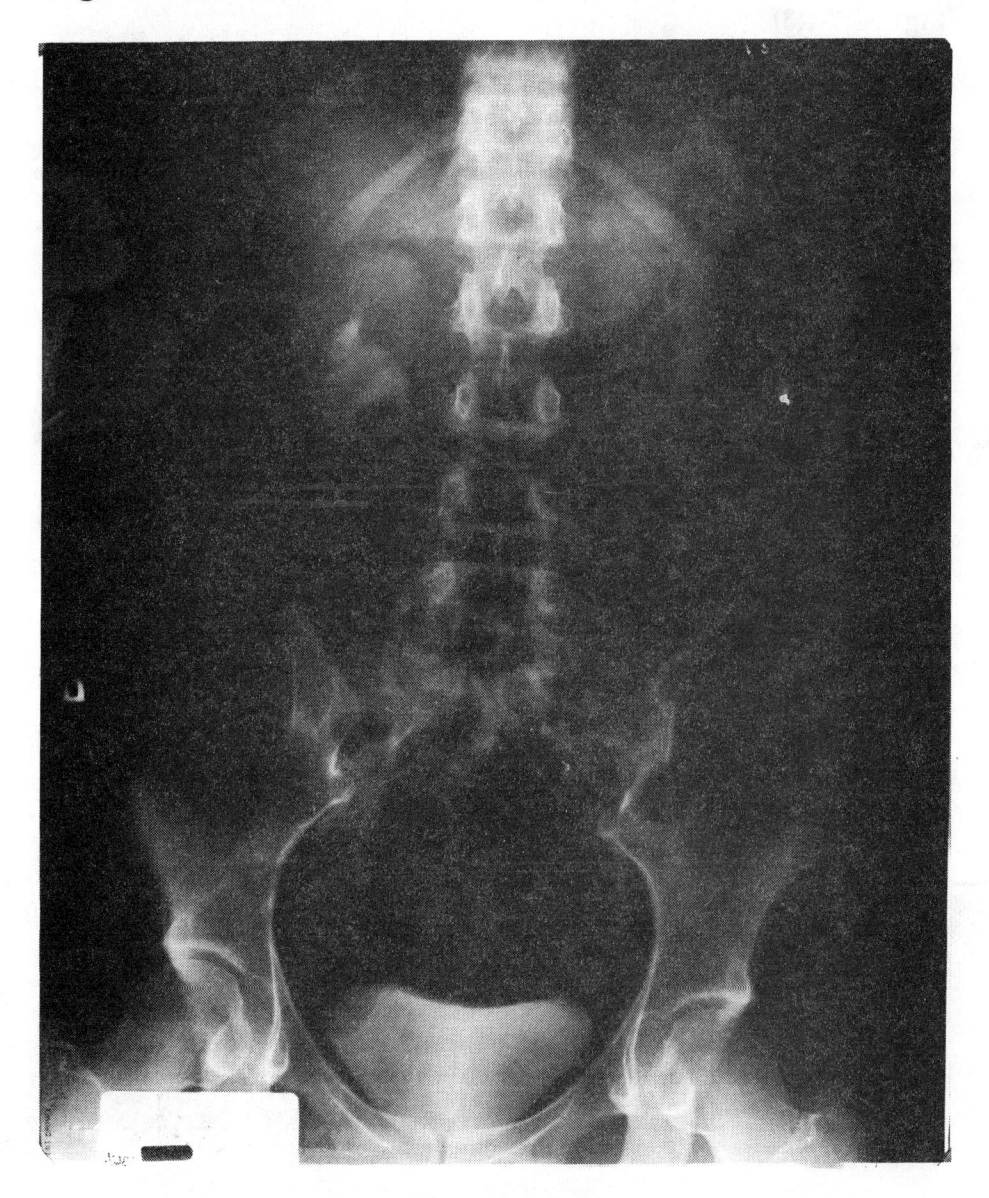

Figure 7-1(3)

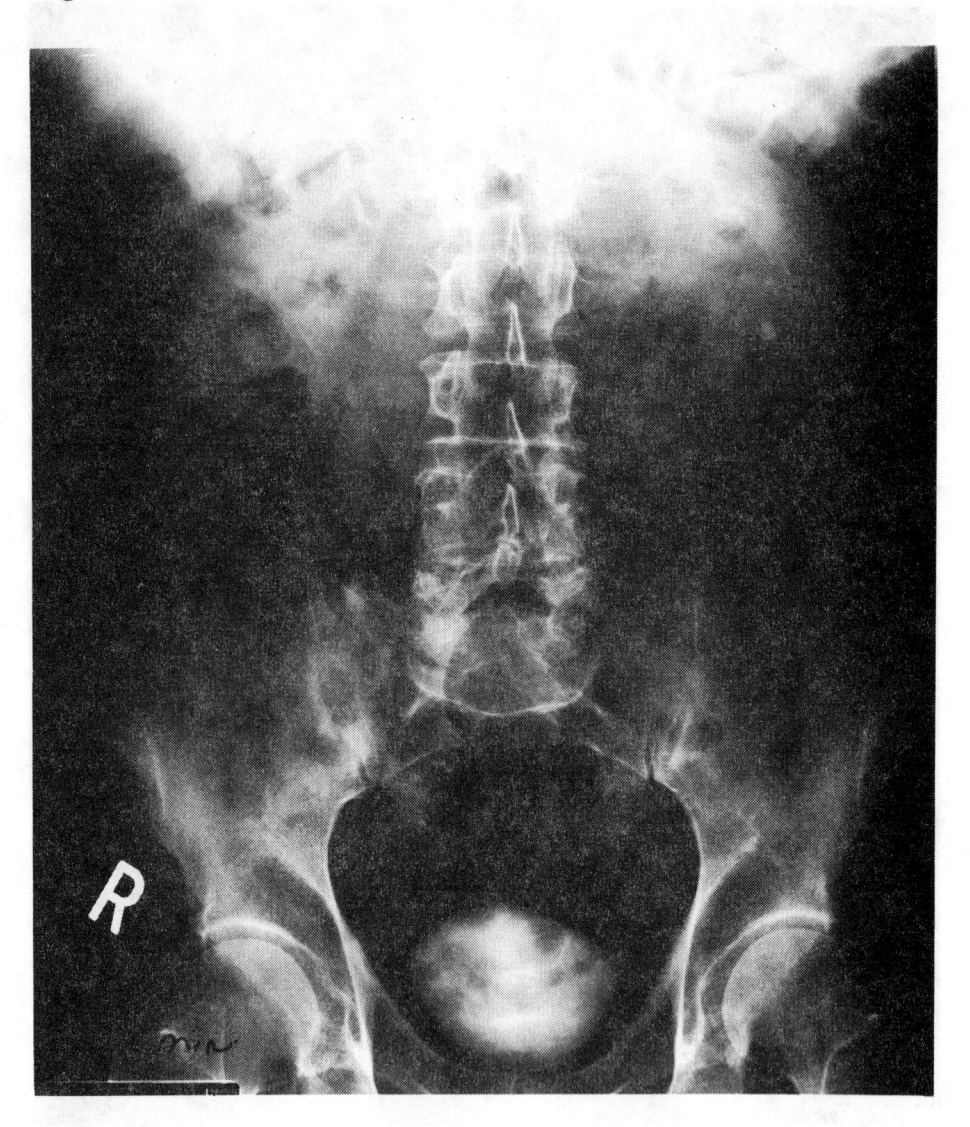

Figure 7-2

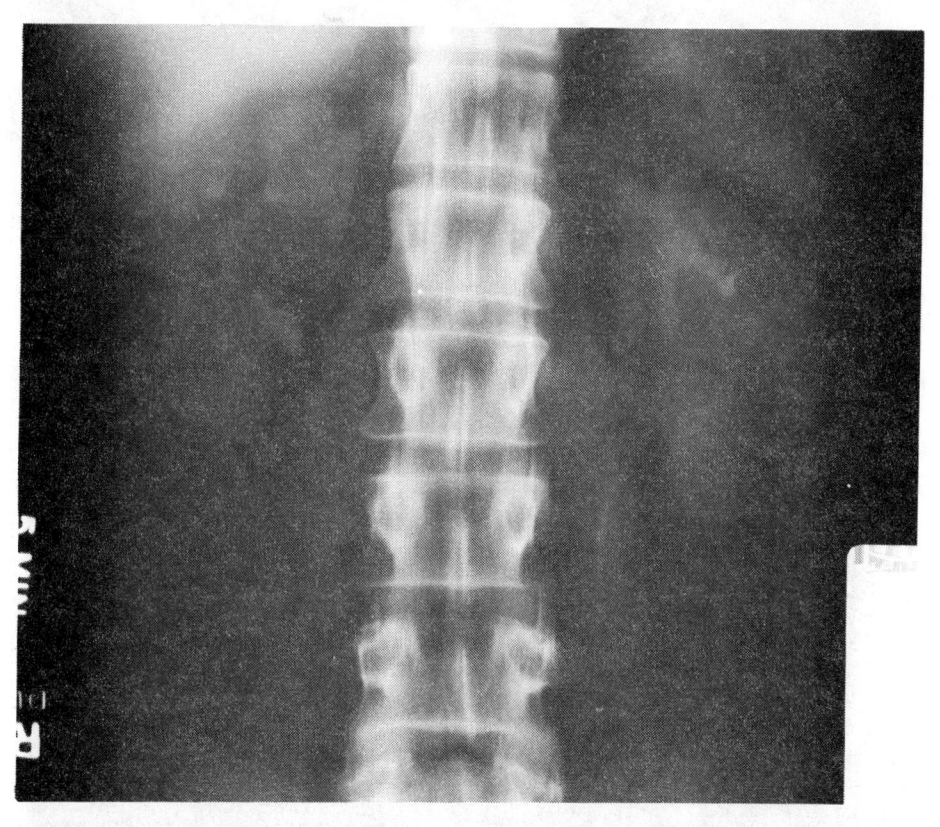

Tomogram: Shown is the tomogram of both kidneys taken at a 3-cm. cut, revealing the dense nephrogram effect outlining each kidney.

Figure 7-3

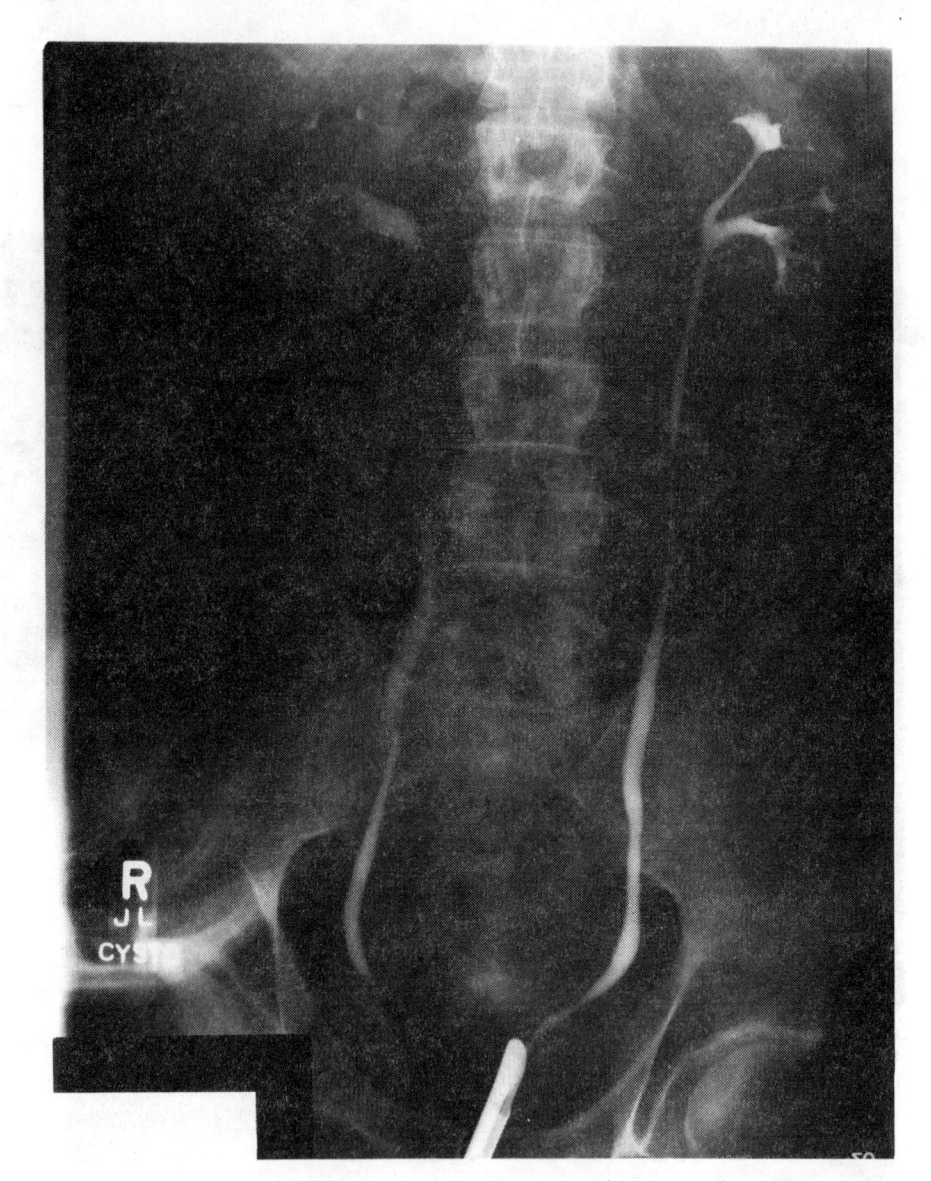

Retrograde pyelogram: This film reveals the cystoscope in the bladder with bilateral retrograde pyelograms showing normal contour of the ureters and upper tracts.

Appendix 7-A 205

Figure 7-4

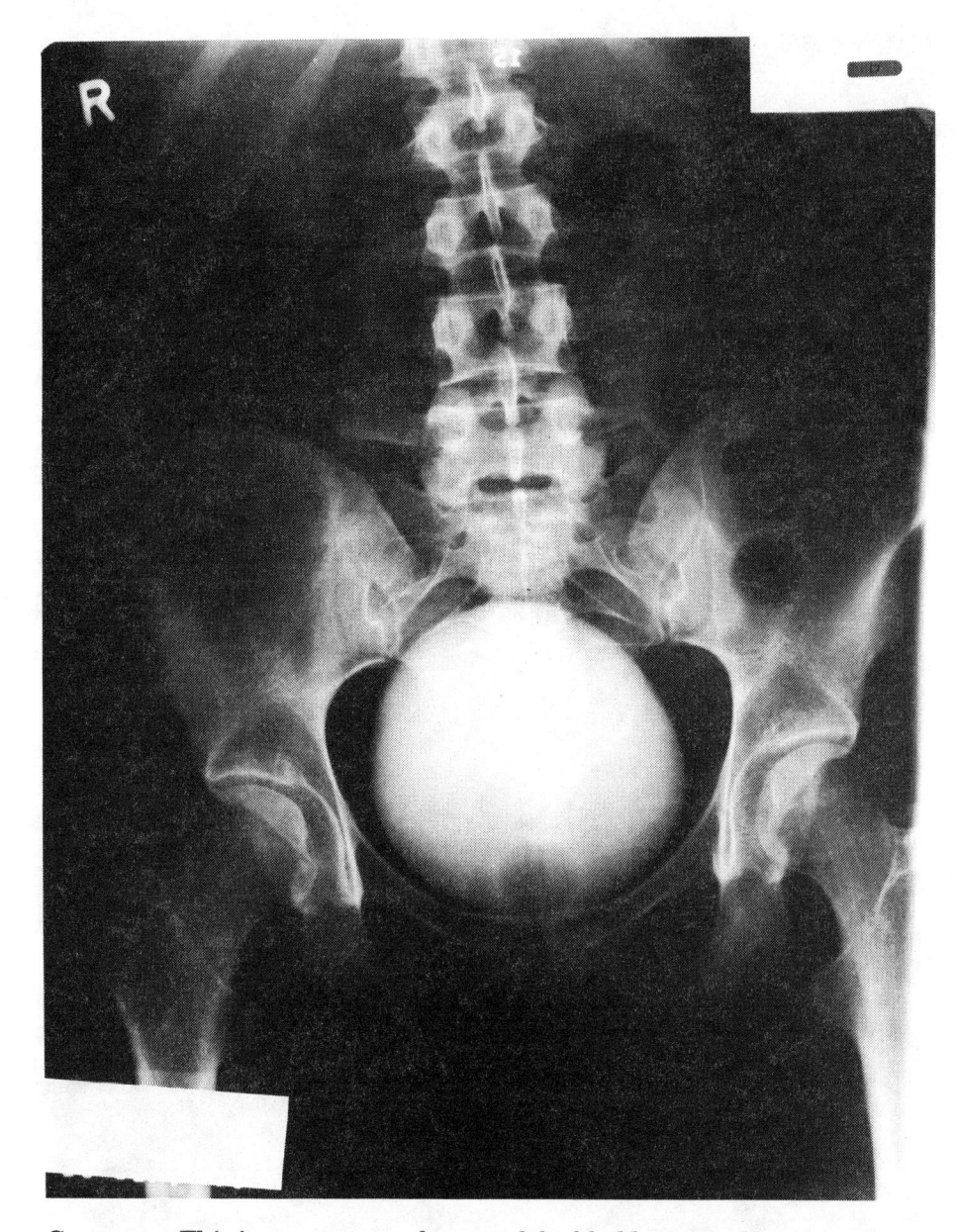

Cystogram: This is a very normal x-ray of the bladder, revealing normal contour of the bladder and without any filling defects. The contrast material is injected through a catheter which is placed in the patient's urethra and the resultant cystogram is as shown. The central round radiolucent area in the cystogram is the Foley catheter balloon filled with air.

206   Radiology of Urinary Tract

Figure 7-5

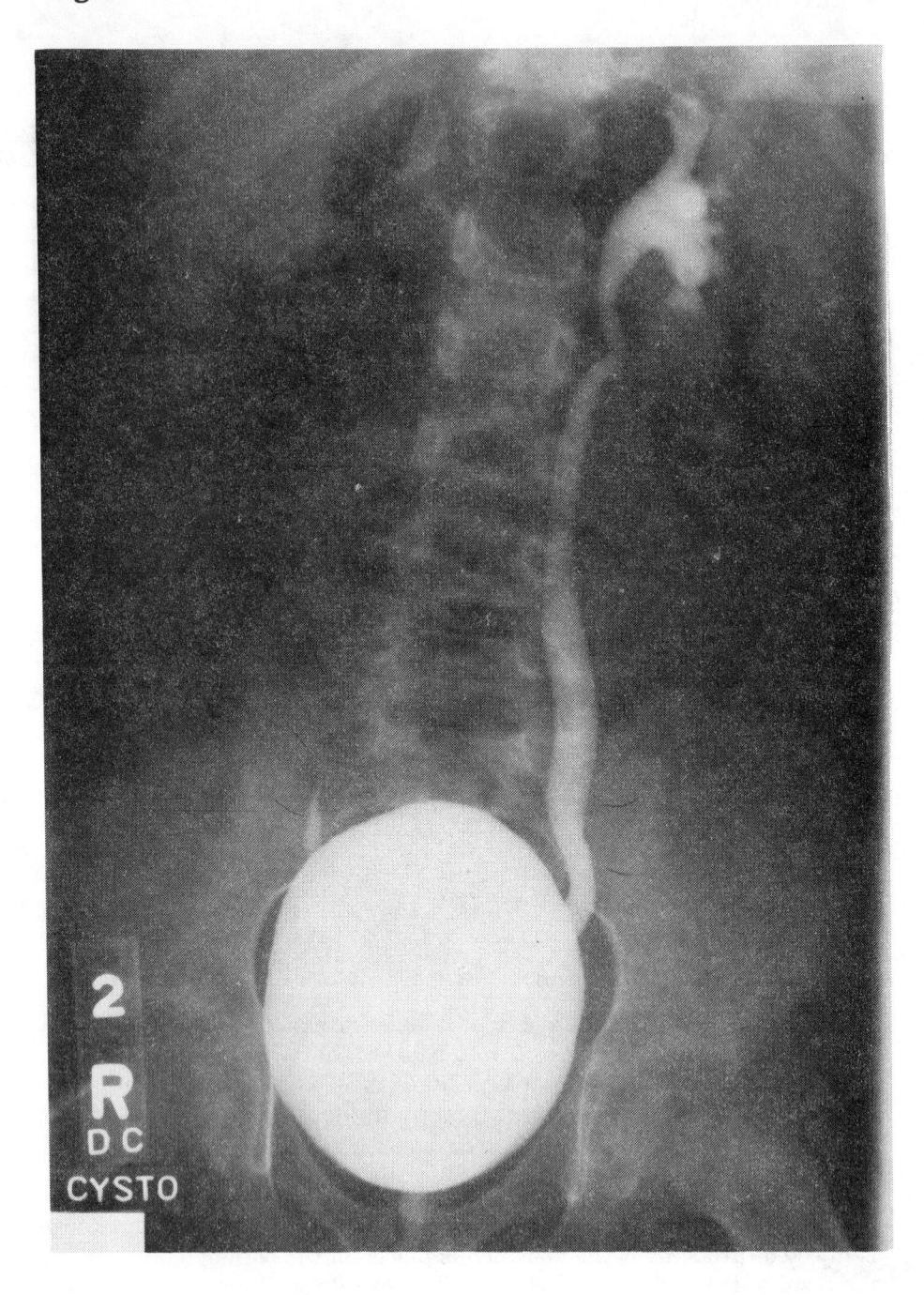

up the right side which minimally outlines the right ureter but does not go into the right kidney.

Appendix 7-A   207

Figure 7-6

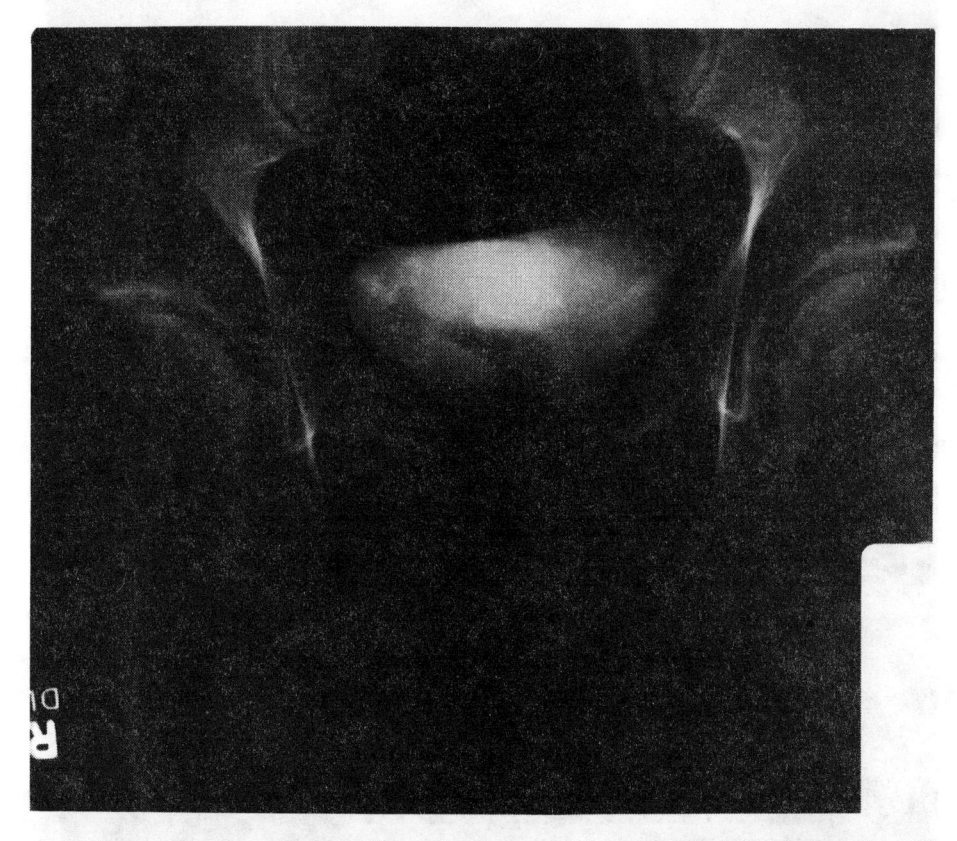

Bladder with filling defect: There is a normal shape of the bladder with both ureters outlined as they come into the bladder at the right side of the bladder. Near the entrance of the ureter into the bladder is the filling defect. The central shadow noted in the bladder is gas in the rectum.

Figure 7-7

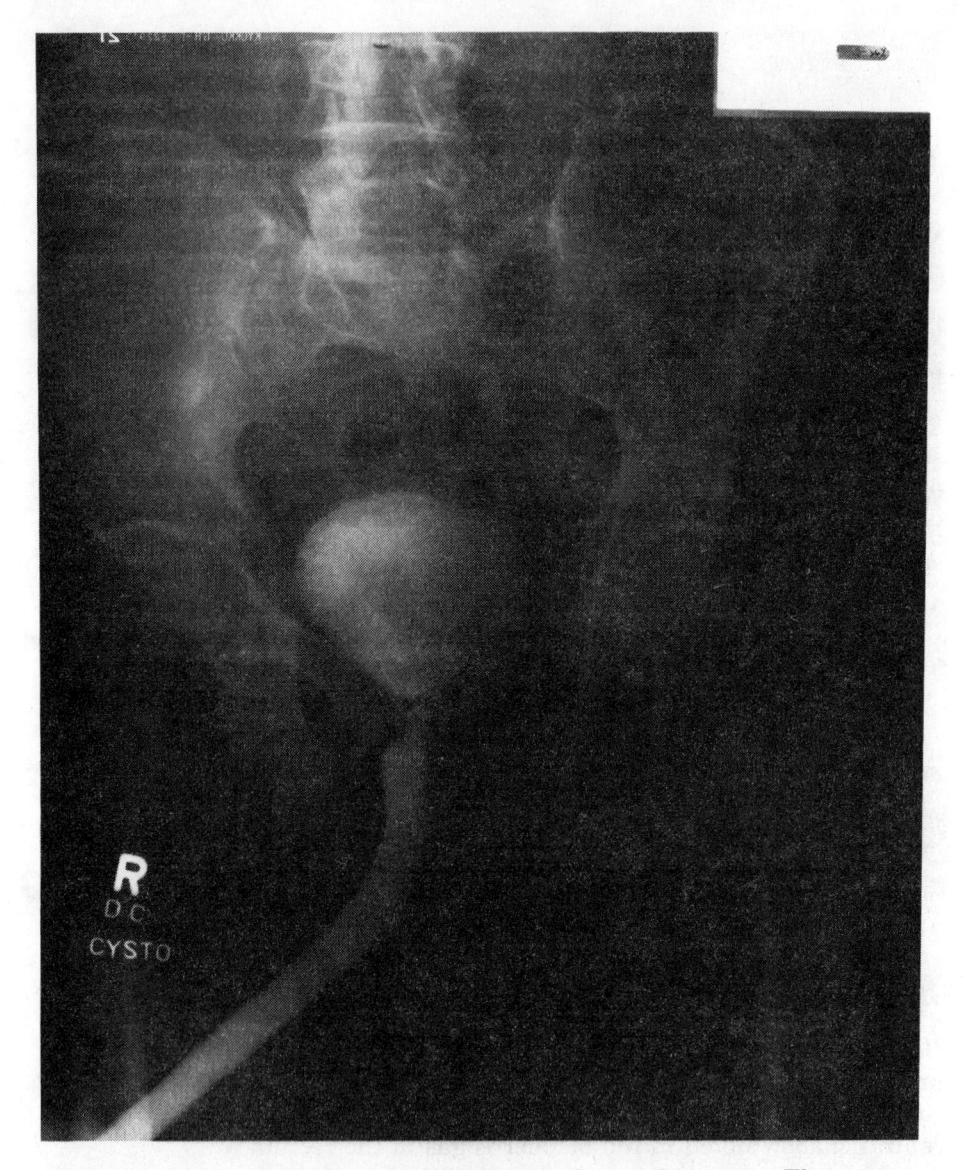

RUG: This is a view of a normal retrograde urethrogram. The contrast medium is injected through the urethral meatus retrograde into the urethra going into the bladder. This particular film reveals a very normal urethra although there is a significant narrowing at the bladder neck. Notice there is some mild extravasation of the contrast medium, but this is considered of no medical consequence.

Figure 7-8

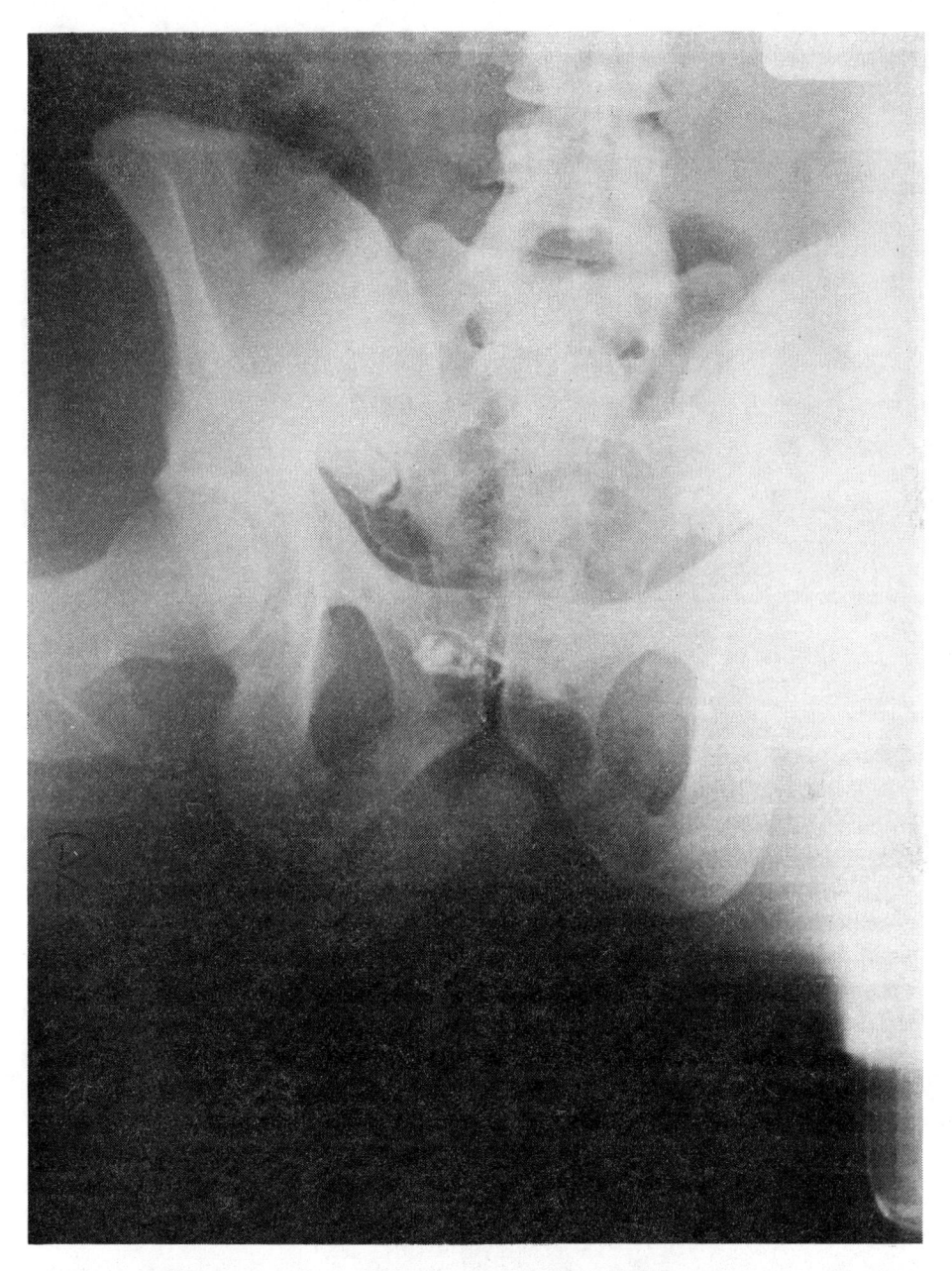

Vasogram: This is a picture revealing dye being injected in the vas and outlining its configuration as it goes into the pelvis back behind the bladder and into the seminal vesicle. This is a normal vasogram.

Figure 7-9

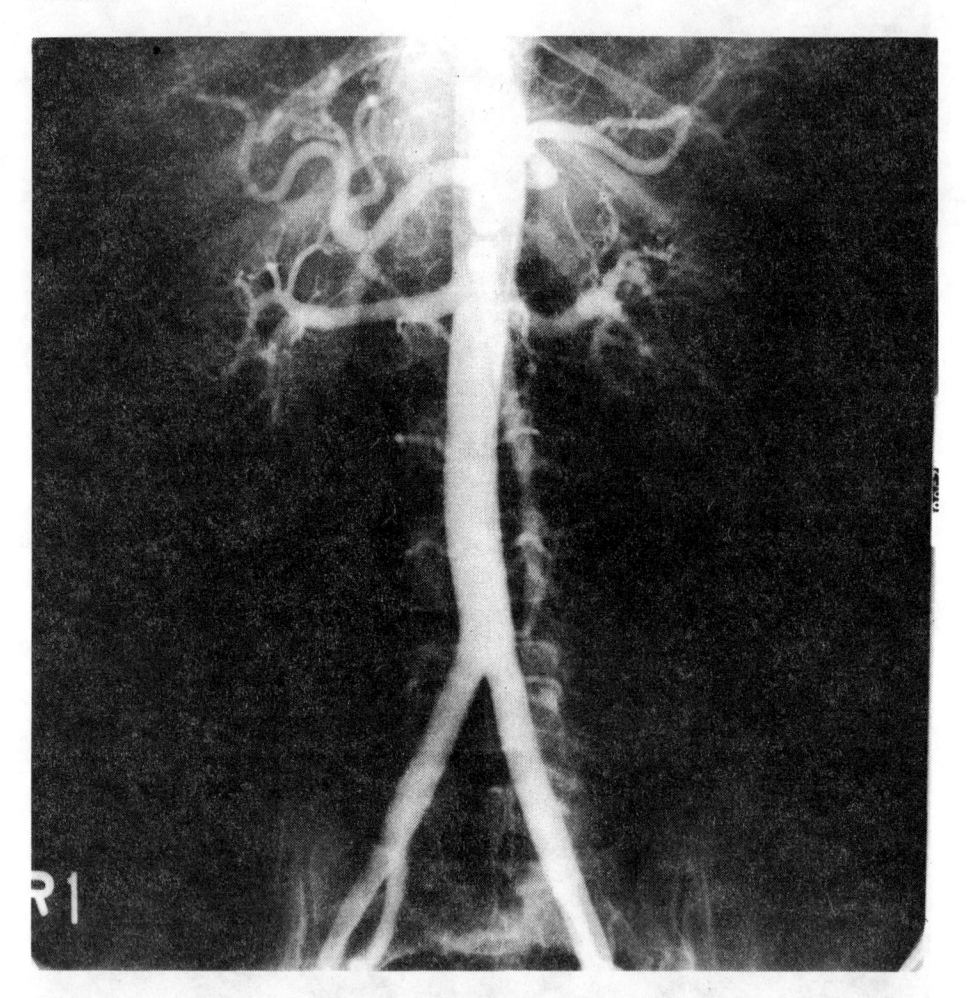

This is a normal arteriogram outlining the abdominal aorta and the renal arteries along with normal renal vasculature on either side. Additionally, the superior mesenteric artery as well as the heptic and splenic arteries are seen.

Figure 7-10

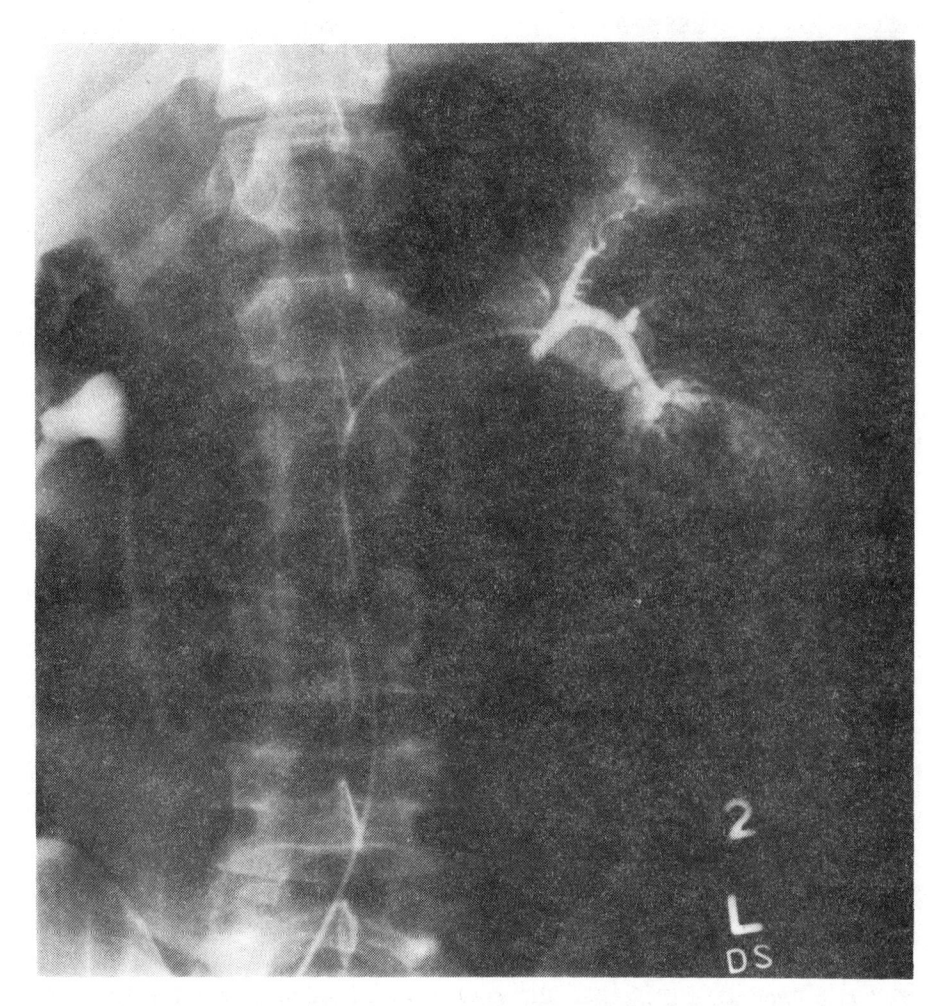

This is a selective left renal arteriogram which reveals a left-lower-pole hypervascular mass demonstrating the areas of the neovascularity and pooling of the contrast medium, highly suggestive of a malignant tumor.

Figure 7-11

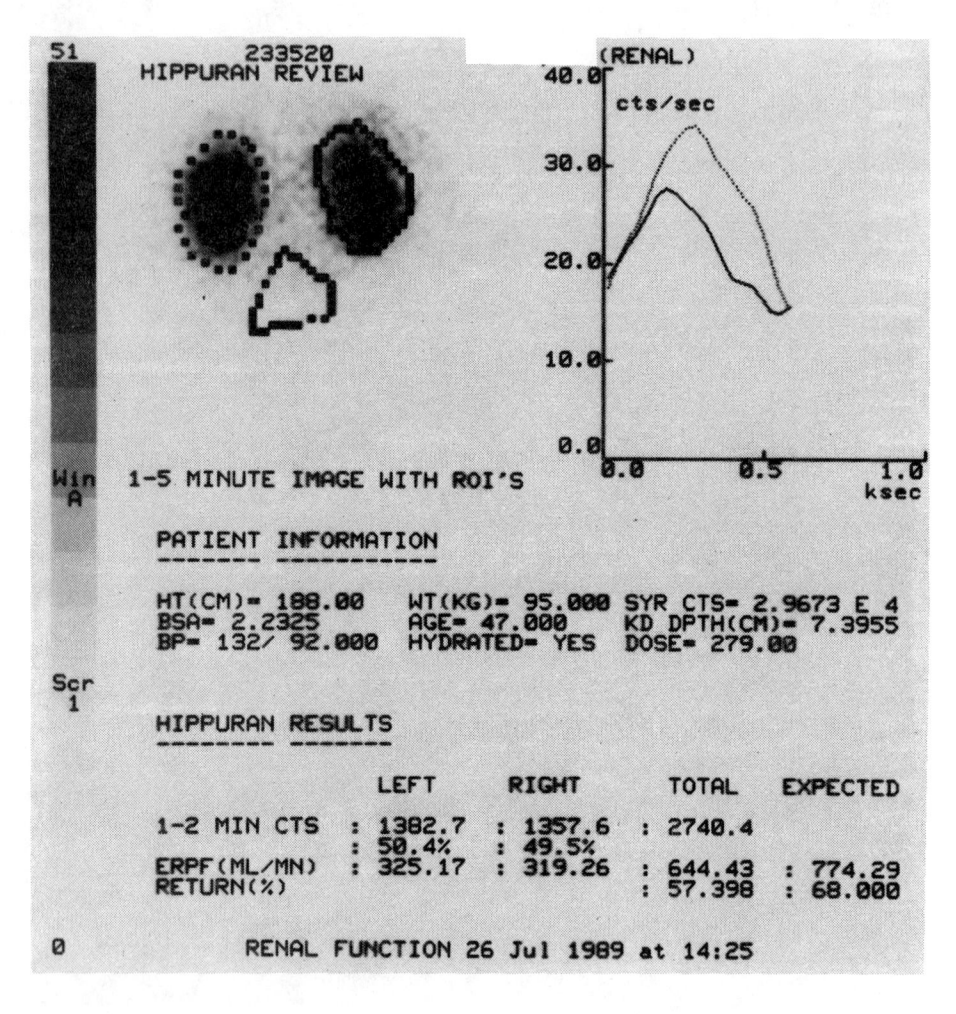

Renal scan: This is a hippuran renal scan showing the uptake of the contrast medium in each kidney along with the plotted curve regarding the expected percentage of hippuran uptake.

Figure 7-12

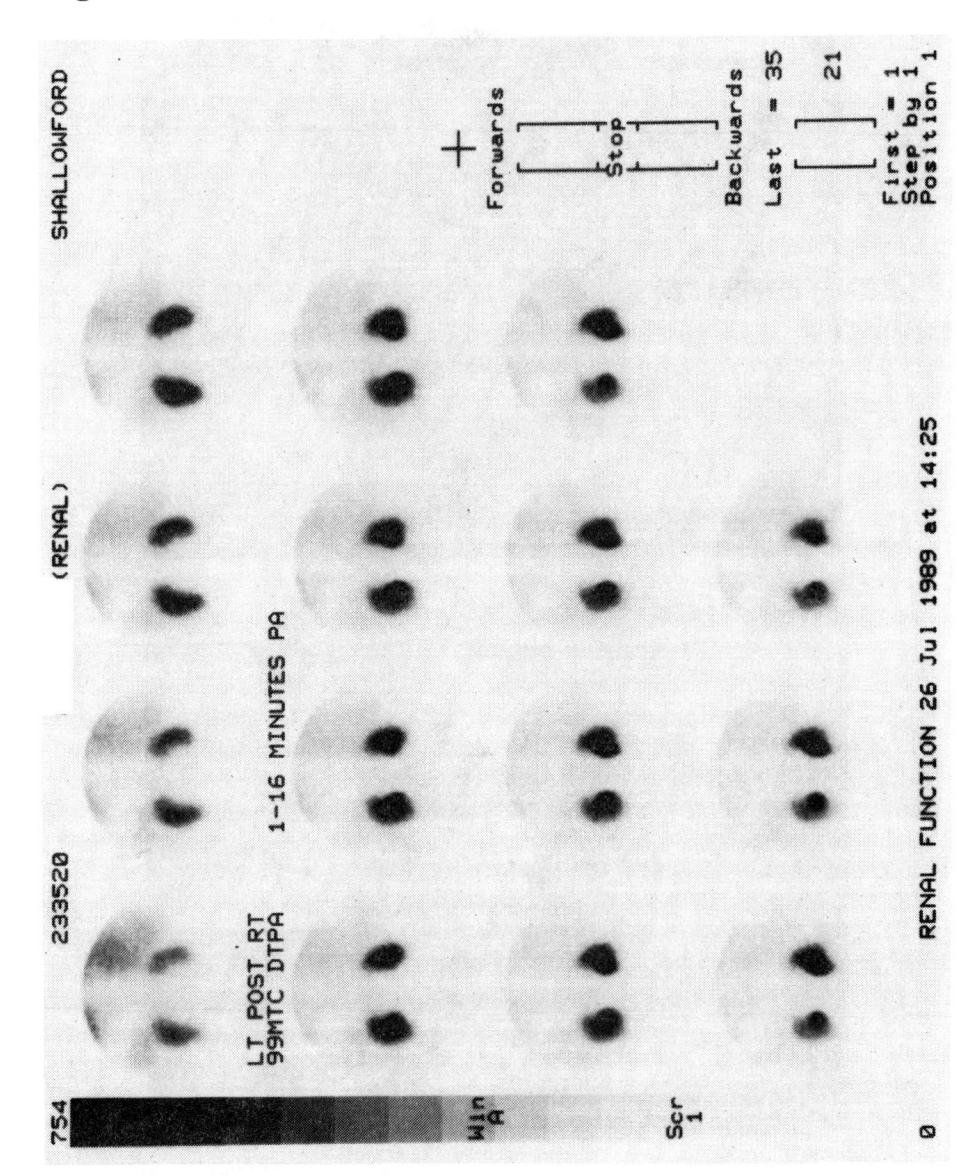

Renogram: Multiple pictures of bilateral uptake of contrast medium in a normal radiorenogram.

214 *Radiology of Urinary Tract*

Figure 7-13

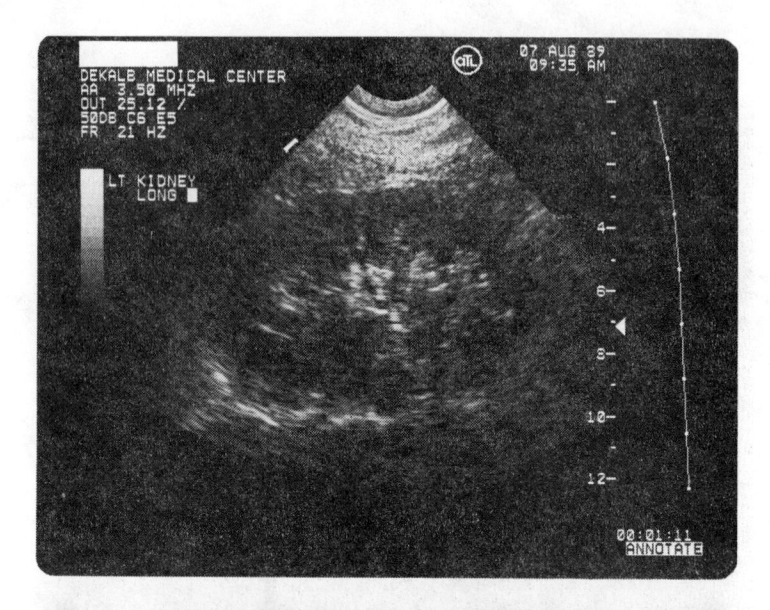

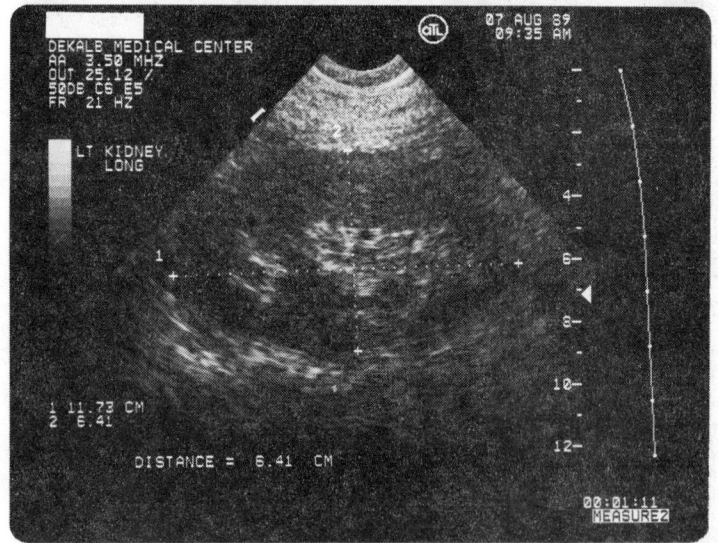

Renal ultrasound: Numerous views of the ultrasound of the left kidney which is normal. I know this looks like a weathermap of the southern United States, but, trust me—it is a renal ultrasound!

Appendix 7-A 215

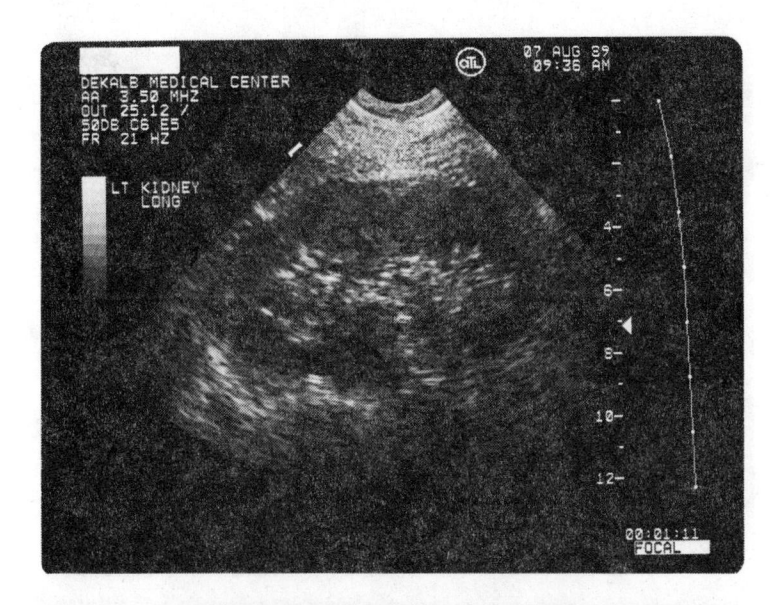

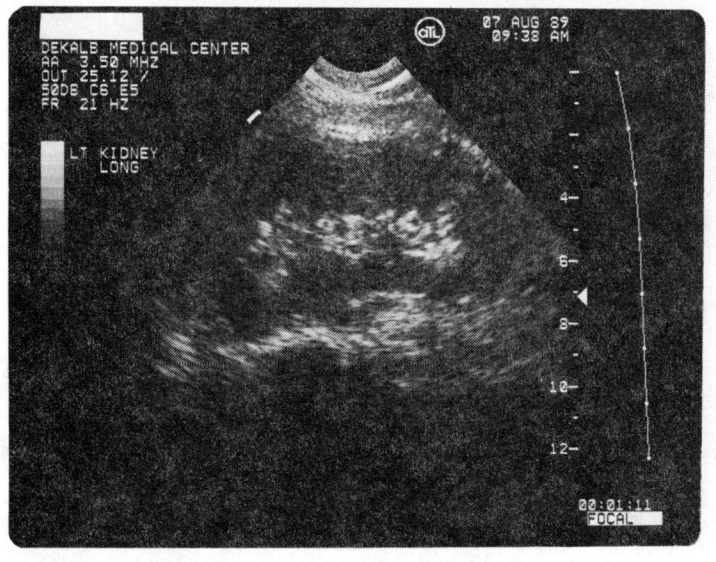

Figure 7-13 (continued)

Figure 7-13 (continued)

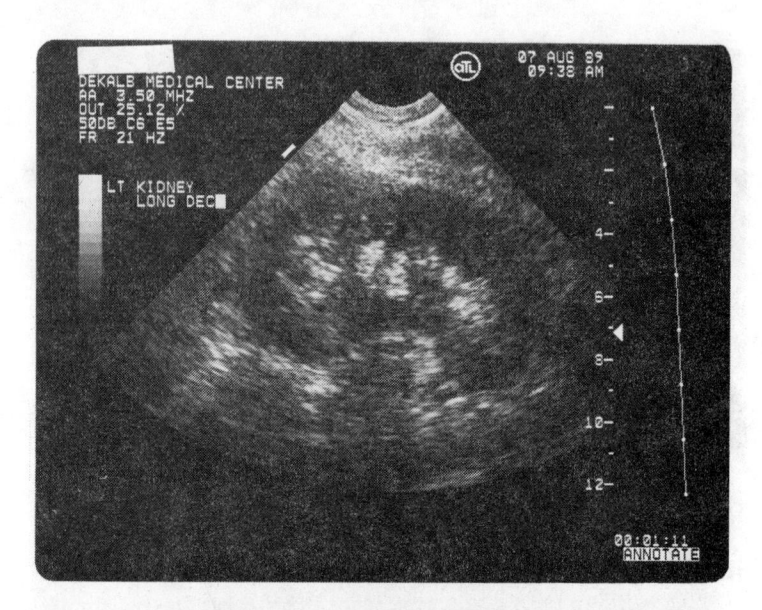

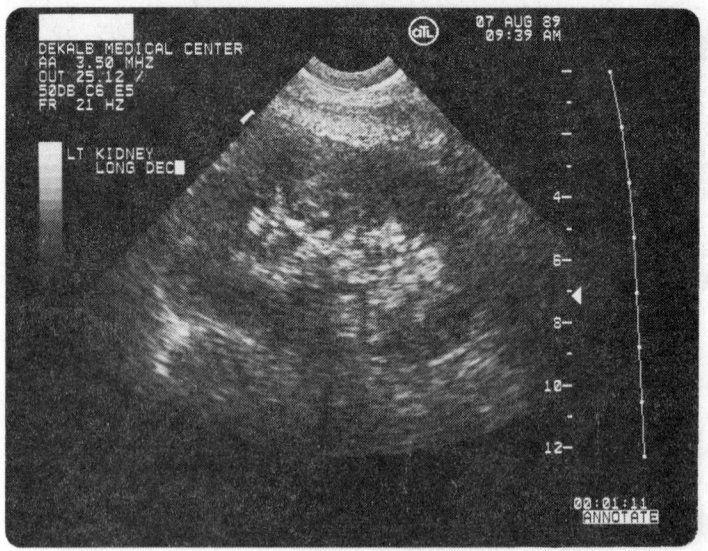

Appendix 7-A 217

Figure 7-14

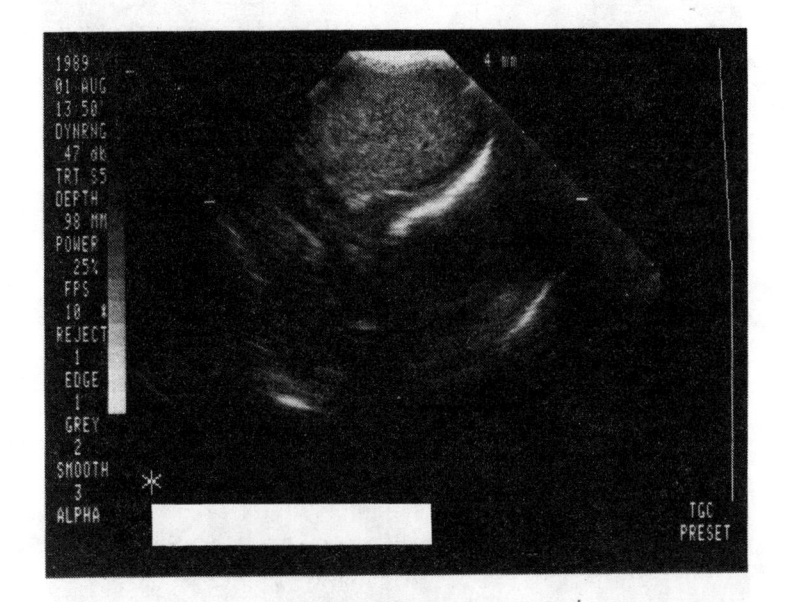

Testicular ultrasound: This is an ultrasound examination which reveals a normal round testicle at the top part of the picture. Notice the normal contour and consistency of the testicle without any abnormal echoes.

Figure 7-15

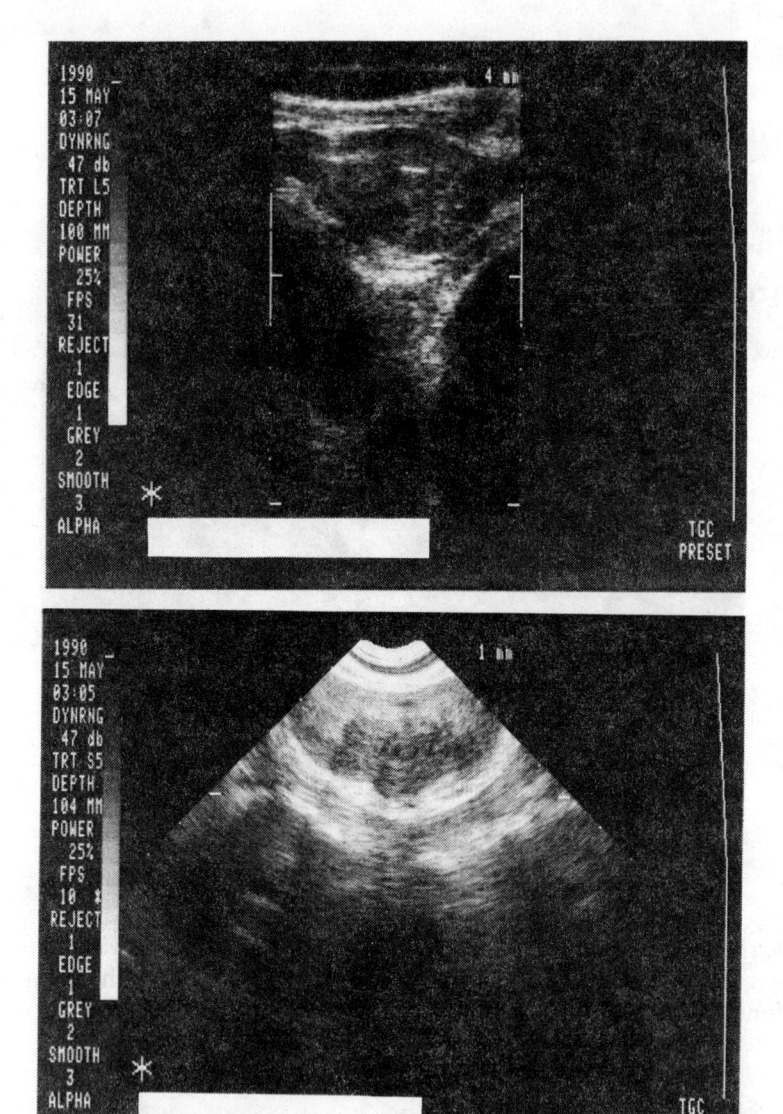

Prostate ultrasound: These two ultrasound examinations reveal a normal prostate in a sagittal and axial view. The prostate is well outlined by the prostate capsule and there are no abnormal echoes nor abnormal configuration of the prostate itself.

Appendix 7-A 219

Figure 7-16

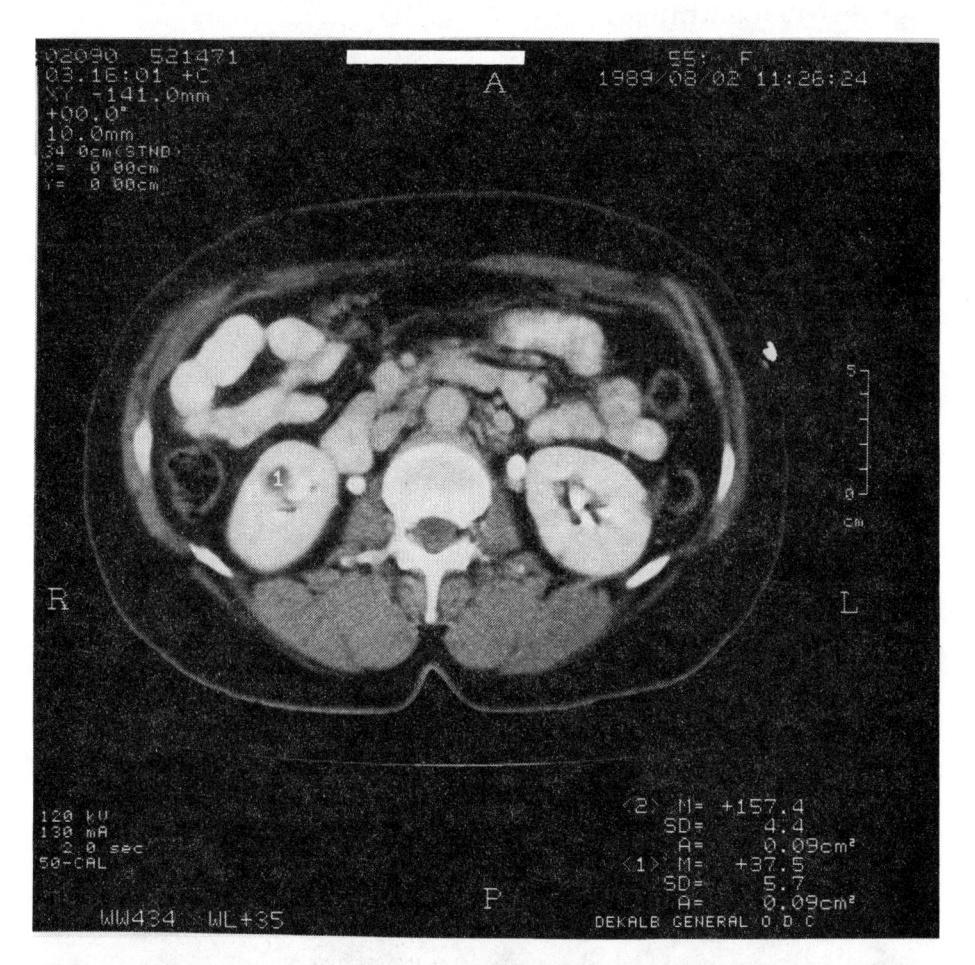

Computerized tomography: Two views of the CT scan of an abdomen showing two normal kidneys with the central vertebral column.

220 *Radiology of Urinary Tract*

Figure 7-16 (continued)

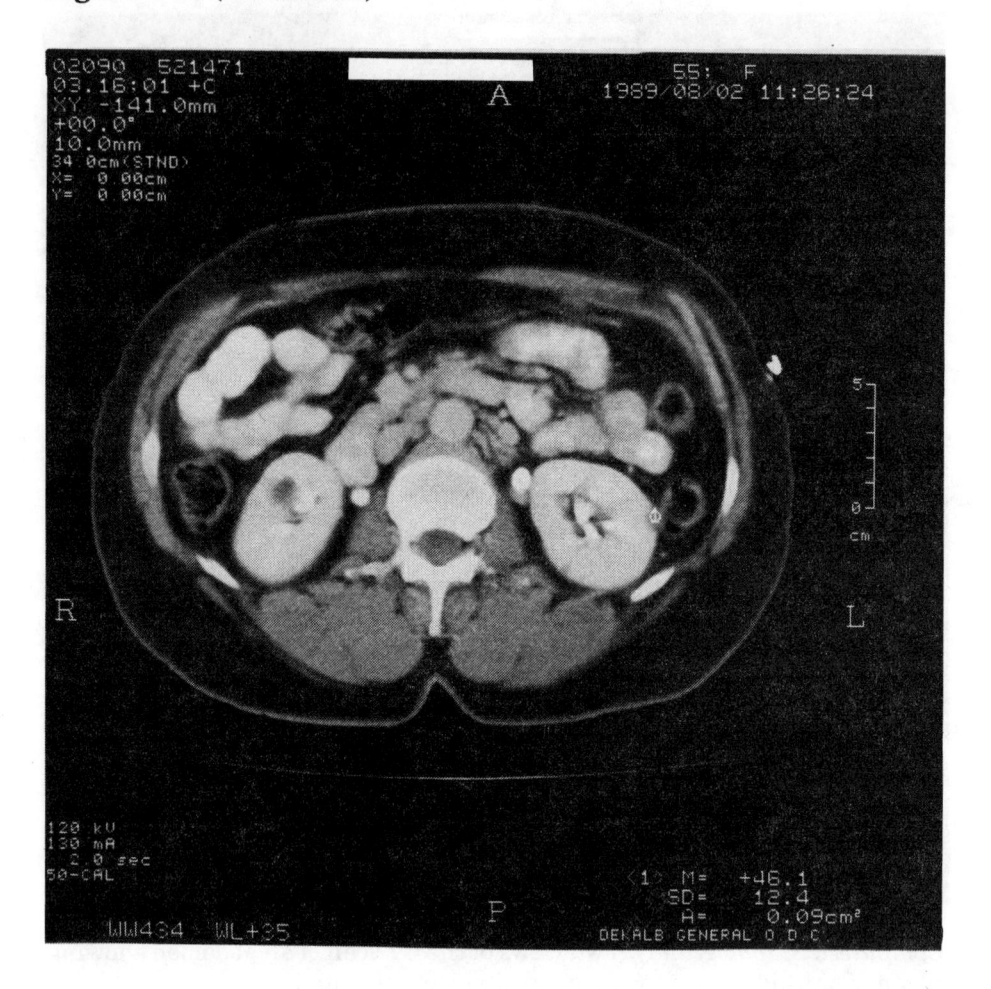

8

Common Urological Surgical Procedures

§8.01 Overview
§8.02 Pyelolithotomy
§8.03 Nephrolithotomy
§8.04 Lithotripsy
§8.05 Percutaneous Nephrostomy
§8.06 Nephrectomy
§8.07 Ureterolithotomy
§8.08 Deligation with Anastomosis
§8.09 Ureteral Reimplantation
§8.10 Vesicourethropexy
§8.11 Vesicovaginal Fistula Repair
§8.12 Cystectomy and Ileal Conduit
§8.13 Open Prostatectomy
§8.14 Radical Prostatectomy
§8.15 Circumcision
§8.16 Vasectomy
§8.17 Insertion of Penile Prosthesis
§8.18 Orchiectomy
§8.19 Detorsion and Orchiopexy
§8.20 Transurethral Resection of Prostate

§8.01 Overview

This chapter involves the surgical procedures most commonly performed by urologists. Of course, any textbook of urology will profoundly discuss all of these procedures in a much more sophisticated manner, but my discussion will provide the reader with a brief overview as to the surgical technique, as well as the indications and common complications which occur with each surgery. I will also include anecdotal observations as the occasion arises. I have chosen what I perceive to be the most commonly employed surgery, but this list is by no means conclusive.

§8.02 Pyelolithotomy

The most common operation regarding the kidney involves stone (calculus) disease. *Pyelolithotomy* means removing a stone from the renal pelvis. With rare exceptions, related to foreign bodies, all calculi are formed in the kidney and then passed down the ureter into the bladder. However, some are trapped and continue to grow in the kidney itself. Fortunately, most calculi remain in the renal pelvis where they are relatively easy to find, but some remain in the calyceal system and are less accessible.

A large renal pelvis calculus presents no challenge to a trained urological surgeon. Of course, pre-operative studies should be performed which would prove the exact location and size of the calculus. Retrograde pyelograms are almost an absolute requirement for the following reasons:

1. To make sure no other calculi are in the ureter
2. To determine whether an intrarenal or extrarenal pelvis exists
3. For evaluation of the ureteropelvic junction which, if obstructive, could be the etiology of the calculus formation

The surgical approach for a pyelolithotomy is through the flank. This is to avoid contaminating the peritoneal contents with infected urine from the calculus. A rib may have to be partially removed for easier access, depending on the body habitus of the patient, but dissection down to the renal pelvis is usually quite easy. Of course, the flank approach accesses the posterior portion of the kidney and makes the surgeon work a little harder to get to the anterior portion where the renal pelvis is located, but this is usually not a difficult problem.

Knowing beforehand whether an intrarenal or extrarenal pelvis (i.e., one that is large and protrudes outside of the kidney parenchyma vis-à-vis a small pelvis which is within the confines of the renal tissue) can assist the surgeon in finding the pelvis more readily.

An incision into the pelvis is made which exposes the calculus, which is then readily grasped and removed. The pelvis is irrigated thoroughly in case other fragments are present and then is closed with the appropriate suture material. Since urine will leak out of any incision in the urinary tract, a surgical drain is placed at the site of the renal pelvis and brought out through the skin wound. This allows egress of the urine and, after seven to ten days when the renal pelvis wound has closed sufficiently to be "urine-tight," the drain can be removed.

The most common complications which occur during the procedure involve entering the pleural cavity during the flank approach or entering the peritoneum during dissection to find the kidney. Usually, these entries are noted at the time, and appropriately repaired and of no consequence. Of course, if a pleural entry occurs resulting in a pneumothorax which is unrecognized by the surgeon, this could be a serious event.

Obviously, damage to the renal artery and vein which is intimately associated with the renal pelvis is a potentially life-threatening complication, and must be immediately repaired.

§8.03 Nephrolithotomy

This surgery is a little more bloody, less accurate, and with a greater risk factor of having complications such as bleeding or severe damage to the kidney or surrounding organs.

The problem in performing the nephrolithotomy is that the x-rays are a one-dimensional view of a three-dimensional organ, and the exact location of a stone in one of the calyces can be extremely difficult to ascertain.

Some techniques involving "fileting" or "splitting" the kidney so as to exactly visualize and remove the stone have been advocated, but, of course, the potential for severe damage to the kidney is quite high in those cases.

Perhaps the most important observation one would make concerning the nephrolithotomy is that this procedure is not done very commonly nowadays. The reason for this, of course, is because of the new technologies which have been advanced regarding the use of the hydroelectric and ultrasonic lithotripter (*see* §8.04).

The main reason for removing any stone is the pain that the patient experiences. The pain occurs because the calculus obstructs the outflow of urine. Calyceal stones rarely cause pain because they ordinarily do not obstruct urinary outflow of any significance. If periodic follow-up x-rays determine that the calyceal calculus is getting larger, nephrolithotomy is indicated because sooner or later this patient will get an infection, and possibly renal abscess associated with the calculus.

The same principles of draining the wound to the outside pertain to nephrolithotomy as to any of the procedures wherein the continuity of the urinary tract has been violated.

There is also great controversy about stenting the ureter after calculus removal, and there are no hard and fast rules or guidelines to follow here. Each patient is individual and different, and of course the surgeon must use his or her best judgment to determine whether a stent is needed.

Nephrolithotomy is best performed by isolating the renal artery and temporarily occluding it so as to allow for optimal renal parenchymal access, vascular control, and tissue cooling.

Finally, the use of the capsule of the kidney is very helpful to facilitate suturing of the nephrolithotomy entrance. This thin veil of tissue is greatly appreciated by the surgeon as a sturdy buttress for the sutures rather than the flabby consistency of the kidney tissue itself.

§8.04 Lithotripsy

This is perhaps the most marvelous advancement in urology today. Cutting for stone, part of the admonitions of the Hippocratic Oath, was a mainstay of urological surgical armamentaria for hundreds of years. It is only in the past decade that the wondrous technology of lithotripsy has virtually made obsolete the surgical approach to renal calculus.

While the physics of the lithotripter is beyond the scope of this text, it is important for the attorney to understand the basic principles and factors involved. The technical aspects of lithotripsy are rapidly changing, and even this paragraph may soon be obsolete. The basic format is that shock waves are generated and then aimed, through a computer-driven guide, at the calculus, and pulsatile shocks are then presented to the stone. Although originally the patient was under general anesthesia and immersed in a "waterbath," newer technology has even changed this approach.

Extracorporeal shockwave lithotripsy (ESWL) is the procedure whereby renal pelvic stones are pulverized and then naturally passed down the ureter. Originally designed for pelvic calculi, newer techniques have evolved wherein ureteral calculi can also be pulverized. Ureteral catheters are usually placed alongside the ureteral stone to create an interface with it and for visualization purposes.

Of course, not every stone or every patient may be a candidate for lithotripsy. For example, an obese patient in whom precise visualization and localization of the calculus is indeterminant will not be amenable to ESWL. Calculi in calyces may also not be amenable because, although they can be pulverized, since they are "trapped" in a calyx, the stone gravel will not pass and will still be trapped, albeit pulverized, in the same location.

Additionally, hydroelectric as well as ultrasonic lithotripsy is available through the ureteroscope or the percutaneous nephroscope. Here, after direct visualization of the calculus has been accomplished, probes are used to actually touch the stone so that the pulse waves can be directed exactly at the stone interface.

The popular stone extraction procedure, performed blindly by generations of urologists, will probably become obsolete. With new techniques of operating room fluoroscopy, flexible and rigid ureteroscopes with their snares, probes, and baskets, the maneuver to extract a small stone from the ureter without open surgery can hardly fail.

§8.05 Percutaneous Nephrostomy

Prior to the advent and availability of the lithotripter, *percutaneous nephrostomy* (PCN) was the rage and vogue of the urologist. Techniques were perfected and new instruments were designed which allowed direct access into the kidney without a surgical exposure.

With the aid of the radiologist and under fluoroscopic guidance, guidewires were introduced into the renal pelvis from the flank position and gradually dilated so that stone baskets, nephroscopes, biopsy forceps, and stents could all be passed into the kidney for appropriate purposes.

Using the hydroelectric or ultrasonic lithotripsy, calculi could be broken up and flushed out or retrieved with a stone basket.

Unfortunately, this type of approach was associated with numerous complications such as bleeding, tissue and organ damage, and perforation of vessels which resulted in a high number of lawsuits. See Chapter 9 for a more complete discussion of the more common complications of the percutaneous nephrostomy.

§8.06 Nephrectomy

Indications for removing a kidney can vary from cancer, stones, trauma, and congenital defects to atrophy, infection, and hypertension.

The approach to the kidney can be via the flank, anterior abdomen, or chest. Some malignancies, because of their involvement of the kidney and surrounding tissues, may require opening the chest and going through the diaphragm to gain access to the vascular pedicle of the kidney.

The prime objective in any nephrectomy is to gain positive control over the renal artery and vein at the earliest opportunity. Finding and tying off the artery first is preferable because if the vein is tied off first, a tremendous amount of blood can be sent to the kidney via the artery and sequestered there. Additionally, if the nephrectomy is being done for cancer, debate continues as to whether the vein should be tied off first so as to prevent the potential spread of malignant cells with manipulation of the kidney. For these reasons, most approaches to the kidney for nephrectomy are via the anterior abdominal approach where the vessels can be easily found prior to manipulation of the kidney.

Since no reconstruction or salvage is required, a nephrectomy is relatively simple surgery. Of course, there are always surgeries which should be easy but turn out to be "horror shows," but, ordinarily taking out the entire kidney is an easy surgical procedure.

The kidney is in a fatty envelope called *Gerota's fascia*. Ordinarily, this fatty "jacket" is not disturbed during the nephrectomy since the objective of the nephrectomy is to remove the entire organ. Even the adrenal gland, intimately associated with the upper pole of the kidney, is removed. Surprisingly, having a normal kidney and adrenal gland on the contralateral side results in no untoward effects from the loss of the bad kidney and its adrenal.

Obviously, the most feared complication from the nephrectomy is laceration, avulsion, or injury to the vasculature. The renal artery and vein are large and very delicate structures which carry a tremendous amount of blood and can easily be torn with resultant severe bleeding. Of course, right next to the renal artery and vein are "Big Red" (the aorta) and "Big Blue" (the vena cava). These are very large vessels and, if one tears into these structures, there is a good possibility that the patient may not survive.

It is also important to understand that sometimes a partial or subtotal nephrectomy may be performed. In cases wherein renal cancer occurs in a solitary kidney, partial nephrectomy may be considered, or, if a large infected stone is confined to an upper or lower pole, a partial nephrectomy may be the appropriate course of action.

§8.07 Ureterolithotomy

This operation, once the most commonly performed urological surgical procedure, is almost obsolete because of the advent of endoscopic procedures. Ureteroscopy, ureteral stents, percutaneous approaches, and ultrasonic, hydroelectric, and extracorporeal shockwave lithotripsy have almost rendered this type of surgery extinct. There is still the rare situation in which, because of the body habitus or medical history of the patient as well as size and location of the stone, the ureterolithotomy may be indicated. Also, if there is an impacted obstructed calculus in the upper-third ureter which cannot be extracted or pushed up into the kidney and a guidewire not passed by it, the indications for ureterolithotomy may be present.

The patient is usually placed on his or her side, the lateral decubitus position, on the operating room table, and a flank incision made down through the musculature into the retroperitoneal area. Finding the ureter may be difficult, and many a urologist (including the author) has searched for over an hour to locate it. When the ureter is located and the stone palpated, the hard work is usually over. A special hook-blade knife is then used to make the incision into the ureter, and the stone is plucked from the ureter. Catheters are then passed proximally into the kidney and distally down the ureter, and irrigating fluid is used to prove the absence of any other small stone fragments. The incision in the ureter is then closed with a few "loosely" tied sutures, and a drain is placed at that site and brought out through the skin.

Interestingly, a number of ureterolithotomies are now being performed as a result of a failed endoscopic procedure. A common urological cause of action is a perforation of the ureter with the ureteroscope during an attempted stone extraction. In this situation, not only is the ureterolithotomy indicated, but proper and adequate drainage of the ureteral perforation is also necessary. While perforation of the ureter with the ureteroscope is not necessarily negligent, if proper drainage is not performed, there may be grounds for a cause of action.

§8.08 Deligation with Anastomosis

Injury to the ureter is relatively common during gynecological surgery, and the urologist is often called upon to repair the damage.

After the appropriate pre-operative studies have been performed to ascertain the exact site of obstruction, surgery will be necessary to repair the damage.

While the ureteral injury may occur because of ligation, electrocautery burn, or transection of the ureter, the surgical repair is usually to excise the damaged portion of the ureter and reanastomose both ends together. Rarely will the removing of an encircling suture allow for the ureter to be revitalized. The most common operation is to approach the most distal normal ureter that the surgeon can find, cut it off at that point, and then reimplant it into the bladder at another location. Since the ureter is somewhat tortuous in its route from the kidney to the bladder, there is usually enough length available to do this. In some instances, however, because there may not be enough length, a *Boari flap* is necessary to connect the bladder to the ureter.

The Boari flap consists of excising a strip of the wall of the bladder and forming it into a tube so as to provide an extension from the bladder to reach the ureter.

All of this surgery is difficult to perform, mainly because it is usually immediately after previous surgery has been done at the same site. Bleeding and tissue edema distort all of the normal anatomy. Happily, the repairs of injured ureters usually are successful.

§8.09 Ureteral Reimplantation

Ureteroneocystostomy is a marvelous combination of syllables which refers to the surgical procedure wherein the ureter is reimplanted into the bladder at a different site than it was previously.

The most common indication for ureteroneocystostomy is vesicoureteral reflux. This is a condition wherein urine in the bladder refluxes backwards up the ureter into the kidney. Because of the high pressure of the refluxing urine, renal damage may and usually does occur.

Ordinarily, the ureter enters the bladder obliquely through its wall so as to create a tunnel (the intramural portion) which, as the bladder fills up with urine, is compressed between the muscular layers and prevents urine from regurgitating backwards up the ureter. Patients with vesicoureteral reflux usually have an abnormal insertion of the ureter into the bladder which lacks the intramural portion, thereby allowing for the reflux.

There are numerous types of ureteroneocystostomy procedures, but the basic technique consists of cutting off the ureter as close to the outside of the bladder wall as possible. The bladder is then pierced and, starting laterally inside the bladder and angling down toward the trigone, a submucosal tunnel is created. The cut end of the ureter is then bluntly pushed through the bladder wall into the newly created tunnel, down toward the trigonal end. There, it is brought out through a small incision made in the bladder mucosa, and sutured to that area. This effectively creates an oblique entrance of the ureter into the bladder which will be compressed as the bladder is filled.

A successful ureteroneocystostomy will prevent urine from refluxing up the kidney, and follow-up cystograms will prove the absence of any reflux.

§8.10 Vesicourethropexy

A common complaint in women who have had multiple pregnancies is *stress urinary incontinence* (SUI). This symptom complex consists of an involuntary leakage of urine whenever the patient coughs, sneezes, laughs, or in any way increases her intraabdominal pressure. Although physicians have told women that the leakage is secondary to a "dropped bladder," indeed the real reason for the urinary leakage is a decrease in the urethrovesical angle. Ordinarily, there is an oblique angle at the junction where the urethra and the bladder meet. If this angle is destroyed, the patient will leak urine involuntarily.

The surgical approach to the loss of the urethrovesical angle is called a *vesicourethropexy*. This classical operation described more than 50 years ago by Drs. Marshall, Marchetti, and Krantz is also known as the Marshall-Marchetti-Krantz procedure (MMK).

In this procedure, an anterior abdominal incision is made, and, remaining extraperitoneally, the prevesical or subsymphyseal space is opened. Because a Foley catheter is inserted into the bladder prior to the surgery, the exact location of the urethrovesical junction can be determined by feeling where the catheter balloon fits against the bladder neck. This area is then sutured to the periosteum of the undersurface of the symphysis pubis. This is accomplished by paralleling the urethra on both sides with individual sutures taken through the tissues, and then passing the needle into the periosteum (lining) of the undersurface of the pubic bone. This increases, elongates, and elevates the urethrovesical angle.

Over the years, numerous other approaches have been described to achieve the same result as the MMK. The most notable and successful is a procedure described by Dr. Thomas Stamey, known as the *endoscopic suspension of the bladder neck* or *Stamey procedure*. This is a slight misnomer, since the surgery is not done endoscopically, but the endoscope (cystoscope) is used during the procedure to accurately determine where the Stamey sutures have been placed.

The Stamey procedure is performed by making an anterior vaginal incision (in the superior wall of the vagina) to expose the urethra, along with a suprapubic abdominal incision. A long needle (similar to a knitting needle) is then passed superiorly from the anterior abdominal incision underneath the symphysis, adjacent to the bladder wall and urethrovesical angle, and then out the vaginal incision. A ligature is passed through the eye of the needle which is then withdrawn superiorly. The needle is then passed downward again, and the other end of the ligature is again passed through the eye of the needle. Then, the needle is again withdrawn superiorly.

Thus, a sling-like affair has been produced with the suture starting from above, going inferiorly underneath the symphysis, adjacent to the urethrovesical junction, out the vagina, and then back up alongside the urethrovesical junction, underneath the symphysis, and out the suprapubic wound. This exact same procedure is performed on the contralateral side of the bladder with the end result of having two sutures in place which, with gentle upward traction, increase, elevate, and elongate the urethrovesical angle.

Both the Stamey and the MMK enjoy remarkable success in resolving SUI in women.

The most common cause of action involved in the MMK results from suturing the Foley catheter in during the procedure. Since multiple sutures are being placed adjacent to the urethra for final placement in the undersurface of the symphysis, it is not unusual for the needle holding the suture to inadvertently enter the urethra and potentially catch the Foley catheter. Ordinarily, after the MMK is terminated and prior to closing the patient, the Foley should be wiggled or even withdrawn so as to prove that it has not been caught by a suture. Unfortunately, this maneuver is not done sometimes, and it is only when the catheter is being removed five days postoperatively that it becomes obvious what has happened. At that time, a certain ingenuity is required to remove the Foley short of having to take the patient back to the operating room for a more involved procedure.

I am aware of one case wherein the surgeon redid the entire MMK procedure when she realized that she had sewn the catheter in—an entirely unnecessary procedure.

The most common cause of action of which I am aware involving the Stamey procedure concerns the entry of the lateral Stamey suture into the bladder. Of course, this is very easy to do, but, since the procedure requires concomitant endoscopic visualization of the bladder interior at the time of the placement of the sutures, it is usually recognized at the time of surgery and resolved.

I am aware of at least three separate instances wherein the surgeon described endoscopically the absence of any suture in the bladder, yet several months later, because of recurrent urinary tract infections, repeat cystoscopy revealed the suture to be in the bladder interior. I can only ascribe this occurrence to migration of the suture through the wall and into the bladder lumen because of the close proximity of the suture to the exterior of the bladder. I do not believe that this was the result of negligence on the part of the urological surgeon.

§8.11 Vesicovaginal Fistula Repair

A connection between the bladder and the vagina is called a *fistula*, and it is one of the most tragic and deplorable medical conditions. There are many causes for a vesicovaginal fistula, but the most common is as a result of gynecological surgery. The end result of the vesicovaginal fistula is a constant urinary leakage from the vagina.

The repair of the fistula is extremely difficult and usually requires more than one procedure. Great controversy exists as to the proper approach—i.e., vaginal or through the bladder—as well as the timing of the surgery. Many advocate repairing the fistula within the first 10 to 15 days of its occurrence, while others suggest waiting six to eight weeks for all of the tissue reaction to subside.

The usual urological approach to the vesicovaginal fistula repair is to enter the bladder from "above"—i.e., through an anterior or suprapubic approach—and visualize the fistula in the interior of the bladder. If it is not a huge hole (and most are usually pinpoint), the area will be difficult to recognize. The hole usually cannot just be sewn together because epithelialization of the fistula tract will not allow the edges to heal. The fistula tract must be totally excised and these new raw edges sutured together. This usually involves the entire muscular layers of the bladder with entrance into the vaginal wall. Each layer is then separately closed, starting with the vaginal wall and then the muscle layers of the bladder, and finally the mucosa (or lining) of the bladder interior. This three-layer closure has a good chance of success. A catheter is then used to drain the bladder and allow for bladder rest.

There are many different described techniques to close fistulae, including the vaginal and combined bladder/vaginal approach. Additionally, there is controversy as to the use of a urethral catheter or a suprapubic catheter to provide drainage. The use of appropriate antibiotics is required as well as the use of an estrogen cream to encourage vaginal healing. All-in-all, vesicovaginal fistula repair is one of the most difficult and demanding surgeries known to urologists.

§8.12 Cystectomy and Ileal Conduit

The most common indication for a total cystectomy is bladder cancer, depending on the clinical staging and histological grading of the tumor. Of course, when the decision is made to perform a cystectomy, another means of diverting and collecting the urine is required. The ileal conduit is a clever way to fashion a new "bladder" for urinary collection.

In the male, because of the location of the prostate gland, total cystectomy (there are a few indications for only a partial or a segmental cystectomy) is a difficult and tedious operation. Total cystectomy in the female is a much easier procedure.

After the bladder has been totally removed, both ureters, which have been cut off from their insertion into the bladder, must be inserted into some artificially created "bladder." In years past, the ureters would have been connected directly to the skin, a so-called cutaneous ureterostomy, and a device placed over each opening for urinary collection. Now, however, the most popular technique used to collect urine is known as the *ileal conduit.* Here, a segment of the ileum containing its own vascular supply is isolated from the intestinal tract. One end of the segment of bowel (the "loop" or "conduit") is sutured closed, and the other is brought out to the skin. Both ureters are implanted into the ileum so that urine can traverse from the kidney down the ureter into the ileum and, thence, into an external collecting device. Although not the most pleasant situation to consider, with modern collecting devices and skin glue, patients can lead a relatively normal life with an ileal conduit.

Interestingly, in spite of the great difficulty in performing this surgery and with the potential for numerous errors and complications to occur, I am not aware of any urological cause of action solely involving the issue of the performance of a cystectomy and ileal conduit. Perhaps patients are so grateful to have survived the threat from bladder cancer that they will tolerate complications more readily than from other surgical procedures.

§8.13 Open Prostatectomy

This is another commonly performed procedure which has decreased in usage because of the ability of urologists to perform this procedure "closed" or "endoscopically." This technique is most definitely a misnomer because the prostate is not removed in an open prostatectomy.

First of all, the word "open" refers to the surgical approach to the prostate from either the suprapubic, retropubic, or perineal approach. The *closed prostatectomy* (*see* §8.20) refers to the endoscopic approach.

Whether open or closed, the surgical procedure is really the removal of a benign tumor in the middle of the prostate and not a prostatectomy. Since this concept may be confusing, it may be advisable to start with the indications for the open prostatectomy.

The anatomical location of the prostate is at the entrance to the bladder, encircling the urethra. As chronological aging occurs, the gland enlarges—usually because of a benign tumor (adenoma) which grows in the middle of the prostate—and may obstruct the outflow of urine from the bladder. Typically, middle-aged men complain of prostatism, a urinary symptom complex composed of frequency, urgency, hesitancy, decreased size and force, and splitting of the urinary stream, post-voiding dribbling, and nocturia.

After determining the cause of the symptoms to be the enlarged prostate, the urologist then makes the decision to remove the obstruction (adenoma), either "open" or "closed." The main criterion as to whether the surgery will be open or closed is the size of the prostate.

Each urologist makes his or her own decision as to how large a gland he or she is able to remove closed (*see* Chapter 9 on Hyponatremia) and if, in palpating the prostate, the urologist believes the gland to be larger than he or she feels comfortable in resecting by transurethral resection, the patient will be advised regarding the open approach. There are also various technical indications for the suprapubic perineal or retropubic approaches, but that discussion is not germane for this text.

When the decision has been made to proceed with the open prostatectomy, the main goal is not to remove the prostate, but merely to remove the obstructing adenoma.

In the suprapubic approach, the surgeon opens the bladder from above, places his or her finger into the prostate, and finds a well-demarcated plane which he or she follows and rather easily scoops out or enucleates the adenoma, leaving the rest of the prostate intact. After the enucleation, catheters are left in the patient to control bleeding. A few sutures are strategically placed near the bladder neck for the same purpose, and the patient is then closed.

Now, it should be apparent why the title "open prostatectomy" is wrong. The procedure should be called a "subtotal prostatectomy" or an "adenomaectomy" for accuracy.

Other than bleeding, which can be quite impressive, the most common serious complications which form the basis for lawsuits from the open prostatectomy are injury to the external urinary sphincter causing urinary incontinence and damage to the rectum. Urinary sphincter damage is easy to do if the surgeon is not extremely careful. As he or she enucleates the adenoma, careless sharp and blunt resection can easily tear or cut the external sphincter.

Damage to the rectum with perforation is also easily done because of the proximity of the delicate rectal mucosa to the prostate. Too rough a dissection or too much pressure from the surgeon's finger can easily result in a tear into the rectal lumen.

Obviously, both of these complications are serious and will commit the patient to more surgery, and it is the rare urologist who will not end up with a lawsuit as a result of these injuries.

§8.14 Radical Prostatectomy

The name of this procedure is actually *prostatoseminovesiculectomy*, but urologists use the term *radical prostatectomy* for convenience. In this operation, the entire prostate, including the seminal vesicles, is removed. The only reason to perform this surgery is for a certain clinical stage of prostate cancer. The types of prostate cancer could cover an entire text, and the interested reader is referred to the medical library for a veritable mountain of texts available concerning this topic. Suffice it to say that after the diagnosis of prostate cancer has been made, and if the clinical staging and tissue grading are such as to make the treatment compatible with surgery as opposed to radiation therapy or chemotherapy, radical prostatectomy is the treatment of choice.

As in the open prostatectomy, there are different approaches to the radical prostatectomy, generally suprapubic or perineal. Either approach is acceptable and depends on the training, experience, and personal preference of the surgeon.

The general task involved in the radical prostatectomy is the *en bloc* removal of all tissue from just proximal to the external sphincter to just proximal to the bladder neck. In this block of tissue are the urethra, prostate, and seminal vesicle. After this extensive dissection has been accomplished, the bladder is then directly connected to the urethra. Amazingly, few patients become incontinent from this surgery. All patients become impotent, however, and this is not as a result of negligence on the part of the surgeon; it is because of the extensive pelvic dissection required to adequately perform the procedure.

Once again, as in the radical cystectomy, because the basic underlying pathology is cancer, it is uncommon for a urological cause of action to arise as a result of complications from the radical prostatectomy.

§8.15 Circumcision

This routine operation on the penis almost needs no description. Interestingly enough, in spite of its commonplace status and probably because of it, it is one of the most common causes of urological medical malpractice. Of course, one's genitalia are a highly charged, emotional area, and any cosmetic result which is less than satisfactory to the patient will form the stimulus to make him go to a lawyer.

Neonatal circumcisions are usually done with a Gomco clamp or other instrument similarly designed. This clamp is applied to the penis so that the foreskin is rapidly excised with excellent hemostasis. Unfortunately, for various reasons, excessive skin may be taken off and, thus, the basis for a lawsuit.

Adult circumcisions are usually performed freehand—i.e., without any Gomco or other clamping device. This type of circumcision rarely results in an excessive removal of skin, although I am aware of some undesirable cosmetic results which have resulted in a lawsuit.

Electrocautery burns to the penis have occurred, especially in neonatal circumcisions, and may result in a terrible injury. I am aware of at least three separate instances wherein sex change operations occurred because of total destruction of the phallus.

§8.16 Vasectomy

This office procedure, performed under local anesthesia, is thought of as simple, but in reality can be associated with severe hemorrhage and, for other reasons, is a common urological cause of action.

Because of the extreme sensitivity of the testicles, great gentleness must be used in palpating the vasa. A small amount of anesthetic is injected under the skin and around each vas, and after that it is a relatively simple matter to isolate a small segment of vas through the scrotal skin incision. A portion of the vas should be excised, and then the proximal and distal ends tied off or cauterized.

Although a properly performed vasectomy invariably results in sterility, the urologist should carefully advise the patient to return for follow-up semen analyses. Ordinarily, the patient is told to return after 10 ejaculations for this check-up. Telling the patient to return in six weeks for his semen analysis without advising him to have a certain number of ejaculations would be violative of the standard of care. There have been patients who have returned in six weeks without having any ejaculations and are surprised to learn that indeed ejaculations must occur in order to empty out the tract. Additionally, the prudent urologist advises the patient to return approximately six to eight months later for another semen analysis in order to monitor whether recanalization has occurred.

Recanalization is the mechanism whereby continuity of the vas deferens is reestablished with the appearance of sperm in the ejaculate. The recanalization is not so much a matter of the two ends of the vas growing back exactly together as much as it is a bridging effect between the two ends. Sperm may leak out of each cut end of the vas and accumulate (sperm granuloma). If these two foci of sperm connect to each other, continuity of the seminal tract may occur, such that live sperm show up in the ejaculate. It is vital, therefore, for the urologist either to bury one or both ends of the cut vas deeper in the scrotum or to separate them sufficiently so that recanalization does not occur. While pregnancy after a vasectomy does not necessarily imply negligence, it is important for the attorney in a wrongful birth action to understand all of the foregoing facts in analyzing the merits of a case.

The most common complication following a vasectomy is hemorrhage. Because of the elasticity of the scrotal skin, a small bleeder in the wound will not have the advantage that tamponade gives in other areas of the body, and the scrotum can continue to fill up with blood until it is the size of a grapefruit! Depending upon each individual set of facts, this could also be a basis for a cause of action.

It is also important to understand that, although the basic surgical principles for performing vasectomy have been utilized for decades, there are always those around who promote other versions of vasectomy. Ideas such as the use of silverclips, injection of a sclerosing solution into the vas, inserting a valve in the lumen of the vas, and others have come and gone. I mention these other methods not necessarily to condemn them, but merely to inform the reader of the need to fully understand the exact manner in which the vasectomy was performed.

§8.17 Insertion of Penile Prosthesis

The problem of impotency is so vast and so devastating that, when it happens to the patient, the so-called solution to the problem is usually insertion of a penile prosthesis. I shall not dwell on the pre-operative evaluation or other indications for the procedure since now the distinction between organic and psychological impotency is becoming more blurred, and prostheses are being inserted for almost any reason regarding impotency.

The original penile prosthesis was a rigid silicone cylindrical tube placed in each of the corpora of the penis. This was succeeded by cylinders with a wire in them so that the phallus could be "bent" downward and did not cause embarrassment from its protrusion. An inflatable prosthesis evolved which included the cylinders and a pump as well as connective tubing to a reservoir with fluid in it. The reservoir was placed subcutaneously in the suprapubic area, and the pump was placed in the scrotum. When the cylinders were inserted in the corpora, by squeezing the pump, fluid from the reservoir would be transferred into the cylinder and cause an erection. The newest model is a self-contained inflatable cylinder which has a valve mechanism in it which, if squeezed properly, can deflate or inflate.

The surgical approach to the insertion of all of these prostheses is identical. The skin of the shaft of the penis is circumscribed and retracted, and the corpus cavernosum is identified and entered. The corpus is readily dilated with the use of specially designed steel rods, and the prosthesis is inserted in the center of each corpus. It is important to make sure that the prosthesis is properly seated with the proximal end on the pubic bone and the distal end under the glans penis.

Scrupulous aseptic technique is mandated when performing this type of surgery because of the high incidence of infections associated with the prosthesis. Measuring the width and the length properly is absolutely necessary (the prostheses come in numerous sizes) because if there is not a proper fit, extrusion of the prosthesis can and does occur.

Lastly, a common complication from this type of surgery is the inadvertent entry into the corpus spongiosum urethra which, if not recognized and repaired properly and promptly, can result in a fistula.

So, while the insertion of a penile prosthesis may appear to be the answer to every man's dream, this surgery is not performed without a high risk of severe complications.

§8.18   Orchiectomy

The two most common reasons for performing orchiectomy are testicular and prostate cancer. The treatment of choice when the diagnosis of testicular cancer is made is to perform a radical orchiectomy and follow this up with other treatment modalities such as chemotherapy or radiation therapy.

In prostate cancer, since androgens (testosterone) are a fuel for exacerbating the cancer, orchiectomy is frequently an alternative treatment given to the patient after initial therapy with oral anti-androgenic medication has failed.

Simple orchiectomy is really just that. A scrotal skin incision is made, and the testicle and its blood supply are readily identified and brought into the wound. The spermatic cord which contains all of the vasculature to and from the testicle is then cross-clamped and divided.

The radical orchiectomy is only slightly more complicated in that an inguinal incision is made so as to gain control of the spermatic vessels in the lower part of the abdomen. After cross-clamping the cord, the testicle is excised. It is not unusual for the urologist to insert a testicular prosthesis into the scrotum after an orchiectomy has been performed.

These procedures rarely, if ever, have any material risk of complications associated with them.

§8.19   Detorsion and Orchiopexy

Torsion of the testicle is really a twisting of the spermatic cord and the testicle. If the torsion is not recognized early and surgically repaired, the testicle will necrose and atrophy because of the vascular occlusion. This is an absolute urological emergency and the diagnosis must be made timely and properly.

With the patient in the operating room, a scrotal incision is made, and the obvious torsion of the spermatic cord is noted. It is simply untwisted in order to allow for the proper blood flow to reestablish. If, after observing the dusky, engorged testicle, it appears to "pink" up and revitalize, nothing more is done (other than an orchiopexy) to help it survive.

Orchiopexy is an operation whereby the base of the testicle is simply sutured into the base of the scrotum so as to prevent it from twisting again. In reality, several sutures are placed rather than one, or else the testicle could conceivably twist again on its longitudinal axis.

The term *bell-clapper deformity* is one which the reader should understand. Ordinarily, the scrotal ligament or gubernaculum testis is a broad band of tissue from the inner wall of the scrotum to the epididymis of the testicle. This immobilizes and prevents the spermatic cord from twisting on itself. With faulty development of this band, the testicle is suspended in the scrotum by the spermatic cord (the "lifeline" of blood vessels, lymphatics, and nerves which is the only connection that the testicle has to the body), much like a bell-clapper. Thus, in instances of torsion of the spermatic cord, urologists will speak of the bell-clapper deformity because of the absence of the scrotal ligament which should have prevented the torsion from occurring. It is also important for the reader to know that numerous articles have been written attesting to the fiction of the bell-clapper deformity. In other words, there is great evidence that no such scrotal ligament exists at all and that torsion of the spermatic cord occurs just because!

As a final note, it is the standard of care when detorting a spermatic cord and either pexing or removing the affected testicle to do an orchiopexy on the opposite testicle. Urological medical malpractice cases have been involved wherein this was not done and subsequent torsion and loss of the opposite testicle have occurred.

§8.20 Transurethral Resection of Prostate

The *transurethral resection of prostate* (TURP) is certainly the most common operation regarding the prostate gland performed by urologists. Its purpose is to remove any obstructing prostate tissue from the urinary channel so as to increase the urinary flow rate for the patient.

The prostate encircles the urethra as it exits from the bladder and, as the adenoma (or carcinoma) grows larger in the center of the prostate, the urethra is more and more restricted. This obstruction gives rise to the symptom complex known as *prostatism*. These symptoms are hesitancy, urgency, frequency, decreased size and force of the urinary stream, the sensation of inadequate emptying of the bladder, nocturia, and post-voiding dribbling.

Under a spinal or general anesthetic, a resectoscope, similar to a cystoscope but with an electrocautery loop, is inserted in the urethra to visualize the prostate. Using the electrocautery loop as a cutting and coagulating tool, the obstructing tissue is removed. The loop makes excursions within the prostatic urethra and "chips" away at the prostate tissue. These prostate "chips" are then sent to the pathologist for histological evaluation. The TURP, as in all endoscopic procedures, must be done with a circulating fluid and, in the interest of preventing hyponatremia, a physiological solution known as *glycine* is used. See Chapter 9 for a more complete discussion of this low-salt syndrome.

Ordinarily, a TURP takes about one hour to perform. This is very important because the incidence of fluid absorption through the open venous sinuses from the surgery can result in a dilutional hyponatremia if a longer time is spent during the resection. The procedure can be very bloody, and the constant flow of irrigating fluid is necessary for proper visualization. Of course, the coagulating current used in conjunction with the resectoscope is important for controlling the bleeding.

At the end of the resection, a large, three-way Foley catheter is inserted in the bladder, and the balloon, having been inflated, is placed with tension at the bladder neck so as to facilitate hemostasis in the prostatic fossa. The three-way catheter, as opposed to the ordinary Foley, is used because it has a separate channel for the constant through-and-through flow of irrigating fluid. This is the *Murphy drip,* and its purpose is to have a continuous flow going into the catheter, circulating in the bladder and then out the catheter so that clots do not form or obstruct the catheter. The management of a postoperative TURP patient and the Murphy drip takes a great deal of skill and experience. Nurses on the urology wing of any hospital where TURPs are performed are usually specially trained in this procedure. Every urologist has spent many long hours at a patient's bedside trying to resolve bleeding, remove clots, reposition the catheter properly, and manipulate the balloon for effective drainage.

Ordinarily, the catheter is left in about three days to allow for the prostatic fossa to start healing. If the Murphy drip can be discontinued on the second day, the Foley catheter is then removed the next day, and the order for SOB written. The abbreviation "SOB" does not stand for the usual epithet we have all heard, but means "string of bottles."

What happens is that the patient is given four or five small containers (bottles) to use for each voided specimen. The urologist or nurse can then visualize the color, consistency, and volume of the urine which has been voided. If the urine is dark, bloody, and full of clots, a catheter may have to be reinserted into the patient, or, if the color gradually improves to a light pink or yellow, then the patient is allowed to go home catheter-free.

The most common complication from a TURP which results in a urological cause of action is damage to the external sphincter with subsequent urinary incontinence.

Absolute knowledge of the area is required before performing TURPs. The external sphincter is very close to the most distal area of the resection, and this is ordinarily noted by the location of the verumontanum. If the resectionist goes too distal to the veru, injury to the sphincter may occur. Although this complication is devastating to the patient, there are new techniques to resolve the incontinence which include injections of silicone into the external sphincter or a prosthesis which acts as an external sphincteric valve.

Hyponatremia, perforation of the bladder or urethra, septicemia, excessive bleeding, and urethral stricture are all complications which can occur after a TURP. More bizarre complications include fracture of the resectoscope sheath and rupture of the bladder, secondary to an explosion of the gas formed during the resection.

9

Common Urological Complications

§9.01 Overview
§9.02 Injury to Ureter during Abdominal Hysterectomy
§9.03 Damage to Urinary Sphincter during TUR
§9.04 Hyponatremia or Low-Salt Syndrome
§9.05 Failure to Diagnose Torsion of the Testicle
§9.06 IVP Dye Reactions
§9.07 Allergic or Toxic Drug Reactions
§9.08 Damage to Internal Organs during the Percutaneous Approach to the Kidney
§9.09 Penile Prosthesis: Infections and Improper Placement
§9.10 Failure to Timely Remove Ureteral Stent
§9.11 Damage to Testicle during Hernia Repair
§9.12 Complications of Vasectomy
§9.13 Urethral Perforation
§9.14 Suture through Catheter after Marshall-Marchetti-Krantz Procedure
§9.15 Potpourri

§9.01 Overview

This chapter is based on my experience as a practicing urological surgeon and as one who has reviewed over 450 urological records for potentially meritorious malpractice claims. Not that I am the world's expert on urological standard of care, but not only has my personal urological experience been somewhat vast, I also have been intensely involved in the urological medical malpractice arena and have had dialogue and colloquy with numerous groups, organizations, and forums for discussing certain potential urological claims. As I describe these common urological complications, I will discuss actual cases in which I have been involved, either as an expert witness or as an attorney, and will also comment on the urological community's approach and standard as I perceive them.

Finally, these topics will not be presented in order of importance or in order of the most common type of urological cause of action. Quite simply, I have just written down a list of what I view to be the most common issues and complications I have found, not only urologically but also medicolegally.

As I discuss the issues and pontificate as to my perception of the standard of care, remember that the standard of care is just that—what one qualified expert articulates the standard of care to be. Obviously, experts view the standard of care differently, which is one reason why we have plaintiffs and defendants. If we all described the standard of care the same way, there might be no conflict because, obviously, the plaintiff's version of the standard of care is diametrically opposite from the defendant's.

I shall try to be as objective as possible in detailing my perception of the urological care, but obviously many readers, particularly the defendant urologist in each case, will not agree with me. Since I am writing this book, however, I get to have it my way.

I also will make a disclaimer up front in that I shall protect the confidentiality of those parties whose cases have been settled or have been dropped and never went to trial. Finally, all of these judgments and perceptions about the issues in cases are my own, not someone's theories to which I subscribe, and certainly have nothing to do with the publisher. I take full responsibility for all of my own statements.

§9.02 Injury to Ureter during Abdominal Hysterectomy

To a urologist, this is the most common complication for which he or she is called upon to intervene. Typically, the gynecologist, during surgery, will tie off, cauterize, clamp, devascularize, or cut the ureter, and within the next 24 to 48 hours, after the patient develops flank pain and fever, will order an intravenous pyelogram (IVP) and make the proper diagnosis.

The urologist will then cystoscope the patient and do a retrograde pyelogram to determine the severity and location of the injury. Immediate surgical intervention is indicated, and invariably the treatment is to operate the patient, excise the damaged segment of the ureter, and reimplant the healthy ureter into the bladder. Plenty of other options exist, from merely deligating the ureter (if a suture has been placed near or around the ureter and has just "tented" or "angled" the ureter) to passing a stent up the ureter for drainage purposes. Additionally, transureterostomy and nephroureterectomy are available, but each particular situation will dictate the appropriate treatment.

Frankly, although I have reviewed numerous records regarding damaged ureters after GYN surgery, in fact the urologist really should not be the expert to contact for an opinion. It is natural to think of the urologist since he or she is the one who usually diagnoses and repairs the damage, but, in fact, the proper expert witness in this case should be a gynecologist.

Urologists are not trained to do gynecological surgery and really should not be asked to describe the standard of care. Since a gynecologist caused the injury, another gynecologist should be the proper person to articulate the standard of care.

Although the most common cause of action arises when damage to the ureter occurs during a routine abdominal hysterectomy and is recognized a few hours later, the case gets juicier when the gynecologist fails to recognize what he or she has done in spite of the patient's post-operative course, and only when a ureterovaginal or ureterocutaneous fistula occurs does the diagnosis become evident.

Of course, not every injured ureter during gynecological abdominal surgery is a result of a departure from the standard of care. Physicians speak of mishaps or maloccurrences, and I agree that some incidents are just that. A surgeon who operates a patient who has never had intraabdominal surgery and does not have scarring or adhesions and then damages the ureter is more likely to have deviated from the standard of care than the surgeon who operates a patient who has had multiple previous surgeries with distorted anatomy and intense scarring.

Obviously, the latter case is difficult surgery with nothing being in the right place and with structures stuck together like cement. There, not cutting into a ureter probably depends more on luck than skill.

But what about the surgeon, knowing he or she is facing a difficult abdominal procedure, who fails to ask a urologist pre-operatively to pass a ureteral catheter up the ureter for identification purposes? Is that a departure from the standard of care? I believe so. It is so simple and so helpful to have the ureters identified during the surgery that it is inexcusable not to have them splinted for identification purposes.

Thus, the damaged ureter during an open gynecological procedure can have all sorts of ramifications. A virgin belly may involve departure from the standard of care, a patient with previous surgery may not, and failure to cannulate the ureters pre-operatively may be another avenue to explore. Each case turns on particulars, and that is why an objective review of the records is paramount.

I was recently asked to scrub in on a case where a patient was undergoing hysterectomy after having had three previous C-sections. The gynecologist made a three-inch-long laceration in the base of the bladder where it was adhered to the uterus. He recognized it, discussed it immediately with the family, and called me in to repair the laceration. The patient and everyone else were understanding and happy. I do not believe that this incident was an example of a departure from the standard of care.

Finally, I have also been involved, as a urologist, in one case wherein I placed catheters up the ureters pre-operatively on an obese patient who had had no previous surgery. In spite of this, the gynecologist still cut into the ureters. Now, with a ureteral catheter staring him in the face, he easily recognized his error and called me back in to repair the laceration. Departure from the standard of care? Proximate cause? Injury? Potential recovery? You make that decision. There was never a lawsuit involved, even after the patient was informed of the incident.

§9.03 Damage to Urinary Sphincter during TUR

This is probably the most common urological complication I have been asked to review from a medicolegal aspect. Enlargement of the prostate is an aging process, and a large percentage of men from age 50 to 70 require some sort of surgical relief for their symptomatology. The *transurethral resection of the prostate* (TUR) is discussed in Chapter 8, but this discussion concerns this most common complication of the TUR and the medicolegal ramifications thereof.

Since the external urinary sphincter is anatomically close to the verumontanum in the prostatic urethra, urologists are taught in their neophyte days to be aware of and thoroughly understand this region anatomically. The surgery is done with an electrocautery "loop" which cuts the obstructing tissue, and if the loop is advanced beyond the anatomical confines of the prostatic urethra, injury to the external sphincter is a distinct possibility.

As the resectionist (the name given the urologist who performs the TUR) inserts the resectoscope into the patient's urethra and begins the resection, he or she is extremely cautious in the manner of manipulating the loop. Urologists use the verumontanum as the most distal landmark of their resection, and if for some reason the excursion of the loop goes beyond the veru, the external sphincter will be injured.

The typical story is of a 65-year-old male who, having suffered with symptoms of prostatism for five years, goes to a urologist who properly evaluates him and then performs the TUR. Ordinarily, a Foley catheter is left in the patient for three or four days after the TUR and, if injury to the sphincter has occurred, the patient experiences a total and constant urinary leakage on removal of the catheter. He is unable to control his stream, and has a "leaky faucet." Urologists call this *total urinary incontinence.* Of course, all sorts of variations on this theme occur, and the patient can either have total urinary incontinence or stress urinary incontinence or even mild and partial urinary incontinence. Frequently, the urologist, in using the electocautery, can burn the sphincter, and when the burned area sloughs off—sometimes many days after the TUR—the leakage can begin.

Also, the total urinary incontinence may improve somewhat as the scarification and healing of the damaged area occur, but in the face of a laceration to the external urinary sphincter, there will always be some and usually a significant element of urinary incontinence.

Of course, the most obvious defense for this injury is that damage to the external urinary sphincter during TUR is a known and accepted complication and one of the risks of the procedure. The defense will maintain that the patient was advised of the risk, that he was willing to accept it, and now that he has sustained the injury, he has no right to sue. This is not a bad defense, and, as a matter of fact, one that will possibly persuade a jury.

Indeed, it is not a clear issue (is any?) as to whether damaging the sphincter is a departure from the standard of care. Some purists believe that urologists are trained to understand the anatomical boundaries of the area and should not violate the landmarks, and therefore every excursion of the loop beyond the verumontanum and into the sphincter is a departure from the standard of care. Others opine that these things happen, even in the best of hands, and doctors are only human and doing the best they can. I guess that is what juries are for!

My most interesting TUR sphincter case involved a gentleman who had a mild neurological problem, walked with a flapping gait, and also had slightly slurred speech. He was undergoing his second TUR by the same urologist (the first one had been performed some 10 years previously) when he was rendered incontinent as a result of damage to the sphincter.

Amazingly, the pathological report of the tissue sent in after the prostate resection described "skeletal muscle fibers consistent with external sphincter." Much to the plaintiff's surprise, however, the defendant's counsel was able to convince the jurors that, in spite of the rather incriminating finding, the main reason for the patient's incontinence was his unusual neurological problem and not the electro-incision into his external sphincter. Thus, it is not who has the best case, but who has the best lawyer!

As a final note to TUR sphincter injuries, it is important for the reader to understand that videocystoscopy is available to actually photograph the external sphincter. This is a rather impressive sight, and if the reader has a client with this problem, he or she should canvass the urological community for one who is able to do a videocystoscopy.

Finally, and this is more of a medical than a legal comment, numerous surgical approaches, from Teflon injections into the sphincter to implantation of artificial sphincters, are available to help these unfortunate men.

§9.04 Hyponatremia or Low-Salt Syndrome

One of the most feared complications from the transurethral resection of the prostate (TUR) is *hyponatremia* ("hypo" means less than, "Na" is the chemical symbol for sodium from the obsolete word "natrium," and "emia" means blood). Thus, hyponatremia is a condition wherein the normal sodium level in the blood is lower because of a dilutional factor from absorption of the irrigating fluid used in the TUR.

As described in Chapter 6, cystoscopy is done with irrigating fluid running through the cystoscope into the bladder so as to distend the bladder for visualization purposes.

Irrigating fluid is also necessary through the resectoscope for the same reason. This irrigating fluid, however, must meet certain stringent requirements and must be optically clear and nonelectrolytic. Saline, the physiological body fluid, is an electrolyte solution which will conduct the electricity, but will also disperse and dissipate it rather than focus it. Water can also be used as irrigating fluid for it will conduct the electricity, but, if absorbed by the body, will cause severe intravascular hemolysis (breakup of the blood cell because of the osmolarity of the water). Thus, a solution is used which is isotonic to the body, optically clear, and conductive. This solution is commercially available and is a 1.5 per cent solution of glycine. This is the solution which the standard of care requires to be used for a TUR.

The absorption of fluid occurs during a TUR and not during a cystoscopy because of the venous plexuses which are opened during the resection. The hydrostatic pressure of the irrigating fluid is higher than the diastolic blood pressure, and therefore the irrigating fluid is forced into the venous sinuses and thus into the body. This absorption of fluid dilutes the normal sodium level in the bloodstream, and hyponatremia or low-salt syndrome is the result.

Even though an irrigating fluid is used which is optically correct, conducts electricity, and will not break up red blood cells, the dilutional effect will still occur if enough of the glycine is absorbed.

So, what happens if your salt level gets low? Remember when Coach What's-His-Name gave you salt pills to take during football practice? He knew that if you lost too much salt you could get sick, have a fit, faint, or—worse—die! And he was right. The symptoms of hyponatremia are mental confusion, muscle cramps, convulsions, coma, and frequently death.

However, the tricky part of diagnosing hyponatremia during a TUR is how to recognize it in a patient who is under either a regional or general anesthetic. Mental confusion and convulsions are very late signs.

The classical signs of hyponatremia are a gradual increase in the venous blood pressure with a slowing of the pulse. This is important for the attorney to understand because it is now becoming obvious that the anesthesiologist who is responsible for monitoring the vital signs during surgery may be more culpable in a hyponatremia case than the urologist.

Thus, the typical case of hyponatremia involves a patient who undergoes a TUR with a spinal anesthetic and, during the procedure, becomes somewhat combative and confused. A serum sodium is drawn on him in the recovery room and found to be markedly low. A 3 per cent solution of salt is given intravenously, but it is too late; he becomes comatose, stays that way for several weeks until he has a cardiac arrest, and dies.

Review of the anesthetic record will reveal the gradually increasing blood pressure and decreasing pulse. In the "remarks" section of the record there may even be a notation about the restlessness of the patient. The duration of the procedure will be over two hours; the universal time allowed for a TUR is one hour plus or minus 15 minutes, and longer TURs can have more absorption of fluid with the potential problem of hyponatremia. The estimated blood loss on the record will be 2000 cc., and the circulating nurse's record will reveal several thousand cc. of irrigating fluid used during the procedure. The urological operative note will detail the significant bleeding which occurred.

All of these factors are important to consider in evaluating each hyponatremia case, and will allow the attorney to make better judgments as to whether the case has merit.

§9.05 Failure to Diagnose Torsion of the Testicle

Torsion of the testicle is one of the most urgent of urological emergencies because a testicle which twists and cuts off its blood supply can become necrotic in a very short period of time. There is a time-honored adage in urology that scrotal swelling in the prepubertal male is torsion until proven otherwise. It is the "proven otherwise" that creates lawsuits. Additionally, torsion can occur at any age and must be heavily suspect in any male with scrotal swelling of a sudden and painful nature. While this text is not the forum to enumerate the differential diagnoses between torsion of the spermatic cord and epididymitis, this is the gravamen of the issues.

The typical missed torsion case involves a patient who sustains the rather sudden onset of pain and scrotal swelling and immediately goes to the local emergency room. There, the physician on call examines the patient, checks his urine, and prescribes an antibiotic for *epididymitis*—an inflammatory process of the epididymis of the testicle (*see* Chapter 5). The emergency room physician may have called the urologist on call for that day and been told to prescribe the antibiotics, or he or she may have relied on his or her own medical judgment to make the diagnosis.

Most commonly, however, the emergency room physician stresses to the urologist on call that he or she should immediately come to the emergency room because of the highly suspected diagnosis of torsion. The urologist may refuse to do so, and the patient is sent home with his antibiotic. It is only some months later after the testicle has died and started to atrophy that the real diagnosis is made.

What went wrong and who is to blame? First of all, one must articulate the standard of care, and the history, physical examination, and laboratory findings are all required components. The suddenness of the onset of the pain and swelling are real tip-offs. Gently palpating the testicle may reveal the epididymis anterior instead of posterior, but the real diagnosis can be made in most emergency rooms today with Doppler or testicular scan—studies which are able to differentiate torsion from epididymitis.

The emergency room physician has a duty to triage the patient. That is, the physician must decide whether the presenting signs and symptoms are such that he or she personally can handle the situation or that he or she needs to call the urologist. Most competent emergency room physicians or even primary care physicians will recognize the possibility of torsion and call in specialists.

What of the situation wherein the emergency room physician sees the patient, properly evaluates him, considers torsion in the differential diagnosis, and then makes the diagnosis of epididymitis? He or she then sends the patient home with antibiotics, and several weeks later, after testicular atrophy occurs, the proper diagnosis is made. Has that physician departed from the standard of care? Physicians can be wrong in their diagnoses and treatment of patients, but if they adhere to the standard of care in making that judgmental decision, there should be no cause of action.

What about the situation where the emergency room physician seriously considers torsion and calls the urologist who, after hearing the clinical facts, decides the patient does not have torsion. Has the emergency room physician satisfied the legal duty to the patient if he or she still believes that torsion is a good possibility and the urologist consultant refuses to come in? These are all questions that have occurred in lawsuits and are difficult to answer, but ordinarily the standard of care requires the emergency room physician to make sure the patient is properly cared for in spite of the inaction of the urologist on call.

The torsion versus epididymitis cases are usually rather well defined. The age of the patient, duration of the symptoms, lack of inflammatory signs, and abnormal Doppler or scan all help to make the proper diagnosis. In spite of all this, however, misdiagnoses continue to be made and prove a fertile ground for the plaintiff's attorney.

§9.06   IVP Dye Reactions

As discussed in Chapter 7, the intravenous pyelogram (IVP) is a commonly performed urographic examination. Because the contrast material used intravenously contains iodine, there is a high incidence of allergic reactions to the "dye" amongst patients. Careful questioning prior to the injection of the dye is required, along with monitoring the patient during the x-ray study. If the patient has a highly allergic history, particularly to iodine or seafood (which has a lot of iodine in it), the IVP should not be performed. If, during the study, the patient exhibits signs of an allergic reaction, such as itching, blotchy red areas on the skin, and shortness of breath, immediate antihistamine measures must be taken. Although the overall fatal incidence of lethal allergic reactions is very small and certainly can happen in the absence of a departure from the standard of care, one case stands out in my mind as a particularly tragic one.

The patient was a 65-year-old man who presented to his family physician with typical symptoms of prostatism. The family physician referred the patient to a large medical center where he was admitted and evaluated for prostate surgery. Because the patient had had a previous history of kidney stone disease, although he was currently asymptomatic, an IVP was ordered. The patient was allergic to the IVP dye, and the records were replete with this positive information.

Because the medical center where the patient was hospitalized was a large medical training facility, a protocol had been prepared for performing IVPs on patients who were allergic to the dye. Among other things, the main component of the protocol was to give an intravenous dose of a steroid prior to the injection of the dye.

After starting the protocol on a Friday evening, the orders were written to give the last dose of the intravenous steroid the next morning and then take the patient to the radiology suite. The physician who wrote these orders then left town for the weekend. Unfortunately, the patient was not taken to the radiology suite for several hours after the last dose of steroid was given, and when the contrast material was given to him, he sustained a massive allergic reaction including a cardiac arrest and death.

A review of the pharmacological properties of the steroid revealed that the useful effect of the drug was only available for one or two hours after it had been given intravenously, and by the time the patient was taken to the x-ray department and given the injection of the contrast medium, all of the steroid was "out of his body." A jury trial resulted in a large plaintiff's verdict.

Many urologists perform IVPs in the office rather than referring the patient to a hospital or to a private radiologist. It is an absolute requirement for any physician performing IVPs to have antiallergic and resuscitative measures handy in case of a reaction. This would be an important piece of information for the plaintiff's attorney to know.

In addition to the informed consent requirements, part of the history which must be taken of each patient undergoing an IVP is careful inquiry concerning previous allergies of any sort as well as any reaction to seafood or shellfish.

It is also important to understand that there are at least two other means of evaluating the kidneys other than the IVP. Renal ultrasound will give a good idea of the contour and density of the kidneys, and retrograde pyelograms will also give information about the renal collecting system. Thus, although important, the IVP is not an indispensable tool.

There are even new iodinated compounds being touted as almost a pure nonallergic medium to be used in patients who present with a questionable allergic history. Even in those instances, I believe subjecting the patient to the potentially lethal risk of an allergic reaction when alternative modalities are available could be construed as a departure from the standard of care.

§9.07 Allergic or Toxic Drug Reactions

While almost any drug or medication can cause an allergic reaction and certainly the standard of care demands that the physician inquire about the allergic history of any patient, there is one drug heavily used by urologists which has been the basis of several lawsuits. *Macrodantin* is a drug which, because it is highly concentrated in the urine, is used daily by urologists. Although not a true antibiotic but rather an antibacterial, Macrodantin is poorly concentrated in the tissues, but very effective as a low-dose urinary antibacterial.

Macrodantin is metabolized in the body and excreted via the kidneys. It is not a strong antibiotic in the sense that it has a therapeutic effect against highly pathogenic organisms, but because of its unique and high urinary concentration, it is effective against most common urinary tract pathogens.

What gets urologists in trouble with Macrodantin is their failure to monitor patients who take this drug. It is common practice for urologists to use Macrodantin on a daily low suppressive dose for months. Used in this manner, Macrodantin is highly effective in keeping many patients infection-free.

But, in these patients who do take long-term Macrodantin, it is imperative to monitor them closely.

The *Physician's Desk Reference* (PDR) is one book which every medical malpractice attorney should own. It is readily available in book stores. The PDR is the "bible" of all prescription drugs sold in the United States. There is even a pocket part for over-the-counter drugs. It is the PDR that most physicians go to for prescribing and using drugs. Although there are package inserts which describe all of the important information about any drug, the physician rarely sees these package inserts and relies rather heavily not only on the pharmaceutical representative who makes calls in his or her office, but also on the PDR.

The following is a typical Macrodantin cause of action which will illustrate the issues involved. Mrs. Smith was treated for a urinary tract infection by Dr. Brown after he had performed cystoscopy on her for recurrent urinary tract infections. The records reflect that Mrs. Smith was given Macrodantin for a total of over 12 months and with approximately 1100 capsules prescribed. The records do not reflect any specific monitoring of her pulmonary or liver function studies. Because of some hemorrhage and after she had been taking the medicine for one year, the patient was admitted to the hospital with the diagnosis of pulmonary fibrosis. She was treated with steroids, but developed a stress ulcer as well as a perforation of a diverticulum. She underwent laparotomy, but eventually died of sepsis caused by the perforated diverticulum and pulmonary fibrosis.

The issues here concern whether the massive prescription of Macrodantin for this patient was appropriate and particularly whether monitoring her pulmonary and liver function should have been performed.

The PDR is very clear about monitoring patients who are on long-term Macrodantin. Certainly, the pharmacy records which were obtained and which revealed over 100 Macrodantin capsules prescribed on a monthly basis support the suggestion that an overindulgence of using this drug occurred. To continue prescribing Macrodantin without monitoring the pulmonary or liver function studies is a departure from the standard of care, and it was this departure which resulted in the patient's developing pulmonary fibrosis and starting the sequence of events which led to her subsequent demise.

The lesson to be learned here is not only that the standard requires monitoring liver function studies and chest x-rays on patients taking Macrodantin, but any physician who prescribes massive doses of any medication should properly evaluate his or her patient periodically.

However, as an alternative to this scenario, I would also like to suggest the incidence of another toxic reaction to a drug in a case which I evaluated but which I believed was not meritorious to pursue.

Stevens-Johnson syndrome is a severe form of an inflammatory, blister-type eruption of the skin and mucous membranes. It is usually violent and of sudden onset. Treatment is usually to no avail, and the patient succumbs secondarily to a fatal respiratory infection. I am aware of at least one case wherein a healthy male, after a proper history was taken, was given a sulfur drug for a prostate infection. Within hours after taking the medication, this unfortunate patient sustained the massive skin, mouth, nose, and eye lesions seen in the Stevens-Johnson syndrome. Despite the rapid diagnosis and institution of appropriate medication, the patient died within 48 hours.

Here, I believe there was no departure from the standard of care, yet because of the allergic and highly toxic reaction to a drug, a patient died.

§9.08 Damage to Internal Organs during the Percutaneous Approach to the Kidney

Popularity of the percutaneous approach to the kidney has birthed an entire new industry in not only urological instrumentation, but also urological medical malpractice cases.

Because of sophisticated radiographic technology along with new urological instrumentation such as endoscopes, guidewires, and ureteral stents, the flank approach to certain urological problems gained huge popularity. Although lithotripsy has now resulted somewhat in a diminution of enthusiasm and requirement for percutaneous approaches to the kidney, there are still many instances where this procedure is appropriately indicated.

Prior to the availability of the lithotripter, the percutaneous procedure was the most popular and least invasive means to remove renal or upper ureteral stones as opposed to surgery. This procedure was performed in the radiology suite by both the radiologist and urologist for the purpose of removing stones. Invariably, as guidewires and instruments were blindly introduced via the flank and into the kidney, perforation of kidneys, arteries and veins, and even bowel occurred. Obviously, this subsequent traumatic occurrence required immediate surgical intervention. Frequently, a nephrectomy was required because of massive bleeding, and other major surgical procedures had to be performed because of injuries to major blood vessels or bowel. Although the popularity of the percutaneous approach to the kidney has subsided somewhat, for several years, because of the complications arising from this procedure, subsequent lawsuits naturally flowed.

One interesting case involved a young man who presented to the emergency room at 9:00 in the evening with severe left ureteral colic. An intravenous pyelogram (IVP) was performed which revealed an obstructed left kidney along with a 4 mm. upper ureteral stone. The patient was admitted to the hospital, and because of the severe pain and obstructive uropathy, the urologist determined that cystoscopy and either stone extraction or pushing the stone back up into the kidney for purposes of a percutaneous removal would be performed the next morning.

At 8:00 the next morning, prior to going to the cystoscopic suite, a KUB (kidney, ureter, bladder x-ray) was taken which revealed that the stone had dropped from the upper ureter into the lower ureter. The urologist neglected to review this x-ray and took the patient to the cystoscopy suite where, after one hour of attempting to find and either remove or push the stone back into the kidney, he was unsuccessful. He transferred the patient to a larger hospital that same day for purposes of a percutaneous removal of the "upper ureteral calculus."

The records further reflect that in the radiology suite that same afternoon in preparation for the percutaneous removal of the "stone," a KUB again revealed the stone to be in the distal ureter. This fact was again overlooked by both the radiologist and the urologist.

During the percutaneous approach to the kidney under fluoroscopic guidance, either the guidewire or the nephroscope itself perforated the renal pelvis, causing significant extravasation of urine into the patient's flank. This fact was immediately recognized, and the patient was taken to the operating room for surgical intervention.

During the procedure, no stone could be found, but the laceration in the renal pelvis was repaired and, as was indicated, a nephrostomy tube was placed in the kidney and brought out through the flank. Approximately one week after the surgical procedure was performed, the patient passed his distal ureteral stone, which was recovered by the nurses. He subsequently was discharged home, was out of work for about six weeks, but responded nicely and convalesced.

Of course, a lawsuit was instituted, and prior to the jury trial a modest settlement was achieved.

This case illustrates not only the fact that the percutaneous approach can be exceedingly difficult and associated with a rather severe complication, but also the fact that two physicians did not objectively evaluate all of the x-rays to see that the upper ureteral stone had indeed descended into the lower ureter.

§9.09 Penile Prosthesis: Infections and Improper Placement

This is probably the currently most popular urological cause of action. The huge impotency problem present in the male population, coupled with technological advances in prosthetic devices, has spawned an unprecedented wave of surgery. The actual surgical implantation of the penile prosthesis is not difficult, but poor training, poor adherence to sterile techniques, and improper patient selection all play roles in causing this litigation.

The different types of penile prostheses are covered in Chapters 6 and 8, and the cases do not necessarily turn on the type of prostheses inserted. This discussion revolves around the cases concerned with the surgical approach to the insertion of the penile prosthesis.

Improper Placement

The most unusual case I have seen involved the crossing over of the prosthesis from the left corpus cavernosum to the right corpus cavernosum. As a surgeon, I still cannot figure out how this happened without being noticed at the time of the original surgery, but, indeed, subsequent surgery on this patient did prove that the left prosthetic cylinder had been placed through the septum between the right and left corporal bodies into the left corpus alongside the right cylinder and then crossing over it. Not only did this cause a severe angulation pushing the head of the penis radically to the left, but the pressure from the crossing-over cylinder eroded a hole in the penile skin.

Of course, the patient refused to go back to the original urologist for reparative surgery, but another urologist reoperated the patient using a videocamera which very nicely showed the prosthesis as it crossed through the septum of each corporal body. Using the videocamera at the time of the second surgery was an excellent tool for the settlement brochure.

Infection

By far, the most common cause of action involving penile prosthesis is the infected prosthesis and failure to timely remove it from the patient.

Every foreign body placed in a patient has a high incidence of being infected and, in spite of using the best possible aseptic technique, infections occur. The crucial issue in any infected penile prosthesis case is not proving where the infection originated or why, but rather when the urologist removed the infected prosthesis. Once again, it is axiomatic—not only in urology, but all the surgical disciplines—that an infected foreign body will rarely become sterile when left in a patient, and the only choice is for the surgeon to remove it.

Alternatively, however, after a prosthesis is inserted, any surgeon is reluctant to immediately remove it if an infection occurs. Trying desperately to save his or her surgery, the urologist will attempt to resolve the infection and avoid removing the prosthesis. This is the judgmental decision that ends up being the basis for the lawsuit. If the urologist waits too long in the belief that he or she can save the prosthesis, he or she may end up with a tremendous infection with disastrous results, as is illustrated in the following case.

The patient underwent an insertion of a self-contained inflatable penile prosthesis because of Peyronie's disease. The involvement of both corpora cavernosa and the proximity of the fibrous Peyronie's plaque to the roof of the corpus spongiosum required the surgeon, in his judgment, to "shave" as much of the fibrous plaque as possible in order to debulk it. The urologist's operative note described that he got "thin" over the urethra and therefore he inserted a Gortex graft (a type of biologically inert material) to buttress the roof of the urethra where he had shaved off the plaque.

Although there is controversy about whether one should excise the Peyronie's plaque or just leave it there, the standard of care is that this is a judgmental decision for the surgeon to make at the time of the surgery.

In this particular instance, the technical aspect of the surgery was performed well, and a Foley catheter was left in the patient for 48 hours postoperatively. The reason for leaving the Foley catheter is that there is so much penile edema that patients cannot void sufficiently, so a catheter is inserted to obviate any urinary retention problems.

In this case, the hospital records reflect that when the catheter was removed as ordered by the urologist, the patient was unable to void, and, in addition, a ballooning of his penis was noted and reported to the urologist. An in-and-out catheterization was ordered to evacuate the bladder, and in another few hours, when the patient again could not void and penile ballooning was again noted, the urologist ordered the Foley catheter to be reinserted and left indwelling. The records also reflect that a few drops of urine were noted to come out of the penile skin incision.

Let us stop for a moment and reflect on the course of treatment thus far. A surgeon has apparently evaluated and properly treated his patient for Peyronie's disease. He has gotten "thin" in his dissection of the plaque off the corpus spongiosum, yet he provided for this by using a graft at that site for buttressing. He left a catheter in his patient post-operatively and appropriately ordered its removal 48 hours later. When the nurses called him to advise that the patient could not void, the urologist appropriately ordered a catheterization, but, here, the departure from the standard of care occurred in that when the urologist was told that a ballooning of the penis occurred, he should have recognized that urinary extravasation was happening.

At subsequent deposition, the urologist testified that he thought the ballooning was a "piss-hard!" What did this urologist mean by a "piss-hard?"

As most readers know, nocturnal and early morning erections are common. Sleep studies, including rapid-eye-movement (REM) studies, have correlated the depth of sleep with the onset of erections. A lay perception of the early morning erection is that a full bladder causes the erection and not the subconscious level of the psyche. The vernacular "piss-hard" is a common erroneous concept so-called because after the male arises with his erection and travels to the bathroom to void, his erection goes away. Urologists, however, know better—there is no correlation between a full bladder and the erection, and no scientific studies have ever promoted that theory.

However, in this case, we now have a ballooning of the penis described by the nurses and the patient which the urologist says was a "piss-hard." In reality, the urine had come down the urethra, trying to escape out the urethral meatus, but because of the swelling of the penis was being forced out through the "thin" roof of the urethra into the surrounding tissues.

The urologist should have realized what was happening and immediately catheterized the patient, but, as it was, a second episode of the exact same mechanics occurred some four to five hours later, at which time finally the Foley catheter was reinserted. Here, again, a few drops of urine were noted to have escaped from the suture line, which was another warning sign that the continuity of the urethra had been disrupted.

As of this juncture, however, the picture was really not totally grim. This scenario occurs not infrequently, and does not always result in infection, loss of the penile prosthesis, and a lawsuit.

The next several days of this patient's clinical course went smoothly, and he was discharged on the Foley catheter with appropriate antibiotics, to be seen in the doctor's office some two weeks later. At that time, the urologist believed the urethra had healed sufficiently to warrant removal of the Foley, a judgment for which he cannot be faulted.

Within 48 hours, however, the patient complained of swelling of the penis when he voided, with urine leaking out of the almost-healed incision site. The urologist again placed the Foley catheter, hoping to divert the infected urine and to allow the urethra to heal. But now, obvious to any urologist, the standard of care demands that something greater than a Foley catheter be done to this patient. It is now imperative that urinary diversion be accomplished so that the fistula site in the urethra is allowed to heal. With the Foley catheter lying in the urethra at the site of the fistula, no substantive healing can occur, and, additionally, the urine has now become infected from the mere presence of the Foley catheter, and the potential for the penile prosthesis to become infected is very great.

Over the next six months, however, the urologist inserted and withdrew the Foley catheter on four separate occasions, each time with subsequent urinary leakage via the fistula site. Finally, a suprapubic cystostomy was performed in order to appropriately and properly divert the urine. The Foley catheter was removed from the patient, and the hope was that the urethrocutaneous fistula would heal.

At this point, however, the infection was rampant and uncontrollable. The time to remove the infected penile prosthesis was now—and, in fact, had passed! However, for the next several weeks, the patient continued to run intermittent temperatures and have inflammatory signs of infection in the phallus, and, yet, the urologist still did not remove the penile prosthesis. Finally, the patient went to another urologist who immediately grasped the situation and removed the infected penile prosthesis which, over the next several weeks and months, resulted in a healing of the urethrocutaneous fistula. The patient additionally underwent closure of the suprapubic cystostomy site and reinsertion of another penile prosthesis some months later.

This case is illustrative of two issues. One is the need for prompt urinary diversion in the face of a urinary fistula, and the other is the timely removal of an infected penile prosthesis.

§9.10 Failure to Timely Remove Ureteral Stent

Ureteral stents are another basis for urological causes of action. Their use is discussed in Chapter 8 and that discussion will not be repeated here. Prior to the advent of the stents, urologists placed catheters up the ureter and left them hanging out of the urethra attached to a Foley catheter—a very messy affair! With the development of internal ureteral stents, patient comfort was improved and the migration of stents out of the ureter was minimal. But, "out of sight, out of mind," and sure enough urologists began forgetting about the indwelling ureteral stents they left behind, and subsequent lawsuits flourished.

One case involved a 70-year-old female with ovarian cancer who had undergone radical cancer surgery with subsequent injury to her ureter. A urologist was called in during the surgery, and he inserted an indwelling ureteral stent after he repaired the ureter.

Postoperatively, the patient did quite well, but the main focus was on her ovarian cancer and her subsequent chemotherapy and radiation therapy. Over the next several months, her convalescence improved, such that she finished all her therapy and appeared to have conquered her cancer. However, the patient soon began experiencing mild urinary tract infections, all of which responded to antibiotic therapy, but which continued to recur. Finally, some *five years later,* another urologist (the patient never saw the original urologist who had inserted the stent), in performing an evaluation on the patient to determine the etiology of her infections, found the stent and readily removed it. Astonishingly enough, the stent was not overly encrusted and easily was withdrawn cystoscopically. An intravenous pyelogram revealed normal upper tracts without any significant damage being done to that ureter or kidney. Subsequent to the removal of the stent, the recurrent urinary tract infections ceased, and the patient survives to this day.

In this instance, a stent was left indwelling for five years without significant damage to the patient. Although an attorney was consulted regarding the possibility of a legal action, because of all the circumstances involved and mainly because of the minimal damage sustained by the patient, no suit was instituted.

Contrast that case with a young woman who, during her pregnancy, had developed an impacted ureteral calculus which required surgical removal. A ureteral stent was placed intraoperatively, and the pregnancy was allowed to continue. Some six weeks postpartum, the patient developed an acute pyelonephritis which was secondary to a yeast septicemia. Yeast is an opportunistic organism frequently associated with any foreign object in the body. Strong antifungal agents were instituted which resolved the infection, but over the next several months, severe fungal infections occurred which required hospitalization.

Her physician finally x-rayed her to determine the etiology of the yeast infection and, at that time, the indwelling stent was recognized. Now, however, the stent was covered with mineral encrustations and could not be simply removed cystoscopically, but required a surgical procedure. Thus, in this instance, the stent caused severe infections, became totally covered with mineral deposits and required drastic surgery for its subsequent removal.

§9.11 Damage to Testicle during Hernia Repair

Because of the thousands of hernia repairs done in this country, it is inevitable that damage to the testicle will occur. This type of case is similar to the ureter damaged during a gynecological surgery case in that, although the urologist is often called upon to opine about this injury, a general surgeon should be called upon to define the standard of care, because it usually is a general surgeon who has performed the herniorrhaphy. Additionally, in certain circumstances, damage to the testicle may not be a result of a departure from the standard of care.

Before one gets involved in the actual injury and loss of the testicle, it is important to understand the anatomy of the area and how the testicle can be injured during a herniorrhaphy.

During the fetus's growth in utero, each testicle is formed as an outgrowth of the kidney, and gradually descends from the renal area retroperitoneally into the pelvis and then into the scrotum. The inguinal canal is a natural "tunnel" which connects the pelvis and the scrotum, and after the testicle descends through it, the tunnel closes off and the normal muscle layers obliterate the channel. If, however, the tunnel does not close off, there is the potential for a loop of bowel to go down the tunnel and create the hernia, which is a term for the herniation of the bowel out of the pelvic cavity into the scrotum.

In addition, the spermatic cord, which is a structure containing testicular nerves, arteries, veins, and the vas deferens, runs in close proximity to the inguinal canal. It is the spermatic cord which must be avoided during herniorrhaphy.

General surgeons are trained to understand the anatomy of the inguinal canal, but frequently damage to the spermatic cord occurs. This can be either a direct clamping or cutting of the cord or an indirect injury such as suturing up the muscle layers of the canal too tightly so that compromise to the vascular structures of the spermatic cord occurs. Whichever is the cause of the injury, the end result is usually an atrophic testicle.

Since the most common cause of testicular damage during a herniorrhaphy is because the muscles of the canal are tightened excessively around the spermatic cord, resulting in ischemia to the testicle, the usual story is that after the hernia repair, the patient experiences a tender, swollen testicle. Although a large percentage of patients will experience some minor testicular tenderness and swelling after a normal herniorrhaphy, it is the significantly swollen testicle of a longer duration that should alert the surgeon to what is happening. Surgeons are reluctant to go back in on their repair to loosen it up—and, indeed, this may not be as easy to do as it sounds—and usually, the general surgeon will "watch it." This is a euphemism for "doing nothing."

Weeks later, after the swollen testicle has subsided, it will continue to shrink and end up being an atrophic, nonviable structure.

I am describing the usual situation in a patient who has not had previous hernia surgery. But, what of the patient who has had recurrent repairs and one who may even have a "mesh" inserted in him for muscular support? Is compromising or directly traumatizing the spermatic cord in those instances a good basis for cause of action? I really do not believe so.

I know of one recent case wherein a general surgeon, in the process of performing herniorrhaphy on a young man who had undergone orchiopexy as a small child some 15 years previously, found that the vas deferens had been cut in half. The general surgeon described both ends of the vas being buried in scar tissue without any continuity. The patient had only a solitary testicle since the contralateral testicle had been removed some years previously during another orchiectomy attempt.

The case got even more interesting when the original urologist who had performed the orchiopexy on the "cut vas" side testified in deposition that he had not injured the vas and that the general surgeon had injured it during the recent herniorrhaphy. So, who did it? The case is still pending, and that is why they have juries.

§9.12 Complications of Vasectomy

The tort of wrongful birth or wrongful life has been promulgated in numerous jurisdictions for a cause of action after a failed vasectomy. Recovery has been somewhat limited, except in the case of a baby with birth defects, because courts have offset the monetary reward by the value of the society and comfort potentially gained from the offspring himself or herself.

Disregarding the actual failure of the vasectomy which is the basis for the wrongful birth tort, this section deals more with the surgical complications of the vasectomy procedure as a cause of action.

The most common surgical complication from a vasectomy is hematoma formation. In the absence of gross disregard for an actively bleeding venule or arteriole, troublesome microcirculation bleeding can occur even in the best of hands. Lacerated blood vessels can spasm and not bleed during the vasectomy, but after the local (or general) anesthetic wears off, the spasmodic vessel relaxes, and significant intrascrotal bleeding can occur. Alternatively, a properly placed suture may untie or slip off the vessel after the procedure has been terminated and cause tremendous bleeding. Some surgeons use electrocautery which cauterizes or burns the small vessels in order to stop bleeding, but the cauterized end of the blood vessel may slough off after a few hours, and brisk bleeding may occur. Additionally, some urologists use surgical clips on the cut end of the vas which also occludes small blood vessels surrounding the vas. These clips may come off, so that bleeding ensues. All of these are reasons why, in the absence of obvious violative technique, I believe hematoma formation may be a difficult case for the plaintiff to win.

I know of one case wherein the patient (and his wife) stated that as he was getting off the examining table in the doctor's office after his vasectomy, blood began streaming out of his scrotal incision and down his leg. The urologist had left the office hurriedly without reexamining the patient, and the patient was sent home with a bulky dressing. The bleeding continued, which required suturing in the emergency room, but the subsequent hematoma formation which had occurred became infected with a resultant loss of the patient's testicle. This clinical course is not quite as simple as the usual postvasectomy hematoma.

It is also important for the attorney to realize in evaluating the postvasectomy hematoma case that even if a large hematoma occurs within the first several hours postoperatively, surgical drainage of that hematoma is usually not the treatment of choice. First of all, the blood in the scrotum is not in a walled-off, localized "pocket." It is usually extravasated throughout the tissues and, thus, no local site can be found in which aspiration will drain off all the blood. If one does incise the scrotum and place a surgical drain in the wound to allow egress of the old blood, this may be a departure from the standard of care. Blood is an excellent culture medium, and by opening up a closed space and inserting a drain into it, bacterial access is allowed, and potential grave complications may occur.

Thus, the treatment of choice for postvasectomy hematoma formation is mere observation and patience. It may take a while and cause several months of patient discomfort, but, in the long run, the body will absorb all the blood, and the scrotum will become normal again.

Infections after a vasectomy are unusual, except in the case of an infected hematoma. Epididymitis, vasitis, and orchitis all may occur even with the use of an antibiotic given at the time of the vasectomy. Unless the circumstances are extraordinarily clear, proving the infection occurred as a result of a departure from the standard of care may be difficult.

I am aware of one case, however, which resulted in a significant jury verdict for the plaintiff after the patient lost his testicle secondarily to a postvasectomy infection. In that case, the urologist used a nonabsorbable silk suture to tie off the vas. The accepted standard of care requires an absorbable suture to be used in the vasectomy; otherwise, the nonabsorbable suture may represent a focus for an infection.

§9.13 Urethral Perforation

Gentleness is a urological maxim. In dealing with the structures involved in a urological evaluation, great damage can be done to the tissues if skill and a gentle touch are not utilized. Using an instrument too large or too roughly in the urethra is the most common reason for injury.

Urethral tears, false passages into the urethra, bleeding, and undermining of the bladder neck are all possible injuries. While these complications do not usually end up in a lawsuit because of the minimal injury, frank perforation of the urethra usually does.

Although pre-existing disease in a urethra may make instrumentation difficult if not impossible, there is almost no excuse—or defense—for a urethral perforation. Most perforations of the urethra occur in the bulbar area where there is an anatomical curve which must be negotiated, but perforation can occur anywhere in the urethra. Undermining the bladder neck with perforation of the urethra at that site is very common, but usually has no significant consequences because of the caliber of the urethra at that particular area.

I am aware of two lawsuits wherein because excessive pressure was used to attempt to insert a urethral dilator into the urethra, perforation of the urethra occurred with entry into the rectum. This injury was recognized rather immediately when a catheter was advanced into the urethra and feces came out the lumen. Each patient in this particular instance required a diverting proximal colostomy, and both cases were settled prior to trial.

§9.14 Suture through Catheter after Marshall-Marchetti-Krantz Procedure

As covered in Chapter 8, the Marshall-Marchetti-Krantz procedure (MMK) is performed in cases wherein patients have stress urinary incontinence with loss of the urethrovesical angle. This surgery is performed by having a Foley catheter inserted in the bladder so that the urologist can feel the Foley catheter balloon which is indicative of the junction of the bladder neck and the urethra. A suprapubic abdominal incision is made, and the subsymphyseal space is opened up. The sutures are passed laterally and adjacent to the urethra at the site of the Foley balloon, and sewn to the undersurface of the pubic symphysis bone.

Standard in the Marshall-Marchetti-Krantz procedure is cystoscopy either before or after the procedure, but, certainly, because of the known frequency with which a suture inadvertently enters the bladder or the urethra, properly determining that the catheter has not been sewn in at the time of the procedure is important.

While most urologists will combine cystoscopy with the MMK, others will deflate the balloon after the procedure and remove it from the urethra so as to determine that it has not been sewn in. While it is probably not a departure from the standard of care to actually have a suture go into the urethra and then through the Foley catheter, the violation of that standard would be when this was not recognized by the urologist. At the time of the surgery, if the catheter has been found to have been sewn into the bladder, removal of the suture is a rather simple procedure and would not destroy the purpose of the surgery. If, however, the urologist fails to recognize that he or she has sewn in the catheter until he or she attempts to remove that catheter, the actual removal of the Foley catheter which has been sewn in will be most difficult and, more frequently than not, would require taking the patient back to the cysto room and placement under general anesthesia.

I am aware of one pending case wherein the gynecologist who performed the MMK, and who failed to recognize the fact that the catheter was sewn in until some days later when she attempted to remove the catheter, took the patient back to the operating room and reopened her, undid her entire procedure, and then reperformed the MMK. The patient sued the gynecologist on the grounds that she had to undergo another general anesthetic and all of the emotional trauma that went with the second surgery. The expert witness in this case opined that it was a departure from the standard of care not to recognize that the catheter had been sewn in until the time came for the catheter to be removed. However, as can be seen, the damages potentially recoverable from this sort of injury are rather negligible.

Ordinarily, the simple suturing in of a Foley catheter during the MMK procedure does not cause any untoward results, and usually will not even affect the surgical repair if the suture is removed and replaced at the time of the MMK. It is the patient who has had the catheter sewn in and not had this recognized and who has to undergo further anesthesia to remove the stitch who may also have the repair compromised when the suture is removed.

The endoscopic urethropexy (Stamey), another procedure utilized to perform urethropexy, requires simultaneous cystoscopy at the time of placing the sutures in order to visualize the bladder neck at the time of suture placement. The urologist can now determine whether there has been an inadvertent entry of the suture into the bladder at that time. I am, however, aware of at least three urological malpractice cases wherein some months after the Stamey had been performed and because of recurrent urinary tract infections, the urologist found that the suture had apparently "eroded" into the bladder. Obviously, this foreign body in the bladder admixed with urine will cause a recurrent infection, and, certainly, encrustations on the suture. In all of these cases, the operating surgeon at the time of the Stamey procedure had dictated that the interior of the bladder was clean and did not have any inadvertent entry of the suture. The only plausible explanation for the subsequent finding of the suture in the bladder is erosion of the suture through the bladder wall because of compression and proximity of the suture to the bladder wall. Opinions vary as to whether this erosion of the suture is a departure from the standard of care, but it is my opinion that it would not be meritorious to proceed with a lawsuit under this set of circumstances.

Another frequent complication regarding Foley catheters is the failure of the Foley catheter balloon to deflate. Ordinarily, this is not as a result of negligence on the part of the endoscopist, but I am aware of at least one products liability lawsuit involving the manufacturer of the Foley catheter because the balloon failed to deflate. The urological manipulations required to remove a Foley catheter when the balloon fails to deflate can be somewhat ingenious, and my personal experience over the years has ranged from passing a spinal needle vaginally into the bladder to pop the balloon, to injecting either or acetone down the lumen to dissolve the balloon, to taking the patient back to the cysto room under anesthesia and inserting a cystoscope after the Foley catheter had been cut off and pushed back into the bladder so that puncture of the balloon could occur cystoscopically.

§9.15 Potpourri

In the preceding sections of this chapter, I have tried to describe the most common urological complications which have resulted in litigation. Obviously, in reviewing all of my records of cases, over the years all sorts of urological mishaps have occurred, some of which did not result in a lawsuit but at least resulted in a review of the record for a potential lawsuit.

This section deals with some of the more singular events in which litigation has occurred, but which are included here, not so much to portend a trend, but rather to continue the colloquy of urological complications and resultant causes of action.

A 15-year-old boy underwent endoscopic surgery for a ureterocele which involved the use of a resectoscope to resect and unroof the mucosal surface of the ureterocele in the bladder. The surgery, according to the operative report, went well, and, although the patient was readmitted to the hospital some 48 hours later because of bleeding which required bladder irrigation over a few hours, no further complications arose. Over the next five years, the patient had multiple episodes of urethritis and urinary tract infections, and was seen by numerous physicians and treated for this problem. Eventually, because of the persistence of the symptoms, as well as some difficulty in actually initiating and maintaining his urinary stream, he was recystoscoped by another urologist. At the time of that cystoscopy, a foreign body was noted in the patient's urethra which was encrusted with minerals, but which appeared to be the broken-off tip of a resectoscope sheath. The exact foreign body was "lost" in the pathology department, but the subsequent treating urologist was able to identify it enough to suggest that it had been a piece of urological instrument, whether a portion of a Foley catheter balloon or the resectoscope sheath, left behind.

The case turned on the fact that the patient had had no other urological instrumentation. He denied that he had inserted any foreign body into his urethra, and, therefore, the only possible explanation for this foreign body was its having been introduced by the urologist, either at the time of the resection of the ureterocele or by agents of the hospital when the Foley catheter had been placed in the bladder in order to irrigate him for postoperative bleeding.

In another case, which occurred in Alabama, a young teenager noted gross hematuria after he had been roller skating and had a minor fall. He went to the urologist who immediately cystoscoped the patient and saw in the bladder grape-like structures that he assumed to be a malignant lesion. He attempted biopsy of this material while the patient was under anesthesia and was told by the pathologist that the specimen was inadequate for a diagnosis.

The urologist then informed the patient's parents that he believed he was dealing with a malignancy and asked permission to operate the patient at that time so that he could get better tissue for a diagnosis. Of course, the parents agreed, and the young man, still under anesthesia, was taken to the operating room where, at open surgery, additional tissue was sent to the pathologist for identification. The record reflects that several more pieces of tissue were sent to the pathologist, and each time the report was "unable to identify the tissue—please submit more."

The urologist then again advised the parents that he was dealing with a very malignant process, and suggested that the patient undergo radical surgery in order to save his life. Of course, the parents agreed, and the urologist performed a cystectomy and prostatectomy which resulted in the patient having an ileal conduit for egress of his urine. Naturally, as a result of the radial cystectomy and prostatectomy, the patient is also impotent.

The patient's clinical course was benign and uncomplicated, and the pathological diagnosis of the tissue was neurofibromatosis, a benign disease and not one with a malignant potential.

Here, the issue was the failure to properly diagnose the patient and, in spite of that, to perform this disfiguring procedure on him. The case went to trial, and resulted in a defendant's verdict based upon the fact that the doctor was able to convince the jury that, in his best judgment, he believed the tissue to be malignant and felt that the proper course at that time was to do the radical surgery.

The final case in this section involves a young woman who went to her urologist for a Stamey procedure to correct her stress urinary incontinence.

At the time of the procedure, the urologist documented that he inadvertently had entered the bladder with the Stamey needle, but felt that it was inconsequential and would heal without any further surgery performed. Within 10 days postoperatively, the patient began leaking urine from her vagina and, when she came back to the urologist complaining of this, he cystoscoped her, identified the vesico-vaginal fistula, and again decided to place ureteral stents up each ureter in order to divert the urine so as to close the fistula. The stents did not work, however, and, within two weeks, the patient again came back to the urologist, noting that she was leaking urine through her vagina. At this time, the urologist then elected to attempt repair of the vesicovaginal fistula and, unfortunately, that surgical repair also broke down.

The urologist then asked another general surgeon to help him reoperate the patient in order to repair the fistula and, indeed, at this procedure, repair of the vesicovaginal fistula was accomplished.

Unfortunately, as a result of all the surgical manipulations, the patient was again incontinent of urine, and had to undergo another surgical procedure for this. This case is still pending, but the issue here is the failure of the physician to properly evaluate and treat the vesicovaginal fistula at the time of its original appearance. Expert testimony has been given, opining that the failure to repair the fistula at the time when it was first noted was a departure from the standard of care, and the modality used by the urologist to divert the urine was not an accepted procedure used by urologists generally.

10

Handling the Plaintiff's Case

Thomas William Malone

§10.01 Introduction
§10.02 Screening
§10.03 Evaluation
§10.04 Settlement or Suit
§10.05 The Complaint
§10.06 Discovery
§10.07 Initial Discovery
§10.08 —Interrogatories and Request for Production of Documents to Defendant Doctor
§10.09 —Interrogatories and Request for Production of Documents to Defendant Hospital
§10.10 Depositions
§10.11 —Deponents
§10.12 —Deposition of the Defendant Doctor
§10.13 —Deposition of Defense Experts
§10.14 Voir Dire
§10.15 Direct Examination
§10.16 Cross-Examination
§10.17 Summation

§10.01 Introduction

Medical malpractice involves an injury resulting from a failure on the part of the physician to exercise a reasonable degree of care and skill. To sustain a malpractice action, the plaintiff must establish the standard of care in the particular circumstances involved, and also must show a negligent departure from the recognized standard in the treatment of the plaintiff. Most importantly, the plaintiff has the burden of proving that the departure from the standard did in fact cause the injuries of which the plaintiff complains.

While some states still hold to the archaic locality rule, most jurisdictions recognize a national standard of care because the training of physicians meets minimal national standards as evidenced by board certifications. There is also immediate availability of transportation to larger and more specialized institutions and the care they offer if the need arises.

Our law has its foundation in the English common law. It would appear that neither Henry VIII nor Parliament was very pleased with the medical profession over 400 years ago. In 1544, in the age of Henry VIII, it was stated: "[F]or although . . . the . . . craft of surgeons have small cunning yet they will take great sums of money and do little therefore and by reason thereof, they do often times impair and harm their patients rather than do them good."

The medical profession has even placed a diagnostic label upon the effects of malpractice. Stedman's medical dictionary defines *iatrogenic* as "an abnormal state or condition produced by the physician in a patient by inadvertent or erroneous treatment".[1]

In 1938, Dr. Richard Cabot, professor of medicine at Harvard, declared that "the greatest single curse in medicine is the curse of unnecessary operations, and there would be fewer of them if the doctor got the same salary whether he operated or not."

Even as early as the 1970s, 1.5 million of 30 million patients hospitalized annually were admitted because of adverse reactions to prescription drugs. In some hospitals, as high as 20 per cent of the patients were admitted because of drug-induced disease.[2] In his work, Martin says: "No physician will deliberately administer a medication that will produce a toxic reaction, but too often he does not fully evaluate the possibility of such a reaction before he prescribes a medication." He goes on to say that "there are no harmless medications, all are potentially hazardous to some extent and all must be prescribed and administered with caution."[3]

Medical malpractice does exist and horrendous injuries do sometimes result. Medical carelessness frequently does not result in any injury at all, just as the careless operation of an automobile does not always result in injury. It is only that small percentage of careless acts which produces an ultimate injury which should give rise to litigation. Unnecessary surgical procedures, careless prescriptions which produce toxic reactions, failures to diagnose treatable pathological states, inept performance of surgical procedures, as well as other acts or omissions can give rise to the legitimate pursuit of a medical malpractice claim against a urological specialist.

Medical negligence cases are difficult, expensive, and frequently lost. Spokespersons for major liability carriers insuring physicians have boasted of a success rate exceeding 90 per cent. The outright hostility of many members of the medical community to the legal profession is at an all-time high in today's "malpractice crisis" climate.

---

[1] T. Stedman, Stedman's Medical Dictionary (1972).
[2] A. Martin, Hazards of Medication (1971).
[3] *Id.* 146.

The filing of frivolous claims has fueled the fire of hostility between the two professions. Neither profession is without members who could best be described as incompetent or foolhardy. The law has its share of practitioners who fit this category.

Careful screening of the potential medical claim is as important to the successful plaintiffs' lawyer's practice as is the actual handling of the case once accepted. Today the success rate on the defense side of a medical malpractice case is not quite as impressive as it was years ago, but the win rate for physicians today certainly exceeds 75 per cent.

When the trial lawyer asks a jury to return a verdict against a health care provider, the task is difficult no matter how strong the case may appear on paper or in the classroom.

The difficulty factor is substantially related to the population of the community where the case will be tried. Cases which succeed in San Francisco, New York, Miami, Atlanta, and other metropolitan areas will frequently be unsuccessful in more rural areas. Venue is an important factor in evaluating a professional liability claim. Time, expense, and pressures associated with a medical negligence case require the damages to be substantial and the liability clear. Even with these points in mind, few will be settled and many will be lost.

§10.02   Screening

Lawyers on the plaintiffs' side who handle a substantial number of medical malpractice claims generally agree that the vast majority of claims are rejected. Even so, statistics show 75 per cent or more of the claims made are ultimately closed by the malpractice carriers without payment. There are many factors to consider when contemplating the handling of a medical malpractice claim.

Since it will take a minimum of $10,000 and often much more for the proper preparation and presentation of the plaintiff's claim, only those cases which have high verdict potential can be handled from a practical standpoint. To underbudget the pursuit of a professional liability claim against a physician destines the claim to failure. Defense resources seem unlimited and the defense will be strong. If the complaining patient had two extra days in the hospital because of erroneous medication or a minor bleeding problem due to a surgical error but is otherwise completely recovered, it is not economically possible to handle the claim. Practical immunity exists for health care providers who have only minimally damaged or inconvenienced their patients.

Professional reputations are at stake, and doctors frequently hold veto power over settlements as a part of their insurance contract. Therefore, the attorney undertaking representation of a plaintiff in a medical negligence claim must be prepared to pursue the case to trial. The potential jury verdict must be high.

§10.03 Evaluation

The careful plaintiff's attorney in taking on a professional liability claim against a physician will meet the plaintiff and the plaintiff's family. Is the plaintiff deserving and will the plaintiff make a good appearance? If the plaintiff is someone with whom the jury will not identify, or who appears hostile or untruthful, or who generally is viewed negatively, other factors must overcome the negative factors in order to justify pursuit of the claim.

If the potential defendant has a bad reputation and has had several cases against him or her settled, or had adverse jury verdicts in the community, or is arrogant, or has changed medical records, or otherwise displays traits that will make him or her disliked by the jury, the plaintiff's case is enhanced.

A consideration of the underlying facts which are claimed to constitute negligence should be closely scrutinized. A departure from the standard of care ordinarily employed by other physicians under the same or similar circumstances must be shown in order to reach the jury. Will physicians disagree regarding the standard of care? If so, careful reflection to determine which side of the issue the jury is likely to believe at the conclusion of the case is necessary. Such cases can certainly be won, but such cases will probably be decided by the jury on the personalities of the parties, the lawyers, and which experts are most believable. An act of omission such as a failure to diagnose is a much more difficult case from the plaintiff's perspective than is a case involving an unnecessary surgical procedure or prescription of a toxic dose of medication.

As basic as it seems, many cases are lost because damages merely happened in the presence of carelessness and not because of any particular act of carelessness. Health care providers, being human, are frequently careless, but the plaintiff must prove a specific act of carelessness caused specific damages. Even the expert witness cannot be expected to fully appreciate proximate cause. This is the responsibility of the attorney handling the claim.

Conscientious physicians willing to serve as expert witnesses are ready to testify in cases where the acts of carelessness have been gross. Expert testimony is required in almost all professional liability claims in order to establish the standard of care. The expert need not always testify that a given act or omission constituted a departure from the standard of care, as that determination can remain within the province of the jury.

An expert witness is a necessity, but he or she need not be a "hired gun." There are many medical-legal advisory groups and physicians throughout the country who advertise their consultation services. Exercise caution when dealing with these consultants, although they do serve a valuable and proper role in many instances.

Expert witnesses can be found at teaching institutions, and among subsequent treating physicians and personal friends of the lawyer or the client, as well as those physicians who have contributed to the medical literature on the subject at hand. Whoever the expert witness may be, his or her personality, credentials, and knowledge of the medical issues of the case must all be considered. An academician is subject to the "ivory tower" criticism; an advertising physician, or one supplied by a consulting service, is subject to the "hired gun" criticism. An expert who is a member of the particular specialty of the defendant doctor is not always a necessity or possibility, even though it is desirable.

A thorough evaluation of all medical records and all available history is necessary to the determination of the validity of a claim in this field. A minimum budget of $2,500 in even the clearest of cases is not overstating the amount involved in making a thorough evaluation of the claim. Copies of medical records can run several hundred dollars, and a physician's time in reviewing these records and consulting with the plaintiff's lawyer does not come cheap!

On the initial contact, many cases can be screened away simply because the facts or magnitude of the injury do not justify the commitment of the time and dollars necessary to pursue the matter further. It is the rare professional liability claim which can be accepted on the basis of an initial client interview.

A proper evaluation must be thorough and must include knowledge of all pertinent facts as well as a general knowledge of the medicine involved. The evaluation of the claim begins with the initial client interview and then should proceed by obtaining all the pertinent facts and records.

Clients can often be confused with regard to the facts as they occurred and particularly with regard to what some health care provider may have said. "Loose-lipped" doctors and nurses have sent more than a few patients to the offices of lawyers even though the cases were totally without merit.

Once medical authorizations have been obtained, the plaintiff's lawyer should proceed to obtain all pertinent records. The records obtained should be complete and should be certified. All records from the hospital, as well as office records of all the treating physicians, should be obtained. Particularly important are the hospital nurses' notes which frequently reveal information not found elsewhere in the record. The record tells a story, and a full appreciation of what was transpiring cannot be had until a mastery of the records is attained.

Today, the reproduction cost for medical records is frequently 50 cents per page and sometimes as high as one dollar per page. Some hospital records covering a long stay can be 1,000 or more pages in length.

A complete narrative from the client and family members should be obtained if at all possible. This is a confidential attorney-client communication and need not be shared with opposing counsel. Frequent reflection and reference to the client's narrative should be made during the evaluation of the hospital records. Reviewing attorneys often fail to attach the proper importance to what the clients are saying in a professional liability claim.

Once all information is obtained, the evaluation process can begin. The evaluator must understand the medical information involved. Most plaintiffs' lawyers turn to basic texts which are readily available in the medical school libraries or medical book stores. Consultants are available to educate the attorney regarding the medical aspects of any claim. The lawyer taking on a professional liability claim against a health care provider should have a basic understanding of the medicine involved in order to have any realistic expectation of successfully handling the claim.

When the lawyer has obtained all the factual information, an understanding of the medicine involved, and an expert, he or she is on the way to accepting the claim.

The lawyer must make certain the expert has given an unequivocal opinion that the health care provider failed to exercise the standard of care ordinarily employed by health care providers generally under the same or similar circumstances. The attorney must make certain the expert can explain exactly how the failure on the defendant's part actually caused the injury or damage to the patient. Only after being satisfied of the facts at hand and the expert's opinion establishing liability and causation should an attorney accept a medical negligence claim.

§10.04 Settlement or Suit

Large settlements are rare before suit is filed and thorough discovery is completed. The attorney handling a professional liability claim against a urologist should consider the advisability of attempts at settlement before the institution of litigation. Once suit is filed and becomes public information, the attitude of the doctor may dictate a vigorous defense. Since such matters as future insurability, cost of future insurance, and reputation in a community may be at risk, even a small settlement may be unlikely.

If settlement before suit is considered, the attorney should refer to the statutes of his or her state and determine if an "Unliquidated Damages Interest Act" exists. The Georgia statute provides that interest at the rate of 12 per cent per annum shall begin to run 30 days following the date of mailing the notice, if upon trial a judgment is for an amount not less than the sum claimed in the demand.[4]

By complying with the prejudgment interest statute at the time of the initial notification, interest has begun to run and delay is no longer a motivating factor for the defense. This of course assumes the demand is reasonable and one which can be expected at trial. The possibility of payment of that amount within 30 days does exist but it is highly unlikely, so for the cost of postage, interest has begun to run.

Settlement brochures and videotape productions designed to produce a settlement have often been effective.

§10.05 The Complaint

While the complaint should comply with notice requirements of the Federal Rules of Civil Procedure or the civil practice act in the particular state, it should not contain any more detail than is necessary. Many times information is developed during discovery which might prove early impressions

---

[4] Ga Code Ann §51-12-14 (1981).

incorrect or which may produce more viable theories of recovery than those contemplated at the stage of filing the complaint.

Tort reform has brought about procedural changes in the field of professional liability litigation, and one of these changes in many states is the "filing affidavit."

Georgia's filing requirement states that in actions for damages alleging professional malpractice, the plaintiff is required to file, with the complaint, an affidavit of an expert competent to testify.[5] The affidavit should set forth specifically at least one negligent act or omission and the factual basis for each claim. Under the Georgia statute, when a case is filed within 10 days of the expiration of the statute of limitations and the plaintiff has alleged that an expert affidavit cannot be prepared, the plaintiff has 45 days after filing the complaint to supplement the pleading with the affidavit. The time may be extended by the trial court on motion after a hearing and good cause is established. The defendant has 30 days to file an answer after the affidavit is filed.

The expert giving an affidavit should be competent in age, soundness of mind, profession, specialty of practice, and, in some states, geographical area. The affidavit should set forth at least one negligent act or omission. The act or omission must be set out specifically and the factual basis for each claim must be set forth. Purely conclusory affidavits should be avoided.

In Georgia, a party may move for summary judgment with or without supporting affidavits.[6] Since an affidavit must be prepared for filing, unless compelling circumstances dictate otherwise, the filing affidavit should be prepared to withstand a motion for summary judgment.

Georgia's requirements for affidavits are substantially similar to the requirements of other jurisdictions.[7] First, the affidavit must be made on personal knowledge. Second, the facts set forth must be admissible as evidence. Third, the affidavit must show that the affiant is competent to testify to the matters stated therein. Fourth, the affidavit must set forth the specific facts showing there is a genuine issue for trial. Fifth, all papers referred to in the affidavit must be sworn or certified and attached to the affidavit. The documents attached provide the premise upon which specific facts set out in the affidavit are based. Sixth, the affidavit and attachments must be filed with the court. And seventh, the affidavit and attachments must be served upon opposing attorneys prior to the day of the hearing.

Safe practice dictates the filing of the complete sworn or certified medical records at the time of filing the complaint. While the records can be voluminous and filing them a burdensome task, the records upon which any expert forms his or her opinions must be a part of the record in order for the trial or appellate court to consider the opinion itself.

The expert affidavit must state the facts gleaned by the expert from the records upon which his or her opinions are based. The expert must set forth

---

[5] Ga Code Ann §9-11-9.1 (1987).

[6] *Id* §9-11-56.

[7] *Id.*

the standard of care which ordinarily should have been employed under the circumstances described in the records.[8] The affidavit must also set forth the causal relationship between the defendant doctor's departure from the standard of care and the plaintiff's injuries. The expert's qualifications should be set forth with some degree of particularity.

In *Humphrey v Alvarado*,[9] the affidavit stated:

> I am a physician licensed to practice medicine in the State of Louisiana . . . and give this affidavit based on my personal knowledge of the facts contained herein. . . . I am familiar with the standard of care of reasonable physicians under circumstances the same or similar to those surrounding the care and treatment of. . . .

The court held this evidence of the expert's qualifications to be minimal but adequate to support his opinion. The minimal nature of the qualifications may very well have led the court into a frame of mind which permitted other holdings not favorable to the plaintiff.

The expert affidavit must set out the parameters of the standard of care and must establish what should have been done and compare that with what was done. The judge may consider any admissible parts of an affidavit, but the affidavit must show the proximate causal relationship between the negligent act or omissions and the injury. In addition, the affidavit must be notarized. Sworn or certified copies of papers must be attached to the affidavit if the papers have not previously become a part of the record.

§10.06 Discovery

Discovery is the process by which the parties gather information relevant to the subject matter of the suit. The method by which this information is obtained can be through written interrogatories, requests for production of documents or things for inspection or other purposes, depositions upon oral examination or written questions, requests for admissions, and requests for physical and mental examinations.

The scope of discovery is regulated in the federal courts.[10] Most jurisdictions have similar rules which define the parameters by which this information can be obtained. In federal court, the scope of discovery is defined by providing:

> Parties may obtain discovery regarding any matter, not privileged, which is relevant to the subject matter involved in the pending action, . . . including the existence, description, nature, custody, condition

---

[8] Humphrey v Alvarado, 185 Ga App 486, 364 SE2d 618 (1988).
[9] *Id* at 487, 364 SE2d at 620.
[10] Fed R Civ P 26.

and location of any books, documents, or other tangible things and the identity and location of persons having knowledge of any discoverable matter.[11]

§10.07 Initial Discovery

Interrogatories and requests for production of documents should be attached to the complaint. These items should elicit information concerning insurance, names of persons with any information relevant to the issues, expert witnesses, existence of statements, whether or not private counsel has been retained, and any similar claims against the defendant and the amount of the resolution of such claim. In a majority of jurisdictions, the request for this information is deemed continuing, which requires the defendant to update the information when it becomes known throughout the litigation. In addition to interrogatories and request for production which would be case-specific, the next two sections provide sample interrogatories and requests which are suggested as basic.

§10.08 —Interrogatories and Request for Production of Documents to Defendant Doctor

The following interrogatories and request for production are directed to the physician.

INTERROGATORIES

1.

Does any insurance agreement exist under the terms of which the person or company issuing the same may be called upon to satisfy all or part of any judgment which may be entered in favor of the Plaintiff in this action?

(a) If such an insurance agreement does exist, what are the limits of liability contained in the terms of any such agreement?

(b) If such an insurance agreement does exist, what are the legal names of any and all parties to the agreement itself or any further or subordinate agreement which in any way relates to the terms of any such agreement?

2.

Please give the name, address, and occupational title of all persons having any knowledge whatsoever about any fact or circumstance surrounding the incident giving rise to Plaintiff's Complaint.

---

[11] *Id* 26(b)(1).

3.

State the name, address, occupational title, and present whereabouts of each person whom you expect to call as an expert witness at the trial of this case, and with respect thereto, state the following:

(a) The subject matter on which the expert is expected to testify;

(b) The substance of the facts and opinions to which the expert is expected to testify; and

(c) A summary of the grounds for each opinion to which the expert is expected to testify.

4.

With respect to each person identified in your answer to the preceding interrogatory next above, please identify each document such person relies upon, if any, to support the opinions to which the expert is expected to testify.

5.

Has any expert or consultant been retained by you for review or consultation in this matter whom you do not expect to use at trial? If so, give the name, address, and occupational title of any such witness.

6.

Please specifically identify all books, journals, articles, or other publications or treatises consulted or relied upon concerning your treatment of Plaintiff, in the defense of the present lawsuit, or which will be utilized in any way in this action.

7.

Describe in detail every claim for damages made against you in any way connected with your professional services, including the name of the claimant, the date of the claim, the resolution of the claim, whether or not the claim was litigated, giving the style and number of the case, and the names of any attorneys involved in any claim, whether litigated or not.

8.

Please give your professional training, qualifications, and experience in detail, including:

(a) Each university or college attended by you, each degree awarded to you, and the date of each degree;

(b) Each hospital with which you have been affiliated at any time up to the present and the nature and inclusive dates of each affiliation and the reason for the termination of any such affiliation;

(c) Each medical society or association of which you have ever been a member and the inclusive dates of your membership;

(d) Each specialty for which you have been certified by specialty or subspecialty board and the date of each certification;

(e) All jurisdictions in which you are licensed with the date of licensure;

(f) All postgraduate education received, including full descriptions and dates; and

(g) A bibliography of all your publications, with titles, dates, and publishers.

9.

Please state the names, job titles, professional designations, and addresses, if known, of every person who in any way assisted or participated in the procedure performed upon Plaintiff by you at (name of hospital) on (date of incident).

10.

Have you given any statement or completed any form or notice of any kind regarding the incident referred to in this Complaint? If so, describe whether or not the report was oral or written, to whom given, in which form, the substance of the same and when the same was made.

11.

Describe in detail your background, training, and experience with the (procedure or type of claim being asserted), including a description of the location where such procedure took place and the number of experiences, as well as any problem whatsoever you have experienced with the (procedure or type of claim), other than the incident which is the subject of this litigation.

12.

Describe with particularity any correction or amplification you deem appropriate or necessary to any entry you made in any medical record pertaining to Plaintiff.

13.

Was the (medical device) which you placed in the (portion of anatomy) of Plaintiff defective in any way? If so, please describe in detail such defect.

REQUEST FOR PRODUCTION OF DOCUMENTS

1.

A copy of any policies of insurance identified in response to Interrogatory No. 1, including, but not limited to, the declaration page.

2.

Copies of all documents identified in response to Interrogatory No. 4.

3.

Copies of all documents identified in response to Interrogatory No. 6.

§10.09 —Interrogatories and Request for Production of Documents to Defendant Hospital

The following interrogatories and requests for production are directed to the hospital.

INTERROGATORIES

1.

Does any insurance agreement exist under the terms of which the person or company issuing the same may be called upon to satisfy all or part of any judgment which may be entered in favor of the Plaintiff in this action?

(a) If such an insurance agreement does exist, what are the limits of liability contained in the terms of any such agreement?

(b) If such an insurance agreement does exist, what are the legal names of any and all parties to the agreement itself or any further or subordinate agreement which in any way relates to the terms of any such agreement?

2.

Please give the name, address, and occupational title of all persons having any knowledge whatsoever about any fact or circumstance surrounding the incident giving rise to Plaintiff's Complaint.

3.

State the name, address, occupational title, and present whereabouts of each person whom you expect to call as an expert witness at the trial of this case, and with respect thereto, state the following:

(a) The subject matter on which the expert is expected to testify;

(b) The substance of the facts and opinions to which the expert is expected to testify; and

(c) A summary of the grounds for each opinion to which the expert is expected to testify.

4.

With respect to each person identified in your answer to the preceding interrogatory next above, please identify each document such person relies upon, if any, to support the opinions to which the expert is expected to testify.

5.

Has any expert or consultant been retained by you for review or consultation in this matter whom you do not expect to use at trial? If so, give the name, address, and occupational title of any such witness.

6.

Describe in detail each and every hospital or surgical manual or other document which contains written policies, procedures, or protocols which in any way deal with the (subject of incident at hospital).

7.

Please state the full name, present address, job title, or description of all employees of the Defendant HOSPITAL who, at any time, participated in the delivery of patient care to Plaintiff while (he or she) was a patient at Defendant HOSPITAL on the (date of incident) and please describe in general terms the nature of the service or activity performed by such employee.

8.

Please describe in detail all committees, investigative personnel, conferences, or any other such people or groups in any way associated with Defendant HOSPITAL having, in any way, discussed the incident concerning the Plaintiff and give the names of all persons known to Defendant HOSPITAL who, in any way, participated in such meetings.

9.

Please describe in detail the credentialing procedure authorizing the performance of any particular surgical procedure at Defendant HOSPITAL.

10.

Please state what accreditation Defendant Hospital has, giving the name or organization or entity awarding such accreditation, the dates Defendant HOSPITAL was accredited, and the basis upon which the accreditation was awarded.

11.

Please describe in detail all corporations having any interest whatsoever in the ownership or management of the Defendant HOSPITAL on (date of incident) and describe the relationship of such corporation to the ownership or operation of Defendant HOSPITAL.

12.

Please identify by name, title, and address each person who participated in the preparation of the responses to these interrogatories.

REQUEST FOR PRODUCTION OF DOCUMENTS

1.

A copy of any policies of insurance identified in response to Interrogatory No. 1, including, but not limited to, the declaration page.

2.

Copies of all documents identified in response to Interrogatory No. 4.

3.

Copies of any reports related to any internal investigation into this incident.

4.

Copies of all manuals, instructional materials, warnings or other labeling which was supplied by the manufacturer of (medical device).

5.

Copies of all documents identified in response to Interrogatory No. 6.

6.

Copies of all correspondence Defendant HOSPITAL or any of its officers, agents, or employees have received from anyone associated with the manufacture of the (medical device) which in any way mentions or relates to employment of the (medical device).

7.

Copies of any manuals, protocols, guidelines, or any other document in the custody, possession, or control of the Defendant HOSPITAL which in any way relates to the accreditation or the accreditation process mentioned in Interrogatory No. 10.

8.

A copy of any and all contracts or agreements in any way relating to the operation or management of the Defendant HOSPITAL on (date of incident).

§10.10 Depositions

The primary object of any deposition is to determine, under oath, what the deponent knows about the issue at hand and, if he or she has any opinions, how he or she arrives at such opinions and upon what he or she bases such opinions. The object of the deposition may be to discover facts of the particular incident. On the other hand, a goal of the deposition could certainly include tying the deponent down so that a later version of factual information is not possible. The object of the deposition could be the cornering of another party. Counsel should certainly have the object in mind long before the deposition begins.

§10.11 —Deponents

Counsel should carefully plan the list of the individuals to be deposed and the sequence with which the depositions will be taken. Just like a story, it is best to begin with those individuals who were present or had knowledge of the event from the beginning. If the negligence occurred during a surgical procedure, the lawyer should take the deposition of each person, nurse, physician, and technician who was present at any time during the operative procedure. These depositions should then be followed by those individuals who were called into the operating room following the careless act. Counsel should never underestimate the value of deposing every individual who might have witnessed the careless act as it is highly unlikely that all of the witnesses will be able to shield the defendant doctor.

§10.12 —Deposition of the Defendant Doctor

Counsel should consider the timing of taking the defendant doctor's deposition. If the careless act or omission was witnessed by several people, counsel should consider taking the defendant doctor's deposition last. More often than not the defendant will attend the factfinding depositions. If the defendant attends these depositions prior to his or her own deposition, he or she can be tied down to his or her testimony when his or her turn arrives. On the other hand, if the doctor is the only witness, other than his or her employees, his or her deposition should be taken first.

It is particularly important to tie the defendant doctor down to the circumstances present at the time of any critical decisionmaking process on his or her part. The doctor's actions and reasons for taking those actions should be clearly established. It is of utmost importance for each question to be clear and succinct, and it is equally important to make certain a responsive answer is provided. It might be necessary to put a long series of questions to establish a clear understanding of the defendant doctor's position on any pertinent matter. Once that understanding is established through a long series of questions, it is vitally important for cross-examination later to conclude the series of questions with the phrase "you will therefore agree . . ." or "it is obviously true that . . ." or "your clear position is. . . ."

Many lawyers insist that the defendant doctor appear at their office for the purpose of the deposition. However, general courtesy usually dictates that clients are deposed in the offices of their respective lawyers. Preferably, the defendant doctor will not be deposed in his or her own office, as that would tend to reinforce the doctor's security and the deposition would be conducted in surroundings familiar to him or her and unfamiliar to examining counsel.

§10.13 —Deposition of Defense Experts

While the strategy and technique to be employed by counsel can be as varied as the personalities and background of lawyers, preparation for the deposition is as important in this area of litigation as in any other place. Proper preparation for the taking of a deposition can cause the deposition to flow smoothly, solidify the position and information of the deponent, and control the further development of the case.

Counsel's initial discovery requests should have called for the curriculum vitae of the defense expert. With this in hand, an in-depth investigation into the background of the expert should be made. All articles written by the expert should be obtained. The articles which were written before the expert's association in your case can be useful. In most instances, the attorney can find an article the expert has written on the issue involved in the particular case. All medical articles are written by the physician with the view that the highest degree of medical care should be rendered to the patient. The defense expert is now being called upon to state that the substandard care rendered in your case is within the acceptable bounds of reasonable conduct. If you are armed with the expert's own article, the expert will be hard pressed to disagree with your position in the case.

Many lawyers today have adopted a practice of sending subpoenas to the experts of opposing parties. The subpoenas command the production of documents and are sometimes used beyond the territorial power of the court issuing the subpoena. It is my belief that this is unethical at best and unlawful at worst. However, the same result can be accomplished by merely sending the deponent a copy of the notice of his or her deposition, and a paragraph can be included in the notice which would request the deponent to bring to the deposition the same items and documents called for by the otherwise invalid subpoena. The difference between the subpoena and the notice is the fact that the subpoena is a court process where the notice is not. Regardless of the procedure utilized, the expert witness should be requested to bring with him or her at least the following:

1. All materials provided to or reviewed by the expert in connection with the case, including but not limited to medical records, depositions, radiology films, reports from other physicians, and any and all other materials relevant to the case
2. All correspondence, tapes, memoranda, notes, reports, and other documents received or generated by the expert in connection with the case
3. The results of all research done by or for the expert relative to the case

4. An accurate accounting of the time spent in review of the case, including preparation time for the deposition and hourly rate charge for such services
5. All invoices, statements, bills, etc., connected with the expert's review of the case
6. A listing of all background sources and other persons, if any, whom the expert consulted in connection with his or her review of the case
7. A complete bibliography and curriculum vitae

The deposition should then proceed to cover at least the following subject matters: the expert's qualifications; how the expert became involved in the case, including the names of the people who contacted him or her; and the approximate dates of contact. Counsel would then want to review all materials furnished to the expert upon which he or she relied in reaching his or her opinion. The expert should be required to clearly state the standard of care which is ordinarily employed under the same or similar circumstances. Thereafter the witness should be carefully examined regarding his or her understanding of the facts upon which he or she is basing his or her opinion. Often the experts for errant doctors will be required to synthesize an entirely new set of facts because the existent facts which can be proven do not permit an honest support by the expert. The expert should be examined regarding his or her rate of pay, and copies of invoices and payments should be reviewed. The expert's prior experience reviewing the cases and his or her court and deposition testimony are also important topics to be explored. It is recommended that the expert be asked if he or she is planning to attend trial if called upon to do so.

§10.14 Voir Dire

Voir dire is the opportunity for the court and/or counsel to examine prospective jurors—to see and hear them respond to questions designed to discover a basis for challenges, either for cause or peremptory. The purpose of voir dire is to select a jury which is free of bias and prejudice and to meet the constitutional requirement that juries be impartial. Although the Seventh Amendment to the United States Constitution does not have an explicit impartiality requirement, an impartial jury is part of the basic right to a jury trial.

Counsel's objective at this stage of the trial is to explain the process of voir dire selection, develop a bond with the jurors, identify bias and prejudice any particular juror might have about the subject matter of the case, the parties, or defense counsel, and educate the jurors to the value of the injury the plaintiff has suffered.

Counsel should take advantage of the initial questions asked of the jurors to put them at ease in responding to questions. Remember, jurors are not familiar with this process and are looking for leadership and information.

In order to put the jurors at ease, counsel must be at ease when asking the questions.

Collective questioning can effectively elicit general information. In order to maximize the effect of collective questioning, it is important to stress the obligation of the juror to assume the question was put individually and the duty of the juror to respond.

Questions posed collectively should relate to any pecuniary interest the jurors might have in the outcome of the case, relationship with any juror to parties, defense counsel, or any members of the firm, familiarity with any witness to be called by the plaintiff and defendant, any knowledge of the lawsuit, and any leaning regarding the subject matter of the suit.

In a medical malpractice case, a general question regarding any connection with the health care industry, any health care dependence, or prejudicial experience with a doctor or hospital must be followed with individual questions. Counsel should use utmost caution before accepting such a person as a juror.

Finally, questions posed to individual jurors regarding any bias or prejudice regarding their views on tort reform, the justice system, and evaluating the plaintiff's injuries are of critical importance. This is the time when counsel can set the theme of the case. All cases should be tried with the theme in mind.

If the plaintiff is seeking a verdict for a large amount of money, now is the opportunity for the attorney to state the amount in open court in the presence of all jurors early and frequently. It does not come easy for most lawyers to mention a figure such as $10,000,000. Likewise, such an expression does not come easy for the jury who is to assess damages for the plaintiff. If the jury is not comfortable with the multimillion-dollar figure after hearing all the evidence and the argument of counsel, such a verdict is not possible. If trial counsel is not at ease with the multimillion-dollar figure, it must be because the case does not justify such an award. Counsel loses credibility in trying to overinflate the value of the case, and no number with which counsel is uncomfortable should be mentioned in the trial.

§10.15 Direct Examination

Direct examination offers counsel the opportunity to use his or her creative talents to prove the case. Leading the witness is generally not allowed except for formalities during initial questions relating to educational background or the general subject matter of the case.

Since counsel will not be able to lead the witnesses, all witnesses, expert or lay, should be thoroughly prepared for their testimony. Counsel can put the "springboard" question but the witness must elaborate.

The medical expert witness's testimony should be prepared to qualify the expert, give his or her opinion regarding the careless acts of the defendant doctor, and describe and illustrate plaintiff's injuries caused by the carelessness. Lay witnesses are effectively used to describe the plaintiff before the incident which will exemplify the contrast with plaintiff's injuries as seen by the jury.

In qualifying the medical expert, counsel should be reluctant to allow defense counsel to stipulate to the expert's credentials. A party is entitled to try the case and prove it as he or she sees fit. The jury should always hear the qualifications of the expert witness and stipulations should be rejected.

In Georgia, questions regarding the deviation from the standard of care and proximate cause must be posed by way of hypothetical questions. Facts and any medical documentary evidence upon which the opinion is based which will be used in the hypothetical question must be in evidence prior to the expert's testimony. The rules of evidence of each state obviously should be consulted with regard to the foundation required for expert testimony. Under the Federal Rules of Evidence, anything ordinarily relied upon by the professional in his or her day-to-day activities would be admissible and could serve as the basis for the hypothetical question.[12]

Finally, the expert should be asked to describe and illustrate the plaintiff's injuries. There are many ways this aspect of the case can be presented. For example, if the plaintiff is totally disabled, a "day in the life" videotape can be prepared and presented as an adjunct to the testimony of a live medical witness. The plaintiff should be presented to the jury prior to playing the tape so that the jury can identify with the plaintiff and reinforce what they are seeing on the tape with their knowledge of someone they have actually met. Questioning the expert during the tape adds variety and keeps the inherent boredom of a videotape to a minimum. Questions should be designed to cause the jurors throughout the tape to think about the injuries and their impact upon the life of the individual they have just met.

If the individual is deceased, a "footprints of life" presentation is used. Through family members, friends, clergy, and coworkers, counsel can effectively "bring the deceased back to life" by using photographs, awards, family films, and any other memorabilia counsel might find from interviews with these witnesses. If the jurors have agreed to place a dollar value on a human life in the voir dire process, the lawyer's job is to present enough evidence that the jury can actually "know" the decedent. In the case of a child, to know the child is to love the child and any dollar value placed by a jury with this frame of mind should be appropriate.

§10.16 Cross-Examination

It is the right of every party to cross-examine witnesses against him or her. The court retains considerable discretion in controlling the right of cross-examination. The English common law rule as to the scope of cross-examination permits counsel to cross-examine witnesses on any subject relevant to any of the issues in the entire case, including facts realting solely to the cross-examiner's own case or affirmative defenses. The English com-

---

[12] Fed R Evid 703.

mon law rule is followed in some jurisdictions. The Federal Rules of Evidence, however, permit cross-examination only to the extent of those matters which had been elicited on direct examination.

Cross-examination is a valuable right but it is not necessary to exercise this right on every witness. When cross-examining, counsel should endeavor to retain control of the witness. Avoid any question on cross-examination which permits the witness to interject new and unknown material into the trial.

While the successful impeachment of an adverse witness through cross-examination is one of the desired goals of the examiner, the practical effect of impeachment is neither clear nor definite. The testimony of a witness who has been impeached is not cancelled out as if the harmful testimony had not been given; rather, it becomes the province of the jury to place whatever weight and credit they choose upon the testimony of a witness who has been successfully impeached.

If the cross-examiner scores sufficient points to convince the jury that the witness has willfully and knowingly sworn falsely, the witness's testimony should be disregarded entirely (unless corroborated by circumstances or other unimpeached evidence). No magic "You win" flag is hoisted when an adverse witness is successfully impeached. The practical effect of a successful impeachment is taken with all of the other matters transpiring during the course of the trial and helps the cross-examiner's position.

Even though the law presumes witnesses to speak the truth, certain jurisdictions usually set forth at least three methods of impeachment:

1. Disproving facts testified to by the witness
2. Contradictory statements previously made by the witness as to relevant matters
3. General bad character of the witness

It should be borne in mind that the jury may also take into account the demeanor of the witness and his or her manner of testifying. This clearly entitles the jury to disbelieve any witness on no more substantial basis than that they do not like "the way they look" or "the way they talk."

A witness's deposition testimony can be used during trial by the cross-examiner only for impeachment purposes. Many times during the trial, the counsel will begin the cross-examination by stating, "Didn't you testify in your deposition. . . ." This is objectionable as irrelevant since what the witness said on another occasion has no value whatsoever unless a difference has first been established in what the witness is testifying to in court. Therefore, cross-examining counsel must first begin with a question which produces an answer he or she feels is inconsistent with prior testimony. Then, counsel can introduce the prior testimony only after laying the proper foundation by establishing familiarity with the deposition with regard to time, place, and so forth. The witness is then read the prior testimony and given an opportunity to explain the inconsistency.

A witness may be impeached by evidence of general bad character as well as proof of a conviction of a crime involving moral turpitude. Showing a conviction is a method of showing bad character. The showing is to be made by record evidence, rather than by reputation, and the judgment of conviction and the indictment or accusation must be shown. Certified or exemplified copies of the judgment are admissible without accounting for the original.

The inexperienced trial lawyer often fails to appreciate the opportunity presented on cross-examination. There is, indeed, a stark difference between the direct question and the one put during cross-examination. The attorney may lead the witness on cross-examination to the point of directing him or her. Never ask the witness "Why," because cross-examination is not an opportunity for the witness to expand and lecture the jury. Tight control of the witness is the objective of the cross-examiner.

The discovery depositions of all opposing witnesses should be carefully studied, and every favorable point gleaned during the discovery deposition should be put into an affirmative interrogatory for trial. The preparatory phrases "You will agree with me, won't you, that . . ." or "It is true that . . ." are excellent tools so that the witness merely voices agreement. If the witness disagrees, then counsel can turn to the deposition and proceed with the impeachment process.

The following *Ten Commandments of Cross-Examination*[13] espoused by the late Professor Irving Younger are most helpful to the effective cross-examiner.

1. Be brief.
2. Use plain words.
3. Use only leading questions.
4. Be prepared.
5. Listen.
6. Do not quarrel.
7. Avoid repetition.
8. Disallow witness explanation.
9. Limit questioning.
10. Save for summation.

Thorough preparation will permit the lawyer to establish pertinent points favoring his or her case through the concessions of other witnesses. The logic of cross-examination is to discredit the witness who has harmed you or to gain concessions from the adverse witness which will be favorable to your case.

---

[13] I. Younger, Ten Commandments of Cross-Examination (National Institute for Trial Advocacy 1975).

§10.17 Summation

The summation or final argument is the opportunity to draw upon all the inner resources of counsel. Commitments should have been obtained on voir dire and now counsel brings all the commitments including the evidence and the damages and the reason together in the summation. Many cases can be won or lost at final argument. The argument should be clear and reasonable and continue logically with the theme which has been displayed throughout the trial.

The plaintiff has the right to open and conclude the closing argument. Some lawyers waive the opening. This is error. The opening is an opportunity to discuss the legal principles with the jury who will be given complex rules of law to apply to the facts. Many jurors fail to fully understand the legal principles involved in such a case and some elaboration on these principles by counsel is clearly appropriate. Illustration, analogy, and discussion are suggested on such complex points as honest errors in judgment, emergency doctrine, burden of proof, preponderance of the evidence, and legal presumptions. The opening segment of the final argument affords an opportunity to challenge opposing counsel on several points such as uncontradicted testimony favorable to the plaintiff. It is also an excellent opportunity to suggest the damages figure and invite the comment of opposing counsel to assist the jury on this very difficult question.

The final segment of the plaintiff's closing argument is devoted to rebuttal of the argument advanced by opposing counsel and efforts to obtain a just and adequate verdict. The talents of trial counsel are valuable throughout the trial but in final argument, if handled appropriately, those talents can make the difference.

11

The Defense Perspective

Robert G. Tanner, Esq.

§11.01 Introduction
§11.02 Defense on Law
§11.03 —Substantive Technicalities
Discovery
§11.04 Marshaling the Facts
§11.05 Exploring the Case: Depositions
§11.06 —Deposition of the Plaintiff
§11.07 —Deposition of the Defendant
§11.08 —Deposition of the Plaintiff's Expert
The Pretrial Phase
§11.09 Evaluating the Case
§11.10 Exhibit Preparation
§11.11 Establishing the Theme of the Defense
The Trial
§11.12 Rejecting the Jury
§11.13 Opening Statement
§11.14 Cross-Examination
§11.15 Direct Examination
§11.16 Closing Argument
Conclusion
§11.17 Conclusion
Appendix 11-A Model Interrogatories
Appendix 11-B Case Summary Chart

§11.01 Introduction

A urological malpractice case is among the most inflammatory that can be presented in a courtroom. The plaintiff alleges injury to a bodily system or function which is uniquely personal and private. Urinary incontinence, disfigurement, sexual dysfunction, psychological harm, and loss of reproductive capacity are common injuries, and lay juries are sympathetic to patients whose lifestyles (if not lives) have been changed radically by such traumas.

There are a host of other perspectives as well. The defendant-physician is outraged by the allegations and/or frightened by the unknown. Overburdened judges are annoyed by any case which promises a prolonged trial and may attempt to pressure counsel into settlement, regardless of the merits. Insurers ideally wish the matter ended with no payment, while the opposition typically has inflated expectations of settlement value or jury verdict. An attorney representing a urologist must look beyond these understandably narrow views to grasp the totality of a complex situation. For the lawyer, the case becomes primarily and predominantly an exercise in the perception of reality—the reality of the severity of injury, of the defendant's explanation of that injury, of problems of the documentation and the opponent's ability to exploit those weaknesses, and of the ultimate ability of a jury to justly weigh the issues.

Given the foregoing, the perceptive lawyer will utilize every legitimate defense. These defenses exist in the substantive and procedural law of the jurisdiction or in the facts of the care rendered. While the diversity of applicable law makes it impossible to comment upon all procedural or substantive defenses, this chapter offers a brief observation on the importance of the assertion of technicalities in any defense, and then examines the flow of the attorney's work from discovery to closing statement. Specific suggestions are offered based upon the reality of daily defense practice, and several model forms are presented as appendixes at the end of the chapter.

§11.02 Defense on Law

That the technicalities of the law favor the defense is so obvious a reality as to be commonly overlooked. Consider, for example, a motion for summary judgment as outlined in Fed R Civ P 56. The rule is neutral and allows either party to move for summary judgment, but the substantive law of all jurisdictions offers defendants more frequent opportunities to prevail on this motion. The same is true of most other motions. Questions of venue, service of process, jurisdiction, and myriad other procedural issues offer advantage principally to the defense. The plaintiff cannot achieve the goal of a large recovery through a motion to change venue; plaintiff's counsel, after all, selected on filing the suit the venue that was either required or believed to be most favorable. The defense, on the other hand, may well make a serious case much more defensible by moving to transfer trial to a more conservative forum if the opportunity arises.

Upon accepting defense of a urological malpractice case, the attorney must consider its procedural component. Is the suit filed in the proper court? Are the parties proper? Has the plaintiff complied with applicable laws requiring arbitration prior to suit or attaching to the complaint an affidavit of an expert witness verifying that the suit is not frivolous? Has the statute of limitations expired as to part or all of the action? Has service of process been perfected?

The last question is especially important in malpractice actions, because frequently service is never perfected as provided by law. In the usual scenario a busy process server appears at the defendant's office only to find that the physician is in surgery; nervous office personnel offer to accept the complaint. The urologist returns later, is handed these papers by a bewildered receptionist and is quickly on the phone to his or her attorney denouncing the legal profession. The physician cannot be expected to grasp the relevance of how the papers came to him or her, but this is one of the first questions counsel should ask. If the statute of limitations has or is about to expire, the attorney should consider how the laws of service of process and expiration of limitations period interrelate and then determine if the service error offers an opportunity to dispose of the case.

The initial procedural review must be ongoing; malpractice litigation is prolonged, and procedural means to dispose of or weaken the plaintiff's case can arise at any time. Venue proper at the outset may be lost by dismissal of parties. Discovery rights may be sacrificed by the failure to meet deadlines, and costs due for appeals or other services may not be timely paid, with disastrous results. If such blunders occur, the urologist's counsel needs to know and act quickly.

This is not to urge that every conceivable technical defense be asserted. Many motions will neither dispose of a case nor meaningfully improve the defense; in such instances there is little point to assert them, and, indeed, the wholesale filing of motions risks the ire of the court. As a general rule, defenses should be asserted to the extent that they reasonably can be anticipated to end the litigation or curtail the opposition's ability to carry the burden of proof. A successful result achieved through the vigorous assertion of such technical defenses is no less welcome to the client than the verdict at trial and certainly is more cost effective.

§11.03 —Substantive Technicalities

A second area wherein the law offers significant advantages to the defense in a urological case is in the very nature of malpractice litigation. A claim for medical malpractice is subject to innumerable rules with subtle interpretations and meanings that have few counterparts. A thorough study of the medical malpractice cases of the jurisdiction in which the action pends is a prerequisite for any attorney undertaking this task.[1]

---

[1] *See generally* Cleveland v Wong, 237 Kan 410, 701 P2d 1301 (1985); Buie v Reynolds, 571 P2d 1230 (Okla Ct App 1977); Perry v Langstaff, 383 So 2d 1104 (Fla Dist Ct App), *petition denied,* 392 So 2d 1377 (Fla 1980); Chiero v Chicago Osteopathic Hosp, 47

For all its complexities, however, the medical malpractice action is, at bottom, a tort action, and it shares with other torts the four fundamental elements of duty, breach of duty, causation, and damages. Keeping in mind these four elements will assist an attorney to organize and understand his or her case, and will often allow him or her to observe when the opposition has erred. There follows a brief general discussion of each of these elements, with examples of particular substantive technical issues which may afford advantage to the defense.

The obligation of a physician to exercise some defined standard of care for the benefit of a patient arises from the establishment of a physician/patient relationship. It is by the voluntary and mutual creation of that relationship that the physician assumes the legal obligation that accompanies treatment of the patient. Given the private nature of the urological system, it would be difficult to imagine many situations in which a urologist has seen the patient without previously establishing the physician/patient relationship, so the existence of this relationship is not frequently a significant question in urological malpractice cases.

Given the physician/patient relationship, a certain duty is imposed upon the physician. That duty is not to guarantee a cure, nor does the law make the physician an insurer of his or her treatment. A bad result in the treatment in and of itself proves nothing. Instead, the law places upon the physician the duty to exercise care commensurate with his or her special skill and training. The measure by which the conduct of a physician is to be judged is the degree of care and skill ordinarily employed by the medical profession under similar conditions and like circumstances to the facts of the case in issue. A professional who professes skill in his or her calling (which a urologist offers by virtue of completing training in that field and practicing as a specialist within it) must in fact be reasonably skillful at it. Whatever represents the usual conduct of a normally skillful member of the profession under the facts of the particular case in litigation becomes the "standard of care" to which the defendant is held. Several actions may represent conduct appropriate under the circumstances and one should avoid the pitfall of accepting that the standard of care can represent only one course of conduct.

This standard is in reality a medical rather than a legal definition. The law merely defines what the conduct must be: practice commensurate with what a physician would expect to observe from a skilled colleague dealing with a certain constellation of presenting symptoms. Medical reality as established by physicians determines what that proper practice actually is. It follows ineluctably that the standard of care must be established by physi-

---

Ill App 3d, 166, 392 NE2d 203 (1979); McMillan v LDLR, 645 SW2d 836 (Tex Ct App 1982). These cases, all involving in whole or in part actions against urologists, arise from a number of jurisdictions and illustrate both the general uniformity with regard to basic malpractice principles in urological litigation as well as some of the differences which can arise amongst the jurisdictions. Needless to say, important principles of law are found in decisions relating to all specialties of medicine.

cians. In almost every conceivable situation, the legal definition of the physician's duty requires that the plaintiff prove through competent expert testimony that there was a departure from an applicable standard of care, either by failing to do the correct thing or by doing the incorrect thing.

On the surface, the standard of care would seem to be a straightforward issue, but problems can arise for the plaintiff which, if properly exploited, may defeat the case. For example, the particular jurisdiction may have a rule which specifies that the standard of care is to be judged by local (i.e., statewide) parameters as opposed to a general (i.e., nationwide) standard. A careless plaintiff's attorney taking a deposition for use at trial and questioning an expert on the incorrect standard may have destroyed his or her own case; defense counsel needs to know this technicality so that objection can be made at the proper time. A similar objection arises when an expert does not testify as to a standard but, rather, states what he or she would do in his or her own practice. In some jurisdictions, such testimony is construed as offering no proof on the relevant standard of care.

Medical malpractice actions are not academic discussions and courts do not expend the considerable time involved in such litigation for the purpose of learning lay jurors' conclusions on the exercise of the care by any particular physician. The question of negligence is meaningless without proof that the alleged violation of a standard of care caused certain injuries. Proximate causation of the injury by the negligence is the next great issue in a malpractice claim. The plaintiff must offer at least some evidence that the injury complained of was directly linked to the alleged failure to exercise the requisite degree of care and skill. The mere possibility of such a link generally is insufficient to carry the plaintiff's burden of proof.

There can be much variation among the jurisdictions on this issue. Questions can arise whether causation of the injury from the negligent act must be testified to by an expert or can be found by a lay jury on its own. Questions such as the probability necessary to establish causation, or whether the incident complained of, if not the sole agent of injury, contributed sufficiently with other things to make it a proximate cause can pose challenges for the plaintiff. Counsel should look carefully at his or her jurisdiction's law on these points.

The last great element of a malpractice tort is damages. It is axiomatic that there can be no tort if the plaintiff has suffered no injury. Furthermore, the damages for which compensation is sought must necessarily be the product of the negligence asserted. All three elements must link. It is generally law that the damages claimed must be susceptible to proof with some reasonable certainty as to their nature, and recovery is not allowed where resort must be made purely to speculation or conjecture. Careful evaluation of the facts will frequently produce evidence of questionable claims for damages.

In sum, these substantive technicalities, used in conjunction with the facts of the case, have offered grounds for directed verdict if not summary judgment on many occasions; they are a potent source of advantage for the defense and should not be overlooked.

Discovery

§11.04 Marshaling the Facts

The defense attorney typically begins work with an information deficit vis-á-vis opposing counsel. The opposing party has already given his or her attorney at least an overview of the treatment rendered and in-depth information concerning the alleged injury. The patient, of course, has access to all physicians seen subsequent to the urologist defendant and can easily obtain their records. On the other hand, defense counsel is unlikely to know anything more than what he or she reads in the complaint, what the urologist has in his or her notes, or what he or she has heard from friends in the medical community. The steps necessary to bridge this information gap are not unique to urological cases, but they are among the most vital actions that the attorney will take.

Obtain a Complete Copy of the Defendant's Office Records

It is impossible to stress too greatly to the defendant that the defense attorney needs a copy of *everything* in the doctor's office file—phone messages, insurance statements, letters from other physicians—in short, every scrap of paper the defendant has ever generated or received on the patient. Office "sign in" sheets and appointment books should be kept as well. The original records must be placed in a secure place (losing them after suit is filed does not impress juries) and several copies should be made. These copies must be legible, and if there is any problem with readability the defendant must be called upon to provide an exact typewritten duplication. It is important to determine who else has already received copies. A request from plaintiff's attorney for a copy of the records often precedes a malpractice case, and it is useful to know at the outset what the opposition already knows.

Interrogatories

Attorneys, not parties, answer interrogatories, and for this reason they are primarily useful as a tool for gathering basic information. (It is rare for an attorney to secure a damaging admission in interrogatories; this form of discovery lacks the spontaneity of deposition, where the client cannot rely upon his or her attorney for advice on every question.) However, within their scope interrogatories are of value. The patient's employment and wage background, residence history, medical expenses, and past and current treating physicians can all be learned through interrogatories. By this means the attorney can decide where to secure additional pertinent records. Additionally, this is an excellent vehicle for securing information to which the defendant is entitled by statute. For example, most states have laws paralleling Fed R Civ P 26 (concerning disclosure of expert witnesses), and any interrogatory modeled as closely as possible on this statute will require the opposition to disclose pertinent information on their experts.

A set of interrogatories which has proved helpful is included in Appendix 11-A as an illustration of what one reasonably can seek by this means of discovery.

Obtain All Other Medical Records

Records from physicians who saw the patient before and after the defendant should be obtained. Again, emphasis is on obtaining complete records. If the case involves hospitalization, copies of the chart generated by the defendant as well as all prior and subsequent charts should be secured. Cost-cutting here is not to be advised, since it is impossible to know at the outset which portions of a hospital record may be significant. Of course, there is no justification for restricting this record gathering to urologists. Information on symptoms significant to the case may appear in the office notes of any specialist.

Obtain Significant Ancillary Information

Data bearing on the patient's condition may be found in sources other than hospital records and physician office notes. Records of employers may be significant if they show the amount of time missed from work; patient insurance or job applications may have significant admissions. Physical therapy and rehabilitation specialists may have useful information in their files, and the same is true of home care nursing services. Diaries of family members may yield helpful data, and, especially insofar as young children are concerned, school records may be informative. In this information-rich age there are many sources of data on a patient beyond just the medical records, and it is always best to err on the side of obtaining too much data from such sources.

Learn the Medicine

Early in the litigation, counsel needs to become knowledgeable about the urology practiced in the case. Whether the focus of the case lies in anatomy, pathology, or surgical technique, the attorney must be able to visualize clearly what was wrong with the patient, what was intended by the physician, and what actually occurred during the treatment. In this effort counsel possesses one of the classic advantages of the defense, for the client is more than able to provide this information. Counsel ought to use the client to ensure that he or she absolutely understands the medical events he or she may someday describe to a jury.

As the attorney learns the medicine, he or she ought to note the areas in which he or she progresses slowly, for it is likely that a jury will have difficulty with many of the same points. Make a list of important ideas and definitions which are difficult to grasp so that extra emphasis can be prepared for presentation to the ultimate factfinder. For example, in almost every urological case, counsel may as well begin at the outset to think through how to explain to the jury the difference between ureter and urethra.

Summarizing the Material

The assembly of legible copies of all relevant records does not in and of itself bridge the information gap. This is accomplished, obviously, only when the records are knowledgeably analyzed. This should be done in consultation with the defendant. Records should be reviewed for information bearing on the two great questions of all malpractice actions and on other particular issues of the individual case.

In any case, two major areas are the patient's pre- and posttreatment status. In reviewing the file, counsel should be aware of and constantly searching for indications of the patient's symptomatology before the care rendered by the defendant. In general, it is advantageous if the records reflect that whatever was done by the defendant was preceded by a lengthy period of conservative but unavailing therapy during which the patient's health rapidly deteriorated. Comparably, the patient's posttreatment course should be examined to isolate all potential evidence indicating that there has been at least significant improvement since the alleged injury. These broad themes are the core of any record review.

At the same time, counsel will examine the file to highlight facts raised by the unique issues of the litigation. For example, the patient who has suffered an operative complication may deny that he or she had any significant complaints prior to surgery; one of the key issues therefore becomes the patient's actual pre-operative complaints. All records in such an action must be scanned carefully for the significant symptomatology. If records of physicians who saw the plaintiff before (and sometimes after) the urologist defendant document major pre-operative symptoms and/or complaints, the defense is well on the way to a successful result. (Any jury is likely to accept as true complaints recorded by a nondefendant physician before the patient saw the defendant; there is no reason for such an uninvolved physician to have charted nonexistent complaints.) The search for this information would be, therefore, extensive, including records of prior hospitalizations, consultants' reports, nurses' admission forms from the hospital admission in question, statements of co-workers and family members, and everything else available.

In some settings the absence of notations may also be important. A lack of notations can indicate either that the condition was not inquired about or that it was inquired of and not reported by the patient. For this reason it is always wise to establish personal contact with other treating physicians to determine both their recordkeeping tendencies and their own recollection of the patient's symptomatology. More often than not, such contacts yield physicians willing to assist the defense. It is best to conduct such visits in person, as opposed to a phone contact; it is simply too easy for a busy physician to fail to thoroughly examine his or her records during a phone query from an attorney about care rendered months or years earlier.

At the conclusion of the record review, counsel ought to have at least as good a knowledge of the patient's medical course as does the patient himself or herself. While this may seem an ambitious goal, it is achievable. Many patients do not have a good recollection of their condition and/or will not take the time to refresh themselves on their course of treatment so as to be able to describe it correctly. The same is often true of plaintiff's experts and, sometimes, of plaintiff's counsel. As the case moves into the deposition phase, it is especially important to be aware whenever an opposing party, witness, or counsel betrays a misunderstanding of the facts.

§11.05 Exploring the Case: Depositions

Modern litigation is, increasingly, trial by deposition, and there is nothing more important to the malpractice defense than this aspect of discovery. Prior and subsequent treating physicians, rehabilitation specialists, nurses, financial experts, family, friends, and others will be deposed by one side or the other. It would be impossible to isolate unifying principles to govern the conduct of all such depositions. It is, however, possible to offer suggestions for use during the three most important depositions in any malpractice case, those of the plaintiff, the defendant, and the plaintiff's expert witness.

§11.06 — Deposition of the Plaintiff

Here there are four objectives: to ensure that the information gap has been closed; to explore the case thoroughly (testing the patient's recollection and ability to articulate); to anticipate and avoid problems; and to conduct a practice cross-examination. These objectives range from the rote to the more creative aspect of the advocate's art.

At its most basic level, a deposition is an opportunity for counsel to confirm what he or she has learned of the patient's background, medical care, and potential damages. This is an opportunity to verify that the initial document gathering has been complete and, if not, to identify the gaps. The patient should be quizzed as to all hospitalizations, outpatient treatments, office treatment, and emergency room visits both before and after the incident in question. Likewise, the patient's general background must be understood. Where has the patient lived for at least several years prior to seeing the defendant? (This information often can be invaluable in finding witnesses.) What is the patient's educational background, employment history, and litigation experience? Finally, do not fail to inquire as to future planned medical care. The rostering of this information can be mechanical but it is nonetheless vital.

Once the basics are confirmed, the case must be thoroughly explored. Counsel needs to understand fully the patient's recollection on all conditions which brought him or her to the defendant urologist. How long had these symptoms been present; had they increased as to area, duration, or intensity prior to seeing the defendant? Had plaintiff tried home remedies? Did they work? More importantly, what does the patient claim was done by the defendant during the office or hospital visits. This is an opportunity which is often sacrificed. Office records may not document certain care rendered, but the plaintiff may recall particular acts by the physician, and all such helpful recollections must be gathered. All quotes—particularly alleged admissions—attributed to the defendant by the patient must be spread upon the record, along with all witnesses present when the words were spoken or at other important times. Finally, the patient's course since leaving the defendant's care should be thoroughly explored. The facts of the situation dictate the extent and duration of this phase of the deposition.

As an attorney explores the case, he or she will usually encounter opportunities to anticipate and avoid problems. The classic example is the opportunity to avoid a battery amendment to a complaint asserting negligence. It frequently happens that an initial claim for negligent surgery will not, in the end, be supported by the evidence; plaintiff's counsel, unable to prove a violation of any applicable standard of practice, then asserts by amendment a battery claim. Such amendments will be allowed by many courts long after the statute of limitations has run. Counsel should keep this in mind at deposition and either take or make the opportunity to render moot such an amendment before it is ever filed—or in fact before opposing counsel has ever thought of it. Thus, the patient should be asked to acknowledge a written consent form (if one exists) and to admit that the symptoms were severe enough to cause him or her to seek out the physician and eagerly accept the treatment offered. In this and other instances, counsel ought to anticipate potential future claims and spend some time laying the groundwork to thwart them.

In most cases, counsel will realize early on what he or she would most like to have the plaintiff admit to the trier of fact, and, conversely, what he or she least wants that factfinder to hear from the opposing party. A deposition is an opportunity to find out what the witness will say in both regards; it is, in fact, a rehearsal for trial cross-examination. It is an appropriate time to thoroughly explore the best case scenario. There is no reason to automatically assume that at least some facts supportive of the defense will not be admitted by a plaintiff, who should be given an opportunity to offer whatever such testimony he or she has. Counsel needs to enter the deposition with a clear understanding of what he or she would most like to hear the plaintiff say, and counsel ought to give the plaintiff an opportunity to say it. By the same token, depositions are the time to ask the questions that can hurt. If there are facts which, if testified to by the opposition, can prove fatal at trial, a deposition is the best place to hear them.

An example of the use of a deposition as practice cross-examination may be helpful. Consider the scenario of a patient presenting with mild complaints such as burning or straining on urination which are diagnosed as a bladder infection. A brief notation in the chart and apparently successful antibiotic treatment is given; the patient is then lost to follow-up, only to re-emerge later as a plaintiff in a malpractice suit claiming failure to diagnose prostate cancer. Here the defense attorney is typically faced with the difficult problem of lack of documentation and serious injury, and here is exactly the case in which counsel should practice cross-examination in the opposition's conference room.

In this example, counsel would attend the deposition with a complete roster of classic symptoms of prostate cancer as well as an inventory of conditions which are not usually part of the classic presentation. He or she should have the same information with regard to bladder infection. The plaintiff is asked to admit or deny the presence of typical symptoms of prostate cancer on each visit to the defendant. If plaintiff claims that these symptoms were present, counsel at least knows what he or she will hear at trial. If the patient denies the classic symptoms, counsel can confidently ask this at trial and argue that the absence of the expected presentation confounded the diagnostic effort. Next, counsel should ask about symptoms which do not usually accompany prostate cancer. Many patients come to a deposition with the idea of overwhelming an attorney with complaints of pain and problems; such people readily claim almost any symptom mentioned. A plaintiff acknowledging symptoms which are not recognizable as reflecting prostate cancer has allowed defense counsel to argue that the diagnostic picture was bizarre.

The same exercise can be followed in reverse with regard to the symptoms of infection. The patient may very well agree that at least some of the classic symptoms of infection were present upon visiting the defendant; if so, the defendant's diagnosis will appear more reasonable. Of course, the plaintiff may agree to none of this, but if so nothing has been lost; counsel at least knows what not to ask at trial.

It is of great value if, prior to the plaintiff's deposition, counsel has been able to completely review all medical records. Through this process counsel will understand when plaintiff is claiming symptoms which are not documented in the records of defendant or other physicians or, alternatively, is testifying in accord with the records. If the former situation develops at deposition, counsel should encourage it, and then at trial present the testimony of the physicians who created the records which contradict the testimony of the patient on the symptomatology at issue.

§11.07 — Deposition of the Defendant

A malpractice defendant's deposition should be an anticlimax. Counsel for the defense has done a perfect job when there are no surprises and plaintiff's counsel learns nothing that he or she does not already know or reasonably could infer from the medical records. In particular, a deposition is successful when the opposition has gained nothing through its practice cross-examination. The key to achieving this is thoughtful preparation before opposing counsel arrives in the conference room.

The first point to establish with the defendant is the location of the deposition—which must be the attorney's office. The urologist may be surprised by such a demand, but fundamental reasons justify it. It is virtually impossible for the average medical practitioner to isolate himself or herself from the flow of office activities. A deposition at the physician's office is invariably interrupted with everything from patient emergencies to nurses needing to say goodnight. Worse, plaintiff's attorney gains unnecessary access to a wealth of information about the defendant. Simply by being in the office, opposing counsel has access to the books and periodicals the defendant receives, and he or she can form an impression of the general flow of work. Giving the deposition in the office deprives the physician of the chance to decline to produce documents on the grounds that he or she has not brought them to the attorney's office. The place to give the deposition is in the lawyer's conference room.

Counsel's next care is to assign to the client two important pre-deposition tasks and to assure their completion. First, the physician must review and thoroughly understand the medical records. A physician will be nervous at his or her deposition, and an individual under stress is likely to overlook supportive notations in his or her own records unless he or she has thoroughly reviewed and organized them. This problem must be minimized by ensuring that the defendant has studied all pertinent records and can easily utilize them during the course of the interrogation.

Second, the defendant should study the general medical literature on the subject matter of the case. It is to be anticipated that opposing counsel will ask the defendant for a textbook definition of whatever condition is involved; it is embarrassing if the defendant is unable to respond fully. The urologist's review should include both the basic anatomy and physiology of the underlying condition, the therapies current at the time the patient was seen, and recent subsequent advances. Even the most able practitioner would be well advised to spend some time in such a session prior to undergoing deposition; it must be assumed that the plaintiff's lawyer will have done the same.

Naturally, defense counsel has much to do as well. Drawing upon his or her knowledge of the case and experience with the plaintiff's attorney, counsel must assess the most likely points of attack and prepare to brief the defendant accordingly. Crucial points must be isolated and an explanation prepared so that the defendant will not misspeak. Significant discoveries from other records and the deposition of the plaintiff must be highlighted so that they can be explained in an unhurried pre-deposition conference. Counsel should have clearly in mind those points on which the defendant needs to be cautioned, and sufficient time must be allowed to cover them and answer the client's questions.

Much of the pre-deposition conference will consist of the defendant's education on the law. In the first instance, it is necessary to explain to the urologist what a deposition is. In particular, the physician needs to understand the concept of impeachment as it relates to transcription of the deposition. Many physicians have absolutely no idea of this danger, nor do they realize how a careless or even humorous answer made in the apparently relaxed atmosphere of a deposition can come back to harm their case before a jury. This needs to be clarified at the outset. There is no reason to assume that a physician, even one who may have given depositions in his or her office, has an understanding of what is coming. Thus it is well to explain the general ground rules: a physician should be advised that he or she must be serious at all times, can take a break when needed, can consult with his or her attorney as appropriate, and must be told that some objections made during the course of the deposition would not prevent him or her from answering a question, whereas others amount to an instruction to say nothing. All of this needs to be explained as one would to any layperson.

It is unreasonable to expect the urologist to have an understanding of the legal elements of a malpractice claim, and he or she needs to be advised of the basic principles (physician/patient relationship, negligence, causation, damages) that frame the issues on which plaintiff must carry the burden of proof; therefore it is important to explain these elements. For example, a full explanation of the significance of proximate cause may prevent a physician's carelessly agreeing that plaintiff's injuries were the result of his or her care when there are other viable theories of causation. It is counsel's task to impart this information so that significant defenses are not inadvertently waived in the deposition.

In particular, it is crucial to explain the criteria by which the question of malpractice is judged in the particular jurisdiction. In most jurisdictions the practice of a physician is judged not by the failure to achieve a perfect result—which is what most doctors believe—but only by the requirement to adhere to a reasonable degree of care and skill such as is appropriate under the particular circumstances of the plaintiff's presentation. The defendant needs to know that his or her treatment is judged by the practice, not by the result. The defendant must in deposition be affirmative that his or her exercise of care and skill for this patient was within reasonable standards of professional conduct; the defense attorney must prepare the physician for this by carefully explaining the underlying legal framework.

Next, the physician must be given the "Golden Rules" of testifying. Tell the truth. Do not volunteer. Do not speculate. The necessity for, and the benefits of, honest answers are known to every experienced advocate and need not be emphasized here. If there is a weak point in the case, the defendant must be prepared to admit it (along with stressing whatever positive aspects exist) if asked an appropriate question. Subject, however, to the obligation to respond truthfully, the defendant must be instructed (urged, cajoled, commanded) to answer only what is asked. It must be explained to him or her in no uncertain terms that volunteering information will only aid the opposition and prolong the deposition. Comparably, the defendant must be admonished not to speculate. He or she will be under oath during the deposition, and if the truthful answer is that he or she does not know, he or she should so state.

The rules of the particular jurisdiction regarding use of textbooks should be explained. The physician must be cautioned not to agree that any textbook is authoritative unless he or she truly feels that it is. The defendant should be cautioned that literature read to him or her is nothing more than the opinion of the author and that he or she is not under any obligation to agree with it. The defendant should be warned about the habits of the plaintiff's attorney and cautioned as to any histrionics that may be expected. The doctor's notes should be reviewed by counsel. Defendants frequently bring with them to depositions their complete file, including correspondence to and from their attorney. This should be removed lest the opposing attorney discover privileged material. Lastly, the defendant must be urged and reminded not to answer any question he or she does not understand and to seek either clarification of the question or a conference with counsel if at any time in the deposition he or she is uncertain what is happening.

§11.08 —Deposition of the Plaintiff's Expert

In many ways this discovery parallels that of the deposition of the plaintiff (*see* §11.06), because the same objectives apply: to determine the background of the witness, to explore the case thoroughly, to anticipate and avoid problems, and to conduct a practice trial cross-examination.

As with other depositions, the deposition of the opposing expert is grounded upon thorough advance preparation. As soon as counsel has determined the identity of plaintiff's expert, at least three sources of information should be tapped. First, search should be made of the medical literature to determine what writings the witness has published touching on the medical issues involved. Secondly, counsel should seek prior depositions given by the witness. It is increasingly common for depositions of expert witnesses in malpractice cases to be stored in central repositories of private defense-oriented organizations. These are available to counsel at nominal fees and can often provide invaluable information, including even sworn testimony in which the witness had advanced the opposite theory to that expected in the current case. Finally, counsel would be well advised to speak with malpractice defense attorneys in the witness's home area. If there is good or bad in the witness's background, local attorneys generally will know it.

Beginning the deposition, counsel needs to establish the data base of the deponent. The witness should be required to roster each and every document he or she has reviewed, to indicate what he or she has learned from other sources, and to state all he or she has done in connection with his or her evaluation. Has the witness created a computer data base on the case or performed a literature search? Has the witness created a file? If so, he or she should be asked to produce it. All records examined by the witness should be examined by the urologist's attorney, who is looking here for two things: first, the witness may have made written notes or comments on the records, and these may prove useful; also, it may appear on careful examination that the records on which the witness claims to have formed opinions are illegible. (This happens more frequently than would be supposed, and it is something that should be silently noted by counsel for potential impeachment at trial.) It is well to ask the total time the deponent claims to have spent on the file.

The core of the deposition consists of learning the opinions held by the adverse expert and the basis for those views. This can be done in both a passive and an active fashion, and indeed it should be done in both, that is, the opinions held by the witness should be explored in the first instance by simply asking him or her what they are. It is impossible to ask such a question too simply. Let the witness state in his or her own words exactly what opinions he or she has. When the witness has finished, counsel should repeat them all and ask if he or she holds any other opinions. The question ought to be asked two or three more times during the course of the deposition, so that at trial it will be impossible for the witness to state that he or she was not given an opportunity to fully recite his or her views in his or her own words. (This can serve as a basis for impeachment if at trial the expert advances a new opinion; at a minimum it prevents the witness from claiming that counsel "put words in my mouth.") The same course should be followed with regard to having the witness state the reasons for each opinion. Once the opinions are learned, the witness is actively cross-examined about them, with counsel suggesting different combinations of facts and theories of the case and learning what responses can be expected.

In conducting such a discovery deposition, counsel ought to remember his or her right to conduct a practice cross-examination. Just as was true for the lay plaintiff, there are certain things one would wish to hear the opposing witness say, and he or she ought to be given an opportunity in deposition to say them. There is no reason to accept as a given that the opposing expert will be critical on every point. The opposition may be willing to concede certain points which, while not considered important by them, might be useful in developing the defense theory of the case. A deposition is the time to see how much help the opposition's expert will give, as well as to learn the worst testimony that is forthcoming.

The deposition must include discovery of the witness's testimony history. How many times has he or she testified for plaintiff's counsel? How many cases has he or she reviewed; how many depositions has he or she given; how many times has he or she appeared in court? What is his or her hourly rate or other compensation arrangement? Has he or she ever been a member of an expert witness service? Such information frequently forms the basis of the cross-examination that will take place at trial. Juries are, rightfully, suspicious of physicians who spend much of their time in court—and not treating patients—and counsel should not overlook this potential source of material to discredit the opposition.

Lastly, the deposition should not end until counsel learns the witness's own malpractice history. Few physicians today have practiced many years without a lawsuit, and the record of the witness's own trials or claims may, if admissible under the law of a particular jurisdiction, be a powerful tool against him or her.

The Pre Trial Phase

§11.09 —Evaluating the Case

Document assembly and analysis, witness identification and deposition, and everything else undertaken in discovery is ultimately intended to allow counsel objectively to evaluate the case. That evaluation is counsel's judgment of an unknown future jury's analysis of the tort elements of negligence, causation, and damages.

These three basic tort elements in fact form an overview of the case and it is useful in evaluating them to prepare a chart listing the fact issues to arise under each element. The witnesses likely to testify on each issue for plaintiff and for defendant can be listed on opposite sides of each fact issue. Next, counsel should consider the documentary evidence. What is plaintiff expected to introduce, and are valid objections available? By the same token, what documents does defense counsel need, and what objections can prevent their introduction into evidence? Documentary evidence which is crucial to the case can be rostered under each element. This simple technique will give counsel a fairly complete outline of the trial, listing the likely witnesses and significant documentary evidence of both sides on the major issues. Such a procedure beneficially forces counsel to summarize the case for himself or herself, and, more importantly, the chart can serve as a guideline for explaining to others what is anticipated in the courtroom. (An example of this chart is offered in Appendix 11-B.)

The role of personalities cannot be overlooked in any pending trial. Idiosyncracies of the judge must be pondered. Counsel's knowledge of the plaintiff's lawyer is vital as well. Most importantly, counsel needs to recall what he or she has learned through the practice cross-examination of the opponent's witnesses. What impressions are they likely to make? Counsel needs to gauge how hard a cross-examination of each witness he or she will be able to conduct without offending the jury. Counsel should also weigh how his or her own witnesses, particularly the defendant, will perform on the stand. All of this is viewed in the light of the probable jury (conservative/liberal; rural/urban, etc.).

In the end, counsel forms an opinion of the probable trial outcome, and good or bad he or she must share that opinion with the defendant. The client must be advised candidly of the likelihood of success or failure. Realism is crucial in these deliberations. The defendant may be needlessly fearful of the case and unduly desirous of settlement. What may appear to a legally unsophisticated urologist as a major crisis may in fact be relatively straightforward litigation with a high likelihood of success. (At the same time, a defendant's extreme fear of the courtroom becomes an element which must be considered as potentially changing the equation.) The reverse may also be true: the defendant may be foolishly confident.

In either situation, counsel must recall that it is his or her function to evaluate the case, not to make the final decision on trial or settlement. Not infrequently counsel will be asked: "What would you do?"—a question which counsel should not answer. Counsel is not the defendant; his or her task is to present the probabilities of success and failure in such a fashion that the client can make an intelligent election. Of course, the case may be one in which settlement is out of the question due to factors beyond the control of the defense (i.e., intransigent plaintiff, excessively unreasonable demand, etc.) in which case the decision to go to trial is clear. It is, however, not the attorney who should make this final decision.

§11.10 —Exhibit Preparation

Once trial is likely, counsel plans how—and not whether—to emphasize his or her evidence visually. Any experienced litigator will grasp that modern juries, heavily influenced by electronic media, are not experienced in the process of absorbing data by listening to strictly verbal explication. (Put another way, jurors did not spend three years extracting a legal education from mind-numbing law school lectures, and it is beyond optimism to expect that any group of laypeople will garner the maximum input from such a presentation.)

Visual aids are crucial to the defense of a urological case. Fortunately, there are innumerable services now available to facilitate counsel's display of his or her evidence. Anatomical charts are common, and talented medical illustrators can be utilized to produce large color pictures of significant portions of the anatomy or critical steps of a surgical process. Such illustrations are valuable throughout the trial, during opening and closing statements as well as during the examination of witnesses. Careful planning is mandatory so that the exhibits show exactly what is intended. Before counsel sits down with an illustrator or selects a slide for reproduction enlargement, he or she needs to have firmly in mind the most significant parts of the case so that they can be emphasized (and less vital matters downplayed) in the illustrations. It is also possible to effectively display much quantitive data.[2]

Just as juries may lose interest in a nonvisual display of evidence, so they may be intimidated by the production of a huge sheath of medical records. By the time the defense rests, there is frequently in evidence a large mass of medical documentation, and it is unlikely that 12 laypeople will ferret through all this technical paperwork. Vital parts of the records therefore should be enlarged into poster form by photo-duplication services so they can be shown to the jury. It is best if all jurors see these records at the same time, and thus the "blow-up" should in fact be *large*. (It is a frequent courtroom blunder for an "enlargement" of a vital record to still be so small that only a few jurors in the first row can see it. Such an exhibit is a waste of the client's money.)

Strategies for the visual exposition of the case are endless, with the creativity of counsel being the only limiting factor. One actual example may illustrate what is suggested here: in urological malpractice cases, the production of urine in too large or too small an amount is commonly a critical issue. If it were favorable to the defense to show that a large amount of urine had been produced over a given number of hours, this point could be accentuated by bringing to trial glass beakers of a size sufficient to contain fluid volume known to have been produced in the relevant time frame. The beakers could be filled with water (perhaps containing a drop of yellow food coloring) to convey an idea of total urine production. Such a demonstration can have

---

[2] For an excellent aid in this area, see E. Tuffy, The Visual Display of Quantitative Information (1983). This source offers an example of unusually creative means of displaying to a jury much quantifiable data.

a much greater impact than simply advising a jury which may or may not be familiar with the metric system that so many cc.'s of urine were produced.

Exhibits, trial demonstrations, and visual displays are and will continue to be a crucial part of the advocate's art. The close marriage of computer technology and video display offers incredible opportunities in the future for counsel willing to spend quality time to develop effective means to exhibit his or her case. Exhibits are a powerful means of persuasion; by the same token they are not the sort of thing which can be planned the afternoon before trial.

§11.11 Establishing the Theme of the Defense

In any well-planned trial one theme unifies all efforts, from deciding which jurors to reject to determining witnesses to call or not to call. This theme is grounded in the burdens placed by the law on the opposite parties. The plaintiff has the burden of proof on all elements of the tort claim, and the failure to prove any one of them is fatal to recovery. The defense has no burden of proof, from which it follows that the theme of the defense is to contend that on at least one of the bedrock elements plaintiff presents no persuasive evidence.

In fact, the theme of a urological malpractice defense can be reduced ultimately to one of three possibilities:

1. There was no failure to exercise reasonable care and skill (no negligence)
2. The actions of the defendant did not cause the injury complained of (no causation)
3. The plaintiff's allegations of damages are not supported by the facts (no damages or greatly reduced damages).

For example, consider a case in which causation of the injury is not disputed and in which plaintiff's expert has given not unreasonable deposition testimony that surgery was improperly performed. Assume further, however, that the credentials of plaintiff's expert are subject to disparagement. The theme of the defense thus becomes "expertise—or the lack thereof," and counsel would plan the trial around that theme. For example, counsel could consider a series of questions for voir dire by which prospective jurors would be asked about their own work expertise. (How was the juror's skill at his or her work obtained and improved? How does the juror judge another's expertise?) Such questions must be carefully crafted to remain within bounds of proper interrogation while still conveying to the jury the idea that lack of expertise is a flaw of plaintiff's case. Counsel could plan his or her opening statement to outline to the jury the gaps in the opposing expert's training and contrast that with the best presentation of the defendant's background. For cross-examination of the opposing expert, counsel might plan to avoid altogether the question of negligence and, instead, concentrate on belittling the witness's motivation for testifying. At its most fundamental level, this theme is an argument to the jury that plaintiff's counsel has not carried the burden of proof on negligence because he or she was forced to rely upon such a poorly trained expert.

Counsel's elaboration of the theme of the defense is perhaps the most important task he or she performs for the client. The theme should offer the most comprehensive explanation of the known events, one that is consistent with all facts and inherently logical. Hopefully such a theme is also the best available to rebut what the opposition must prove. Once the theme is finalized, trial preparation is organized around it. Every witness and document which supports the theme must be arrayed, and every legal argument and potential jury charge which supports it should be held in readiness. An attorney who is about to commence trial should have a firm idea at the very outset where he or she intends to be at the end. Put another way, counsel at the beginning of trial ought to be almost as ready to give his or her closing argument as he or she is to give the opening outline. Counsel will be ready to do just that once the theme of the defense has been established.

The Trial

§11.12 Rejecting the Jury

Juries are rejected, not selected. In a civil case, each side typically has a set number of challenges to be exercised at counsel's discretion; by the exercise of these challenges counsel removes prospective jurors from the panel. The final jury is not selected but, rather, the factfinding body represents the pool of jurors that both sides feared least. This distinction is important when planning the interrogation of prospective jurors because it highlights the proper issue. Counsel need not worry about which jurors he or she wants; he or she is not going to choose them. Instead, the focus should be on the correct question: which jurors should be stricken. It is only by the latter means that counsel can exercise a choice (albeit a negative one).

Counsel for the urological malpractice defendant does not desire precisely the jurors that the opponent wants. Consequently, counsel needs to consider the case from the perspective of the plaintiff. The goal should be to determine who the opposition would most like to have on the panel and to strike them.

It is intuitively obvious who are jurors favored by a plaintiff in urological malpractice litigation. Plaintiff comes to court for cash compensation, not for critical scrutiny of the evidence. Opposing counsel convinced himself or herself prior to the trial of the merits of his or her case and has at least evidenced that conviction by spending a good deal of money getting the matter to court; if given a choice, plaintiff's counsel would invariably skip proof of negligence and concentrate on what is for him or her the "fun" part of the case: damages. Plaintiff has no reason to relish the prospect of his or her proof being critically dissected by an analytical panel and will seek to avoid such jurors. The opposition does not wish to have on the panel individuals whose occupations require them to absorb and evaluate by listening large amounts of data. Nor does plaintiff's attorney have any reason to desire a jury capable of looking for subtleties of the case or of attending to definitional distinctions. Plaintiff's counsel does wish to have a jury which is easily persuaded (and hence facilitates his or her carrying of the burden of proof) and without any experience in or concept of the value of money (thus facilitating an increased verdict). Such individuals would be prime candidates for exercise of a strike by defendant's counsel.

There are other considerations as well. In any medical malpractice case there are general issues which must be explored and which may form the basis for further strikes. These would include any dissatisfaction on the part of a juror with the medical profession as a whole or with urology in particular. In each of these instances it is well to inquire concerning the status of other members of the prospective juror's family. Any juror with a family member who has had serious dissatisfaction with the medical profession would be favored by the plaintiff and therefore should be removed by the defense. Jurors who have suffered urological diseases or problems must be carefully considered, but not automatically rejected. They may be well pleased with their care and grateful to the medical profession—in which event the opposition will certainly strike them.

Finally, in voir dire counsel should whenever possible begin advancing the theme of the case. If the theme is that plaintiff's causation evidence is speculative and therefore unworthy of belief, counsel might attempt several questions designed to inquire how jurors make decisions at their own jobs. (Do you guess when you do not know, Mr. Juror? Does your job require you to be certain before you take action, Ms. Juror? What do you do if you simply have no data?) The information gained will be useful, and the jury will have been introduced to the theme counsel intends it to hear often in the coming days.

If any prospective juror admits to some bias or prejudice in response to questioning, this must be followed up carefully with a view toward having the judge remove the individual. Such questioning should be done in a leading fashion, with counsel inserting into his or her question the "magic words" sufficient in the jurisdiction to cause disqualification and the juror asked if that is what he or she is saying. Never give the juror a chance to talk at length under this circumstance, because the answer may taint others. If the court has been successfully urged to remove this juror from the panel, counsel has gained, in effect, an extra strike at the opponent's expense.

Numerous questions can be asked on any voir dire, but endless interrogation risks jury fatigue and the annoyance of the trial judge. Below are a series of questions forming a basic core which the author has used in over 100 malpractice trials. Brief comments are given as to the purpose of each question.

1. IS THERE ANYONE HERE WHO IN THE PAST HAS SUED A DOCTOR, A HOSPITAL, A DENTIST, A NURSE, OR ANY PROVIDER OF HEALTH CARE SERVICES?

COMMENT: The obvious concern is the bias of any juror who has had adverse dealings with the medical profession sufficient to cause a suit. It should be noted that the question is not restricted to malpractice; contractual or fee disputes or any other type of litigation with a physician can cause prejudice and must be discovered.

2. IS THERE ANYONE IN YOUR FAMILY WHO HAS EVER SUED A DOCTOR, A HOSPITAL, A DENTIST, A NURSE, OR ANY PROVIDER OF HEALTH CARE SERVICES?

COMMENT: Adverse experiences of the juror's spouse, parent, or child can be just as prejudicial to the defense as those of the juror himself or herself.

3. IS THERE ANYONE HERE WHO HAS EVER BEEN SERIOUSLY DISSATISFIED WITH THE CARE YOU HAVE RECEIVED FROM A DOCTOR, A HOSPITAL, A NURSE, A DENTIST, OR ANY HEALTH CARE PROVIDER?

COMMENT: At this point the question is made more specific, to focus on dissatisfaction with medical care. That area of prejudice is so fundamental as to justify some repetition; more timid jurors who have not yet brought to light certain experiences often do so when the question is repeated in a slightly different form.

4. IS THERE ANYONE IN YOUR FAMILY WHO HAS BEEN SERIOUSLY DISSATISFIED WITH THE CARE RECEIVED FROM A DOCTOR, A HOSPITAL, A NURSE, A DENTIST, OR ANY PROVIDER OF HEALTH CARE SERVICES?

COMMENT: It is well to define "family" in the broadest terms, including parents, aunts and uncles, brothers and sisters, children, grandparents, and grandchildren.

5. HAS ANY JUROR HERE EVER SUFFERED ANY SIGNIFICANT UROLOGICAL PROBLEMS REQUIRING TREATMENT BY A PHYSICIAN? IF SO, PLEASE EXPLAIN.

COMMENT: It is important to understand the experience that each juror has had with the organ system at issue. The nature of the juror's symptoms needs to be understood; it is imperative that some member of the jury not sit in the jury room during the deliberation and offer the fellow jurors a grizzly story of his or her own illness. It is well to know whether the patient was satisfied with the treatment and thankful to the medical profession for that treatment. If there was satisfaction, counsel can confidently expect that the plaintiff's attorney will strike this particular juror.

6. IS THERE ANY JUROR WHO HAS USED THE SERVICES OF A UROLOGIST FOR ANY REASON?

COMMENT: This "catchall" question should reveal anything that has been missed about the jury's urological background.

7. IS THERE ANY JUROR WHO HAS EVER EXPERIENCED THE CONDITION OF _____?

   COMMENT: This question particularizes the voir dire to the exact condition with which counsel is dealing. It is well to inquire also if family members of the juror have had the condition or anyone knows anything about it.

8. DOES ANY JUROR HAVE ANY LEGAL TRAINING? IF SO, PLEASE EXPLAIN.

   COMMENT: Jurors with any legal knowledge generally believe they know more than they do and thus pose a real risk. (Plaintiff's attorney as well usually has little desire for these people to serve.)

9. IS THERE ANY JUROR HERE WITH ANY MEDICAL TRAINING? IF SO, PLEASE EXPLAIN.

   COMMENT: Defense counsel confidently can expect that the opposition will wish to eliminate anyone with medical knowledge, but identifying such jurors allows defense counsel to explore with them their experiences and perhaps elicit comments helpful to the defense, e.g., "Did you find that patients invariably died as a result of the underlying condition?"

10. IS THERE ANY JUROR HERE WHO KNOWS OR HAS USED THE SERVICES OF _____?

    COMMENT: All the medical witnesses who will testify should be listed. It is crucial that defense counsel not be called upon to cross-examine a plaintiff's expert who also is a treating physician of one of the jurors.

Many other general questions might be asked as part of a general voir dire—for example, whether any of the jurors have ever been plaintiffs or defendants in suits, or have ever been represented by plaintiff's counsel or utilized his or her services. Such general questions are not unique to urological cases and should be a part of every attorney's usual voir dire; they need not be considered here.

§11.13 Opening Statement

The jury has heard hints of the theme of the defense during the rejection process. During opening statement, the jury is told the theme bluntly and directly. It is the first office of the opening statement to establish the theme and the principal supports for it in the mind of the jury. This includes an explanation of both the strong points of the defense as well as the weak points of the plaintiff's case. If there is weakness in the defense case, and if it is certain that the opposition knows it, then this needs to be addressed in the opening statement, putting the problem in the best light possible.

The latter situation represents one instance in which even well-prepared counsel may not know at the outset what he or she will have to tell the jury in closing argument. It sometimes happens that the opposition has failed to discover harmful facts which may yet be learned during the course of the trial. Defense counsel hardly will want to discuss them at this point! In this uncomfortable situation, counsel's best tactic is to make a nonspecific opening statement outlining the evidence in such fashion as will allow him or her to maintain credibility with a jury however the facts later develop.

Counsel should also recall that while during direct examination he or she will be restricted to a traditional question and answer format—and subject to objection for leading the witness if he or she strays from it—there is no provision against "leading" in an opening statement. Counsel here can outline interrelated points, give definitions, and establish anatomical facts which do not readily lend themselves to a more formal question and answer presentation. Complicated concepts should be discussed during the opening statement so that the jury will have some grasp of them before they are required to listen to the choppy presentation of direct examination. As long as counsel is stating evidence which will in fact be offered, he or she is on safe ground for the opening statement; this time offers an excellent opportunity to put before the jury evidence on an uninterrupted basis.

§11.14 Cross-Examination

In the flow of the trial, the plaintiff's attorney of course presents his or her evidence first, which gives defense counsel the opportunity early on to exercise the highest calling of the advocate's art, cross-examination. Many cases are won or lost by the end of the plaintiff's evidence, with the result that cross-examination is all important.

The basic rules of cross-examination apply to urological as well as all other malpractice cases. The most fundamental principle is that cross-examination is not foreordained to be a hostile confrontation. There is nothing to prevent an amiable cross-examination, and this approach should always be considered. Most witnesses fall somewhere on a continuum ranging from total hostility to those whose testimony can be thought of as quite helpful. If counsel has prepared properly, he or she will know where on the continuum each of the plaintiff's witnesses is to be found, and this assessment will dictate the approach at trial.

For example, if opposing counsel has not fully understood the theme of the defense, he or she may present a witness who concedes certain very major points. The witness will make other points which are not helpful, but defense counsel must be a realist and accept that he or she cannot attack the credibility of this witness and then later ask the jury to accept selected points which are beneficial. In such a situation, a nonconfrontational examination is justified, one ignoring what was harmful and reemphasizing the advantageous points so they can be adopted later.

The second basic principle of cross-examination is to skip it if there is nothing to be gained. The plaintiff often calls witnesses whose testimony is straightforward and whose background does not render them subject to attack. Friends and neighbors may be called to testify about physical limitations of the plaintiff, while employers may be called to establish the factual basis for a damage claim (lost wages, medical bills, etc.). Such witnesses have little reason to do anything but tell the truth as they perceive it, and an attack on them risks the ire of the jury and should never be carried out unless there is a specific and very pressing reason. At the other extreme, plaintiff may call a hostile witness whose background or reputation simply makes him or her unassailable. The best course of action is to get such an individual off the stand as soon as possible. There are times when the wisest examination is to conduct none.

The paramount rule of cross-examination has been read by every attorney and then understood by those who have breached it: Do not ask a question to which the answer is unknown. No experienced attorney will ask such a question on cross-examination save under unusual circumstances. Many attorneys have concluded that, under the logic of the facts, either a yes or no answer must aid his or her case and have posed questions without knowing the answer; such efforts more often than not produce entirely unanticipated responses which prove harmful. Cross-examination cannot be conducted on the basis of serendipity.

For this reason, the discovery depositions of plaintiff and plaintiff's experts are of great importance during cross-examination. If those depositions were carried out with trial cross-examination in mind, counsel has a prepared outline for questioning the witness. The witness can be asked those points which he or she has previously conceded, and counsel can reasonably expect that the answers will be identical. If they are not, the basis for immediate impeachment is at the attorney's hand. (Counsel should have page and line number of all significant points readily available for this purpose.) Admissions found in the pleadings, interrogatories, requests to admit, or documentary evidence may also offer a safe basis for questioning.

Counsel always should recall that it is rare for any cross-examination to annihilate a witness. Plaintiff's attorneys do not routinely offer up witnesses—either lay or expert—whose testimony is so unbelievable, whose credentials are so poor, or whose perjury is so blatant that an inspired cross-examination will destroy the opposition's case. In most instances, counsel must be satisfied to glean a few points from each witness. These points accumulate, and if at the end of plaintiff's case cross-examination has kept the theme of the defense viable in the jury's mind, counsel has served his or her client well.

§11.15 Direct Examination

The facts of the given case dictate which witnesses are called for presentation of defense evidence. For example, if unreasonable injury claims have been made by the plaintiff, it is incumbent upon the defendant to call other physicians who have seen the patient and whose recollections and records allow them to state that the injuries claimed are absent or are greatly exaggerated. As another example, office personnel may be necessary witnesses to establish what occurs (or does not occur) in routine office practice. However, in the typical case the core of the defense will be the urologist defendant and at least one expert witness. In presenting this core defense, three general purposes must be served: The jury must be reassured about the defendant's qualifications; the points raised by the opposition must be rebutted; and the theme of the defense must be reiterated.

Jurors are understandably attentive to the background of any defendant-physician before them. For this reason, direct examination of a defendant must include underscoring his or her credentials. Direct examination is not a time for modesty. Everything good that can be stated about the physician's training, internship, residency, and continuing education should be emphasized. Residency programs often involve work at several hospitals or training—however brief—under distinguished leaders of the specialty. A careful attorney will do more than just ask the client to describe his or her training. Rather, counsel will guide the defendant through a detailed description of three or four years of intensive concentration under nationally known urologists with specialized extra training in areas pertinent to the suit.

Contributions to the literature, Board certifications, and membership in and offices held in professional societies should all be enumerated. Hospital staff affiliations and positions of leadership within the hospital should be rostered. By merely becoming a specialist in urology, a physician has amassed a fairly extensive curriculum vitae, and it is up to counsel to share all of this with the jury. A jury which believes that a physician is well grounded in medicine is much more likely to accept that physician's testimony. Of course, the same points should be established with each of the defense experts.

If the defense expert's credentials are especially impressive, it may be advantageous to question him or her about them at the conclusion of this testimony. By the time defense witnesses are presented, most jurors have come to assume that the first portion of any doctor's testimony will consist of a recitation of professional achievements, to which the jurors may not attend. It is possible to catch the jury's interest by directing the witness immediately to the principal causation and/or negligence issues. After the witness has stated his or her opinions on the central issue, he or she can then be questioned about qualifications. Ending such testimony with a recital of prestigious affiliations and accomplishments puts an exclamation point to the witness's direct examination.

In rebutting the plaintiff's contention, counsel will draw upon all records which are helpful and upon relevant recollections. However, counsel must also learn to work with and from records which do not exist. The trial of a medical malpractice case often focuses upon document interpretation, with the plaintiff taking the position that if something is not written it never happened. Counsel can be confident that if something which would have been helpful to the defense is absent or misstated in the records, this documentation will become a centerpiece of the plaintiff's case. (Indeed, it is clear that many plaintiff's attorneys will simply not accept cases in which the documentation is thorough, with the result that much of the career of any defense counsel will be spent defending weak documentation.)

Defense counsel needs to reject out of hand the idea that "If it is not documented it was not done." Many things which do not lend themselves to documentation must have transpired in the normal course of urological practice, and counsel's job at trial is often to explain this fact. Consider as an example a patient's claim that unauthorized surgery was performed. In the absence of a consent form, and without documentation that surgery even was discussed with the patient, there would still be numerous routine acts which would have been completed before the patient ever reached the operating room and which would have alerted the patient to what was happening. At some point the patient was subjected to sterilization procedures, including shaving. Given the nature of anatomy significant to urological operations, such shaving would hardly go unnoticed. At some point the patient would have been placed in special operating room garb. At a later point the patient would have been taken from his or her room and transported to a presurgical holding area where, presumably, additional routine procedures were followed. While some or all of these steps may be missing from the record, counsel can establish them by appropriate testimony from relevant individuals; nurses and orderlies can testify that a routine would be followed or the patient could never have entered the operating room. Such testimony allows counsel to argue that since the customary steps must have taken place it would be unreasonable to believe that the patient went through all of the process objecting to surgery but was heeded by no one. Documentation of a specific act may not exist, but that is no evidence in and of itself that the act did not happen.

Alternatively, counsel may reject plaintiff's case by capitalizing upon the absence of records. The argument can be made that the absence of documentation is evidence for the absence of any significant ongoing problems. This is not an unreasonable argument, and it is one which is frequently persuasive. Jurors often accept the premise that if a patient appeared to be doing well there would be little reason at the time for detailed documentation of that fact. However counsel confronts the presentation of direct evidence, he or she is certain to spend time overcoming recordation flaws, and this must be something which is given careful attention.

Finally, and fundamentally, counsel should advance through his or her own witnesses his or her theme of the case. This should not be difficult since counsel will not, save in the most extreme circumstances, offer any witness who would not view the case in accord with the defense theme. The witnesses need to be fully advised of the theme of the case and urged to recite it at every opportunity, on direct examination and cross-examination as well. Jurors prefer to see witnesses hold their own on cross-examination, and they can become annoyed if defense counsel makes numerous speaking objections. The best witness is one who can be allowed to battle the plaintiff's attorney on the issues. This can be achieved, obviously, only by thorough advance preparation of the witness, explaining not only the defense theme but the likely points of attack. In any such preparation it is crucial to ensure that the witnesses are familiar with all documentary evidence and have been warned about any potential stumbling points in their own depositions.

§11.16 Closing Argument

Closing argument is the final occasion to present the defense theme. It is counsel's opportunity to pull together the strands of his or her case, interrelating the concessions gained on cross-examination, the testimony elicited on direct examination, and significant documents into a coherent summary which demonstrates wherein plaintiff is unable to carry the burden of proof. It is of course also an opportunity to give rebuttal to those strong points offered by the opposition and where possible to posit for the opponent questions which he or she cannot answer. This look backward over the evidence is a well-understood function of the closing argument.

What is often overlooked is the function of the closing argument as a look forward to the court's charge. In any medical malpractice case, the substantive law will offer helpful principles on which counsel can expect a jury instruction. By way of illustration, these principles include the presumption that medical services are correctly performed, a rule that the presumption can be overcome only through the testimony of expert witnesses, that the standard of care to which the defendant is held is not that of individual physicians but, rather, of some professional group (either a local or a national standard), and that an unfortunate result from medical treatment does not in and of itself establish negligence. Counsel may be entitled to a charge that the law does not require a physician to obtain perfect results for his or her patient or that the jury cannot assess the care in hindsight. There may be other favorable principles that the court must charge touching on causation issues. Long before trial, counsel will have prepared his or her requests for charge in accordance with the law of the jurisdiction and will by the time of closing have a general idea as to what the court is likely to instruct.

Given this knowledge, counsel can consider planning his or her closing argument around favorable portions of the charge. It is especially effective if counsel can interrelate the evidence the jury has heard with the legal principles they soon will hear from the court. This has the effect of reinforcing those points with at least some of the jurors. The defense gains credibility because the factfinders' last input before retiring to deliberate is to hear in effect a theme of the defense delivered from the bench.

Conclusion

§11.17 Conclusion

Chapters are written in general; cases are tried in particular. It is therefore inevitable that many of the ideas contained in this discussion would not be applicable to any given litigation. Candor requires the author to admit that he has never had a case in which he has done everything discussed herein, nor is it conceivable that a case should exist which would materially benefit from every such step.

What are contained herein are not standards of care but, rather, proposals for consideration to counsel contemplating the defense of a urological malpractice case. Attorneys will find in their own trial experience and detailed knowledge of the law of their jurisdictions the truest guides to the defense of such an action. Above all else, counsel needs to retain a sense of realism about everything he or she does. Such realism, manifested through intelligent hard work, may not prevail in every case, but it will deserve the gratitude of the defendant and the respect of opposing counsel and the court.

Appendix 11-A

MODEL INTERROGATORIES:

1.

Please state the name, current residence address, age, date of birth, and social security number of the person or persons answering these interrogatories. If the person or persons allegedly injured by the acts complained of in the complaint is/are different from the person or persons providing the above information, please provide the same information for the allegedly injured person or persons.

2.

Please itemize all special damages that are claimed by or on behalf of the person or persons allegedly injured by the acts complained of in the complaint.

3.

State the name, address, and present whereabouts of each and every physician, osteopath, chiropractor, or other practitioner of the healing arts who has expressed an opinion, either orally or in writing, as to the subject matter of the within litigation.

4.

If the allegedly injured person or persons presently suffer(s) as a result of the injuries complained of in the complaint, please state how and in what respect.

5.

If the allegedly injured person or persons is/are presently under the care of a physician or other practitioner of the healing arts, please state (as to each such physician or other practitioner):

(a) The date such care began;
(b) The last date the practitioner was seen;
(c) The purpose or condition for which the practitioner was seen.

6.

To your knowledge, information, or belief, have any hospitals, physicians, surgeons, or other practitioners of the healing arts made any report, statement, or bill concerning examination or treatment of the allegedly injured person or persons since the incident complained of?

7.

If so, please describe each such report, statement, or bill, giving as to each:

(a) The date;
(b) The person making the report;
(c) The form of the report (whether oral or written);
(d) The person, firm, or corporation to whom the report was rendered;
(e) The location of the report and the name of the person having custody, possession, or control thereof.

NOTE: Disregard subparts (d) and (e) of the preceding interrogatory if a copy of each such report is attached to the answers to these interrogatories.

8.

If the allegedly injured person or persons was/were employed at the time of the acts complained of in the complaint, please state:

(a) The employer or employers;
(b) The duties on behalf of each employer;
(c) The earnings from each employer.

9.

If the allegedly injured person or persons is/are presently employed, please state:

(a) The employer or employers;
(b) The duties on behalf of each employer;
(c) The earnings from each employer.

10.

If the alleged injuries have prevented the allegedly injured person or persons from working at any time since the date of the incident complained of, please state:

(a) The date or dates of inability to work because of the alleged injury;
(b) The earnings, if any, lost by reason of such inability to work.

11.

To your knowledge, information, or belief, are there any photographs, drawings, or other illustrative-like matter depicting or illustrating either any of the alleged injuries or objects or devices allegedly causing such injuries and forming the subject matter of any issues in the within action.

12.

If the answer to the preceding interrogatory is in the affirmative, please give the following information:

(a) The date made;
(b) By whom it was made;
(c) A description of such illustrative matter;
(d) The present location and the name of the person having possession, custody, or control;
(e) Will you voluntarily produce each such photograph or drawing and permit its inspection and copying at the expense of the defendant?

13.

To your knowledge, information, or belief, are there any diaries, written notes, written recollections, or other narrative or diary style writings summarizing in any way either any of the alleged injuries or any contact with defendant.

14.

If the answer to the preceding interrogatory is in the affirmative, please state the following information:

(a) The date made;

(b) By whom it was made;

(c) A description of such written matter;

(d) The present location and the name of the person having possession, custody, or control;

(e) Will you voluntarily produce each such written item and permit its inspection and copying at the expense of the defendant?

15.

Please list all documents relied upon to demonstrate and support facts relevant to all claims of negligence, breach of contract, and any other wrong claimed in the within matter, showing for each:

(a) The date made;

(b) By whom it was made;

(c) A description of such document;

(d) The present location and the name of the person having possession, custody, or control;

(e) Will you voluntarily produce each such written item and permit its inspection and copying at the expense of the defendant?

16.

Please list the name, address, and occupation of all persons having knowledge, either directly, indirectly, or hypothetically, and whether of a lay or expert character, of any of the relevant facts, events, circumstances, or issues formed by the subject matter of this litigation. For each said person, please give a brief statement of the nature and content of such knowledge.

17.

For each person whom plaintiff expects to call as an expert witness at the trial of the within matter, please state the following:

(a) Name, office address, and medical specialty, if any;

(b) Subject matter on which said person is expected to testify;

(c) Substance of the facts and opinions to which said person is expected to testify;

(d) Basis for the witness's opinions.

18.

Please specify and itemize each and every ground of battery, negligence, breach of contract, or any other wrong for which it is contended the defendant is liable in this action.

19.

For each item of special damages claimed, including all medical expenses, lost wages, hospital bills, physician bills, medication bills, etc., please state the following:

- (a) Whether said item was covered by insurance of any kind or nature or any other form of third-party payor obligation;
- (b) Whether said item was compensated as a result of such insurance or obligation;
- (c) Whether said item was covered as a result of workers' compensation coverage or any other disability supplement or support of any kind;
- (d) Whether said item was compensated as a result of such coverage as referred to in subpart (c) above.

20.

Have you at any time by any means recorded any conversation with the defendant or anyone acting on the defendant's behalf? If so, please state the following:

- (a) Type of recording (cassette tape, etc.);
- (b) Date of recording;
- (c) Length of recording;
- (d) Person recorded;
- (e) Name of person having possession of such recording;
- (f) Contents of recording.

Appendix 11-B

CASE SUMMARY CHART
NEGLIGENCE

Defendant Witnesses			Plaintiff Witnesses
Dr. Smith	FACT ISSUE ONE:	(Example, improper pre-operative testing)	Dr. Jones
Dr. Smith	FACT ISSUE TWO:	(Example, improper surgical approach)	Dr. Jones
Dr. Smith Nurse A	FACT ISSUE THREE:	(Example, failure to prescribe timely antibiotic to prevent debilitating infection)	Dr. Jones

CAUSATION

Dr. White	FACT ISSUE ONE:	(Example, whether surgery was required regardless of absence of test)	Dr. Black
	EVIDENCE:	Office notes	
Dr. White	FACT ISSUE TWO:	(Example, whether the surgical approach increased likelihood of infection)	Dr. Black
	EVIDENCE:	Hospital chart	

Defendant Witnesses			Plaintiff Witnesses
Dr. Blue	FACT ISSUE THREE:	(Example, whether the alleged antibiotic delay was cause of development of infection)	Dr. Green
	EVIDENCE:	Consultant's report (hearsay problem?)	

DAMAGES

Defendant Witnesses			Plaintiff Witnesses
Neighbors who have knowledge of plaintiff's improved health	Pain and suffering lost wages		Wife, employer
	FACT ISSUE ONE:	Medical expenses	
	FACT ISSUE TWO:	Lost wages	
	FACT ISSUE THREE:	Pain and suffering	

12

Evolution of Hospital Liability

§12.01 Overview
§12.02 Immunity
§12.03 —Charitable Immunity
§12.04 Agency
§12.05 —Principal and Agent
§12.06 —Respondeat Superior
§12.07 —Apparent Agency
§12.08 —Borrowed Servant
§12.09 —Agency by Necessity
§12.10 Expert Witness
§12.11 Corporations
§12.12 Joint Commission on Accreditation of Healthcare Organizations
§12.13 Corporate Practice of Medicine
§12.14 —Physician Credentialing
§12.15 —Independent Contractors
§12.16 —Substantial Evidence Test
§12.17 —Fairness
§12.18 —Antitrust
§12.19 —Grounds, Buildings, and Vendors
§12.20 Consolidated Omnibus Budget Reconciliation Act (COBRA)

§12.01 Overview

The purpose of this chapter is to help the reader understand the role the hospital plays in the total picture of health care rendered to the patient. No longer will the public perceive the hospital as a brick and mortar edifice wherein physicians practice their craft. The hospital is now recognized as a business entity with corporate obligations and fiduciary responsibilities. The fact that a physician is not a direct agent (or employee) of the hospital will not release the hospital of its duty to the public.

There are numerous reasons to hold hospitals responsible for acts of persons functioning within its structure. The sociological evolution of the hospital as a governing being allowing certain activity to occur within its domain gives rise to the belief that the hospital must be held responsible for those individuals and activities it regulates and condones. Other reasons relate to procedural issues such as statute of limitations problems or standing. Additionally, the "deep-pocket" theory may be a valid reason to include a hospital in the health care malpractice field. Finally, since physicians as a whole appear to have difficulties in disciplining their ranks, the hospital must exercise its ability to monitor and credential its professional staff. The failure of the hospital generally to do so has made it a target for monetary recovery. Not only will the individual physician be the target, but, for reasons described in this chapter, so will the hospital.

§12.02   Immunity

It is a general rule that everyone is liable for his or her own conduct. The exception to this rule is the concept of immunity. In the area of hospital law, exemption from liability is applied to eleemosynary institutions, governmental agencies, and public hospitals. *Eleemosynary* is one of those awesome words not often found in today's context. In ancient England, any possessions belonging to the church were considered eleemosynae. The "eleemosyna regis" was the penny ordered to be paid for every plow in England to support the poor, and the eleemosynarius was the chief officer who received the eleemosynary rents and distributed them for charitable uses.

§12.03   —Charitable Immunity

Today's modern use of the word *eleemosynary* refers to any charitable purpose. An eleemosynary corporation is one which is created for charitable purposes although the immunity usually available for such institutions has been abrogated in almost all jurisdictions. The basis for these exemptions generally rest on artificial arguments which are often unrealistic and arbitrary. The liability immunity appears to stem from *Jensen v Maine Eye & Ear Infirmary*,[1] a 1910 case which declared that a "purely charitable institution cannot be made liable for damages for the negligent acts of its employees." Were it not so, charitable institutions of all kinds would ultimately cease or become greatly impaired in their usefulness. This legal doctrine was decided in the days when hospitals were supported mainly by private benefactors, and the

---

[1] 107 Me 408, 78 A 898 (1910).

courts sought a legal basis to protect these institutions against money judgments.

At least five different legal theories have been advanced to justify the immunity of charitable institutions from liability for tort. These theories include the trust fund theory, the inapplicability of respondeat superior, implied waiver, governmental function, and public policy.

Trust Fund Theory

The trust fund theory is based upon a statement in the common law that "to give damages out of a trust fund would not be to apply it to those objects which the author of the fund had in view, but would be to divert it to a completely different purpose." A judgment against a charitable institution could conceivably bankrupt it. Additionally, allowing such an institution to be sued would discourage gifts to the institutions, thereby diminishing the funds available for such charitable purposes.

Inapplicability of Respondeat Superior

The inapplicability of respondeat superior is another example of a charitable institutional immunity. The respondeat superior rule is the principle of agency law whereby the master is held answerable for the acts of its agent or servant. It is founded on the duty which rests on every person in the management of his or her own affairs, whether by himself or herself or by his or her agents or servants. The question of liability depends frequently on whether the person treating the patient is an agent or servant of that master. In the 1914 case of *Schloendorff v The Society of New York Hospital*,[2] the court stated,

> It is true I think of nurses as of physicians that in treating a patient they are not acting as the servants of the hospital. The superintendent is a servant of the hospital, the assistant superintendent, orderlies and the other members of the administrative staff are servants of the hospital, but nurses are employed to carry out the orders of the physicians to whose authority they are subject. The hospital undertakes to procure for the patient the services of a nurse. It does not undertake through the agency of nurses to render those services itself.

This legal doctrine, promulgated in 1914, withstood the test of time regarding the inapplicability of the doctrine of respondeat superior, thereby leaving hospitals immune from tort liability.

Implied Waiver Theory

The implied waiver theory is that anyone accepting the bounty of a charitable institution impliedly waives any claims against it for the negligence of its agents and servants. It was not until the 1939 California case of *Silva v*

---

[2] 211 NY 125, 105 NE 92 (1914).

Providence Hospital [3] that strong exception to this waiver doctrine was taken by the court which declared that admission to a hospital is no proof of an intention not to charge it with responsibility for wrongdoing.

Governmental Function

The governmental function exemption for charitable institutions is exemplified under the theory that "the king can do no wrong." This was an early common law doctrine which evolved into the legal theory of sovereign immunity.

Some states hold that the duty of a municipality to conserve the public health is governmental in nature. Consequently, the establishment of a hospital for that purpose by a city is considered to be a governmental activity, and its operation is held to also be a purely governmental function exercised under the police policy of the state. Thus, the city is not liable in tort for injuries caused by the acts of the hospital's officers, agents, or employees in the discharge of their functions. On the other hand, it has been held that a municipal corporation that operates and maintains a hospital for compensation acts in a quasi-private manner within the scope of its proprietary powers and so cannot avoid liability.

Whether or not governmental immunity applies in cases of state or municipal hospitals depends on whether the particular jurisdiction defines the operation of a hospital as a governmental or proprietary function. If the function is described as proprietary—i.e., a function which could also be provided by the private sector—the immunity will not apply. The distinction between governmental and proprietary functions is often unclear, and different jurisdictions have classified the operation of a hospital as both governmental and proprietary and have therefore either allowed or disallowed liability.

Questions of governmental immunities in the federal government are governed by the Federal Tort Claims Act, ch 753, 60 Stat 842, which states: "The United States shall be liable respecting the provisions of this Act relating to tort claims, in the same manner and to the same extent as a private individual under like circumstances, but shall not be liable for interest prior to judgment or for punitive damages." However, even this immunity is being eroded.

Public Policy

A final legal theory for immunity of a charitable institution from liability was based on public policy. Courts held that it would be against public policy to hold a charitable institution liable for the negligence of servants who were selected with due care. It was felt that hospitals perform a function in ministering to the poor and sick without pecuniary profit to themselves; therefore, the patient who accepts those services, if injured therein by the negligence of an employee, must look for redress to such employee alone and not to the institution.

---

[3] 14 Cal 2d 762, 764, 97 P2d 798, 800 (1939).

Current Trend in Charitable Immunity

As a final note to the discussion of charitable immunity, one must be slightly amused as the evolution of hospital liability makes a complete circle. Now, on the basis of Good Samaritan acts as well as eleemosynary grounds, most states have declared physicians immune from any liability in doing purely charitable acts, and some jurisdictions are holding purely charitable institutions immune from liability, also.

The Georgia Medical Malpractice Act of 1987[4] eliminates liability for health care providers who voluntarily and at no charge provide care to patients, as long as that care is not grossly negligent or wanton and willful in its misconduct.

§12.04 Agency

A brief discussion is required for definition of terms and delineation of doctrines under agency principles. While this is not meant to be a complete course in the law of agency, perhaps a refresher of some of the terms and doctrines will help make the reader more aware and understand the nexus between the physician and the hospital.

§12.05 —Principal and Agent

Agency is a consensual fiduciary relationship between one person (the agent) who agrees to act for or under the direction or control of another (the principal). One may employ another to do his or her work, sell his or her goods, or acquire property on his or her behalf, all to the same effect as if the principal were doing this enterprise. The basic idea of making the agent's actions binding on the principal and conversely of giving the principal the benefit of rights acquired by the agent seems to have been settled very early in common law. Further, according to the *Restatement (Second) of Agency* §1 (1957), an agent is anyone who has manifested consent to act in a fiduciary relationship on behalf of another and subject to his or her control. The servant, on the other hand, is an agent employed by a master to perform service in his or her affairs, and whose physical conduct is controlled or is subject to the right of control by the master.

Additionally, the *Restatement* also provides that a master is subject to liability for the torts of his or her servants committed while acting in the scope of their employment. Thus, we now have the doctrine of vicarious liability. This liability applies when a master/servant relationship exists between two parties and the injury complained of resulted from an act which occurred while the servant was acting within the scope of the employment. In determining whether the negligent tortfeasor was the agent of the third party to be held liable, the court will look at a variety of factors such as whether

---

[4] Ga Code Ann §51-1-29 (1987).

the agent was engaged in a distinct business or was a part of the principal's business, the customs with regard to the supervision of the agent, the degree of skill exercised by the agent, the duration of that relationship, and the basis of compensation. Thus, if the court determines that the negligent tortfeasor was the servant of the third party, then the court must determine whether the servant was acting within scope of his or her employment. This determination involved a consideration of many of the same factors that were examined initially to determine whether the master/servant or principal/agent relationship existed.

Finally, once the court has found that the negligent tortfeasor was the servant or agent of the principal and that the tortfeasor was acting within the scope of employment at the time the injury occurred, the principal will be held liable for the injury.

§12.06 —Respondeat Superior

Bing v Thunig [5] is the leading case which established that where the appropriate master/servant relationship exists between a physician and a hospital, vicarious liability will be the basis of recovery against the hospital. Before discussing *Bing* in such detail, let us review the theory of respondeat superior. The terms of *principal, agent,* and *vicarious liability* are almost synonymous and intermingled with the theory of respondeat superior.

The *Restatement of Agency* §2 (1957) says: "A master is subject to liability for the torts of his servants committed while acting in the scope of their employment." The hospital's duty in respondeat superior situations arises from the responsibility it accepts for the physician's action. Literally translated as "Let the master answer," respondeat superior imposes vicarious liability on the master for negligent acts committed by the servant.

Respondeat superior is a Latin term for the principle of vicarious liability. The doctrine means that an employer is liable to a third party for the tort of an employee committed within the scope of employment. There are three elements to this theory:

1. Was the tort committed?
2. Was the person who committed the tort an agent or employee of the defendant-employer?
3. Was the tort committed within the scope of employment?

Justification for this theory is the employer's right to control the employee, but really the basis for holding the employer vicariously liable is simply the fact that the employer has either insurance coverage or the superior financial means to compensate the plaintiff. Of course, the employee who committed the tort can also be held individually and personally liable, and the employer also has the right of indemnification, but this right is exercised

---

[5] 2 NY2d 656, 143 NE2d 3, 163 NYS2d 3 (1957).

infrequently because of insurance coverage. Of course, if the employer and the employee are insured by different insurance companies, then there is an incentive for indemnification.

While this discussion is limited to the very strict employer/employee relationship, as will be seen later in the chapter under other theories such as apparent agency, independent contractor, or direct liability, the hospital may still be held liable.

In the seminal case of *Bing v Thunig,* the court first announced the theory on which to hold hospitals liable for the torts of their employees. *Bing* involved the actions of two nurses who failed to inspect linen placed underneath a patient which subsequently ignited and burned the patient. Rejecting the doctrine of charitable immunity which allowed hospitals to avoid this liability, the court turned to respondeat superior as the basis for the hospital's liability. *Bing* says,

> The doctrine of Respondeat Superior is grounded on firm principles of law and justice. Liability is the rule, immunity, the exception. It is not too much to expect that those who serve and minister to members of the public should do so as do all others subject to that principle and within the obligation not to do injury through carelessness.
>
> Present-day hospitals, as their manner or operation plainly demonstrates, do far more than furnish facilities for treatment. They regularly employ on a salary basis a large staff of physicians, nurses and interns, as well as administrative and manual workers, and they charge patients for medical care and treatment, collecting for such services, if necessary by legal action. Certainly, the person who avails himself of "hospital facilities" expects that the hospital will attempt to cure him, not that its nurses or other employees will act on their own responsibility. Hospitals should, in short, shoulder the responsibilities borne by everyone else. There is no reason to continue their exemption from the universal rule of Respondeat Superior.[6]

Some jurisdictions adhere to the rule that institutions created and controlled by the state or its subdivisions such as state asylums or county hospitals or municipal hospitals and the like are not liable for the negligence of their agents in the absence of statutory provisions to the contrary. In these states, the doctrine of respondeat superior does not apply.

Medical versus Administrative Acts

The vicarious liability imposed on a hospital for the negligent ministerial acts of professionals but not for their negligent medical acts was based in the exemption given to the hospital from the doctrine of respondeat superior. Many early cases held that hospitals could not be held vicariously liable for the acts of a professional because a lay hospital administrator could have no right of control over the medical acts of a professional person. When the

---

[6] *Id* at 659, 143 NE2d at 6, 163 NYS2d at 5.

professionals stopped acting in their professional roles, the reason for the exemption disappeared.

Florida is among the jurisdictions which have considered the distinction between medical and administrative acts in deciding whether a hospital will be vicariously liable for the acts of a negligent physician. In *City of Miami v Oats*,[7] the Supreme Court of Florida affirmed a judgment imposing liability on a hospital for burns the plaintiff received when an intern brought a heated cautery instrument in contact with some alcohol-saturated surgical gauze lying on the plaintiff's stomach. The *Oats* court initially said that the city would be liable because the maintenance and operation of a hospital is a corporate and not governmental function of the city. The court, then, went on to say:

> Aside from all this, the negligence complained of in this case was such that it could not be said that the intern was exercising his professional skill and judgment in applying the healing art when he did the act complained of and which caused the injury. It did not require any knowledge or skill of medicine or surgery for anyone of ordinary intelligence to know that if one saturates . . . gauze . . . with a large quantity of high-grade alcohol and then brings a red-hot iron into close proximity . . . the gauze pads will immediately ignite and burn.

The distinction between administrative and medical acts represents an effort by courts to circumvent the immunity which was given charitable and governmental hospitals for the negligence of their professional employees. If, however, a court finds that a physician was not an employee of the hospital but was rather an independent contractor, the need for the distinction between administrative and medical acts is obviated. It was the New York Court of Appeals decision in 1957 in *Bing* which abolished the distinction between medical and administrative acts. While many courts followed New York in abolishing the distinction, a few jurisdictions still retain it. The Supreme Court of Georgia is among the minority of courts that retain the distinction, and the Georgia court reaffirmed its position as recently as 1980 in *Moore v Carrington*.[8] The *Moore* court wrote that "a noncharitable hospital is liable for the negligence of its nurses, orderlies and other employees in the performance of mere administrative or clerical duties which . . . do not require the application of specialized technique . . . and which are not performed under the direct supervision of attending physicians."

One jurisdiction has abolished the administrative/medical distinction for nurses, but not for physicians. In *Bernardi v Community Hospital Association*,[9] the Supreme Court of Colorado abolished the distinction between administrative and medical acts for cases involving the negligence of nurses.

---

[7] 152 Fla 21, 24, 10 So 2d 721, 723 (1942).

[8] 155 Ga App 12, 270 SE2d 222 (1980).

[9] 166 Colo 280, 443 P2d 708 (1968).

However, the court expressly limited its holding to those cases in which a nurse acted outside the presence of a physician.

§12.07 —Apparent Agency

The next definition of terms is rather confusing and has many synonyms. *Apparent agency, agency by estoppel, apparent authority,* and *ostensible agency* are all the same. *Black's Law Dictionary* defines *apparent authority* as follows: "In the law of agency, such authority as the principal knowingly or negligently permits the agent to assume." The *Restatement (Second) of Agency* §8 (1957) says, "The power to affect the legal relations of another person by transactions with third persons professedly as agent for the other arising from and in accordance with the other's manifestations to such third persons." *Agency by estoppel* is defined as: "One created by operation of law and established by proof of such acts of the principal as reasonably lead to the conclusion of its existence." This arises where the principal by negligence in failing to supervise the agent's affairs allows the agent to exercise powers not granted to him or her, thus justifying others in believing the agent possesses the requisite authority. *Ostensible agency* is defined as one which exists where the principal intentionally or by want of ordinary care causes a third person to believe another to be his or her agent who is not really employed by him or her. The court in *Lloyd's Casualty Insurer v Farrar* said: "An apparent agent is one that the principal either intentionally or by want of ordinary care induces third persons to believe is his agent, although neither expressed nor implied authority has been conferred." Thus, the reader may be somewhat less confused by the terminology and perhaps a recapitulation of case law may be more demonstrative for definitional purposes.

In *Capan v Divine Providence Hospital,*[10] the court held that:

> First, the changing role of the hospital in society creates a likelihood that patients will look to the institution rather than the individual physician for care. Thus, a patient today frequently enters the hospital, seeking a wide range of hospital services, rather than personal treatment by a particular physician. It would be absurd to require such a patient to be familiar with the law of Respondeat Superior, so as to inquire of each person who treated him whether that person is an employee of the hospital or an independent contractor.

Thus, if a hospital holds out a physician as working on behalf of the institution—i.e., in its emergency room, lab, or radiology suite—even though the provider may not technically be an employee for purposes of imparting vicarious liability to the institution, it will be assumed by the court that such an employment relationship actually exists.

Where the public perceives the hospital to be an institution furnishing physicians and staff or treatment, the hospital is generally considered to

---

[10] 270 Pa Super 127, 130, 410 A2d 1282 (1979).

have a duty to the patient on the basis of apparent authority. Several cases illustrate this theory. In a Michigan case, a physician working for a clinic referred an infant to an outside independent physician for removal of a leg cast. During this removal, the infant sustained injuries, and the court found the original clinic liable on an "ostensible agency theory." In a Delaware case, a private physician substituting for the regular emergency room physician in a hospital negligently applied a leg cast to a patient. After noting that the physician had not been paid a salary by the hospital nor been subject to any hospital control, the court found the hospital liable on the basis of "ostensible agency."

Finally, a recent Georgia case more fully defines the doctrine of ostensible or apparent agency. *Brown v Coastal Emergency Services, Inc* [11] was granted certiorari by the Georgia Supreme Court and is a case where Mr. Brown was injured in an automobile accident and taken to the emergency room at Richmond County Hospital doing business as University Hospital in Augusta, Georgia. He was treated in the emergency room by two physicians and later in the hospital by two physician employees of University Hospital. Brown alleged negligent treatment by these physicians and sued University Hospital and Coastal Emergency Services on the basis of ostensible agency. The trial court granted the motion for summary judgment for both Coastal and the hospital because the doctors were independent contractors and not employees, and the court of appeals agreed with Coastal, but held "allegation of ostensible agency as to the hospital was not pierced by the facts" and denied the motion for summary judgment for the hospital. The Georgia Supreme Court heard the case and held:

> There may have been a time when all the world knew hospitals were structures where physicians treated and cared for their patients. In such a society, one would be hard pressed to show that he justifiably relied on the hospital to care for his illness or injury through doctors employed for that purpose. But, the situation has evolved, and most modern hospitals hold themselves out to the public as providing many health-related services, including the services of physicians. A patient is likely to look to the hospital, not just to a particular doctor he comes into contact with through the hospital.
>
> The doctrine can seldom apply to the customary situation in which a patient consults his own physician who then has him admitted to a hospital. In such a case, there is no representation or holding out by the hospital to the patient. The hospital does not furnish him a doctor, he obtains his own.[12]

Finally, *Pamperin v Trinity Memorial Hospital* [13] concluded that:

---

[11] 181 Ga App 893, 354 SE2d 632, *affd,* 257 Ga 507, 361 SE2d 164 (1987).
[12] *Brown,* 257 Ga at 509, 361 SE2d at 166.
[13] 144 Wis 2d 188, 423 NW2d 848 (1988).

When a hospital holds itself out to the public as providing complete medical care, a hospital can be held liable under the doctrine of apparent authority for negligent acts of the physicians retained by the hospital to provide emergency room care, irrespective of the fact that the person who committed the negligent act was an independent contractor. By holding themselves out as providing complete care, hospitals have created the appearance that the hospital itself through its agents or employees treats emergency room patients. When a hospital does not inform incoming patients which if any care or services are provided by independent contractors a patient should be able to look to the hospital for the negligence of the physician retained by the hospital to provide medical care. However, because complete medical care consists of both direct care and support services, liability should attach regardless of whether the hospital is negligent in treating the patient directly or assisting in treating the patient by providing support services invisible to the patient.

We therefore hold that Trinity can be held liable under the doctrine of apparent authority for the negligence of its physicians who provide care incident to the admission of a patient to an emergency room irrespective of the fact that the specific physician who committed the negligent act was an independent contractor.

§12.08 —Borrowed Servant

Another doctrine which must be discussed is the "borrowed servant" theory. A recent Georgia case, *Ross v Chatham County Hospital Authority*,[14] illustrates this. In this case, the plaintiff sued a surgeon and the Chatham County Hospital Authority for malpractice, alleging that an instrument was left in him after abdominal surgery. The hospital's liability was predicated on the negligence of an employee who assisted the surgeon. The issue before the Georgia Supreme Court was under what circumstances the hospital employee becomes the employee of the surgeon, so as to impute the negligence of the employee to the surgeon under the rule of respondeat superior. The court held that a hospital may escape liability under the borrowed servant doctrine only if it has yielded the control of the employee to the surgeon who has then assumed immediate supervision. In addition, the borrowed servant doctrine only applies to employees when performing tasks involving professional skill and judgment. Therefore, a hospital may not escape liability if the employee negligently performs clerical or administrative tasks.

In *Ross*, the court concluded that the surgeon has primary responsibility for seeing that no foreign object was left in the patient's body. In addition, the court noted that the evidence showed that the local standard of care at the time of this particular surgery did not include the counting of sponges, instruments, and other items used during an operation. Thus, using the bor-

---

[14] 184 Ga App 660, 362 SE2d 390 (1987), *revd*, 258 Ga 234, 367 SE2d 793 (1988).

rowed servant doctrine, the court made the physician "the captain of the ship" (a theory no longer in vogue) and immunized the hospital. But the court concluded further that the hospital also might be liable for the patient's injuries based on some negligent administrative act, since counting sponges is a clerical function requiring no medical judgment. Thus, the court reversed the summary judgment for the hospital and concluded that there were factual issues to be resolved by the lower tribunal.

Another Georgia case illustrating the borrowed servant issue is *Runnels v Coleman*.[15] Here, Annabelle Runnels sued St. Joseph's Hospital after a surgical towel was left in her abdomen during an abdominal hysterectomy. The hospital moved for summary judgment on the basis that hospital employees were "borrowed servants" whose negligence should be attributed to the "surgeon" as "captain of the ship." The court ruled that the issue was not whether the employee was performing administrative functions, but whether the surgeon was exercising immediate personal supervision over the employee, and therefore denied the hospital's motions.

In *Reed v Adventist Health Systems/Sunbelt, Inc*,[16] a patient was admitted to the hospital for a hip-nailing. Following surgery, the patient discovered a burn on her right leg and subsequently filed suit against the hospital and others. The trial court granted the hospital's motion for summary judgment, but the court of appeals held that when a hospital yields control of its employees to a surgeon in the operating room and the surgeon personally supervises those employees, the surgeon becomes the employees' master, and their negligence during the course of the master/servant relationship is imputed to the surgeon. The evidence showed that the surgeon was present and in control of the operating room personnel during the entire procedure and, therefore, the court affirmed the trial court's order, holding the hospital not liable for negligent operation of the equipment used during the hip-nailing procedure.

A final example of the borrowed servant theory is found in *Hudmon v Martin*.[17] Here, a patient sued a nurse who improperly prepared a solution which injured the patient. Although the scrub nurse was employed by the hospital, she had been assigned to assist the doctor at surgery and was considered under his control. The court held that such an arrangement put her in the position of a borrowed servant, and the physician was responsible for her negligence.

§12.09 —Agency by Necessity

Agency by necessity or emergency applies to unique and special areas when the agent's authority arises independent of agreement between him or her and the principal. Because of the necessity of the situation without

---

[15] No CV 187-102 (D Augusta Div 1988).
[16] 181 Ga App 750, 353 SE2d 523 (1987).
[17] 315 So 2d 516 (Fla Dist Ct App 1975).

the agent's fault or neglect, if some sudden and unexpected emergency arises and if the agent in good faith adopts the course which seems best to him or her under all the circumstances, those acts will bind the principal. Thus, if a physician, an agent of the hospital, acts outside the scope of his or her authority under an employment contract, but in an emergency situation, the principal may be held liable if the agent acts negligently. An example of this is when a radiologist suddenly performs a tracheostomy in the radiology department which is outside the ordinary scope of his or her employment.

§12.10 Expert Witness

The concept of the expert witness in hospital case law can be illustrated by a Missouri case, *Robbins v Jewish Hospital*.[18] Here, a plaintiff brought an action to recover damages from the hospital after a hip fracture she sustained while a patient in the hospital. The court of appeals held that, having accepted plaintiff as a patient, the hospital owed plaintiff the specific duty of exercising reasonable care to protect the patient from injuring herself. The hospital's duty was proportional to the patient's needs—i.e., such reasonable care and attention as her condition required. Numerous other legal, not factual, issues arose, most of which are not germane to this discussion, but the issue of "expert witness" is of interest. The hospital claimed that the patient did not introduce an expert medical witness to establish the professional standard of care required. The court ruled that where the conduct in question involves unique knowledge, skill, or ability peculiar to those educated and trained in a particular profession, expert testimony is essential for the guidance of lay jurors. In this particular case, no special knowledge, education, or experience was required to recognize that the dangers the nurse sought to avoid might well occur if the patient in some way was not properly restrained which, in this case, she was not.

Compare that case to the Missouri case of *Ackerman v Lerwick, M.D. and Missouri Baptist Hospital*.[19] Here, the widow and five children of a patient who died from a pulmonary embolus three days post-operatively brought a wrongful death action against the surgeon and hospital. The claim against the hospital was that the hospital was negligent in obtaining the patient's consent to surgery. The court held that the hospital which furnished the consent form to the patient had no duty to make a *further* oral inquiry of the patient as to whether the risks had been explained to him, where the form which the patient had signed *said* that risks had been explained and the patient had read the form and signed it.

---

[18] 663 SW2d 341 (Mo 1981).
[19] 676 SW2d 318 (Mo 1984).

§12.11 Corporations

Because of the potential size of any corporation, a hospital as a corporation now may have liabilities never before imagined. Previous discussion in §§12.04 to 12.09 concerned the liability of a hospital under agency principles. This section includes other bases of hospital liability under the corporate umbrella. *Direct liability* is a synonym for *corporate liability* and is separate from any vicarious liability ordinarily expected in the master/servant relationship.

Most hospitals are organized under corporate structure. The general business corporation act of each state gives the hospital its legal entity and hospitals may operate as a profit or nonprofit corporation. A profit corporation is organized to earn a profit and pays income to shareholders, while a nonprofit corporation is organized primarily to render a service and does not distribute its income to shareholders. Additionally, the nonprofit corporation uses its profits and reinvests its income for institutional purposes. The major advantage of hospital corporate status is the limited liability of its shareholders, owners, or members of the corporation, under which they are not held personally liable for the actions of the corporation.

Corporations have express and implied powers. The express powers are granted by the articles of incorporation and bylaws, whereas the implied powers are those which are reasonably necessary to carry out the express powers. If a corporation performs an act outside its powers, it is said to perform *ultra vires*. For example, if an officer of a corporation performs an act which is outside the express powers of that officer, that act is considered to be ultra vires and voidable.

The bylaws of a hospital are adopted by the governing board and include items such as the purpose of the hospital, along with the specifics of the administration of the hospital such as members, officers, duties, quorum requirements, frequency of meetings, etc. Another set of bylaws may be developed by the hospital staff which may establish the framework for the operation of the medical staff and its accountability to the governing board. These bylaws will include qualifications and procedures for appointment and reappointment to the medical staff, along with delineation of privileges, committee meetings, and mechanisms for effective communication between and amongst the different departments. The medical staff may also adopt rules and regulations related to the role of the medical staff in the care of patients and various departments in the hospital.

The governing board is the major decisionmaking body of the hospital and, in the case of a private hospital, the governing board will be the board of directors. In the case of a public hospital, the governing board is called the board of trustees. Most state incorporation statutes regulate the duties and responsibilities of these governing boards. Additionally, the governing board may appoint an executive committee which is responsible for the day-to-day operation of the hospital. The authority of the executive committee as well as the governing board is either expressed or implied. The express authority is granted by the articles of incorporation, whereas the implied authority exercises that power necessary to carry out the express authority.

The hospital administrator is the chief executive officer of the hospital, appointed by the governing board. He or she is responsible for planning and developing the policies and procedures of the hospital and organizes the administrative functions as well as facilitates the effective communication between the medical staff and the administration of the hospital.

The medical staff of the hospital is made up of those physician members properly credentialed by the governing board of the hospital. The functions and duties of the medical staff are specified in the bylaws and ordinarily are categorized into active, associate, courtesy, consulting, and honorary membership. These categories carry with them various responsibilities and privileges. Ordinarily, the medical staff will also elect officers who perform day-to-day functions of the medical staff and serve as liaison between the medical staff and the administration.

The medical aspects of the hospital are monitored by various hospital committees. Each medical staff member is required by the bylaws to serve on a committee. Committee function ranges from the Executive Committee to the Credentials, Mortality and Morbidity, Utilization Review, Operating Room, Housekeeping, Infection Control, etc. Most jurisdictions provide a shield for the content of the committee meetings based on each state's peer review act, but there are instances wherein this veil has been pierced to allow the information sought to be divulged.

§12.12 Joint Commission on Accreditation of Healthcare Organizations

Hospitals are regulated in numerous ways by state and federal programs as well as voluntary compliance with requirements of the Joint Commission on Accreditation of Healthcare Organizations (JCAHO). This nonprofit organization is dedicated to improving the quality of care in health care settings. The JCAHO has been widely recognized for its dynamic leadership role in developing standards and adapting its accreditation and survey processes to address important changes and issues in the delivery of health services. Accreditation by the JCAHO is voluntary, and the decision to be surveyed is made by the governing board of the hospital. The accreditation process provides access to the JCAHO information resources along with identification of areas in which performance may improve. Additionally, on-site education and consultation is given along with documentation of the hospital's responsibility for effective performance in delivering care. The accreditation and survey processes of the JCAHO focus on identifying the hospital's strengths and weaknesses and on providing assistance in correcting the identified weaknesses.

§12.13 Corporate Practice of Medicine

Historically, a corporation, not being a person, could not be licensed and therefore could not practice medicine. In addition, ownership in a clinic where physicians who were licensed to practice medicine and who were employed by that clinic's corporation was illegal.

In prior years, courts have supported this corporate practice of medicine doctrine because of theories involving:

1. The physician/patient relationship
2. The possibility of interference with this relationship by a corporation
3. The fear of commercial exploitation of the medical profession
4. The possible danger of having nonphysicians in charge of physicians regarding medical decisions

The erosion of this doctrine has become very apparent, as most states have now enacted statutes authorizing the formation of professional corporations. These corporations generally must have licensed health care providers as officers or employees. Thus, we see the evolution to the hospital as a corporate entity and to its liabilities.

The duties of the corporate entity hospital toward the patient and the medical staff have been broadened by sociological advances. Not only do hospitals now have a duty to provide quality care for their patients, but additional duties required to be provided include proper credentialing and monitoring of the physician and nonphysician staff, and the provision and maintenance of proper facilities, whether they be administrative (such as building and parking lots) or professional (such as x-ray equipment or laboratory instruments).

Additionally, the hospital is required to maintain its own accreditation according to accepted standards, to protect and give physicians due process in the peer review process, to provide for incompetent patients, to make proper subcontracts with other providers, and to provide protection from theft from patients and the need to safeguard patients from physical hazards. In addition, hospitals have now been required to guarantee safe transfer of the patient to another facility. This list will continue to grow as inventive plaintiffs' attorneys continue to provide reasons for hospital liability.

The leading case initiating corporate liability as a theory to hold a hospital liable came in 1965 in *Darling v Charleston Community Memorial Hospital*.[20] Here, the patient had a cast applied to his broken leg by the emergency room physician and subsequently had his leg amputated below the knee because of complications secondary to the cast being too tight. The patient brought suit against the physician and the hospital and, at trial, obtained a jury verdict against the hospital which was offset by the amount of the settlement made previously with the physician.

The defendant hospital in *Darling* argued that it was bound only by the standard of care customarily offered by hospitals. However, the court recognized the hospital's own role in the overall treatment of the patient, including the credentialing and monitoring of the physician staff. The hospital

---

[20] 217 NY 24, 111 NE2d 253 (1965).

argued that: "A hospital is powerless under the law to forbid or command any act by a physician or surgeon in the practice of his profession." The court concluded that the hospital was liable in not only finding that the nurses were not the "borrowed servants of the physician, but had independent responsibilities themselves, but also found that the hospital should have monitored the physician and exercised reasonable care in the credentialing process of its physician staff." Thus, for the first time, *Darling* did not impose liability on the hospital for the negligence of the physician practitioner who was an independent contractor; rather, it applied liability on the hospital for its own negligence in the failure to select and monitor its staff more carefully.

Darling suggests that the hospital has the following duties:

1. To select and monitor only qualified physicians on its staff
2. To supervise the medical staff
3. To supervise the treatment which a patient is given

It took many years for other jurisdictions to appreciate and take the position that *Darling* embraces.

Whether or not the hospital is liable for the negligence of its medical staff or other personnel involved in the care of patients depends upon the relationship to the hospital. To hold the hospital responsible, it must be shown that the employer has the right of control over the manner in which the services are to be performed. Jurisdictions vary in the application of this theory. Since the relationship between a physician and his or her patient is a personal one, the hospital is usually not liable for those physician acts; however, that position is being eroded. In some jurisdictions, it is held that the mere fact that a nurse is employed and paid by the hospital does not establish the relationship between the hospital and the nurse unless the nurse is acting for the benefit of the hospital and not in the course of treatment. Other jurisdictions make no distinction based on the nature of the nurse's act; the hospital is held liable for his or her negligence completely.

§12.14 —Physician Credentialing

New applicants for medical staff privileges at a hospital must go through a credentialing process. The hospital has an application form which is filled out by the applicant and then other information is obtained such as letters of recommendation from peers or previous supervisors. The credentials committee of the hospital evaluates the application and then refers it to the specific department to which the applicant is applying for privileges. For example, a new urologist would apply for privileges in the Department of Urology, and a new family practitioner would apply for privileges in the Department of Family Practice. Once the department reviews and decides on the applicant, the credentials committee then passes that information on to the executive committee, which reviews all of the information again and, if it agrees with the credentials committee and the department below it, refers the application on to the hospital's governing body for a final decision.

One of the byproducts of the *Darling* case discussed in §12.13 is found in *Joiner v Mitchell County Hospital Authority*,[21] a 1971 case. Here, the court held that "the hospital must act in good faith and with reasonable care in the selection of a physician, and it has fulfilled its obligation and cannot be held liable when it selects an authorized physician in good standing in its profession." The hospital contended that it was not liable because it had left screening of medical staff candidates to existing members of the medical staff, yet the court stated that a hospital cannot escape liability merely because a physician was licensed in the state and recommended by other staff physicians. It must ensure that the medical staff properly determines the physician's competence before granting privileges.

In an Illinois case, *Cronic v Doud*,[22] six patients sued Dr. Doud, alleging unnecessary rib resection surgery for thoracic outlet syndrome, and also sued the hospital, claiming that the hospital had failed to properly review and supervise Dr. Doud's work. The court said that the hospital was put on notice of possible malpractice by Dr. Doud because rib resection surgeries increased dramatically with his coming on staff and, therefore, the hospital should have investigated and probably limited Dr. Doud's surgical privileges.

The case of *Johnson v Misericordia Community Hospital*[23] illustrates the standards of investigations, election, and evaluation of physician applicants for hospital privileges. In *Johnson,* the hospital was found negligent in granting orthopedic surgery privileges to the physician who unsuccessfully attempted to remove a pin from the patient's hip, thereby damaging the femoral nerve and causing permanent paralysis of the leg. Another recent case demonstrating this theory is *Rule v Lutheran Hospitals & Homes Society of America.*[24] Here, the hospital was successfully sued for the birth of a child with cerebral palsy, not on the basis of vicarious liability, but on the independent theory for breach of the hospital's duty to use care in granting and/or continuing hospital staff privileges to one it had reason to know was not qualified.

§12.15 —Independent Contractors

An *independent contractor* is one who has sole control over the means and methods of the work to be accomplished, even though the employer who hires the independent contractor retains the right of power of approval over the final result of the work.

---

[21] 125 Ga App 1, 186 SE2d 307 (1971).
[22] 168 Ill App 3d 665 (1988).
[23] 99 Wis 2d 708, 301 NW2d 156 (1981).
[24] 835 F2d 1250 (1987).

There are some exceptions to the general rule that the employer of an independent contractor is not liable for the independent contractor's torts. Some duties of the employers are nondelegable, as established by statute, and the employer will be liable in these instances. For example, when an enterprise owes duties to the public, the performance of that duty cannot be delegated. Another example is when the work of the independent contractor is inherently dangerous—i.e., crop dusting, use of dynamite, etc. In these instances, the employer cannot be insulated from liability.

In the health care field, a physician is generally considered to be an independent contractor. In a New Mexico case, *Cooper v Curry*,[25] the plaintiff was blinded because of cataract surgery in both eyes, and she then sued her physician as well as the hospital, claiming that the hospital had a duty to obtain her informed consent prior to the procedures performed on her. A jury verdict for the hospital occurred because the court instructed the jury not to find against the hospital because of the independent contractor theory. On appeal, the lower court's verdict was upheld.

Interestingly, the dissent in *Cooper* noted that the distinction between an employee and an independent contractor was no longer viable. Because the public views the hospital as an entity, the hospital should be held liable, regardless of whether a physician is considered a contractor because the hospital creates the entity of a medical unit, approves bylaws, credentials medical staff, and reviews the staff performance and holds them accountable for their actions.

Changing factual circumstances as to the practice of medicine in the hospital role have eroded the doctrine of independent contractor and expanded the doctrines of respondeat superior and apparent agency. Patients, by going to the emergency room of a hospital, no longer choose their own physicians. The patients take the physician who happens to be on call at that particular emergency room. In addition, physicians will tell their patients to go to the emergency room on weekends or whenever the physician is off duty, which further enhances the respondeat superior doctrine.

The Eleventh Circuit Court of Appeals[26] held that bylaws of the Hospital Authority of Gwinnett County which exclude Doctors of Osteopathy from its medical staff do not violate due process, equal protection, or Georgia's antidiscrimination statute. Three appellants, each of whom had completed medical education and training accredited by the American Osteopathic Association and were licensed to practice medicine in Georgia as Doctors of Osteopathy (DOs), challenged the constitutionality of the bylaws of the Gwinnett Hospital Authority which allowed only allopathic physicians (MDs) to be admitted to the medical staff. The Eleventh Circuit affirmed the district court which held that the bylaws do not violate equal protection or due process under the Fourteenth Amendment or the Georgia Constitution. The court also held that the bylaws do not violate the antidiscrimination provisions of Ga Code Ann §31-7-7(A) (1984).

---

[25] 92 NM 417, 589 P2d 201 (1978).
[26] Silverstein, DO v Gwinnett Hosp Auth, No 87-8926 (11th Cir Dec 27, 1988).

The court noted the recognized distinctions between osteopathic and allopathic postgraduate specialty training, for example, a D.O. has not served an AMA-approved residency. Those distinctions provided a rational basis for a hospital to restrict its staff to MDs. In addition, the bylaws were not arbitrary or unreasonable.

While it is true that hospitals have a duty to credential and monitor their professional staff, physicians must also be given proper due process if their privileges are to be curtailed, revoked, or suspended. Substantive and procedural safeguards must be available to physicians trying to regain staff privileges. Such reasons as failure of the physician to have proper credentials, to comply with the hospital bylaws regarding medical recordkeeping or committee or staff meeting attendance, as well as poor interpersonal interactions may be adequate substantive reasons for the actions against a physician.

Procedural due process requirements which must be given to the physician include but are not necessarily limited to the following: providing timely notice of the action, allowing an opportunity to be heard, allowing discovery and for independent counsel to be present at the hearing, allowing for cross-examination by the physician, allowing for an appeal, and providing final written notice of the adverse decision.

Robinson v Magovern,[27] a Pennsylvania case, concerned a thoracic surgeon who was denied staff privileges as a result of the hospital's determination that : (1) the surgeon had serious personality flaws; (2) the surgeon's multiple staff appointments would impair his ability to provide high-quality care or to instruct residents; (3) the surgeon lacked interest in the thoracic surgeon residency program; and (4) denial of privileges would save scarce operating room resources for other surgeons who could make greater contributions to the hospital. The court held that his denial of staff privileges was based on fair application of criteria as set forth in hospital bylaws.

§12.16 —Substantial Evidence Test

Under the "substantial evidence test," recommended review action will be upheld as long as that action is supported by "substantial evidence." This terminology means that as long as the decision to make a recommendation against a physician was made on a "rational basis," the decision may be supported by the courts. A California case of *Gill v Mercy Hospital & the Medical Staff of Mercy Hospital*[28] illustrates the substantial evidence test.

Dr. Gill, who had been granted provisional privileges at Mercy Hospital under a monitoring program, asked to be released from this program when he had satisfied the requested requirements. The executive committee recommended the removal of this requirement for certain procedures, but continuation of it with respect to others. A committee was formed to hear the evidence and eventually decided against Dr. Gill. The California Court of

---

[27] 521 F Supp 842 (WD Pa 1981).
[28] 199 Cal App 3d 889, 245 Cal Rptr 304 (1988).

Appeals reviewed the proceedings on the basis of the substantial evidence test, noting that "when an appellate court is reviewing a quasi-judicial decision of a governing body of a private hospital, the function of the appellate court is to review the entire record to determine whether the decision is supported by substantial evidence."

The court held that the testimony offered regarding the monitoring reports of Dr. Gill's performance was sufficient to provide substantial evidence to support the decision against Dr. Gill. Additionally, although Dr. Gill claimed that he was precluded from having an attorney represent him at the hearing, under California law, it is possible to have a fair hearing without being represented by counsel. Additionally, Dr. Gill was denied discovery of certain documents involving the monitoring report on one case in which he was involved, but the court held that, while he should have been supplied with that one report, the trial court did not rely on the evidence of that report, and therefore his denial of the discovery of that document was moot. Finally, Dr. Gill also charged that the hospital administrator attended the review committee's meetings concerning him, but the court held that the presence of the hospital administrator at the hearing committee was harmless and that Dr. Gill had failed to provide any evidence to indicate that the administrator had acted improperly during the hearing.

Another case illustrative of the substantial evidence case is *Sywak v O'Connor Hospital*.[29] In *Sywak*, an ad hoc investigative committee was formed to conduct an investigation into Dr. Sywak's allegedly disruptive behavior. Dr. Sywak was given notice of specific charts that the committee was interested in, but, when Dr. Sywak met with the committee, several other cases were reviewed, none of which involved the charts that had been previously identified to him. Additionally, Dr. Sywak attended another meeting, at which time he was presented with another group of cases about which he had not been notified prior.

After Dr. Sywak's privileges were suspended by the hospital, he filed suit and the trial court agreed that he had been denied a fair hearing because he had been given "new and different" charts other than those that had been the subject of previous investigations.

The hospital appealed and the court of appeals reversed, finding that Dr. Sywak had not been denied a fair hearing despite the fact that some of the cases used against him were different than those discussed with him during the investigative process. The court held that the medical staff bylaws placed the "burden of proof" on the doctor challenging the prior adverse decision and that this burden of proof provision did not deny a physician a fair hearing since it compelled the medical staff's recommendation to be supported by "substantial evidence." The court further held that a committee hearing in the nature of a "de novo" proceeding was proper in which to receive new evidence. And, if a de novo hearing is properly conducted, prior recommendations of previous committees will become irrelevant. Thus, it did not matter

---

[29] 199 Cal App 3d 423, 244 Cal Rptr 753 (1988).

whether the executive committee considered certain evidence to decide a recommendation brought to it by the hearing committee because, if a "de novo" committee heard new evidence brought to it, this de novo hearing satisfied due process requirements.

§12.17 —Fairness

Lasko v Valley Presbyterian Hospital[30] demonstrates the doctrine of "fairness." In this case, Dr. Lasko had his admitting privileges at the hospital suspended. During a hearing concerning this issue, Dr. Lasko attempted to ask questions of the panel concerning: (1) bias; or (2) any financial or competitive conflicts of interest. The chairman of the committee denied his request to ask these questions and advised Dr. Lasko that he was free to offer any evidence of bias, but that he did not have the right to ask any questions. The court of appeals ruled that the refusal to allow Dr. Lasko to ask questions violated his right to a "fair hearing." The court stated as follows:

> An individual who is being expelled or excluded from a private institution which controls important economic interests such as a private hospital is entitled to a fair procedure by which to challenge the action taken. . . . [O]ne whose right to practice his or her livelihood is being revoked or suspended has a right to a tribunal which meets the prevailing standards of impartiality.

In this case, while the hospital bylaws addressed the issue that "no staff member who has actively participated in the consideration of the adverse recommendation shall be appointed a member of this hearing committee," the bylaws did not specifically provide for questioning of the hearing panels. Basic notions of fairness dictate that an individual whose right to practice his or her livelihood is at risk certainly has a right to examine the members of the tribunal for possible bias against him or her.

Even if the medical staff bylaws were complied with, and case law indicates that the bylaws must be followed, efforts must also be made to make sure that hearings are "fair," and this is the test by which hospital actions will be judged.

§12.18 —Antitrust

Whereas numerous cases can be used to demonstrate that a hospital authority may restrict a staff member's privileges by reasonable and nondiscriminatory rules and regulations, a unique approach employing the vehicle of the Sherman Antitrust Act has been used successfully by plaintiffs' attorneys.

The Sherman Act, enacted over 90 years ago, was aimed at protecting competition in the economy to keep prices at a reasonable level. There are several

---

[30] 180 Cal App 3d 519, 522, 225 Cal Rptr 603 (1986).

activities that could violate the act, including price-fixing and the creation of a monopoly. Congress did not intend to compromise any state's ability to regulate its own commerce. Actions taken by the state are immunized from federal antitrust scrutiny. The "state action" doctrine, first promulgated in 1943, has suddenly gained intense medical prominence. *Parker v Brown*,[31] a California raisin-grower case, showed that a state can create a program and enforce it, thereby bypassing federal laws. A frequently quoted statement from that case, however, is: "A state does not give immunity to those who violate the Sherman Act by authorizing them to violate it." It was not until 1980 that the United States Supreme Court adopted a two-pronged test to determine whether state regulation of antitrust activities could be shielded from federal scrutiny. Here, the court said that the state regulation must be "clearly articulated and affirmatively expressed." In addition, the second prong is that the policy must be "actively supervised" by the state. Hence, the groundwork has been laid for the current medical denial-of-privilege cases.

In 1982, the United States Supreme Court decided in *Arizona v Maricopa County Medical Society*[32] that federal antitrust laws applied to physicians. Also, in 1982, in *Jefferson Parish Hospital District #2 v Hyde*,[33] the United States Supreme Court held that an exclusive contract between an anesthesiology group and a hospital which excluded other anesthesiologists from serving patients did *not* violate §1 of the Sherman Act. However, the case itself was important to demonstrate that the relationships among hospitals, physicians, and the total health care industry were subject to the same antitrust restrictions as those engaged in commerical activities.

No current writings concerning antitrust litigation in the physician peer review arena would be complete without discussing the *Patrick* case.[34] Here, Timothy Patrick, a surgeon, declined an invitation by other physicians to join them as a partner in the Astoria Clinic. He thereafter experienced difficulties in his professional dealings with the clinic physicians, culminating in peer review proceedings to terminate his privileges at Astoria's only hospital on the ground that his care of patients was below the standard of care. Dr. Patrick filed suit, alleging that the defendant physicians had violated the Sherman Antitrust Act by initiating and participating in the peer review proceedings in order to reduce competition rather than to improve patient care. Ultimately, the district court entered judgment against the defendant doctors for $650,000, trebled under the Sherman Act to $1,950,000, plus $90,000 in punitive damages, $20,000 in compensatory damages, and $228,000 in attorney's fees, for a total of $2,288,000. The court of appeals reversed on the ground that the defendant physicians' conduct was immune from scrutiny of the federal antitrust act because of the state action doctrine

---

[31] 317 US 341 (1943).
[32] 457 US 332 (1982).
[33] 104 S Ct 1551 (1984).
[34] Patrick v Burget, 486 US 94 (1988).

wherein Oregon had articulated a policy in favor of peer review and had actively supervised that process.

Dr. Patrick appealed to the United States Supreme Court, which held that the state action doctrine does not protect Oregon physicians from federal antitrust liability because the "active supervision" prong of the test used to determine whether private parties may claim state action immunity requires that state officials have and exercise power to review such parties' competitive acts and disapprove those that fail to accord with state policy. The Court found that this requirement was not satisfied in this case because there was no showing that the state Health Division, the state Board of Medical Examiners, or the state judiciary reviewed private decisions regarding hospital privileges. Lastly, the Court held that the argument that effective peer review is essential to the provision of quality medical care and that any threat of antitrust liability will prevent physicians from participating openly and actively in peer review proceedings essentially challenges the wisdom of applying the antitrust laws to the sphere of medical care.

The physician bears the burden of proving that he or she was a member of the protected class, was qualified for the position held, and was discharged while a person outside of the class with equal or lesser qualifications was retained. In *Zaklama v Mount Sinai Medical Center*,[35] the appellate court found that Dr. Zaklama, a resident anesthesiologist who was discharged from the program, successfully showed that his discharge was based on discriminatory reasons.

§12.19 —Grounds, Buildings, and Vendors

It should be noted at this time that hospitals have significant liability that may lie outside the scope of this chapter. As in any commercial structure, hospitals are liable for slip-and-fall accidents, injuries secondary to poorly maintained or repaired facilities, and the criminal activities that may occur in dimly lighted parking areas, etc. Those areas of direct liability will not be discussed here.

Hospitals do have direct liability in such areas as contracts with subcontractors, proper licensing and accreditation, and even patient transfer. A large fertile area for liability is with the radiologist, anesthesiologist, and pathologist (RAP) population of the hospital. These contracts are held to high scrutiny under various theories from antitrust to independent contractor, and where an injury occurs as a result of an act or omission by a physician member or employee of one of these "subcontractors" in the hospital, direct liability may occur.

Oltz v St Peter's Community Hospital[36] concerns issues which arose after Helena, Montana's only general hospital, St. Peter's Community Hospital, signed an exclusive contract in 1980 with an anesthesiology group. St. Peter's

---

[35] 842 F2d 291 (11th Cir 1988).
[36] (9th Cir 1980).

also terminated a contract agreement with nurse anesthetist Oltz who had been administering anesthesia at that hospital and recieved 90 per cent of his billings directly from the hospital since 1974.

Oltz sued the hospital and the anesthesiologist (who settled out of court of $462,500). In 1987, a United States District Court found the hospital guilty of conspiring with the anesthesiologists to restrict Nurse Oltz's trade and awarded him $421,831 in lost income. The Ninth Circuit Court of Appeals affirmed the trial court's findings, but ordered the damages issue to be retried because the lost income was "excessive."

While this case may be viewed as a garden variety Sherman Antitrust Act case, it also stands for the premise that hospitals can now be held to a greater degree of responsibility in antitrust cases as a means of protecting the interest of patients in the communities they serve.

§12.20 Consolidated Omnibus Budget Reconciliation Act (COBRA)

The Consolidated Omnibus Budget Reconciliation Act of 1986 (COBRA), also known as the "Anti-Dumping" law, is designed to prevent hospitals from transferring patients who have not been medically screened, who are not stable, or who are in active labor. This act will mainly affect emergency rooms, but can affect any hospital transfer. Violators of COBRA suffer stiff penalties. Not only can patients sue the hospital, the receiving hospital may recover financial losses from a transfer and, in addition, federal fines may apply.

Interestingly, the definition of *transfer* as provided by COBRA is

> the movement (including the discharge) of a patient outside the hospital's facilities at the direction of any person employed by (or affiliated or associated directly or indirectly) with the hospital, but does not include such movement of a patient who: (a) has been declared dead, or (b) leaves the facility without the permission of any such person.

Thus, one could see that the transfer of a patient would include the actual discharging of a patient from the hospital and the potential liability associated with that discharge.

Because the act provides a cause of action to "any individual who suffers harm as a direct result of a participating hospital's violation of a requirement of the section," there is a strict liability interpretation which bears discussion. A mere violation of the act may trigger strict liability which, as opposed to a negligence cause of action, may not require an expert to establish that liability. Such strict liability items may include transferring any nonstable patient, one who has not been medically screened, one who is in labor, one transferred to a facility without qualified personnel, or transfer via unqualified transportation.

The negligence standards may apply in situations involving the stabilization of the patient or in determining whether an emergency situation exists.

Whether strict liability or negligence is the issue, COBRA will affect hospital emergency departments specifically, and the transfer of patients, for whatever reason, will come under much closer scrutiny.

Cases

A

Ackerman v Lerwick, MD & Missouri Baptist Hosp, 676 SW2d 318 (Mo 1984) §**12.10**

American Motorcycle Assn v Superior Court of Los Angeles County, 28 Cal 3d 578, 578 P2d 899, 146 Cal Rptr 182 (1978) §**1.34**

Arizona v Maricopa County Medical Socy, 457 US 332 (1982) §**12.18**

B

Berlin v Nathan, 64 Ill App 3d 940, 21 Ill Dec 682 (1978) §**1.38**

Bernardi v Community Hosp, 166 Colo 280, 443 P2d 708 1968 §**12.06**

Bing v Thunig, 2 NY2d 656, 143 NE2d 3, 163 NYS2d 3 (1957) §**12.06**

Boyce v Brown, 51 Ariz 416, 77 P2d 455 (1938) §**1.03**

Breddice v Doctors Hosp, 50 FRD 249 (DC 1970) §**1.39**

Brown v Coastal Emergency Servs, Inc, 181 Ga App 893, 354 SE2d 632, *affd*, 257 Ga 507, 361 SE2d 164 (1987) §**12.07**

Buie v Reynolds, 571 P2d 1230 (Okla Ct App 1977) §**11.03**

Bull v McCuskey, 96 Nev 706, 615 P2d 957 (1980) §**1.38**

C

Capan v Divine Providence Hosp, 270 Pa Super 127, 410 A2d 1282 (1979) §**12.07**

Carr v Pac Tel Co, 26 Cal App 3d 537, 103 Cal Rptr 120 (1972) §**2.23**

Carson v Maurer, 120 NH 925, 424 A2d 825 (1980) §**1.44**

Cate v Gordon, 40 Conn Supp 15, 478 A2d 631 (1984) §**2.08**

Chandra v Sprinke, 678 SW2d 804 (Mo 1984) §**1.39**

Chiero v Chicago Osteopathic Hosp, 47 Ill App 3d 166, 392 NE2d 203 (1979) §**11.03**

Cleveland v Wong, 237 Kan 410, 701 P2d 1301 (1985) §**11.03**

346　CASES

Cohen v Miami, 54 FRD 274 (1972) §2.24
Combs v Hargis Bank & Trust Co, 234 Ky 202, 27 SW2d 955 (1930) §1.26
Comforti v Beekman Downtown Hosp, 79 AD2d 968, 435 NYS2d 284 (1981) §2.24
Cooper v Curry, 92 NM 417, 589 P2d 201 (1978) §12.15
Cronic v Doud, 168 Ill App 3d 665 (1988) §12.14

D

Darling v Charleston Memorial Hosp, 217 NY 24, 111 NE2d 253 (1965) §12.13
Dillon v Legg, 68 Cal 2d 728, 441 P2d 912, 69 Cal Rptr 72 (1968) §1.30
Dunn v Beck, 80 Mont 414, 260 P 1047 (1927) §1.03
Duren v Suburban Community Hosp, 24 Ohio Misc 2d 25, 482 NE2d 1358 (1985) §1.44

E

Emory Clinic v Houston, 258 Ga 434, 369 SE2d 913 (1988) §1.39

F

Ferriter v Daniel O'Connell's Sons, 381 Mass 507, 413 NE2d 690 (1980) §2.14
Firestone Tire & Rubber Co v Pinyan, 155 Ga App 343, 270 SE2d 883 (1980) §1.28

G

Gill v Mercy Hosp & the Medical Staff of Mercy Hosp, 199 Cal App 3d 889, 245 Cal Rptr 304 (1988) §12.16
Gillette v Tucker, 67 Ohio St 106, 65 NE 865 (1966) §1.21
Girard v Weiss, 160 Ga App 295, 287 SE2d 301 (1981) §2.08
Grippe v Momtazee, 705 SW2d 551 (Mo Ct App 1986) §2.20

H

Hall v Ervin, 642 SW2d 724 (Tenn 1982) §2.18
Hanna v Martin, 49 So 2d 585 (Fla 1950) §1.26
Hayes v Brown, 108 Ga App 360, 133 SE2d 102 (1963) §1.25
Heath v Swift Wings, Inc, 40 NC App 158, 252 SE2d 256 (1979) §1.21
Herrerro v Atkinson, 227 Cal App 2d 69, 38 Cal Rptr 490 (1964) §1.36
Howard v Walker, 242 Ga 406, 249 SE2d 45 (1978) §2.06
Hudmon v Martin, 315 So 2d 516 (Fla Dist Ct App 1975) §12.08
Humphrey v Alvarado, 185 Ga App 486, 364 SE2d 618 (1988) §10.05

J

Jefferson Parish Hosp Dist No 2 v Edwin G Hyde, 466 US 2 (1984) §12.18
Jensen v Maine Eye & Ear Infirmary, 107 Me 408, 78 A 898 (1910) §12.03
Johnson v Flex-O-Lite Mfg Corp, 314 SW2d 75 (Mo 1958) §1.27

Johnson v Misericordia Community Hosp, 99 Wis 2d 708, 301 NW2d 156 (1981) §12.14

Joiner v Mitchell County Hosp Auth, 125 Ga App 1, 186 SE2d 307 (1971) §12.14

Jones v Griffith, 870 F2d 1363 (7th Cir 1989) §2.08

Jordan v Long Beach Community Hosp, 201 Cal App 3d 1402, 248 Cal Rptr 651 (1988) §1.44

Judd v Rowley's Cherry Hill Orchards, 611 P2d 1216 (Utah 1980) §1.28

K

Kaileha v Hayes, 556 Haw 306, 536 P2d 568 (1975) §2.08

Kansas Malpractice Victims Coalition v Bell, 243 Kan 333, 757 P2d 251 (1988) §1.44

Kozar v Chesapeake & Ohio RR, 449 F2d 1238 (DC Cir 1971) §1.26

L

Lamar v Graham, 598 SW2d 729 (Tex Ct App 1980) §2.17

Lasko v Valley Presbyterian Hosp, 180 Cal App 3d 519, 225 Cal Rptr 603 (1986) §12.17

Ledford v Cent Medical Pavilion, Inc, 531 F Supp 793 (WD Pa 1982) §2.08

M

Mateo v Rish, 86 AD2d 736, 446 NYS2d 598 (1982) §2.18

Mayfield v Ideal Enters, Inc, 157 Ga App 266, 277 SE2d 62 (1981) §1.27

McKee v Williams, 23 Ohio App 3d 187, 492 NE2d 461 (1985) §2.17

McMillan v LDLR, 645 SW2d 836 (Tex Ct App 1982) §11.03

Miami v Oates, 152 Fla 21, 10 So 2d 721 (1942) §12.06

Mitchell v McGee, 51 So 2d 198 (Miss 1951) §2.17

Moore v Carrington, 155 Ga App 12, 270 SE2d 222 (1980) §12.06

Moss v Bjornson No 16894 (Idaho Dec 1988) §1.47

N

Natanson v Kline, 186 Kan 393, 350 P2d 1093, *clarified,* 187 Kan 186, 354 P2d 670 (1960) §1.23

Nicholson v Hugh Chatham Memorial Hosp, 300 NC 295, 266 SE2d 818 (1980) §2.14

O

Oltz v St Peter's (9th Cir 1980) §12.19

P

Pamperin v Trinity Memorial Hosp, 144 Wis 2d 188, 423 NW2d 848 (1988) §12.07

Parker v Brown, 317 US 341 (1943) §12.18

Patrick v Burget, 486 US 94 (1988) §12.18

Peace v Weisman, 186 Ga App 697, 368 SE2d 319 (1988) §1.03

Perry v Langstaff, 383 So 2d 1104 (Fla Dist Ct App), *petition denied,* 392 So 2d 1377 (Fla 1980) §11.03

Phillips v Mease Hosp & Clinic, 445 So 2d 1058 (Fla 1984) §2.17

Piper Aircraft Co v Reyno, 454 US 235 (1981) §2.10
Price v Neyland, 115 US App DC 355, 320 F2d 674 (1963) §1.24

R

Reed v Adventist Health Systems/Sunbelt, Inc, 181 Ga App 750, 353 SE2d 523 (1987) §12.08
Rice v Rinaldo, 67 Abs 183, 119 NE2d 657 (Mass 1951) §1.03
Robbins v Jewish Hosp, 663 SW2d 341 (Mo 1981) §12.10
Robinson v Magovern, 521 F Supp 842 (WD Pa 1981) §12.15
Rodriques v Carroll, 510 F Supp 547 (ND Tex 1981) §1.38
Rose v Pfister, 607 SW2d 587 (Tex Ct App 1980) §2.25
Ross v Chatham County Hosp Auth, 184 Ga App 660, 362 SE2d 390 (1987), *revd*, 258 Ga 234, 367 SE2d 793 (1988) §12.08
Rowell v McCune, 188 Ga App 528, 373 SE2d 243 (1988) §2.17
Rule v Lutheran Hosps & Homes of Am, 835 F2d 1250 (1987) §12.14
Runnels v Coleman, No CV187-102, (D Augusta Div 1988) §12.08

S

Salgo v Leland Stanford, Jr, Univ Bd of Trustees, 154 Cal App 560, 317 P2d 170 (1957) §1.23
Schloendorf v Society of NY Hosp, 211 NY 125, 102 NE 92 (1914) §§1.23, 12.03
Silva v Howe, 608 SW2d 840 (Tex Ct App 1980) §2.17
Silva v Providence Hosp, 14 Cal 2d 762, 97 P2d 798 (1939) §12.03
Silverstein, DO v Gwinnett Hosp Auth, No 87-8926 (11th Cir Dec 27, 1988) §12.15
Smith v Dept of Ins, 507 So 2d 1080 (Fla 1987) §1.44
South Carolina Ins Co v James C Greene & Co, 290 SC 171, 348 SE2d 617 (1986) §2.20
Southwest Community Health Servs v Smith, 107 NM 196, 755 P2d 40 (1988) §1.39
Stevens v FAA's Florist, Inc, 169 Ga App 189, 311 SE2d 856 (1983) §2.12
Sywak v O'Connor Hosp, 199 Cal App 3d 423, 244 Cal Rptr 753 (1988) §12.16

T

Terrell v West Paces Ferry Hosp, Inc, 162 Ga App 783, 292 SE2d 433 (1982) §1.25
Texas & Pac RR v Behymer, 189 US 468 (1903) §1.21
Turcotte v Dewitt, 333 Mass 389, 131 NE2d 195 (1955) §1.26

V

Vaughan v Menlove, 3 Bing (NC) 467, 132 Eng Rep 490 (1887) §1.21

W

Walden v Coleman, 105 Ga App 242, 124 SE2d 313 (1962) §2.14
Whitlock v Haj-Murad, Civ Action No 87-1-1476 (Ga 1989) §2.24
Williams v Physicians & Surgeons Community Hosp, 249 Ga 588, 299 SE2d 705 (1982) §2.27

Woodward v Keenan, 79 Mich App 543, 261 NW2d 80 (1977) **§2.08**

Z

Zaklama v Mt Sinai Medical Center, 842 F2d 291 (11th Cir 1988) **§12.18**

Statutes

United States Code

28 USC §2678 **§1.48**
42 USC §§11101-11152 **§1.48**
47 USC §406 **§1.48**

State Statutes

Colo Rev Stat §13-21-102(1)(A) (1986) **§1.27**
Colo Rev Stat §13-21-102(4) (1986) **§1.27**
Ga Code Ann §9-2-61 (1985) **§2.12**
Ga Code Ann §9-11-9.1 (1987) **§10.05**
Ga Code Ann §9-11-9.1(A) (1987) **§2.24**
Ga Code Ann §9-11-56 (1987) **§10.05**
Ga Code Ann §9-10-31 (1983) **§2.09**
Ga Code Ann §24-7-8 (1985) **§3.03**
Ga Code Ann §24-9-40 (1985) **§3.24**
Ga Code Ann §24-10-71 (1985) **§3.03**
Ga Code Ann §31-7-7(A) (1984) **§12.15**
Ga Code Ann §31-7-143 (1983) **§1.39**
Ga Code Ann §51-1-29 (1987) **§12.03**
Ga Code Ann §51-12-5 (1987) **§1.27**
Ga Code Ann §51-12-5.1(E)(2) (1987) **§1.27**
Ga Code Ann §51-12-5.1(F) (1987) **§1.27**
Ga Code Ann §51-12-5.1(G) (1987) **§1.27**
Ga Code Ann §51-12-14 (1981) **§10.04**
Kansas HB 2025, §1(H) (1987) **§1.27**
Okla Stat Ann tit 23, §9(A) (West 1987) **§1.27**

Authorities

A

1 Am Jur 2d *Abatement, Survival and Revival* §§41, 48, 51-68 (1962) **§2.28**

57A Am Jur 2d *Negligence* §305 (1989) **§1.25**

61A Am Jur 2d *Pleadings* §149 (1981) **§2.28**

Ansell, *Trends in Urological Manpower in the United States in 1986*, J Urol 138 (1987) **§4.03**

C

Cambell, Urology (1978) **§4.09**

Curran, *A Further Solution to the Malpractice Problem: Corporate Liability and Risk Management in Hospitals*, 310 New Eng J Med 704 (1984) **§5.32**

G

J. Gillenwater, Adult and Pediatric Urology (1987) **§4.09**

H

M. Hill, H. Rossen, & W. Soggs, Torts for Law School and Bar Examinations (3d ed 1975) **§1.21**

Hospital Corporate Liability: An Effective Solution to Controlling Private Physician Incompetence?, 32 Rutgers L Rev 342 (1979) **§5.32**

M

A. Martin, Hazards of Medication (1971) **§10.01**

P

Peters, *Hospital Malpractice: Eleven Theories of Direct Liability*, 52 Trial 82 (Nov 1988) **§5.32**

1982 Prosser, Cases and Materials on Torts (7th ed 1982) **§1.06**

W. Prosser, Handbook of the Law of Torts (5th ed 1982) **§1.02**

R

Restatement (Second) of Agency (1957) §§**5.32, 12.05, 12.06, 12.07**
Restatement (Second) of Torts (1977) §§**1.26, 1.31, 1.33, 2.28**

S

Shrager, *Screening and Preparing the Medical Negligence Case*, Trial, Aug, 1988 §**2.28**
Socioeconomic Fact Book for Surgery (P. Politser & E. Cunico eds 1988) §**4.03**
T. Stedman, Stedman's Medical Dictionary (1972) §**10.01**
B. Stewart, Operative Urology (1982) §**4.09**
Survey of Urology Practice, Urology Times, Sept, 1988 §**4.07**

T

E. Tanagho & J. McAninch, Smith's General Urology (12th ed 1988) §**4.09**
Trail & Maney, *Jurisdiction, Venue and Choice of Law in Medical Malpractice Litigation*, 7 No 4 J Legal Med 403 (1986) §**2.28**
E. Tuffy, The Visual Display of Quantitative Information (1983) §**11.10**

W

Weiss & Mills, Atlas of Genitourinary Tract Disorders (1988) §**4.09**
E.D. Whitehead, Current Operative Urology (1984) §**4.09**

Y

I. Younger, Ten Commandments of Cross-Examination (National Institute for Trial Advocacy 1975) §**10.16**

Index

A

ABANDONMENT OF PATIENT
  Malpractice considerations
    §§1.03, 1.09
ABBREVIATIONS
  Medical records §3.23
ACCREDITATION COUNCIL FOR GRADUATE MEDICAL EDUCATION (ACGME)
  Urology specialization §4.03
ACETYLCHOLINE
  Physiology §5.19
ADC VAN DISSEL PATTERN
  Medical records §3.07
ADMINISTRATOR
  See HOSPITAL ADMINISTRATOR
ADMITTING AND ATTENDING PHYSICIANS
  Medical records §§3.02, 3.14
ADRENAL GLANDS
  Anatomy §5.03
  Surgical procedures §8.06
AFFIDAVITS
  Defense perspective §11.02
  Malpractice considerations §1.38
  Plaintiff's case, handling §10.05

AFFIDAVITS, *continued*
  Procedures in malpractice
    litigation §§2.06, 2.24
AFFIRMATIVE DEFENSES
  Procedures in malpractice
    litigation. See PROCEDURES
    IN MALPRACTICE
    LITIGATION
AGENCY
  Apparent agency. See
    APPARENT AGENCY
  Hospital liability. See
    HOSPITAL LIABILITY
  Restatement of Agency. See
    RESTATEMENT OF
    AGENCY
ALCOHOL AND DRUG PROBLEMS
  Malpractice considerations
    §§1.08, 1.16
  Physiology §5.26
  Procedures in malpractice
    litigation §§2.04, 2.19
ALLERGIC REACTIONS
  Common urological
    complications §§9.06, 9.07
  Radiology of the urinary tract
    §§7.02, 7.04, 7.06

ALTERED RECORDS
  See LOST OR ALTERED RECORDS

AM ADMIT
  Medical records §3.02

AMBULATORY CENTERS
  Medical records §3.05

AMERICAN ASSOCIATION OF CLINICAL UROLOGISTS (AACU)
  Urology specialization §4.10

AMERICAN BAR ASSOCIATION (ABA)
  Malpractice considerations §1.19

AMERICAN BOARD OF UROLOGY (ABU)
  Urology specialization §§4.03, 4.05, 4.08, 4.10

AMERICAN COLLEGE OF SURGEONS (ACS)
  Urology specialization §4.03

AMERICAN MEDICAL ASSOCIATION (AMA)
  Hospital liability §12.15
  Malpractice considerations §§1.19, 1.20
  Urology specialization §4.04

AMERICAN UROLOGICAL ASSOCIATION (AUA)
  Urology specialization §§4.03, 4.10

ANASTOMOSIS
  See DELIGATION AND ANASTOMOSIS

ANATOMY, PHYSIOLOGY, AND LABORATORY TESTS
  Generally §5.01
  Adrenal glands §5.03
  Impotency
  –generally §5.23
  –drugs §5.26
  –physical causes §5.25
  –psychological causes §5.24
  Kidneys

ANATOMY, PHYSIOLOGY, AND LABORATORY TESTS, *continued*
  –generally §5.04
  –external anatomy §5.06
  –internal anatomy §5.05
  Laboratory tests. See LABORATORY TESTS
  Male reproductive system §5.21
  Micturition, see Urine transport and micturition, this heading
  Nephrology and urology §5.15
  Penis §5.12
  Prostate gland §5.11
  References §5.32
  Retroperitoneum §5.02
  Seminal vesicles §5.14
  Sexual dysfunction
  –generally §5.22
  –other §5.27
  Testicular and spermatic cord structures §5.13
  Urinary storage system
  –generally §5.09
  –urethra §5.10
  Urinary transport system
  –generally §5.07
  –ureter §5.08
  Urine formation §5.16
  Urine transport and micturition
  –generally §5.17
  –bladder §5.19
  –urine transportation §5.18
  –voiding urine §5.20
  Urology, see Nephrology and urology, this heading

ANEMIA
  Laboratory tests §5.30

ANESTHESIOLOGISTS AND ANESTHETISTS
  Anatomy §5.11
  Common urological complications §§9.04, 9.14, 9.15
  Hospital liability §§12.18, 12.19
  Medical records §3.12
  Surgical procedures §§8.16, 8.20

ANESTHESIOLOGISTS AND
ANESTHETISTS, *continued*
   Urogenital tract evaluation and treatment §§6.02, 6.05, 6.10
ANGIOGRAPHY
   Radiology of the urinary tract §7.10
ANNUITIES
   Malpractice considerations §1.44
   Procedures in malpractice litigation §2.27
ANTEGRADE PYELOGRAPHY
   Radiology of the urinary tract §7.05
ANTIBIOTICS
   Common urological complications §§9.05, 9.07, 9.10, 9.12
   Defense perspective §11.06
   Laboratory tests §5.29
   Urogenital tract evaluation and treatment §6.04
"ANTI-DUMPING" LAW
   See CONSOLIDATED OMNIBUS BUDGET RECONCILIATION ACT (COBRA)
ANTITRUST LAW
   Malpractice considerations §1.40
APPARENT AGENCY
   Hospital liability §§12.07, 12.15
APPORTIONMENT
   Malpractice considerations §§1.27, 1.32, 1.46
ARBITRATION
   Defense perspective §11.02
ASSAULT AND BATTERY
   Defense perspective app 11-A
   Malpractice considerations §1.23
   Medical records §3.17
ASSUMPTION OF THE RISK
   Malpractice considerations §1.33
   Procedures in malpractice litigation §§2.19, 2.23

ATHEROSCLEROSIS
   Physiology §5.25
ATTENDING PHYSICIAN
   See ADMITTING AND ATTENDING PHYSICIANS
ATTORNEYS AND ATTORNEY'S FEES
   Common urological complications §§9.01, 9.04, 9.05, 9.10, 9.12
   Defense perspective, generally this heading
   Hospital liability §§12.13, 12.16, 12.18
   Malpractice considerations §§1.01, 1.06-1.08, 1.12, 1.17-1.19, 1.21, 1.24, 1.28, 1.35, 1.40, 1.43
   Medical records §§3.02, 3.08
   Physician and attorney relationships. See PHYSICIAN AND ATTORNEY RELATIONSHIPS
   Plaintiff's case, handling §§10.01-10.04, 10.11-10.17
   Procedures in malpractice litigation §§2.01, 2.02, 2.04-2.06, 2.09, 2.12, 2.17, 2.24-2.27
   Radiology of the urinary tract §§7.02, 7.11
   Surgical procedures §§8.04, 8.15, 8.16
   Urology specialization §§4.03, 4.09
AUTOPSY REPORTS
   Medical records §3.03
AZOSPERMIA
   Radiology of the urinary tract §7.09

356 INDEX

B

BANKRUPTCY
Procedures in malpractice litigation §2.19
BATTERY
See ASSAULT AND BATTERY
BED WETTING
See ENURESIS
BELL-CLAPPER DEFORMITY
Surgical procedures §8.19
BENEFACTORS
Hospital liability §12.03
BENEFITS
See SOCIAL SECURITY DISABILITY BENEFITS
BIAS
See PREJUDICE
BILLS
Attorneys and attorney's fees. See ATTORNEYS AND ATTORNEY'S FEES
Medical bills. See MEDICAL BILLS
BIOPSY
Common urological complications §9.15
Physiology §5.15
Surgical procedures §8.05
Urogenital tract evaluation and treatment §§6.05, 6.10
BIOPSY INSTRUMENTS
Urogenital tract evaluation and treatment §§6.05, 6.10
BIRTH DEFECTS
Common urological complications §9.12
BLADDER
Anatomy §§5.07-5.11, 5.14
Common urological complications §§9.02, 9.09, 9.13-9.15
Defense perspective §11.06
Laboratory tests §5.29

BLADDER, *continued*
Physiology §§5.17-5.20, 5.25
Radiology of the urinary tract §§7.04, 7.06-7.08 app 7-A
Surgical procedures §§8.02, 8.08-8.13, 8.20
Urogenital tract evaluation and treatment §§6.02, 6.03, 6.05-6.07, 6.09, 6.10
BLOOD TRANSFUSIONS
Medical records §§3.05, 3.09
BLOOD UREA NITROGEN (BUN)
Laboratory tests §5.31
BOARD CERTIFICATION
Defense perspective §11.15
Urology specialization. See UROLOGY SPECIALIZATION
BOARD OF TRUSTEES
Hospital liability §12.11
BOARI FLAP
Surgical procedures §8.08
BOWEL
Anatomy §5.06
Common urological complications §9.08
Radiology of the urinary tract §7.07
Surgical procedures §8.12
BREACH OF CONTRACT
Defense perspective app 11-A
BREACH OF DUTY
Defense perspective §11.03
Malpractice considerations §1.04
Procedures in malpractice litigation §2.03
BURDEN OF PROOF
Defense perspective §§11.02, 11.03, 11.07, 11.11, 11.12
Hospital liability §§12.16, 12.18
Malpractice considerations §§1.24, 1.25
Plaintiff's case, handling §§10.01, 10.17

INDEX

BYLAWS
Hospital liability §§12.11, 12.15, 12.17

C

CALCULI
See RENAL STONES

CANCER
Common urological complications §9.10
Defense perspective §11.06
Malignancies. See MALIGNANCIES
Procedures in malpractice litigation §2.03
Radiology of the urinary tract §§7.02, 7.03, 7.07, 7.11
Surgical procedures §§8.06, 8.12, 8.14, 8.18
Urogenital tract evaluation and treatment §§6.03, 6.06

CAPSULE
Anatomy §§5.04, 5.06, 5.09, 5.11
Physiology §§5.15, 5.16
Surgical procedures §8.03

CARE
See STANDARD OF CARE

CASTS
Laboratory tests §5.29

CATHETERS
Foley catheters. See FOLEY CATHETERS
Ureteral catheters. See URETERAL CATHETERS
Urethral catheters. See URETHRAL CATHETERS

CAUSATION
Defense perspective §§11.03, 11.07, 11.09, 11.11, 11.12, 11.15 app 11-B
Malpractice considerations §1.05
Procedures in malpractice litigation §§2.02, 2.03

CAUSE OF ACTION
Common urological complications §§9.01, 9.07, 9.09-9.12, 9.15
Malpractice considerations §§1.02, 1.05-1.07, 1.18, 1.22, 1.37, 1.38
Medical records §§3.02, 3.22
Procedures in malpractice litigation §§2.08, 2.13, 2.14, 2.16, 2.17, 2.23
Radiology of the urinary tract §7.02
Surgical procedures §§8.07, 8.10, 8.12, 8.14, 8.16

CERTIFIED REGISTERED NURSE ANESTHETIST (CRNA)
Medical records §3.12

CHARTS
See MEDICAL RECORDS

CHEMOTHERAPY
Common urological complications §9.10
Surgical procedures §§8.14, 8.18

CHIEF COMPLAINT (CC)
Medical records §3.05

CHILDREN
Infants. See INFANTS
Minors. See MINORS

CHIROPRACTORS
Defense perspective app 11-A

CHOLINESTERASE
Physiology §5.19

CIRCUMCISIONS
Anatomy §5.12
Surgical procedures §8.15

CLAIMS
See LIQUIDATED CLAIMS

CLOSING ARGUMENT
Defense perspective §11.16

CODE OF ETHICS
Malpractice considerations §1.20

358   INDEX

COLLATERAL SOURCE
   Malpractice considerations §1.31
   Procedures in malpractice litigation §2.04
COLON
   Anatomy §5.06
COLOSTOMIES
   Common urological complications §9.13
COMMUNICATION
   Malpractice considerations §1.07
   Medical records §§3.01, 3.15
COMPARATIVE NEGLIGENCE
   Malpractice considerations §1.32
COMPENSATORY DAMAGES
   Hospital liability §12.18
   Malpractice considerations §§1.06, 1.26, 1.27, 1.29
COMPLAINT
   Plaintiff's case, handling §10.05
COMPLICATIONS
   See UROLOGICAL COMPLICATIONS, COMMON
COMPROMISE AND SETTLEMENT
   Procedures in malpractice litigation. See PROCEDURES IN MALPRACTICE LITIGATION
COMPUTERIZED TOMOGRAPHY (CT)
   Radiology of the urinary tract §7.13 app 7-A
CONCEALMENT
   Procedures in malpractice litigation §§2.15-2.17
CONFERENCES
   Malpractice considerations §1.19
CONGENITAL UROLOGICAL PROBLEMS
   Urology specialization §4.01
CONJUGAL RIGHTS
   Procedures in malpractice litigation §2.14
CONSENT
   See MUTUAL CONSENT
CONSENT FORMS
   See HOSPITAL CONSENT FORMS
CONSOLIDATED OMNIBUS BUDGET RECONCILIATION ACT (COBRA)
   Hospital liability §12.20
CONSORTIUM
   See LOSS OF CONSORTIUM
CONTINUING MEDICAL EDUCATION (CME)
   Urology specialization §4.06
CORPORATE PRACTICE OF MEDICINE
   Hospital liability. See HOSPITAL LIABILITY
CORPORATIONS
   Hospital liability §12.11
COUNCIL OF MEDICAL SPECIALTY SOCIETY (CMSS)
   Urology specialization §4.03
COUNTERSUITS
   Malpractice considerations §1.38
COURT APPEARANCES
   Malpractice considerations §1.19
COURT ORDERS
   Procedures in malpractice litigation §2.03
COWPER'S GLANDS
   Anatomy §5.10
   Physiology §5.21
CREATININE
   Laboratory tests §5.31
CREDENTIALING
   Hospital liability §12.14
CREDIBILITY OF PHYSICIAN
   Defense perspective §11.14
   Medical records §3.02
CROSS-EXAMINATION
   Defense perspective §11.14
   Hospital liability §12.15

CROSS-EXAMINATION, *continued*
  Plaintiff's case, handling §10.16
CURRENT PROCEDURAL
    TERMINOLOGY (CPT)
    MANUAL
  Medical records §3.04
CYSTECTOMY AND ILEAL
    CONDUIT
  Common urological
    complications §9.15
  Surgical procedures §8.12
CYSTOGRAPHY
  Radiology of the urinary tract
    §7.06 app 7-A
CYSTOSCOPES
  Common urological
    complications §§9.02-9.04,
    9.07, 9.08, 9.10, 9.14, 9.15
  Radiology of the urinary tract
    §7.04
  Surgical procedures §§8.10, 8.13,
    8.20
  Urogenital tract evaluation and
    treatment §§6.05, 6.10
  Urology specialization §4.01
CYSTOSTOMY
  Common urological
    complications §9.09
  Urogenital tract evaluation and
    treatment §6.02
CYSTOURETHROSCOPES
  Urogenital tract evaluation and
    treatment §6.05

D

DAMAGES
  Common urological
    complications §9.14
  Compensatory damages. See
    COMPENSATORY
    DAMAGES

DAMAGES, *continued*
  Defense perspective §§11.03,
    11.07, 11.09, 11.11, 11.14 app
    11-A, 11-B
  Hospital liability §§12.03, 12.09
  Injuries. See INJURIES
  Malpractice considerations. See
    MALPRACTICE
    CONSIDERATIONS
  Medical records §3.02
  Nominal damages. See
    NOMINAL DAMAGES
  Pecuniary damages. See
    PECUNIARY DAMAGES
  Plaintiff's case, handling §§10.03,
    10.04, 10.07
  Procedures in malpractice
    litigation §2.03
  Property damages. See
    PROPERTY DAMAGES
  Punitive damages. See
    PUNITIVE DAMAGES
DATA BANK INFORMATION
  Malpractice considerations §1.40
DATE OF DISCOVERY
  Plaintiff's case, handling of. See
    PLAINTIFF'S CASE,
    HANDLING OF
  Procedures in malpractice
    litigation §§2.15-2.18
DEATH
  Common urological
    complications §§9.04, 9.06
  Disability. See DISABILITY
  Malpractice considerations
    §§1.26, 1.39
  Medical records §3.14
  Wrongful death and survival.
    See WRONGFUL DEATH
    AND SURVIVAL
DEFECTS
  See BIRTH DEFECTS
DEFENDANT PHYSICIANS
  Malpractice considerations §1.18

DEFENDANTS
  Procedures in malpractice litigation §2.05

DEFENSE ON LAW
  Defense perspective. See DEFENSE PERSPECTIVE

DEFENSE PERSPECTIVE
  Generally §§11.01, 11.17
  Case summary chart app 11-B
  Defense on law
  –generally §11.02
  –substantive technicalities §11.03
  Depositions. See DEPOSITIONS
  Discovery. See DISCOVERY
  Model interrogatories app 11-A
  Pre-trial phase
  –case evaluation §11.09
  –exhibit preparation §11.10
  –theme of the defense, establishment of §11.11
  Trial
  –closing argument §11.16
  –cross-examination §11.14
  –direct examination §11.15
  –opening statement §11.13
  –rejecting jury §11.12

DEFENSES, PROCEDURAL
  Procedures in malpractice litigation §2.24

DELIGATION AND ANASTOMOSIS
  Surgical procedures §8.08

DEMOGRAPHICS AND SOCIOECONOMICS
  Procedures in malpractice litigation §2.02
  Urology specialization §4.07

DEPOSITIONS
  Discovery. See DISCOVERY
  Plaintiff's case, handling of. See PLAINTIFF'S CASE, HANDLING OF
  Procedures in malpractice litigation §2.05

DERIVATIVE ACTIONS
  Procedures in malpractice litigation §2.14

DETORSION AND ORCHIPEXY
  Common urological complications §9.11
  Surgical procedures §8.19

DIABETES MELLITUS
  Laboratory tests §5.29
  Physiology §5.25

DIALYSIS
  Urology specialization §§4.01, 4.03

DIETARY THERAPY
  Medical records §3.15

DIFFERENTIAL COUNT
  Laboratory tests §5.30

DIP STICKS
  Laboratory tests §5.29

DIRECT EXAMINATION
  Defense perspective §11.15
  Plaintiff's case, handling §10.15

DISABILITY
  Defense perspective app 11-A
  Malpractice considerations §1.28
  Medical records §3.15
  Procedures in malpractice litigation §2.17

DISCHARGE SUMMARY
  Medical records §§3.02, 3.16

DISCLOSURE, DUTY OF
  Malpractice considerations §1.23

DISCOVERY
  Date of discovery. See DATE OF DISCOVERY
  Defense perspective, marshalling the facts §11.04
  Depositions
  –generally §11.05
  –defendant §11.07
  –plaintiff §11.06
  –plaintiff's expert §11.08

INDEX 361

DISCOVERY, *continued*
  Plaintiff's case, handling of. See PLAINTIFF'S CASE, HANDLING OF
DISFIGUREMENT
  Defense perspective §11.01
DISPOSITION
  Medical records §3.05
DISTRESS
  See EMOTIONAL DISTRESS
DOCUMENTARY EVIDENCE
  Defense perspective §§11.14, 11.15
DRUG PROBLEMS
  See ALCOHOL AND DRUG PROBLEMS
DUTY
  Breach of duty. See BREACH OF DUTY
  Defense perspective §11.03
  Malpractice considerations §1.03
  Procedures in malpractice litigation §2.03
DYES
  See IODINE
DYSFUNCTION
  See SEXUAL DYSFUNCTION

E

EDEMA
  Common urological complications §9.09
  Surgical procedures §8.08
EDUCATIONAL COUNCIL FOR FOREIGN MEDICAL GRADUATES (ECFMG)
  Urology specialization §4.04
EJACULATION
  Physiology §§5.21, 5.23, 5.24, 5.26
  Surgical procedures §8.16
EJACULATORY DUCTS
  Anatomy §5.14

EJACULATORY DUCTS, *continued*
  Radiology of the urinary tract §7.09
ELECTROCAUTERY
  Anatomy §5.04
  Common urological complications §9.12
ELECTROENCEPHALOGRAPH (EEG)
  Physiology §5.24
ELEEMOSYNARY INSTITUTIONS
  Hospital liability §§12.02, 12.03
ELEMENTS OF MALPRACTICE ACTION
  Malpractice considerations. See MALPRACTICE CONSIDERATIONS
EMBOLIZATION
  Anatomy §5.04
EMOTIONAL DISTRESS
  Common urological complications §9.14
  Malpractice considerations §§1.26, 1.30
  Medical records §3.25
  Physiology §§5.23, 5.24
  Procedures in malpractice litigation §§2.14, 2.25
EMPLOYMENT
  Defense perspective §§11.04, 11.06
  Malpractice considerations §1.26
  Medical records §3.04
ENDOCRINE GLANDS
  Anatomy §5.03
ENDOSCOPES
  See CYSTOSCOPES
ENDOSCOPIC URETHROPEXY
  See STAMEY PROCEDURE
ENEMAS
  Urogenital tract evaluation and treatment §6.10

ENTEROSTOMAL THERAPY
  Medical records §3.15
ENURESIS
  Physiology §5.19
EPIDIDYMIS
  Anatomy §5.13
  Common urological
    complications §9.05
  Malpractice considerations §1.24
  Physiology §5.21
  Radiology of the urinary tract
    §7.12
  Surgical procedures §8.19
EPIDIDYMITIS
  Common urological
    complications §9.12
ERECTION
  Common urological
    complications §9.09
  Physiology §§5.23-5.25, 5.27
  Surgical procedures §8.17
  Urogenital tract evaluation and
    treatment §6.11
ESTOPPEL
  Procedures in malpractice
    litigation §2.19
ETHICS
  See CODE OF ETHICS
EVALUATIONS
  Plaintiff's case, handling §10.03
EVIDENCE
  Defense perspective §§11.03,
    11.04, 11.06, 11.09-11.16 app
    11-B
  Documentary evidence. See
    DOCUMENTARY EVIDENCE
  Hospital liability §12.16
  Malpractice considerations
    §§1.03, 1.04, 1.06, 1.19, 1.24,
    1.25, 1.27, 1.31, 1.39, 1.42
  Medical records §§3.01, 3.03, 3.25
  Plaintiff's case, handling §§10.01,
    10.05, 10.14-10.17

EVIDENCE, *continued*
  Procedures in malpractice
    litigation §§2.02, 2,17, 2.20,
    2.26
  Radiology of the urinary tract
    §§7.06, 7.08
  Urology specialization §4.09
EXAMINATIONS
  See PHYSICAL
    EXAMINATIONS
EXCRETORY UROGRAPHY
  Radiology of the urinary tract
    §7.02
EXEMPLARY DAMAGES
  See PUNITIVE DAMAGES
EXHIBITS
  Defense perspective §11.10
EXOCRINE GLANDS
  Anatomy §5.03
EXPERTS
  See WITNESSES, EXPERT
EXTRACORPOREAL
    SHOCKWAVE
    LITHOTRIPSY (ESWL)
  Surgical procedures §8.04

F

FAMILY HISTORY (FH)
  Medical records §3.05
FEDERAL RULES OF CIVIL
    PROCEDURE
  Defense perspective §§11.02,
    11.04
  Plaintiff's case, handling §10.05
FEDERAL RULES OF EVIDENCE
  Plaintiff's case, handling §§10.15,
    10.16
FEDERAL TORT CLAIMS ACT
  Hospital liability §12.03
  Malpractice considerations §1.43
FEDERATION LICENSING
    EXAMINATION (FLEX)
  Urology specialization §4.04

FELLOWSHIP PROGRAMS
  Urology specialization §4.03
FERTILIZATION
  Physiology §5.21
FILTRATION
  Physiology §5.16
  Ultrafiltration. See
    ULTRAFILTRATION
FINAL NOTATION
  See IMPRESSION
FOLEY CATHETERS
  Common urological
    complications §§9.03, 9.09,
    9.10, 9.14, 9.15
  Surgical procedures §§8.10, 8.20
  Urogenital tract evaluation and
    treatment §§6.02, 6.08
FOLLICLE STIMULATING
    HORMONE (FSH)
  Physiology §5.21
FOREIGN MEDICAL GRADUATE
    (FMG)
  Educational Council for Foreign
    Medical Graduates (ECFMG).
    See EDUCATIONAL
    COUNCIL FOR FOREIGN
    MEDICAL GRADUATES
    (ECFMG)
  Urology specialization §4.03
FRAUD
  Malpractice considerations
    §§1.20, 1.39
  Procedures in malpractice
    litigation §§2.15, 2.17
FUNERAL EXPENSES
  Malpractice considerations §1.26

G

GENERAL BUSINESS
    CORPORATION ACT
  Hospital liability §12.11
GENITALIA
  Medical records §3.05

GENITALIA, *continued*
  Surgical procedures §8.15
  Urology specialization §4.10
GENITOURINARY TRACT
  Radiology of the urinary tract
    §7.02
GLOMERULAR FILTRATION
    RATE (GFR)
  Physiology §5.16
GLOSSARY
  Urology specialization §4.02
GLYCINE
  Surgical procedures §8.20
GOMCO CLAMP
  Surgical procedures §8.15
GONORRHEA
  Urogenital tract evaluation and
    treatment §6.04
GOOD FAITH
  Hospital liability §§12.09, 12.14
GOVERNMENT
  Medical records §3.01
GOVERNMENTAL FUNCTION
  Hospital liability §12.03
GYNECOLOGISTS
  Common urological
    complications §§9.02, 9.11,
    9.14

H

HEALTH CARE QUALITY
    IMPROVEMENT ACT OF
    1986
  Malpractice considerations §1.40
HEARSAY RULES
  Medical records §3.03
HEMATOMAS
  Anatomy §5.04
  Common urological
    complications §9.12

HEMOGRAMS
  Laboratory tests. See
    LABORATORY TESTS
HEMOSTASIS
  Anatomy §§5.04, 5.11
  Surgical procedures §8.15
HERNIAS
  Common urological
    complications §9.11
HERNIORRAPHY
  Common urological
    complications §9.11
HIPPOCRATIC OATH, THE
  Malpractice considerations §1.23
  Surgical procedures §8.04
"HIRED GUNS"
  Plaintiff's case, handling §10.03
HISTORY OF PRESENT ILLNESS
    (HPI)
  Medical records §3.05
"HOLD HARMLESS CLAUSE"
  Malpractice considerations §1.36
HOME CARE
  Medical records §3.05
HOMEOSTASIS
  Physiology §5.16
HOSPICE CARE
  Medical records §3.05
HOSPITAL ADMINISTRATOR
  Hospital liability §12.11
HOSPITAL CONSENT FORMS
  Defense perspective §§11.06,
    11.15
  Medical records §3.17
HOSPITAL LIABILITY
  Generally §12.01
  Agency
  –generally §12.04
  –agency by necessity §12.09
  –apparent agency §12.07
  –borrowed servant §12.08
  –principal and agent §12.05
  –respondeat superior §12.06

HOSPITAL LIABILITY, *continued*
  Consolidated Omnibus Budget
    Reconciliation Act (COBRA)
    §12.20
  Corporate practice of medicine
  –generally §12.13
  –antitrust §12.18
  –fairness §12.17
  –grounds, buildings, and vendors
    §12.19
  –independent contractors §12.15
  –physician credentialing §12.14
  –substantial evidence test §12.16
  Corporations §12.11
  Expert witness §12.10
  Immunity
  –generally §12.02
  –charitable immunity §12.03
  Joint Commission on
    Accreditation of Healthcare
    Organizations (JCAHO) §12.12
HOSPITAL RECORDS
  Medical records. See MEDICAL
    RECORDS
HUMAN RESOURCES, STATE
    DEPARTMENT OF
  Malpractice considerations §1.03
HUSBAND AND WIFE
  Malpractice considerations §1.03
  Procedures in malpractice
    litigation §2.14
HYPERTENSION
  Radiology of the urinary tract
    §7.11
  Surgical procedures §8.06
HYPONATREMIA
  Common urological
    complications §9.04
  Surgical procedures §8.20
HYSTERECTOMIES
  Common urological
    complications §9.02

I

IATROGENIC
  Plaintiff's case, handling §10.01
ILEAL CONDUIT
  See CYSTECTOMY AND ILEAL CONDUIT
ILLUSTRATIONS
  Urogenital tract evaluation and treatment app 6-A
IMMUNITY
  Hospital liability. See HOSPITAL LIABILITY
  Sovereign immunity. See SOVEREIGN IMMUNITY
"IMPACT RULE"
  See "ZONE OF PHYSICAL DANGER"
IMPEACHMENT
  Defense perspective §§11.07, 11.08, 11.14
  Medical records §§3.02, 3.05
  Plaintiff's case, handling §10.16
  Urology specialization §§4.05, 4.09
IMPLIED WAIVER THEORY
  Hospital liability §12.03
IMPOTENCY
  Anatomy, physiology, and laboratory tests. See ANATOMY, PHYSIOLOGY, AND LABORATORY TESTS
  Common urological complications §§9.09, 9.15
  Physiology §§5.22-5.26
  Surgical procedures §§8.14, 8.17
  Urogenital tract evaluation and treatment §6.11
  Urology specialization §4.01
IMPRESSION
  Medical records §3.05
IMPRISONMENT
  Procedures in malpractice litigation §2.17

INCOME
  See LOSS OF INCOME
INCONTINENCE AND RETENTION
  Common urological complications §§9.03, 9.15
  Defense perspective §11.01
  Physiology §5.17
INFANTS
  Physiology §5.20
INFECTIONS
  Common urological complications §§9.07, 9.09, 9.10, 9.12, 9.14, 9.15
  Defense perspective §11.06
  Laboratory tests §§5.29, 5.30
  Surgical procedures §§8.02, 8.03, 8.06, 8.10, 8.17
  Urogenital tract evaluation and treatment §6.10
INFERTILITY
  Physiology §5.21
  Urology specialization §§4.01, 4.09
INFORMED CONSENT
  Malpractice considerations §1.23
  Medical records §3.17
INITIAL DISCOVERY
  Plaintiff's case, handling of. See PLAINTIFF'S CASE, HANDLING OF
INJURIES
  Anatomy §§5.04, 5.14
  Common urological complications, generally this heading
  Damages. See DAMAGES
  Defense perspective §§11.01, 11.03, 11.06, 11.07, 11.11, 11.15 app 11-A
  Hospital liability §§12.03, 12.05-12.10, 12.19
  Legal injuries. See LEGAL INJURIES

366 INDEX

INJURIES, *continued*
  Malpractice considerations
    §§1.02, 1.03, 1.05, 1.06, 1.12,
    1.18, 1.25-1.27, 1.32, 1.34,
    1.36-1.38, 1.45, 1.46
  Physiology §5.25
  Plaintiff's case, handling §§10.01,
    10.03, 10.05, 10.14, 10.15
  Procedures in malpractice
    litigation §§2.02-2.04, 2.13,
    2.16, 2.17, 2.20-2.23, 2.25, 2.27
  Radiology of the urinary tract
    §§7.06, 7.10
  Surgical procedures §§8.06, 8.08,
    8.13, 8.15
INPATIENT HOSPITALIZATION
  Medical records §3.02
INSTRUMENTS USED IN
    EVALUATION AND
    TREATMENT OF THE
    UROGENITAL TRACT
  Generally §6.01
  Biopsy instruments §6.10
  Cystoscopic instruments §6.05
  Illustrations app 6-A
  Lithotrites §6.07
  Penile prostheses §6.11
  Resectoscopes §6.06
  Stone baskets and ureteroscopes
    §6.09
  Ureteral catheters §6.03
  Urethral catheters §6.02
  Urethral sounds §6.04
  Urethrotomes §6.08
INSURANCE
  Defense perspective §11.04 app
    11-A
  Hospital liability §12.06
  Malpractice considerations
    §§1.30, 1.41-1.43, 1.45
  Medical records §§3.04, 3.16, 3.25
  Payments. See PAYMENTS
  Plaintiff's case, handling §§10.01,
    10.02, 10.04, 10.07, 10.09
  Procedures in malpractice
    litigation §§2.08, 2.27

INTERCOURSE, SEXUAL
  See SEXUAL ACTIVITY
INTERNAL REVENUE SERVICE
    (IRS)
  Procedures in malpractice
    litigation §2.27
INTERNATIONAL
    CLASSIFICATION OF
    DISEASES (ICD) MANUAL
  Medical records §3.04
INTERNISTS
  Anatomy §5.01
  Defense perspective §11.15
  Hospital liability §12.06
  Laboratory tests §5.28
  Medical records §3.02
  Physiology §5.15
  Urogenital tract evaluation and
    treatment §6.01
  Urology specialization §4.03
INTERROGATORIES
  Defense perspective. See
    DEFENSE PERSPECTIVE
  Plaintiff's case, handling of. See
    PLAINTIFF'S CASE,
    HANDLING OF
  Procedures in malpractice
    litigation §2.05
INTERVIEWS
  Procedures in malpractice
    litigation §2.02
INTRAUTERINE DEVICE (IUD)
  Procedures in malpractice
    litigation §2.18
INTRAVENOUS PYELOGRAPHY
    (IVP)
  Common urological
    complications §§9.06, 9.08,
    9.10
  Radiology of the urinary tract
    §§7.02, 7.03 app 7-A
  Urology specialization §4.01
INVOICES
  Plaintiff's case, handling §10.13

INDEX

IODINE
  Common urological complications §9.06
  Radiology of the urinary tract §§7.02, 7.06-7.09, 7.11
ISCHEMIA
  Common urological complications §9.11

J

JOINT AND SEVERAL LIABILITY
  Malpractice considerations. See MALPRACTICE CONSIDERATIONS
JOINT COMMISSION ON ACCREDITATION OF HEALTHCARE ORGANIZATIONS (JCAHO)
  Hospital liability §12.12
  Medical records §§3.01, 3.03, 3.05, 3.15
JOURNAL OF UROLOGY
  Urology specialization §4.08
JOURNALS
  See TEXTS AND JOURNALS
JUDGES AND JURIES
  Common urological complications §§9.03, 9.06, 9.08, 9.11, 9.12
  Defense perspective §§11.01, 11.04, 11.08-11.15
  Hospital liability §§12.13, 12.15
  Malpractice considerations §§1.03, 1.06, 1.12, 1.24, 1.25, 1.27-1.29, 1.31, 1.39-1.42, 1.44, 1.47
  Medical records §3.25
  Plaintiff's case, handling §§10.01, 10.03, 10.05, 10.14-10.17
  Procedures in malpractice litigation §§2.04, 2.09, 2.12, 2.25, 2.27

K

KIDNEYS
  Anatomy, physiology, and laboratory tests. See ANATOMY, PHYSIOLOGY, AND LABORATORY TESTS
  Common urological complications §§9.06-9.08, 9.10
  Radiology of the urinary tract §§7.01-7.03, 7.05, 7.10-7.12
  Surgical procedures §§8.02-8.06, 8.09
  Urogenital tract evaluation and treatment §6.03
KIDNEY STONES
  See RENAL STONES

L

LABORATORY TESTS
  Hemograms
  –generally §5.30
  –chemical analysis of blood §5.31
  Overview §5.28
  Urinalysis §5.29
LAPAROTOMY
  Common urological complications §9.07
LASER
  Urogenital tract evaluation and treatment §6.07
LAST CLEAR CHANCE DOCTRINE
  Malpractice considerations §1.32
LAWSUITS, REASONS BEHIND
  Malpractice considerations. See MALPRACTICE CONSIDERATIONS
LAWYERS
  See ATTORNEYS AND ATTORNEY'S FEES
LEGAL INJURIES
  Malpractice considerations §1.26

LEYDIG CELLS
  Physiology §5.21
LIABILITY
  Hospital liability. See
    HOSPITAL LIABILITY
  Joint and several liability. See
    JOINT AND SEVERAL
    LIABILITY
  Malpractice considerations
    §§1.03, 1.14, 1.23, 1.24, 1.27,
    1.32, 1.34, 1.37, 1.40, 1.41, 1.46
  Plaintiff's case, handling
    §§10.01-10.05, 10.09
  Procedures in malpractice
    litigation §§2.02, 2.03, 2.20,
    2.24
  Products liability. See
    PRODUCTS LIABILITY
  Vicarious liability. See
    VICARIOUS LIABILITY
LIAISON COMMITTEE ON
    MEDICAL EDUCATION
    (LCME)
  Urology specialization §4.03
LIBRARIAN
  Medical records §§3.03, 3.04
LICENSES
  Hospital liability §12.13
  Malpractice considerations
    §§1.16, 1.39
  Medical records §3.01
  Urology specialization §4.04
LIQUIDATED CLAIMS
  Malpractice considerations §1.29
LITHOTRIPSY
  Common urological
    complications §9.08
  Extracorporeal shockwave
    lithotripsy (ESWL). See
    EXTRACORPOREAL
    SHOCKWAVE
    LITHOTRIPSY (ESWL)
  Surgical procedures §8.04
  Urology specialization §4.01

LITHOTRITES
  Urogenital tract evaluation and
    treatment §6.07
LIVER
  Common urological
    complications §9.07
LOCALITY RULES
  Malpractice considerations §1.03
LOOPOGRAM
  Radiology of the urinary tract
    §7.07
LOSS OF CONSORTIUM
  Procedures in malpractice
    litigation §2.14
LOSS OF INCOME
  Defense perspective §11.14 app
    11-A, 11-B
  Procedures in malpractice
    litigation §2.27
LOST OR ALTERED RECORDS
  Medical records §3.25
LOW-SALT SYNDROME
  See HYPONATREMIA

M

MACRODANTIN
  Common urological
    complications §9.07
MALE REPRODUCTIVE SYSTEM
  Physiology §5.21
MALIGNANCIES
  Common urological
    complications §9.15
  Laboratory tests §5.31
  Physiology §§5.26, 5.27
  Surgical procedures §8.06
MALPRACTICE
    CONSIDERATIONS
  Generally §1.01
  Assumption of the risk §1.33
  Burden of proof §1.24
  Code of ethics §1.20
  Collateral source §1.31

MALPRACTICE CONSIDERATIONS, *continued*
  Common urological
    complications §§9.01, 9.08
  Comparative negligence §1.32
  Countersuits §1.38
  Damages
  –generally §1.26
  –categories §1.27
  –pain and suffering §1.28
  –pre- and post-judgment interest §1.29
  Defense perspective, generally this heading
  Elements of action
  –generally §1.02
  –breach of duty §1.04
  –causation §1.05
  –damages §1.06
  –duty §1.03
  Health Care Quality Improvement Act of 1986 §1.40
  Informed consent §1.23
  Joint and several liability
  –generally §1.34
  –contribution §1.35
  –indemnity §1.36
  –tort reform, see Tort reform, this heading
  Laboratory tests §5.31
  Lawsuits, reasons behind
  –generally §1.07
  –abandonment §1.09
  –attorneys §1.17
  –egregious conduct §1.11
  –failure to refer §1.10
  –incompetent doctors §1.08
  –litigious society §1.12
  –organized medicine §1.16
  –patients' expectations §1.13
  –patients' rights §1.15
  –technological failures §1.14
  Medical records §§3.01, 3.22
  Negligent infliction of emotional distress §1.30

MALPRACTICE CONSIDERATIONS, *continued*
  Peer review §1.39
  Physician and attorney relationships
  –generally §1.18
  –interprofessional relationships, statement on §1.19
  Plaintiff's case, handling §§10.01, 10.03, 10.05
  Procedures in malpractice litigation. See PROCEDURES IN MALPRACTICE LITIGATION
  Radiology of the urinary tract §§7.02, 7.06
  References §1.48
  Releases §1.37
  Res ipsa loquitur §1.25
  Several liability, see Joint and several liability, this heading
  Standard of care
  –generally §1.21
  –substandard care, reasons for §1.22
  Surgical procedures §§8.15, 8.19
  Tort reform
  –generally §1.41
  –attorney's fees §1.43
  –collateral source §1.42
  –joint and several liability §1.46
  –limitation of awards §1.44
  –pre-screening panels and arbitration §1.47
  –statutes of limitations §1.45
  Urology specialization §4.01

MANAGED CARE ORGANIZATIONS
  Medical records §3.05

MARRIED PERSONS
  See HUSBAND AND WIFE

MARSHALL-MARCHETTI-KRANTZ PROCEDURE (MMK)
  Common urological complications §9.14

MARSHALL-MARCHETTI-
    KRANTZ PROCEDURE
    (MMK), continued
  Surgical procedures §8.10
MEDIA EXPOSURE
  Malpractice considerations
      §§1.07, 1.12
MEDICAL BILLS
  Defense perspective §11.14
MEDICAL LITERATURE
    ANALYSIS AND
    RETRIEVAL SYSTEM
    (MEDLARS)
  Urology specialization §4.09
MEDICAL RECORDS
  Abbreviations §3.23
  Altered records, see Lost or
      altered records, this heading
  Defense perspective §§11.04,
      11.06, 11.10, 11.15
  Function §3.01
  Hospital records
  –generally §3.02
  –admission note, history, and
      physical §3.05
  –ancillary records §3.15
  –anesthesia record §3.12
  –certified copies §3.03
  –circulating nurse's records §3.19
  –consent forms §3.17
  –consultation notes §3.14
  –discharge summary §3.16
  –doctor's orders §3.07
  –emergency room records §3.22
  –graphic sheet §3.18
  –laboratory data §3.09
  –medication sheets §3.21
  –nurses' notes §3.08
  –operative notes §3.11
  –pathology report §3.20
  –patient information sheet §3.04
  –progress notes §3.06
  –recovery room record §3.13
  –x-ray data §3.10
  Lost or altered records §3.25

MEDICAL RECORDS, continued
  Office records §3.24
  Plaintiff's case, handling §§10.03,
      10.13
  Sample forms app 3-A
MEDICAL REPORTS
  Malpractice considerations §1.19
MENTAL HEALTH
  Medical records §3.05
MICROSCOPIC ANALYSIS
  Laboratory tests §5.29
MICTURITION
  See URINE TRANSPORT AND
      MICTURITION
MINORS
  Defense perspective §§11.04,
      11.12
  Infants. See INFANTS
  Malpractice considerations §1.45
  Physiology §5.19
  Procedures in malpractice
      litigation §2.14
MISCONDUCT
  Hospital liability §12.03
  Malpractice considerations §1.06
MURPHY DRIP
  Surgical procedures §8.20
MUTUAL CONSENT
  Malpractice considerations §1.03

N

NASOGASTRIC (NG) TUBES
  Medical records §3.18
NATIONAL BOARD OF
    MEDICAL EXAMINERS
    (NBME)
  Urology specialization §4.04
NATIONAL LIBRARY OF
    MEDICINE
  Urology specialization §4.09

INDEX 371

NEGLIGENCE
  Defense perspective §§11.03, 11.06, 11.07, 11.09, 11.11, 11.12, 11.15, 11.16 app 11-A, 11-B
  Hospital liability §§12.03, 12.06-12.10, 12.13, 12.14, 12.20
  Malpractice considerations §§1.01, 1.03, 1.05, 1.17, 1.21-1.23, 1.25, 1.26, 1.30, 1.32, 1.33, 1.35, 1.36
  Medical records §§3.14, 3.17, 3.25
  Plaintiff's case, handling §§10.01, 10.03, 10.05, 10.11
  Procedures in malpractice litigation §§2.03, 2.13, 2.17-2.23
  Surgical procedures §§8.07, 8.10, 8.14, 8.16

NEPHRECTOMY
  Surgical procedures §8.06

NEPHROLITHOTOMY
  Surgical procedures §8.03

NEPHROLOGY AND UROLOGY
  Physiology §5.15
  Radiology of the urinary tract §§7.10, 7.11, 7.13

NEPHRON
  Anatomy §5.05

NEPHROSTOMY
  See PERCUTANEOUS NEPHROSTOMY

NOMINAL DAMAGES
  Malpractice considerations §§1.06, 1.27

NONRESIDENTS
  See RESIDENTS AND NONRESIDENTS

NOTICES OF TERMINATION
  Malpractice considerations §1.03

NURSES
  See PHYSICIAN AND NURSE RELATIONSHIPS

O

OCCUPATIONAL THERAPY
  Medical records §3.15

OFFICE RECORDS
  Medical records §3.24

OFFSET
  Common urological complications §9.12
  Malpractice considerations §1.42

OPENING STATEMENT
  Defense perspective §11.13

OPEN PROSTATECTOMY
  Surgical procedures §8.13

OPERATING ROOM TECHNICIAN
  Medical records §3.19

ORCHIECTOMY
  Common urological complications §9.11
  Surgical procedures §8.18

ORCHIOPEXY
  See DETORSION AND ORCHIOPEXY

ORCHITIS
  Common urological complications §9.12

ORDER FOR REPRODUCTIONS
  Medical records §3.03

ORDERLIES
  Defense perspective §11.15
  Hospital liability §§12.03, 12.06

ORDINARY PRUDENCE
  Malpractice considerations §1.21

OSMOSIS
  Physiology §5.16

OSTEOPATHS
  Defense perspective app 11-A

OUTPATIENT HOSPITALIZATION
  Defense perspective §11.06
  Medical records §3.02

P

PANCREAS
  Anatomy §5.06
PAPAVERINE
  Physiology §5.25
PAST MEDICAL HISTORY (PMH)
  Medical records §3.05
PATHOLOGISTS
  Common urological
    complications §9.15
  Hospital liability §12.19
  Medical records §3.03
PATIENTS
  Physician and patient
    relationships. See
    PHYSICIAN AND PATIENT
    RELATIONSHIPS
PAYMENTS
  Defense perspective §11.01
  Malpractice considerations
    §§1.03, 1.31
  Medical records §3.16
  Plaintiff's case, handling §10.04
  Procedures in malpractice
    litigation §2.27
PECUNIARY DAMAGES
  Malpractice considerations
    §§1.27, 1.43
PEER REVIEW
  Malpractice considerations §1.39
PELVIS, RENAL
  Anatomy §§5.08, 5.09
  Common urological
    complications §§9.08, 9.11
  Physiology §§5.17, 5.25
  Radiology of the urinary tract
    §§7.02, 7.09
  Surgical procedures §§8.02, 8.05
  Urogenital tract evaluation and
    treatment §6.03
PENILE PROSTHESIS,
    INSERTION OF
  Common urological
    complications §9.09

PENILE PROSTHESIS,
INSERTION OF, *continued*
  Physiology §5.27
  Surgical procedures §8.17
  Urogenital tract evaluation and
    treatment §6.11
PENIS
  Anatomy §5.12
  Common urological
    complications §9.09
  Physiology §§5.23-5.25, 5.27
  Radiology of the urinary tract
    §7.08
  Surgical procedures §8.15
  Urogenital tract evaluation and
    treatment §6.02
PERCUTANEOUS
    NEPHROSTOMY
  Surgical procedures §8.05
  Urogenital tract evaluation and
    treatment §6.03
PERITONEUM
  Surgical procedures §8.02
PERJURY
  Defense perspective §11.14
PEYRONIE'S DISEASE
  Common urological
    complications §9.09
  Physiology §5.27
PHYSICAL EXAMINATIONS
  Malpractice considerations
    §§1.03, 1.24
  Medical records §§3.05, 3.16, 3.25
PHYSICAL THERAPY
  Defense perspective §11.04
  Medical records §3.15
PHYSICIAN AND ATTORNEY
    RELATIONSHIPS
  Defendant physicians. See
    DEFENDANT PHYSICIANS
  Defense perspective §§11.04 app
    11-A
  Malpractice considerations. See
    MALPRACTICE
    CONSIDERATIONS

PHYSICIAN AND ATTORNEY
RELATIONSHIPS, *continued*
  Plaintiff's case, handling §10.03
  Procedures in malpractice
    litigation §§2.04, 2.06, 2.08
  Subsequent treating physicians.
    See SUBSEQUENT
    TREATING PHYSICIANS
PHYSICIAN AND NURSE
    RELATIONSHIPS
  Defense perspective §§11.04,
    11.05
  Medical records §3.08
PHYSICIAN AND PATIENT
    RELATIONSHIPS
  Abandonment of patient. See
    ABANDONMENT OF
    PATIENT
  Common urological
    complications §9.07
  Defense perspective §§11.03,
    11.07, 11.15
  Hospital liability §12.07
  Malpractice considerations
    §§1.03, 1.07-1.16, 1.20
  Medical records §§3.01, 3.05-3.07,
    3.16, 3.24
  Plaintiff's case, handling,
    generally this heading
  Procedures in malpractice
    litigation §§2.02-2.04, 2.20
  Radiology of the urinary tract
    §7.02
PHYSICIAN ASSISTANT (PA)
  Medical records §3.12
PHYSICIAN'S DESK
    REFERENCE (PDR)
  Common urological
    complications §9.07
PHYSICIAN'S FEES
  Malpractice considerations §1.19
PHYSICIAN'S VISITS
  Medical records §3.02

PHYSIOLOGY
  See ANATOMY, PHYSIOLOGY,
    AND LABORATORY TESTS
PLAINTIFF'S CASE, HANDLING
    OF
  Generally §10.01
  Complaint §10.05
  Cross-examination §10.16
  Depositions
    –generally §10.10
    –deponents §10.11
    –deposition of defendant doctor
      §10.12
    –deposition of defense experts
      §10.13
  Direct examination §10.15
  Discovery §10.06
  Evaluation §10.03
  Initial discovery
    –generally §10.07
    –interrogatories and request for
      production of documents to
      defendant doctor §10.08
    –interrogatories and request for
      production of documents to
      defendant hospital §10.09
  Procedures in malpractice
    litigation §2.04
  Screening §10.02
  Settlement or suit §10.04
  Summation §10.17
  Voir dire §10.14
PLATELETS
  Laboratory tests §5.30
PLEADINGS
  Defense perspective §11.14
  Malpractice considerations
    §§1.27, 1.28
  Medical records §3.03
  Procedures in malpractice
    litigation §§2.19, 2.23
POST-ANESTHESIA RECOVERY
    ROOM RECORD (PARR)
  Medical records §3.13

PREGNANCIES
  Common urological
    complications §9.10
  Physiology §5.21
  Surgical procedures §§8.10, 8.16
PREJUDICE
  Defense perspective §11.12
  Hospital liability §12.17
  Plaintiff's case, handling §10.14
PRETRIAL PHASE
  Defense perspective. See
    DEFENSE PERSPECTIVE
PRIAPISM
  Physiology §5.27
PRIMA FACIE CASES
  Malpractice considerations §1.25
PRINCIPLES OF MEDICAL
    ETHICS
  Malpractice considerations §1.20
PRIVACY, RIGHT TO
  Malpractice considerations §1.23
PROCEDURES IN
    MALPRACTICE LITIGATION
  Generally §2.01
  Affirmative defenses
  –generally §2.19
  –assumption of the risk §2.23
  –comparative negligence §2.22
  –contributory negligence §2.20
  –last clear chance §2.21
  Compromise and settlement
  –generally §2.25
  –settlement brochure §2.26
  –types of settlement §2.27
  Defendants §2.05
  Derivative actions §2.14
  Elements of consideration
    regarding a potential case
    §2.03
  Experts §2.06
  Initial interview §2.02
  Plaintiffs §2.04
  Procedural defenses §2.24
  References §2.28
  Requirements

PROCEDURES IN
MALPRACTICE LITIGATION,
continued
  –generally §2.07
  –forum non conveniens §2.10
  –jurisdiction §2.08
  –prior dismissals §2.12
  –service of process §2.11
  –venue §2.09
  Statute of limitations
  –generally §2.15
  –foreign body §2.18
  –tolling §2.17
  –torts §2.16
  Wrongful death and survival
    §2.13
PROCESS
  See SERVICE OF PROCESS
PRODUCTS LIABILITY
  Malpractice considerations
    §§1.14, 1.27, 1.41
PROOF
  See BURDEN OF PROOF
PROPERTY DAMAGES
  Malpractice considerations
    §§1.26, 1.27
  Procedures in malpractice
    litigation §2.03
PROPERTY, REAL AND
    PERSONAL
  See REAL AND PERSONAL
    PROPERTY
PROSTATECTOMY
  Common urological
    complications §9.15
  Open prostatectomy. See OPEN
    PROSTATECTOMY
  Radical prostatectomy. See
    RADICAL
    PROSTATECTOMY
PROSTATE GLAND
  Anatomy §5.11
  Common urological
    complications §§9.03, 9.06,
    9.07

PROSTATE GLAND, *continued*
  Defense perspective §11.06
  Laboratory tests §§5.29, 5.31
  Physiology §§5.17, 5.21, 5.25, 5.27
  Radiology of the urinary tract §§7.09, 7.12
  Surgical procedures §§8.12-8.14, 8.18, 8.20
  Transurethral resection of the prostate (TURP). See TRANSURETHRAL RESECTION OF THE PROSTATE (TURP)
  Urogenital tract evaluation and treatment §§6.02, 6.05, 6.06, 6.10
PROSTATISM
  Common urological complications §9.06
  Surgical procedures §8.20
PROSTHESIS
  Common urological complications §9.09
  Penile prosthesis, insertion of. See PENILE PROSTHESIS, INSERTION OF
  Urogenital tract evaluation and treatment §6.11
  Urology specialization §4.01
PROXIMATE CAUSE
  Common urological complications §9.02
  Defense perspective §§11.03, 11.07
  Malpractice considerations §1.05
  Medical records §3.02
  Plaintiff's case, handling §§10.03, 10.15
  Procedures in malpractice litigation §2.03
PRUDENCE
  See ORDINARY PRUDENCE
PSYCHOLOGICAL HARM
  Defense perspective §11.01

PUBERTY
  Physiology §5.21
PUBLIC POLICY
  Hospital liability §12.03
PUNITIVE DAMAGES
  Hospital liability §§12.03, 12.18
  Malpractice considerations §§1.06, 1.27
PYELOGRAPHY
  Antegrade pyelography. See ANTEGRADE PYELOGRAPHY
  Retrograde pyelography. See RETROGRADE PYELOGRAPHY
PYELOLITHOTOMY
  Surgical procedures §8.02
PYURIA
  Laboratory tests §5.29

R

RADIATION THERAPY
  Common urological complications §9.10
  Surgical procedures §§8.14, 8.18
RADICAL PROSTATECTOMY
  Surgical procedures §8.14
RADIOLOGISTS
  Common urological complications §§9.06, 9.08
  Medical records §3.10
  Surgical procedures §8.05
RADIOLOGY OF THE URINARY TRACT
  Generally §7.01
  Angiography §7.10
  Antegrade pyelography §7.05
  Computerized tomography §7.13 app 7-A
  Cystography §7.06 app 7-A
  Excretory urography §7.02
  Loopogram §7.07
  Radionuclides §7.11

RADIOLOGY OF THE URINARY TRACT, *continued*
   Renal ultrasound §7.12 app 7-A
   Retrograde pyelography §7.04 app 7-A
   Tomography §7.03 app 7-A
   Urethrography §7.08 app 7-A
   Vasogram §7.09 app 7-A
RADIONUCLIDES
   Radiology of the urinary tract §7.11
RAPID EYE MOVEMENT (REM)
   Common urological complications §9.09
REABSORPTION
   Physiology §5.16
REAL AND PERSONAL PROPERTY
   Procedures in malpractice litigation §2.16
RECANALIZATION
   Surgical procedures §8.16
RECTUM
   Anatomy §§5.09, 5.11, 5.14
   Common urological complications §9.13
   Physiology §5.19
   Surgical procedures §8.13
   Urogenital tract evaluation and treatment §6.10
RED CELL COUNT
   Laboratory tests §5.30
REFERENCES
   Anatomy, physiology, and laboratory tests §5.32
   Malpractice considerations §1.48
   Procedures in malpractice litigation §2.28
REHABILITATION SPECIALISTS
   Defense perspective §§11.04, 11.05
RELEASES
   Malpractice considerations §1.37

RELIGIOUS BELIEFS
   Medical records §3.05
RENAL ARTERIES
   Anatomy §§5.06, 5.13
   Common urological complications §9.08
   Physiology §§5.15, 5.16
   Surgical procedures §§8.02, 8.03, 8.06
RENAL PELVIS
   See PELVIS, RENAL
RENAL STONES
   Anatomy §5.08
   Common urological complications §§9.06, 9.08, 9.10
   Radiology of the urinary tract §7.02
   Surgical procedures §§8.02-8.07
   Urogenital tract evaluation and treatment §§6.03, 6.07, 6.09
RENAL ULTRASOUND
   Radiology of the urinary tract §7.12 app 7-A
RENIN
   Physiology §5.16
REQUESTS TO ADMIT
   Defense perspective §11.14
REQUIREMENTS
   Procedures in malpractice litigation. See PROCEDURES IN MALPRACTICE LITIGATION
RESECTIONS
   Common urological complications §§9.03, 9.15
   Transurethral resection of the prostate (TURP). See TRANSURETHRAL RESECTION OF THE PROSTATE (TURP)
   Transurethral resection (TUR). See TRANSURETHRAL RESECTION (TUR)

RESECTOSCOPES
  Common urological
    complications §§9.04, 9.15
  Surgical procedures §8.20
  Urogenital tract evaluation and
    treatment §6.06
  Urology specialization §4.01
RESIDENCY PROGRAMS
  Defense perspective §11.15
  Urology specialization §§4.04,
    4.05
RESIDENTS AND
    NONRESIDENTS
  Defense perspective §§11.04,
    11.15
  Procedures in malpractice
    litigation §2.08
RES IPSA LOQUITUR
  Malpractice considerations §1.25
RES JUDICATA
  Procedures in malpractice
    litigation §2.19
RESPIRATORY THERAPY
  Medical records §3.15
RESPONDEAT SUPERIOR
  Hospital liability §§12.03,
    12.06-12.08, 12.15
RESTATEMENT OF AGENCY
  Hospital liability §§12.06, 12.07
RESTATEMENT OF TORTS
  Malpractice considerations
    §§1.26, 1.31, 1.33
  Procedures in malpractice
    litigation §2.20
RETENTION
  See INCONTINENCE AND
    RETENTION
RETROGRADE PYELOGRAPHY
  Common urological
    complications §§9.02, 9.06
  Radiology of the urinary tract
    §7.04 app 7-A
  Surgical procedures §8.02

RETROGRADE PYELOGRAPHY,
continued
  Urogenital tract evaluation and
    treatment §6.03
RETROPERITONEUM
  Anatomy §5.02
REVERSIONARY TRUSTS
  Procedures in malpractice
    litigation §2.27
REVIEW OF SYSTEMS (ROS)
  Medical records §3.05
RISKS
  Malpractice considerations
    §§1.02, 1.07
  Medical records §§3.01, 3.17
  Surgical procedures §§8.03, 8.17,
    8.18

S

SAME-DAY SURGERY
  Medical records §3.02
SAMPLE FORMS
  Medical records app 3-A
SCHOOL RECORDS
  Defense perspective §11.04
SCREENING
  Plaintiff's case, handling §10.02
SCROTUM
  Anatomy §§5.12, 5.13
  Common urological
    complications §§9.05, 9.11,
    9.12
  Radiology of the urinary tract
    §7.09
  Surgical procedures §§8.16,
    8.17-8.19
  Urogenital tract evaluation and
    treatment §6.11
SCRUB NURSE
  See OPERATING ROOM
    TECHNICIAN
SECRETION
  Physiology §5.16

SEMEN
   Physiology §§5.21, 5.23
   Surgical procedures §8.16
SEMINAL VESICLES
   Anatomy §5.14
   Physiology §5.21
   Surgical procedures §8.14
SEMINIFEROUS TUBULES
   Anatomy §5.13
   Physiology §5.21
SEPTICEMIA
   Common urological complications §9.10
   Surgical procedures §8.20
SERVICE OF PROCESS
   Defense perspective §11.02
SETOFFS
   Malpractice considerations §1.05
SETTLEMENT
   Compromise and settlement. See COMPROMISE AND SETTLEMENT
   Defense perspective §11.09
   Plaintiff's case, handling §10.04
SEVENTH AMENDMENT OF US CONSTITUTION
   Plaintiff's case, handling §10.14
SEVERAL LIABILITY
   See JOINT AND SEVERAL LIABILITY
SEXUAL ACTIVITY
   Physiology §§5.21, 5.22, 5.27
   Urogenital tract evaluation and treatment §6.11
SEXUAL DYSFUNCTION
   Anatomy, physiology, and laboratory tests. See ANATOMY, PHYSIOLOGY, AND LABORATORY TESTS
   Defense perspective §11.01
SHERMAN ANTITRUST ACT
   Hospital liability §12.18
***SOAP* PATTERN**
   Medical records §3.06

SOCIAL HISTORY (SOC)
   Medical records §3.05
SOCIAL SECURITY ACT
   Malpractice considerations §1.43
SOCIAL SECURITY DISABILITY BENEFITS
   Malpractice considerations §1.03
SOCIOECONOMICS
   See DEMOGRAPHICS AND SOCIOECONOMICS
SOVEREIGN IMMUNITY
   Hospital liability §12.03
SPEECH THERAPY
   Medical records §3.15
SPERMATIC CORD STRUCTURES
   See TESTICULAR AND SPERMATIC CORD STRUCTURES
SPERMATOGENESIS
   Physiology §5.21
SPERMATOZOA
   Anatomy §5.13
   Azospermia. See AZOSPERMIA
   Physiology §5.21
SPLEEN
   Anatomy §5.06
SPOLIATION
   Medical records §3.25
STAMEY PROCEDURE
   Common urological complications §§9.14, 9.15
   Surgical procedures §8.10
STANDARD OF CARE
   Defense perspective §11.03
   Hospital liability §§12.10, 12.13
   Malpractice considerations. See MALPRACTICE CONSIDERATIONS
STATE DEPARTMENT OF HUMAN RESOURCES
   See HUMAN RESOURCES, STATE DEPARTMENT OF

STATUTE OF LIMITATIONS
　Defense perspective §§11.02, 11.06
　Hospital liability §12.01
　Malpractice considerations §1.45
　Plaintiff's case, handling §10.05
　Procedures in malpractice litigation. See PROCEDURES IN MALPRACTICE LITIGATION
STENOSIS
　Urogenital tract evaluation and treatment §6.04
STENTS
　Common urological complications §§9.02, 9.08, 9.10, 9.15
　Urogenital tract evaluation and treatment §6.03
STERILITY
　Physiology §§5.21, 5.22
　Surgical procedures §8.16
STERILIZATION
　Defense perspective §11.15
STEVENS-JOHNSON SYNDROME
　Common urological complications §9.07
STONE BASKETS AND URETEROSCOPES
　Urogenital tract evaluation and treatment §6.09
STONE DISEASE
　Urology specialization §4.01
STOP ORDERS
　Medical records §3.21
STRESS URINARY INCONTINENCE (SUI)
　Common urological complications §§9.03, 9.14, 9.15
　Surgical procedures §8.10

SUBPOENAS
　Malpractice considerations §§1.18, 1.19
　Medical records §§3.03, 3.24
　Plaintiff's case, handling §10.13
SUBSEQUENT TREATING PHYSICIANS
　Malpractice considerations §1.18
SUBSPECIALIZATION
　Anatomy §5.01
　Physiology §5.15
　Urology specialization §4.08
SUMMARY JUDGMENTS
　Defense perspective §11.02
　Hospital liability §§12.07, 12.08
　Plaintiff's case, handling §10.05
SUPERINTENDENTS
　Hospital liability §12.03
SURGICAL PROCEDURES
　Generally §8.01
　Circumcision §8.15
　Cystectomy and ileal conduit §8.12
　Deligation with anastomosis §8.08
　Detorsion and orchiopexy §8.19
　Insertion of penile prosthesis §8.17
　Lithotripsy §8.04
　Nephrectomy §8.06
　Nephrolithotomy §8.03
　Open prostatectomy §8.13
　Orchiectomy §8.18
　Percutaneous nephrostomy §8.05
　Pyelolithotomy §8.02
　Radical prostatectomy §8.14
　Transurethral resection of the prostate (TURP) §8.20
　Ureteral reimplantation §8.09
　Ureterolithotomy §8.07
　Vasectomy §8.16
　Vesicourethropexy §8.10
　Vesicovaginal fistula repair §8.11

SURVIVAL
  See WRONGFUL DEATH AND
    SURVIVAL
SYSTEMS FOR ANESTHETIC
    RESPIRATORY
    ASSESSMENT (SARA)
  Medical records §3.12

T

TELEPHONE ORDER (T.O.)
  Medical records §3.07
TERMINATION
  See NOTICES OF
    TERMINATION
TESTICULAR AND SPERMATIC
    CORD STRUCTURES
  Anatomy §5.13
  Common urological
    complications §§9.05, 9.11,
    9.12
  Physiology §5.21
  Surgical procedures §§8.16, 8.18,
    8.19
TESTICULAR ULTRASOUND
  Radiology of the urinary tract
    §7.12
TESTIMONY
  Common urological
    complications §9.15
  Defense perspective §§11.03,
    11.06-11.08, 11.11, 11.14-11.16
  Malpractice considerations
    §§1.18, 1.19
  Plaintiff's case, handling §§10.03,
    10.12, 10.15-10.17
  Procedures in malpractice
    litigation §2.13
TESTOSTERONE
  Physiology §5.21
  Surgical procedures §8.18
TEXTS AND JOURNALS
  Urology specialization §4.09

THERAPEUTICS
  Urology specialization §4.01
THERAPY
  See PHYSICAL THERAPY
THIRD PARTIES
  Defense perspective app 11-A
  Hospital liability §12.05
  Malpractice considerations
    §§1.03, 1.42
  Medical records §3.01
  Procedures in malpractice
    litigation §2.14
TOMOGRAPHY
  Computerized tomography (CT).
    See COMPUTERIZED
    TOMOGRAPHY (CT)
  Radiology of the urinary tract
    §7.03 app 7-A
  Urology specialization §4.01
TORSION OF THE TESTICLE
  Common urological
    complications §9.05
  Malpractice considerations §1.24
TORTFEASORS
  Hospital liability §12.05
"TORT OF OUTRAGE"
  Malpractice considerations §1.30
TORT POLICY WORKING
    GROUP
  Malpractice considerations §1.41
TORT REFORM
  Hospital liability §§12.03, 12.05
  Malpractice considerations. See
    MALPRACTICE
    CONSIDERATIONS
  Plaintiff's case, handling §§10.05,
    10.14
  Procedures in malpractice
    litigation §§2.04, 2.16, 2.17,
    2.27
  Restatement of Torts. See
    RESTATEMENT OF TORTS

INDEX 381

TOTAL URINARY
    INCONTINENCE
  Common urological
    complications §9.03
TRANSFERRAL OF PATIENT
  Medical records §3.02
TRANSPLANTATION
  Urology specialization §4.01
TRANSURETHRAL RESECTION
    (TUR)
  Anatomy §5.10
  Common urological
    complications §§9.03, 9.04
  Physiology §5.25
  Urogenital tract evaluation and
    treatment §§6.02, 6.06
TRANSURETHRAL RESECTION
    OF THE PROSTATE (TURP)
  Surgical procedures §8.20
  Urogenital tract evaluation and
    treatment §6.06
TRIAL
  Defense perspective. See
    DEFENSE PERSPECTIVE
TRUSTEES
  See BOARD OF TRUSTEES
TRUST FUND THEORY
  Hospital liability §12.03
TRUSTS
  Reversionary trusts. See
    REVERSIONARY TRUSTS

U

ULCERS
  Common urological
    complications §9.07
ULTRAFILTRATION
  Physiology §5.16
ULTRASOUND
  Renal ultrasound. See RENAL
    ULTRASOUND
  Surgical procedures §8.07

ULTRASOUND, *continued*
  Testicular ultrasound. See
    TESTICULAR
    ULTRASOUND
  Urogenital tract evaluation and
    treatment §§6.07, 6.10
  Urology specialization §4.01
ULTRA VIRES
  Hospital liability §12.11
UNIFORM CONTRIBUTION
    AMONG TORTFEASORS
    ACT
  Malpractice considerations §1.35
UNLIQUIDATED DAMAGES
    INTEREST ACT
  Plaintiff's case, handling §10.04
URETERAL CATHETERS
  Urogenital tract evaluation and
    treatment §6.03
URETERAL REIMPLANTATION
  Surgical procedures §8.09
URETEROLITHOTOMY
  Surgical procedures §8.07
URETEROSCOPES
  See STONE BASKETS AND
    URETEROSCOPES
URETERS
  Common urological
    complications §§9.02, 9.08,
    9.10, 9.15
  Defense perspective §11.04
  Radiology of the urinary tract
    §§7.02-7.04, 7.07, 7.09
  Surgical procedures §§8.02-8.04,
    8.07, 8.09, 8.12
  Urogenital tract evaluation and
    treatment §§6.03, 6.05, 6.09
URETHRAL CATHETERS
  Urogenital tract evaluation and
    treatment §6.02
URETHRAL PERFORATION
  Common urological
    complications §9.13

URETHRAL SOUNDS
   Urogenital tract evaluation and treatment §6.04
URETHRITIS
   Common urological complications §9.15
URETHROGRAPHY
   Radiology of the urinary tract §7.08
URETHROTOMES
   Urogenital tract evaluation and treatment §6.08
URINALYSIS
   Laboratory tests §5.29
URINARY STORAGE SYSTEM
   See ANATOMY, PHYSIOLOGY, AND LABORATORY TESTS
URINARY TRANSPORT SYSTEM
   Anatomy, physiology, and laboratory tests. See ANATOMY, PHYSIOLOGY, AND LABORATORY TESTS
   Radiology of the urinary tract. See RADIOLOGY OF THE URINARY TRACT
URINE FORMATION
   Physiology §5.16
URINE TRANSPORT AND MICTURITION
   See ANATOMY, PHYSIOLOGY, AND LABORATORY TESTS
UROGENITAL TRACT
   See INSTRUMENTS USED IN EVALUATION AND TREATMENT OF THE UROGENITAL TRACT
UROGRAPHY
   See EXCRETORY UROGRAPHY
UROLOGICAL COMPLICATIONS, COMMON
   Generally §§9.01, 9.15
   Allergic or toxic drug reactions §9.07

UROLOGICAL COMPLICATIONS, COMMON, *continued*
   Damage to urinary sphincter during transurethral resection of the prostate (TURP) §9.03
   Hernia repair, damage to testicle during §9.11
   Hyponatremia §9.04
   Injury to ureter during abdominal hysterectomy §9.02
   Internal organ damage during percutaneous approach to kidney §9.08
   Intravenous pyelogram (IVP) dye reactions §9.06
   Marshall-Marchetti-Krantz (MMK) procedure, suture through catheter after §9.14
   Penile prosthesis, infections and improper placement §9.09
   Torsion of the testicle, failure to diagnose §9.05
   Ureteral stent, failure to timely remove §9.10
   Urethral perforation §9.13
   Vasectomies, complications with §9.12
UROLOGY
   Nephrology and urology. See NEPHROLOGY AND UROLOGY
   Surgical procedures. See SURGICAL PROCEDURES
UROLOGY SPECIALIZATION
   Board certification
   –generally §4.05
   –recertification §4.06
   Demographics and socioeconomics §4.07
   Glossary §4.02
   History §4.01
   Licensure §4.04
   Making of a urologist §4.03
   Standard texts and journals §4.09
   Subspecialization §4.08

UROLOGY SPECIALIZATION, *continued*
   Urological societies §4.10

V

VAGINA
   Anatomy §§5.08-5.10
   Surgical procedures §8.11
   Urogenital tract evaluation and treatment §6.02
VAS DEFERENS
   Anatomy §5.13
   Common urological complications §9.11
   Radiology of the urinary tract §7.09
   Surgical procedures §8.16
VASECTOMIES
   Common urological complications §9.12
   Procedures in malpractice litigation §2.17
   Surgical procedures §8.16
VASITIS
   Common urological complications §9.12
VASOGRAM
   Radiology of the urinary tract §7.09 app 7-A
VENUE
   Defense perspective §11.02
VERBAL ORDER (V.O.)
   Medical records §3.07
VESICOURETHROPEXY
   Surgical procedures §8.10
VESICOVAGINAL FISTULA REPAIR
   Common urological complications §9.15
   Surgical procedures §8.11
VICARIOUS LIABILITY
   See RESPONDEAT SUPERIOR
VINDICTIVE DAMAGES
   See PUNITIVE DAMAGES
VITAL SIGNS
   Medical records §§3.05, 3.13, 3.18, 3.22
VOIR DIRE
   Defense perspective §§11.11, 11.12
   Plaintiff's case, handling §10.14

W

WAGE BACKGROUND
   Defense perspective §11.04
   Loss of income. See LOSS OF INCOME
WAIVERS
   Implied waiver theory. See IMPLIED WAIVER THEORY
WHITE CELL COUNT
   Laboratory tests §5.30
WITNESSES, EXPERT
   Common urological complications §§9.01, 9.02, 9.14
   Defense perspective §§11.04-11.09, 11.11, 11.12, 11.14-11.16 app 11-A, 11-B
   Hospital liability §12.10
   Malpractice considerations §§1.04, 1.18, 1.21, 1.30, 1.39, 1.41, 1.47
   Plaintiff's case, handling §§10.03, 10.07, 10.11-10.16
   Procedures in malpractice litigation §§2.06, 2.08, 2.10
   Radiology of the urinary tract §7.08
WORKERS' COMPENSATION LAWS
   Defense perspective app 11-A
   Malpractice considerations §1.43

WRONGFUL BIRTH
  Common urological
    complications §9.12
WRONGFUL DEATH AND SURVIVAL
  Hospital liability §12.10
  Procedures in malpractice
    litigation §2.13

Z

"ZONE OF PHYSICAL DANGER"
  Malpractice considerations §1.30
"ZONE OF PSYCHIC DANGER"
  Malpractice considerations §1.30